SECOND CHANCES
6th edition

First published in 1979 by the Macmillan Press Ltd.

This edition published 1987 by

Careers and Occupational Information Centre
Moorfoot
Sheffield S1 4PQ
Tel: (0742) 753275.

Conversion and Typesetting by Cambridge Composition

ISBN 0 86110 435 8

Printed in Great Britain.

SECOND CHANCES
6th edition

The annual guide to adult education and training opportunities

ANDREW PATES, MARTIN GOOD

CAREERS AND OCCUPATIONAL INFORMATION CENTRE

Index of advertisers

Acknowledgements

A book like this is quite impossible to write without the help and co-operation of hundreds of people. We are very pleased to be able to thank again, the many people who have willingly supplied information and often volunteered ideas and information beyond what was asked for.

We would like to extend an extra thanks to a number of people who have done even more and have taken time to think about the book and given us ideas, information and suggestions to help with the continuing development of *Second chances*.

In particular we would like to thank Dorothy Eagleson and Elisabeth Gerver, the compilation team: Liz Blackadder, Elspeth Cardy, Lesley Crichton, Clare Fowler, Julie O'Connor, Sheila Raynor, Jan Sellers, Mark Sutton, Wendy White, and many others too numerous to mention who gave their time freely to ensure this book is as up to date as possible.

The Editors

Contents

What's in the book

Second chances exists to help anyone over 16, who wants to use the rich supply of education and training opportunities (ET) available.It can help if you

- have retired and are looking for worthwhile things to do
- missed the chance of higher education and want it now
- want an interesting spare time activity
- have been made redundant or want to change your job or career
- never learned to read, write or spell well enough
- want to develop new skills for your job
- never went to school
- have come to live in the UK from abroad
- want to return to work after a break (maybe raising a family)
- want to meet people or just want a change
- have any other reason.

The opportunities are there. You just need to find them.

HOW THE BOOK WORKS

It does not give a complete list of every opportunity there is but helps you find out where to go for help and who to talk to. There are four parts:

Part 1: Users
Different reasons for wanting ET and some of the facilities for those with special needs (studying with children, unemployment, courses for women only etc).

Part 2: Providers
Main types of provision (university, adult and further education, training etc).

Part 3: Money
All about money; why you need it and where to get it.

Part 4: Subjects and places
Chapter *41 Qualifications* describes the range; *42 Things to study* tells you where to find information on many different subjects; and the *Gazeteer: places to study* is a county by county list of the main colleges and centres.

USING THE INFORMATION

Although the information here has been checked thoroughly, things do change quickly. Courses are cancelled, people move on, addresses and phone numbers alter, courses are put on at short notice. Always check locally.

USERS

1 Advice and help

This chapter explains the sources of advice and help that are generally available if you are thinking about education or training. Listed here are providers of general advice and information or national information services – there are many other places that will help you with specific queries about their own work.

WHAT DO YOU NEED TO KNOW?

- what's on and where?
- how much does it cost?
- can you get a grant?
- how do you get in?
- does it lead to any qualification?
- will it get you a job afterwards?
- is it the right thing for you?
- do you want to do it?
- will you cope with it if you start?

The first five questions can be answered with hard facts; any of the agencies listed in this chapter should be able to answer them. The last four are more difficult; what you really need to do is to work through them with someone, and come to your own conclusions. Some of the services here will be better at helping you than others. Some are good at giving information but don't have the time or skills to help you to work through your decisions; some vary a good deal depending on who you see; and some may know a lot about one type of education or training, or about what's available in one area, but not know much about other, different opportunities. As with all agencies, it's up to the users to make sure that the service they get is good. That's easier if you can ask the right questions in the first place.

EDUCATION GUIDANCE SERVICES

There are a number of local services which provide information on education and training to adults in their areas. They work in different ways, using different types of staff. Have a few questions in mind before you go. For example:

- Do they have, or can they get, accurate information about all kinds of opportunities available, or are they better informed about some than others?

- Can they help you make up your mind if you're not sure what you want?
- Can they help if you have problems with studying or learning?
- Will they contact places on your behalf if you can't get anywhere by yourself?
- Can they advise about money? (how much will you need and where could you get it?)
- Do they charge a fee?

This list of services is as complete as it can be at present. It's possible that some may have closed by the time you come to use them, since they are very vulnerable to cuts, even when well established. It is also possible that there are others. If a new one is set up in your area it should make itself known and may well publicise its services in public libraries, Citizens' Advice Bureaux and other public places.

A directory of services is also published every year by the Educational Counselling and Credit Transfer Information Service (ECCTIS).

★ **SEND FOR** *The directory of educational guidance services for adults*, free from ECCTIS, PO Box 88, Walton Hall, Milton Keynes MK7 6DB. Tel: (0908) 368921. (Multiple copies cost 25p each.)

Local Education Guidance Services for Adults

England

Avon

Avon Network (*Education Guidance Centre for Adults*), Quay Street, Bristol BS1 2JL. Tel: (0272) 299822.
Open Monday to Friday 9 am to 5 pm and Saturday 10 am to 4 pm.
Get in touch preferably by phone first.
Ask for Mr Stephens.

Bath Educational Advisory Service, City of Bath College of Further Education, Avon Street, Bath BA1 1UP. Tel: (0225) 312191 ext 209.
Get in touch by appointment over the phone between 9 am and 5 pm.
Ask for John Manley.

Norton Radstock College of Further Education, South Hill Park, Radstock, Bath BA3 3RW. Tel: (0761) 33161.
Open according to demand.
Ask for Anne Doveton.

South Bristol Technical College, Marksbury Road, Bedminster, Bristol BS3 5JL. Tel: (0272) 661105.
Open according to demand.
Ask for Christine Higgott.

Bedfordshire

Education Advice Centre, Adult Education Centre (Bedford College of Higher Education), 10 Rothsay Gardens, Bedford. Tel: (0234) 47914.
Open Monday to Friday 9 am to 5 pm except two weeks at Easter, Christmas and summer.
Offers information and advice, especially on basic, adult and further education and MSC courses. Adult = 16 and over.
Ask for Hilary Ferry.

Drop In Advice and Counselling Service, Charles Street Adult Education Centre, Charles Street, Luton LU2 0EB. Tel: (0582) 38348.
Open Monday to Friday 9 am to 5 pm, Monday and Tuesday 7.30 to 9.30 pm, or by appointment.
Get in touch by phone or post for an appointment or by calling in.
Ask for Stephen Macdonald.

Challney Community College, Stoneygate Road, Luton LU4 9TJ. Tel: (0582) 599921.
Get in touch by calling in or by phone.
Ask for Mr M Berrill.

Berkshire
Reading Educational Guidance Service for Adults (*REGSA*), Reading Adult College, 18 Cross Street, Reading RG1 1SW. Tel: (0734) 581754.
Open Tuesday, Wednesday and Friday 9.30 am to 4.30 pm; Thursday 9.30 am to 7.30 pm; Saturday 9.30 am to 12.30 pm.
Offers information and advice on hobbies and interests.
Ask for Steve Pass or Avril Ison.

Reading University, Whiteknights, Reading RG6 2AH. Tel: (0734) 875123.
Get in touch by phone for an appointment.
Ask for Roger Clark.

Buckinghamshire
Education Information Service for Adults, Youth & Community Department, County Hall, Aylesbury HP20 1UZ. Tel: (0296) 395000 ext 8193.
Offers a central referral point for the county's education guidance services.
Ask for George Cook.

Cambridgeshire
Education Desk, Cambridge Jobcentre, Guildhall Chambers, Guildhall Place, Cambridge. Tel: (0223) 64941.
Open Monday 10 am to 1 pm.
Ask for Ruth Hawthorn.

Peterborough Education Guidance Service for Adults (*PEGS*), Community Education, Touthill Close, City Road, Peterborough PE1 1UJ. Tel: (0733) 310101 ext 247.
Ask for Jill Navid.

Isle College, Wisbech PE13 2JE. Tel: (0945) 582566.
Open Monday to Friday 9 to 9.30 am and Monday to Thursday 6.30 to 7 pm. Answerphone available for appointments.
Ask for Peter Clow.

Cheshire
North Cheshire College, Museum Street Centre, Museum Street, Warrington WA1 1HU. Tel: (0925) 814343.
Get in touch by calling in or phoning.
Open Wednesday 9am to 4pm.
Ask for Dr Ken Kilbey.

West Cheshire College of Further Education, Eaton Road, Handbridge, Chester CH4 7ER. Tel: (0244) 677677.
Get in touch by phone for an appointment.
Ask for Mr F Griffiths or Mr A Burgen.

Cleveland
Hartlepool College of Further Education, Stockton Street, Hartlepool TS25 7NT. Tel: (0429) 275453.
Get in touch by calling in or phoning.
Ask for Mr Brian Lamb.

Longlands College of Further Education, Douglas Street, Middlesbrough TS4 2JW. Tel: (0642) 248351.
Get in touch by phone.
Ask for Alan Wilby.

Cornwall

Advice Service for Adult Education (*NETWORK*), Department of Continuing and Adult Education, Hayne Corfe Centre, Sunningdale, Truro TR1 3ND. Tel: (0872) 74503.
Open Monday to Friday mornings, 50 weeks per year.
Offers a central contact point for a network of advisers.
Ask for John Hurst.

Restormel Adult Continuing Education Centre, Mid-Cornwall College of Further Education, Westmoor Annexe, Priory Road, St Austell PL25 8AB. Tel: (0726) 67911.
Open Tuesday 9 am to 1 pm.
Ask for Colin Eddy.

Derbyshire

Derby College of Further Education, Wilmorton, Derby DE2 8UG. Tel: (0332) 73012.
Get in touch by phone first.
Ask for John Barnes.

Devon

Advice Service for Adult Education (*NETWORK*), Herondyke, West Charleton, Kingsbridge TQ7 2AA. Tel: (054853) 289.
Get in touch by phone at any reasonable time (home address).
Ask for Bob Pim.

East Devon College of Further Education, Bolham Road, Tiverton, Devon EX16 6SH. Tel: (0884) 254247/9.
Get in touch by phone first.
Ask for Ron Yates.

Dorset

Weymouth College, (1) Cranfield Avenue, Weymouth. Tel: (0305) 774911 ext 259. (2) Newstead Road, Weymouth. Tel: (0305) 774911 ext 236.
Get in touch by calling in.

Durham

New College Durham, Framwellgate Moor Centre, Durham DH1 5ES. Tel: (0385) 62421.
Get in touch by phone first.
Ask for Ruby Coldicott.

Essex

Harlow College, College Gate, The High, Harlow CM20 1LT. Tel: (0279) 441288.
Get in touch by phone first or drop in Wednesday morning.
Ask for Ms B Hayes.

Gloucestershire

Guidelines (Educational Guidance Service for Adults) Gloucestershire College of Arts and Technology (Cheltenham). Tel: (0242) 573794.
Ask for Anne Clement or John Hurley.

Gloucestershire College of Arts and Technology (Gloucester). Tel: (0452) 426528.
Get in touch by phone first or drop in at one of the advertised times.
Offers information, advice with emphasis on educational opportunities for the unemployed.
Ask for Vareta Bryan.

Mid-Gloucestershire Technical College, Stratford Road, Stroud, Gloucestershire GL5 4AH. Tel: (04536) 71408.
Get in touch by phone first.
Ask for Kit Tyrell.

Royal Forest of Dean College, Cinderford, Gloucestershire GL14 2JY.
Get in touch by phone first.
Offers to visit people living in rural areas.
Ask for Alyson Laverick or Linda Audsley. Tel: (0594) 26365

Hampshire
Portsmouth College of Art, Design and Further Education, Winston Churchill Avenue, Portsmouth PO1 2DJ. Tel: (0705) 754287.
Open Monday to Friday 9 am to 4 pm for public information sessions. Tuesday and Wednesday 2.30 to 4 pm, Wednesday 6.30 to 8 pm, Friday 10 am to 12 for counselling guidance service.
Get in touch by calling in. Phone first for personal appointment.
Ask for R Morgan.

Southampton Educational Information Centre for Adults, c/o The Argyle Centre, Argyle Road, Southampton SO2 OBQ. Tel: (0703) 332676.
Get in touch by phone first.
Ask for Angelina Clarina-Biga.

Hereford and Worcester
Education Guidance for Adults.
Get in touch by appointment.
For Worcester tel: (0903) 353366 ext 3475.
Ask for Janet Hazzard.
For Kidderminster tel: (0562) 66631.
Ask for Rose Stephens.

Hertfordshire
Educational Guidance for Adults, Hatfield Polytechnic, PO Box 109, Hatfield AL10 9AB. Tel: (07072) 79499.
Open during term time – Monday to Friday, 9 am to 4.30 pm.
Get in touch phone for an appointment, Tuesday to Friday, 9.30 am to 4.30 pm. On Mondays there is a phone-in advisory service.
Ask for Anne Burke.

Humberside
Educational Guidance Service for Adults (*EGSA*), c/o Careers Information Centre, Careers Office, Union Street, Hull HU2 8HB. Tel: (0482) 223081 ext 240.
Open all times of year except December. Telephone during office hours. Counselling by appointment.
Get in touch by phone, by post or by calling in.
Offers an annual booklet of courses currently available.
Ask for Felicity Redfern.

East Yorkshire College of Further Education, West Street, Bridlington, North Humberside YO15 3EA. Tel: (0262) 672676.
Open 9 am to 9 pm Monday to Friday.
Get in touch by calling in.
Ask for Fred Baker.

Kent
Educational Guidance Service for Adults, Dartford Adult Education Centre, East Hill House, East Hill Drive, Dartford, Kent. Tel: (0322) 21897.
Get in touch by phone.
Ask for Angela McGowan.

Victoria Centre for Adult Education, Darnley Road, Gravesend, Kent. Tel: (0474) 534051/534026.
Get in touch by calling in between 10 am and 12 Monday to Friday or by phone for an appointment.
Ask for Denise Ross.

Lancashire

EGSA, Stand 18, Nelson and Colne College, Scotland Road, Nelson BB9 7YT. Tel: (0282) 603151.
Open Monday to Friday, 9 am to 4.30 pm and Monday to Thursday 7 to 8 pm.
Ask for Wyn Smith.

Educational Information and Counselling Service for Adults, Lancashire Polytechnic, Preston PR1 2TQ. Tel: (0772) 22141.
Get in touch by phone or post.
Ask for Tony Goddard.

Lincolnshire

Educational Guidance Service, Castlegate Centre, Castlegate, Grantham NG31 9AP. Tel: (0476) 66273.
Open Monday to Friday 9 am to 4.30 pm.
Get in touch preferably by phone.
Ask for Hector Young.

LONDON – GREATER

BBC Radio London, Education Advice Line, 35a Marylebone High Street, London W1A 4LG. Tel: (01) 486 7040.
Open all year round on Thursday, 3 to 5 pm.
Get in touch by phone.
Offers information and advice. The last Thursday in every month is for information on the Open University. To check for changes look in the current Radio Times, London edition.
Ask for Patsy Brown.

Croydon

Educational Guidance Service, Room G37, Croydon College, College Road, Fairfield, Croydon Surrey CR9 1DX. Tel: (01) 760 5885.
Get in touch by calling in Tuesday, Wednesday or Thursday, 10 am to 1 pm, during term time, or telephone Tuesday or Wednesday 9 to 10 am for an appointment.
Ask for Jackie Sadler.

Haringey

Haringey Adult Education Service, White Hart Lane Centre, Wood Green, London N22. Tel: (01) 888 0952.
Get in touch by calling in Monday to Friday, 9.30 am to 4 pm; 6.30 to 9.30 pm Monday to Thursday; or phone between 9 am and 5 pm, Monday to Friday.
Ask for Mr Day.

Richmond

Learning Information Service for Adults (*LISA*), The Clifden Centre, Clifden Road, Twickenham, Middlesex. Tel: (01) 891 5907 ext 403.
Open Monday to Thursday 9 am to 8 pm, Friday 9 am to 4 pm (term times), Monday to Friday 9 am to 4 pm (out of term).
Get in touch preferably by phone first.
Ask for Karen North.

LONDON – INNER

Camden

Camden Adult Learning Advice (*CALA*), 58 Phoenix Road, London NW1 1EU. Tel: (01) 388 4666.
Open throughout the year except two weeks at Christmas, Easter and August. Drop-in times Monday, Wednesday and Friday, 10 am to 1 pm, open for appointments 2 to 4 pm.
Get in touch by phone, post or by calling in.
Ask for Val Forsyth, Baden Prince or Ann Short.

Greenwich
Greenwich Education and Training Advice Centre (*GRETA*), 12/14 Wellington Street, Woolwich, London SE18 6PF. Tel: (01) 854 2993.
Open Monday to Friday, 10 am to 4 pm and Saturday 10 am to 12 noon.
Offers advice and counselling service for education and training. Adult = at least 19.
Ask for Ruth Bird or Hansa Sehdev.

Hackney
Hackney Education Advice Service, Edith Cavell School, Enfield Road, London N1 5AZ. Tel: (01) 254 4180.
Open Call in Monday, Tuesday, Wednesday, Friday, 10 am to 2 pm. Other times by telephone appointmtment.
Offers free information and advice on all post-school education and training in Hackney Borough and beyond.
Ask for Paddy Maynes.

Hammersmith and Fulham
Education and Training Advice for Adults, 241 King Street, London NW6 9LP. Tel: (01) 741 8441.
Open Monday to Friday 9.30 am to 3 pm and 6 to 8pm.
Get in touch by phone or by calling in.
Offers information, advice and counselling; also prepared to talk to groups about education.
Ask for Sue Thurston or Sue Bradley.

Islington
Education Advice Service for Islington Adults (*EASIA*), 12 Barnsbury Road, Islington NW1 0HB. Tel: (01) 278 3761/2.
Get in touch by calling in Monday, Tuesday, Thursday 10 am to 12 noon and 2 to 4 pm. Wednesday only, 5 to 7 pm by appointment. Other times, phone for appointment.
Ask for Gloria Elliott, Geraldine Bailey or Geoff Biggin.

Kensington and Chelsea
Kensington and Chelsea Advice for Adults, 51 Goldborne Road, London W10 5NR. Tel: (01) 968 8532.
Get in touch by calling in Tuesday 2 to 4.45 pm, Wednesday 10 am to 12.45 pm and 2 to 4.45 pm. Other times, telephone for appointment.

Lambeth
Lambeth Educational Opportunities (*LEO*), 166A Stockwell Road, London SW9. Tel: (01) 733 3155.
Open Monday, Tuesday, Thursday 10 am to 2 pm, Wednesday 4 to 7 pm.
Ask for Brenda Bryan.

Southwark
Information and Advice Network on Southwark Educational Training (INSET), 175 Rye Lane, Peckham, London SE15 4TL. Tel: (01) 635 9111.
Open Call in 10 am to 12 noon and 2 to 4 pm, Monday, Tuesday, Wednesday and Friday; or phone Monday to Friday.
Ask for any adviser.

Tower Hamlets
Tower Hamlets Education Advice Ltd (*THEA*), The Education Shop, 75 Roman Road, London E2. Tel: (01) 981 3164.
Open Tuesday 2 to 5 pm; Wednesday 10 am to 5 pm; Thursday, Friday, Saturday 10 am to 1 pm.
Get in touch by phone, by post or by calling in.
Offers information and counselling on all aspects of adult education and training to local people. Adult = 16 and over.
Ask for Kevin Burton or Joy Andries.

Wandsworth

Wandsworth Education Shop, 86 Battersea Rise, London SW11 1EJ. Tel: (01) 350 1790.
Get in touch by calling in Monday 4 to 7 pm; Wednesday 1 to 4 pm; Friday 10 am to 1 pm. Other times, phone for appointment.
Ask for Ros Gillham.

Westminster

Westminster and City Educational Guidance Service for Adults, c/o Beauchamp Lodge, 2 Warwick Crescent, London W2 6NE. Tel: (01) 289 0339. (May move to 36 Church St NW8.)
Get in touch by calling in if possible, but it is best phone for appointment.
Ask for John Brown, Caroline Fry or Ricardo Salva.

MANCHESTER – METROPOLITAN DISTRICTS

Manchester

Manchester Educational Advice Service, 9 Anson Road, Victoria Park, Manchester M14. Tel: (061) 224 8241.
Get in touch by phone or by post.
Offers information, guidance and counselling by means of a linked network of advisers.
Ask for Melanie Tebbutt.

Central Area Office, Moseley Road Centre, Fallowfield, Machester M14 6WQ. Tel: (061) 224 8241.
Ask for Letitia Opie.

South Area Office, The Birtles Centre, South Manchester Community College, Town Centre, Wythenshawe, Manchester M22 5RF. Tel: (061) 499 1455.
Ask for Ethney Freeman.

North Area Office, Miles Platting Community Education Centre, Holland Street, Miles Platting, Manchester M10 7AF. Tel: (061) 205 3594.
Ask for Jane Barrett.

Tameside

Tameside Education Advice Service for Adults, Warrington House, Church Street, Ashton-under-Lyne OL6 7PR. Tel: (061) 330 6911.
Open Monday to Friday 9 am to 4.30 pm and Tuesday evenings 5 to 7 pm.
Offers advice plus weekly advice sessions in local Jobcentres and libraries.
Get in touch by calling in.
Ask for Liz Green or Mary Shiner.

Wigan

Contact for Learning and Educational Opportunities (*CLEO*), Education Department, Gateway House, Standishgate, Wigan WN1 1XL. Tel: (0942) 827912.
Open Monday to Friday, 9 am to 5 pm (evening appointments by arrangement).
Get in touch by phone, by post or by calling in.
Ask for Bridget Fielding.

MERSEYSIDE METROPOLITAN DISTRICTS

Knowsley

Educational Advice Service for Adults, Knowsley Central Tertiary College, Rupert Road, Huyton Merseyside L36 9UT. Tel: (051) 489 2002.
Open everyday 9 am to 5 pm, 6 to 8 pm except public and college holidays.
Get in touch by phone, by post or by calling in.
Ask for Alan Maw.

Norfolk

Educational Guidance for Adults in Kings Lynn and West Norfolk (EGAL), Orchard Hall, Room 0409, NORCAT, Tennyson Avenue, Kings Lynn, Norfolk PE30 2QW. Tel: (0553) 761144 ext 287.

Ask for Paul Richards or John Holden.

Northamptonshire

Educational Guidance for Adults in Northamptonshire, The Military Road Centre, Military Road, Northampton NN1 3ET. Tel: (0604) 28259/2804/30311.

Get in touch by phone any weekday for an appointment on Tuesday, Wednesday or Thursday.

Ask for Gil Smith or Luise Heron

Nottinghamshire

Open University East Midlands Regional Enquiry Service, The Octagon, 143 Derby Road, Nottingham NG7 1PH. Tel: (0602) 473072.

Open Monday to Friday 9 am to 5 pm. Closed public holidays and for a week at Easter.

Get in touch by phone, by post or by calling in.

Offers information about Open University courses. Further discussion available about local provision if Open University courses are not suitable or relevant.

Ask for Christine Simmons if writing, a member of the Regional Enquiry Service if phoning.

Oxfordshire

Links in Information Services on Education (LIAISE) offers educational guidance throughout the county. The LIAISE index is avaliable in libraries, colleges and centres. Gives details of over 4000 courses and contact names for further information and guidance. Offers an advisory service in the summer in libraries and other centres. Get in touch via the Open University (see below).

Open University, Southern Region, Regional Enquiry Service, Foxcombe Hall, Boars Hill, Oxford OX1 5HR. Tel: (0865) 730731.

Open Monday to Friday 9 am to 5 pm.

Get in touch by phone or post, or by calling in.

Offers information about all Open University courses and other adult education provision where relevant. Is a contact for LIAISE.

Ask for Stephanie Clennell.

Somerset

Somerset Adult Education Advisory Service, Open University (South West Region), 41 Broad Street, Bristol BS1 2EP. Tel: (0272) 299641.

Open normal office hours.

Ask for Jeff Jones.

Yeovil College Education Guidance Service, Ilchester Road, Yeovil, Somerset BA21 3BA. Tel:(0935) 23921 ext 212.

Open by appointment, normal working hours and Monday evenings in college term-time only.

Offers a series of interviews with trained counsellor including aptitude and ability testing (a fee of £6 – waived in cases of hardship – is charged for this service for non-students of the college); also information and advice (free).

Ask for Mark Sutton.

Staffordshire

Educational Guidance Service for Adults, Stoke-on-Trent Technical College, Loughton Centre, Lightwood Road, Stoke-on-Trent. Tel: (0782) 319406.

Suffolk

Suffolk Educational Advisory Service for Adults, Education Department, Grimwade Street, Ipswich IP4 1LJ. Tel: (0473) 55801 ext 4414.

Get in touch initially by phone or post; interviews may then be arranged.

Offers advisory and referral service to any adult wanting to continue in education. This is a central contact point and there is a network of advisers.

Ask for N Williams.

Surrey *see* Sussex – West.
Sussex – East *see* Sussex – West.

Sussex – West
Educational Advisory Service for Adults, The Open University, Wyvern House, 230/232 London Road, East Grinstead, West Sussex. Tel: (0342) 27821. Covers West and East Sussex, Surrey and Kent.
Ask for Regional Enquiry Service.

TYNE AND WEAR
Newcastle-upon-Tyne
Linked Educational Advisory Service for Adults (*LEASA*), College House, Northumberland Road, Newcastle-upon-Tyne NE1 8ST. Tel: (091) 232 9735.
Open throughout the year excluding two weeks at Christmas and Easter – Monday to Thursday, 10 am to 12 noon and 2 to 4 pm. (At other times by appointment.)
Get in touch by phone, by post or by calling in.
Offers a network service for the north east region.
Ask for Margaret Locke.

South Tyneside
Linked Educational Advisory Service for Adults, South Tyne & Wear (*LEASA*), Centre for Continuing Education, 3 Green Terrace, Sunderland SR1 3PZ. Tel: (091) 5676474. Also at West Park Community Centre, Whitehall Street, South Shields. Tel: (091) 456 8093.
Open Monday to Friday 10 am to 4 pm.
Get in touch by phone or by calling in.
Ask for Mick Murray.

WEST MIDLANDS – METROPOLITAN DISTRICTS
Birmingham
Adult Learners Enquiry Centre (*ALEC*), c/o City of Birmingham Polytechnic, Faculty of Education, Westbourne Road, Edgbaston, Birmingham 18. Tel: (021) 454 3550 or 233 2260.
Open Monday to Friday, 9.30 am to 4.30 pm in term time.
Get in touch by phone, by post or by calling in.
Offers information, advice and counselling on all aspects of education and training. Operates kiosk in central library Tuesday 5 to 7 pm, Thursday 12 to 2 pm. Tel: (021) 233 2260. Adult = left school.
Ask for any advisor

Wiltshire
The Adult Guidance Unit, Old College Building, Victoria Road, Swindon SN1 1PT. Tel: (0793) 618866.
Open Monday to Thursday 9.30 am to 4 pm.
Get in touch by phone.
Offers guidance and information on careers and education for those over 19, library facilities.
Ask for head of unit.

Education Guidance Service for Adults, West Wiltshire Adult Guidance Service. A network service.
Get in touch by phone for appointment. Contact either Keith Hopper tel: (022 14) 66241, or David Larmour tel: (022 14) 66516.

YORKSHIRE – SOUTH
Rotherham
Educational Guidance for Adults, The Guardian Centre, Howard Street, Rotherham S65 1DD. Tel: (0709) 374902 or 382121 ext 3657.
Open throughout the year.

Get in touch by phone, by post or by calling in. Central referral and resource agency on education and training opportunities throughout the Rotherham area. *Live and Learn* booklet produced annually identifying contacts in network.
Ask for Robert Wood (co-ordinator).

Sheffield
Sheffield Educational Information Service for Adults (*SEISA*), AUEW House, Furnival Gate, Sheffield S1 3SL. Tel: (0742) 735360.
Open Monday to Friday 8.30 am to 4 pm. Specialist advisers available 11.30 am to 2.30 pm on Wednesdays.
Ask for Frank Lipman.

YORKSHIRE – WEST
Bradford
Educational Advisory Service for Adults (*EASA*), Central Library, Princes Way, Bradford BD1 1NN. Tel: (0274) 753658.
Open throughout the year, Monday to Friday, 9.30 am to 12.30 pm and 1 to 4 pm; at other times by appointment.
Get in touch by phone, by calling in or by post.
Ask for Vivienne Rivis.

Calderdale
Education Guidance Service for Adults, Education Shop, 2 Crossley Street, Halifax. Tel: (0422) 42106.
Open Monday to Friday 8.45 am to 4.45 pm.
Get in touch by phone, by post or by calling in.
Offers information and advice on learning and training opportunities. Adult = over 14 (with school's permission).
Ask for Tony Lilley.

Leeds
Drop-in Education & Advice Centre, 54 The Corn Exchange, Vicar Lane, Leeds LS1 7BR. Tel: (0532) 459816.
Open Monday to Thursday, 9.30 to 12.30 pm and 1.30 to 5 pm, Friday 9.30 am to 12.30 pm.
Offers education advice as well as welfare rights information and drop-in basic education provision; emphasis on basic education up to O-level.
Ask for Jane Riddell.

Education Advice for Adults, Bramley Community Centre, Waterloo Lane, Bramley, Leeds 13. Tel: (0532) 556231. Also at Upper Wortley Centre, Ashley Road, Leeds 12. Tel: (0532) 798435.
Open Monday and Wednesday, 9 am to 12 noon; Thursday 9 am to 12.30 pm. Contact by phone at other times on (0532) 560664.
Offers referral service for all local education and training opportunities.
Ask for Reg Cliffe, Mary Myers or Tim Phelan.

Wakefield
Bretton Hall Continuing Education Unit, Bretton Hall College of Higher Education, West Bretton, Nr Wakefield WF4 4LG. Tel: (092 485) 261.
Get in touch by phone or post only for an appointment.
Ask for Don Sissons.

WALES

Clwyd
Education for Adults Referral Service (*EARS*), Adult Education Office, Rhyl High School, Grange Road, Rhyl, Clwyd. Tel: (0745) 31609.
Open all year, Monday to Friday, 8.30 am to 4.30 pm.
Get in touch by phone or post for an appointment near your home.

Offers information on all aspects of education (formal and informal), training courses, grants, allowances and ways to use leisure time. The service now has a closer liaison with Clwyd library and with the WEA. Adult means beyond school.
Ask for Jackie Yeomans.

SCOTLAND

NETWORK Scotland Ltd, Dowanhill, 74 Victoria Crescent Road, Glasgow G12 9JQ. Tel: (041) 357 1774.
A service which answers postal and telephone enquiries about learning opportunities for adults throughout Scotland and which will either provide information or refer enquirers to a relevant agency.
Ask for Isabel Mather or Joan Rees.

Lothian
Education Information and Advice Service, Kirk O'Field College Adult Learning Centre, Edinburgh University Settlement, 29 Guthrie Street, Edinburgh EH1 1JG. Tel: (031) 226 3801.
Open on appointment basis only.
Get in touch by phone or post.
Ask for Tony Graham.

Area Careers Office, South Bridge Centre, Infirmary Street, Edinburgh EH1 1LT. Tel: (031) 556 4110.
Offers educational guidance on a part-time basis.
Ask for Carole Barnes.

NORTHERN IRELAND

Belfast
Educational Guidance Service for Adults, Room 208, Bryson House, 28 Bedford Street, Belfast BT2 7FE. Tel: (0232) 244274.
Open all year, Monday to Friday 9 am to 5 pm, Tuesday 9 am to 6 pm.
Get in touch by phone, by post, or by calling in (for appointment).
Offers professional guidance and information on eduction and training.Adult = over 19 and having left school for at least a year. An optional initial registration fee of £1.
Ask for Dorothy Eagleson.

THE CAREERS SERVICE

The careers service is run by the Local Education Authority (see *15 Some notes about the system*). It mainly provides advice for school and college leavers – an increasing number of the latter are mature students. In addition many services would like to move towards an all age guidance service and this is the policy of their professional body – The Institute of Careers Officers. Some services such as Birmingham, Coventry and Sheffield already have a policy of working with adults and have several careers officers for that work. Some will see adults if they call in; others have a policy of not offering a service because they have insufficient resources to devote to it. You will have to ask and see what the local policy is. All careers offices are under great pressure because of the high level of unemployment and the huge numbers of young people they deal with. It is still worth asking since the careers service is a major source of educational and vocational guidance.

They also have good collections of information and reference books, so if you can't find one of the books listed here in your local library, do ask them. They sometimes also produce their own information about courses, facilities and jobs in the area. Their reference books are also likely to be up to date, which won't always be the case with library collections.

Advanced Further Education Information Service
Run by the careers service in the summer to help people find college places for advanced and higher education, particularly once exam results are known. Many careers services will have access to daily updated information through Prestel and will offer immediate and expert help. For more information:

★ **ASK** at the local careers office.

INFORMATION SERVICES

Higher Education Information Service (HEIS)
The Service provides course information about opportunities in higher and professional education throughout the UK, and is described more fully in *22 Getting a degree: higher education*. For full details of the Service:

★ **WRITE TO** HEIS, Middlesex Polytechnic, 114 Chase Side, London N14 5PN. Tel: (01) 886–6599.

ECCTIS
The Educational Counselling and Credit Transfer Information Service is currently being developed as a national computerised information service. The development work is being done at the Open University under contract from the Department of Education and Science. At present, the ECCTIS information bank has details of all higher education courses (including advanced further education) in the UK. It also has information about non-advanced further education courses in the south west of England, East Anglia and Northern Ireland leading to qualifications (other than GCE); this is being gradually extended throughout the country. Information on all certified higher and further education courses in Northern Ireland is now available. This can be accessed through Prestel, or by telephoning the Educational Guidance Service for Adults on Belfast 244274.

At present the service is free. You can phone or write with specific queries about courses or for general information about the ECCTIS facilities. Prestel *21161 describes the service and offers a response frame for enquiries; direct on-line searching of the information bank is available through a Gateway Prestel page *8881888#, which also offers a course vacancies service in August and September.

★ **ASK** ECCTIS, PO Box 88, Walton Hall, Milton Keynes MK7 6DB. Tel: (0908) 368921.

GOVERNMENT AGENCIES

Training Access Points (TAP)

The MSC is currently looking at ways of improving public access to information and advice about education and training opportunities related to employment needs. Computerised Training Access Points (TAP) are to be introduced into places such as public libraries, jobcentres and other high street locations. These will provide information on what is available at both national and local level.

In addition, a TAP Network agent will be available in each area to provide further help to people unsure of what they want to do.

During 1987 the TAP service is likely to become available in Banbury, Enfield, Bristol, Dudley, Coventry, Northampton, Cambridge, Chesterfield, Nottingham, Norwich, Kirklees, Wakefield, West Cumbria, Blackpool and Fylde, Newcastle upon Tyne, Clwyd, Cwnbram, Newport, Swansea, Glasgow, Strathclyde region, the Highlands, Dundee and the Isle of Wight.

Each area will have a minimum of five TAP points. Details of how to contact the network will be advertised locally.

PROVIDERS THEMSELVES

One of the greatest problems adults have is that they are so often special cases. The usual rules of entry often don't apply to them. Receptionists tend to know only the standard answers and might say no when their bosses might have said yes. So always ask to see someone from the department concerned with a course. Give the reception staff enough information to enable them to find the person you want to talk to. It's normal for people in education – teachers, heads of department and sometimes even administrative staff – to talk to prospective students to help them find out what's available and appropriate.

If you want an alternative view of what the place is really like, ask the people who are students there already. If you're brave enough, just ask people you see around. If not, ask the secretary of the students' union to fix up for you to have a chat with some students on the course you're interested in. Or ask if they publish an alternative prospectus.

Open colleges

Many colleges and other institutions that provide education for adults are aware of the difficulties that may face adults trying to return to education. Some are experimenting with different ways of making access more easy and are often called things like Open College to emphasise the greater openness to the public – including adults. Open college schemes do however vary enormously in their approach. Those we know of are discussed in more detail in *18 Adult Routes*; it is worth adding that where an open college has been set up, there is likely to be a more helpful attitude to adult students. This may well include staff with the job of providing help and guidance to people looking for the right course. Some of them are also closely linked with the local education guidance service for adults.

Student services officers
An increasing number of colleges have a college counsellor or student services officer. Their job is mainly to help students already at the college with a range of problems that might affect their studies. However, if you are hoping to attend a particular college and you can foresee that you will have problems with child-care, money, some aspect of studying etc, the student services officer would probably be happy to talk to you.

OTHER ORGANISATIONS

Libraries
The library can get you information but they can't usually supply a person to help you work through it. Go to the information desk and ask for any course pamphlets, books and other information you need. If they don't have them, ask where you can get them. Libraries often collaborate with the local adult or community education services. The more they are asked, the more they will do.

They should also have all the books listed in *Booklist*.

Citizens' Advice Bureau
Like the library, they are not experts in the subjects you're asking about, but in getting information for you to use. For instance, they should know if there is an education guidance service for adults in your area. And they should be able to help if you're having difficulties getting information on your financial entitlements. For a list of CABs:

★ **LOOK AT** *Social services year book* (see *Booklist*).

National Advisory Centre on Careers for Women
Offers advisory interviews – for more details see *6 Women*.

★ **WRITE TO** National Advisory Centre on Careers for Women, Drayton House, 30 Gordon Street, London WC1H OAX. Tel: (01) 380 0117.

National Institute of Adult Continuing Education (NIACE)
A national body which does a lot of useful work in adult education and has a good information service for any information on the subject. Its library, which has an information and database, is open to anyone interested.

★ **ASK** NIACE, 19b De Montfort Street, Leicester LE1 7GE. Tel: (0533) 551451.

Scottish Institute of Adult Education (SIAE)
Serves as an information centre for all aspects of the education of adults in Scotland. Membership is open to individuals who receive a variety of information services including use of the library.

★ **ASK** SIAE, 30 Rutland Square, Edinburgh EH1 2BW. Tel: (031) 229 0331 or 229 0311.

HELP YOU PAY FOR

There are a number of vocational guidance services which charge a fee. They advertise in some newspapers and usually provide vocational guidance and assessment tests and a written report.

For a detailed list giving prices, methods used and services offered:

★ **LOOK AT** *Guidelines for the redundant manager,* Sue Webb, £6.25 (£5.00 to members) plus p & p from Professional Publishing Ltd, 7 Swallow Place, London W1R 8AB. Tel: (01) 409 3322.

NATIONAL UNION OF STUDENTS

All full- and part-time students at colleges of further education, higher education, polytechnics and universities in Britain and Northern Ireland are eligible to join NUS. About 95 per cent of full-time students become members of NUS automatically because their local college student union is affiliated to the national union. Membership of the college union is usually automatic. People who find that their local union is not part of the national union may take out individual membership for £5 per year.

How can NUS help you?

Local student unions

If you have questions about a particular college or are already at a college, the first point of contact should be the president or an officer of the college's student union. The president is a student at the college elected by other students; in larger institutions he or she may do the job full-time. Local union officers are trained to advise on problems over course or welfare matters. If the problem is beyond their scope it can be referred to a regional officer.

Regional officers

NUS has eight regional officers who are full-time staff. They will be in touch with what's happening in all the colleges in their area and should have a good idea of the policies of LEAs on things like grants. If you are not already at a college or if your query is a general one try the regional office.

NUS headquarters

NUS nationally has a research department which deals with questions or enquiries on almost any problem that students or would-be students can face. NUS is passionately in favour of an open system of education for all and is always willing to help anyone who is finding the doors closed. They are prepared to deal with individual enquiries – but do try the regional office first. They are particularly good at providing information and advice on problems related to:

- Grants – contact the Grants Officer.
- Welfare rights and benefits – contact the Research Officer-Finance.
- Housing rights – contact the Housing Officer.
- Colleges or courses – contact the Education Officer.
- Overseas students – contact the Overseas Student Officer.

Publications

NUS student welfare manual
Published annually, this provides detailed information about most of the difficulties you may face as a student. Even where it can't provide the answers, it can usually suggest other sources of help. Its advice on grants and finance is second to none. It costs £7.50, but every college union should have a copy.

NUS grants survey
Another annual publication, this includes details of the grants policies of every LEA in the country – who they will give money to, what for, how much and why. Many libraries will have a copy.

National student
Is a magazine published every month during term time and is free to NUS members through colleges. Non-members can subscribe.

★ **WRITE TO** NUS Publications Department, Nelson Mandela House, 461 Holloway Road, London N7 6LJ for a list of NUS publications (enclose sae).

Alternative prospectuses
An increasing number of universities, polytechnics and colleges have an alternative prospectus, written by students to give an inside view and tell you what it's really like to be a student there. They vary from highly polemical critiques of the whole education system to views of what the food is like. The prospectuses are obtained direct from the students' union at the college concerned. They may cost, possibly up to £1.00.

★ **ASK** the students' union at the college you're interested in.

NUS services

A student union membership card can entitle you to cheap, or sometimes free entry to lots of places or events (such as plays or concerts). College unions may negotiate discounts with local shops but NUS also run a National Student Discount Scheme – but you have to buy the special discount card. College unions will have details.

Benefits of student union membership

Membership of your college student union enables you to take part in decisions that may affect you. The union can help in disputes with the college and co-ordinate the student voice on the college's governing body and academic board (both very powerful bodies in any college). Once you are a member it's up to you to make sure they are representing your interests.

More information

In local colleges, ask for the student union president or secretary.

NUS national headquarters
National Union of Students, Nelson Mandela House, 461 Holloway Road, London N7 6LJ. Tel: (01) 272–8900.

Regional offices

East Anglia: Bill Rammell, c/o Hatfield Polytechnic Student Union, PO Box 109, Hatfield, Herts. Tel: (07072) 72207.

East Midlands: James Walker, c/o Loughborough Student Union, Ashby Road, Loughborough, Leicester. Tel: (0509) 239754.

London: Vaughan West, c/o University of London Student Union, Malet Street, London WC1. Tel: (01) 631 3541.

North East Region: Nick Gash, c/o Teesside Polytechnic Student Union, Borough Road, Middlesborough, Teesside. Tel: (0642) 249079.

North West Region: Gill Stewart, c/o Bowland Annexe, University of Lancaster, Bailrigg, Lancaster. Tel: (0524) 35638.

South East Region: Sarah Gilmore, c/o Surrey University Student Union, Guildford, Surrey GU2 5XF. Tel: (0483) 575189.

South West Region: David Johnson, c/o University of Bristol Student Union, Queens Road, Clifton, Bristol 8. Tel: (0272) 734970.

West Midlands Region: Paul Kent, c/o University of Birmingham Union, Edgbaston, Birmingham B15 2TU. Tel: (021) 472 1841.

Mature student societies

Many larger student unions have mature student societies or someone responsible for representing older students.

2 Studying

It's different from school
Some basic study skills
Extras that often aren't covered
Adult realities
Courses to help with studying
Books on studying

IT'S DIFFERENT FROM SCHOOL

Once you've left school, whether you are 16 or 99, the key fact about learning is that *you* organise it, in *your* way, and it has to fit in to *your* life. What your teachers think does not matter – their job should be to be available, for you to refer to, to help you to gauge your progress and to give guidance when you want it. If you need outside pressure to help you learn, they can supply that – if you don't want it they shouldn't give it.

Unfortunately it still often happens that you may be told to learn things without being told *how*. Yet there are techniques of studying which can themselves be learnt and which can help the rest of your learning. So, learning about *how* to learn is an important part of any studying we do as adults.

Learning is a natural human activity which all of us do all our lives. We never stop. As children we learn to walk, talk, understand where we are, and what everything around us is for; as adults we learn many new skills (working, using the launderette, driving etc). Learning is not something you only do at school. The only difference between normal everyday learning and being educated or trained is that in the second case you do it self-consciously, on purpose. But learning is itself a set of techniques you can learn to be better at, by doing study skills courses or reading books about it. There is a list of some relevant books at the end of the chapter; they may help you once you've decided to take the plunge. But they sometimes make it seem even harder than it is, so some other thoughts are included which might help you study other books on studying. There is also a short section on skill learning (learning practical things, or manual jobs) which no study books ever seem to mention.

SOME BASIC STUDY SKILLS

Efficient reading is fast reading

But don't take too much notice of books that tell you to speed up your eye-movements. Your eyes move quickly if you read quickly, not the other way round. Just try to read quickly; don't pause over bits you find hard – finish reading and go back to them later. And never read more than you have to. If you're told to read a book, but you only need one chapter of it for the work you're doing – don't read the rest.

Note-taking

Very important and very personal. Your notes have to be a way of reminding yourself of what you've already learned. Practise making notes of things that don't matter – conversations with friends, TV programmes. See how short you can make them. Look at them four weeks later. Do they remind you of the occasion they're about? If so, they're okay.

Passing exams

A matter of technique as much as knowledge. You need to know in advance what sort of exam it is (essay, multiple choice etc), what questions you're likely to be asked and how much time you'll have to do them. Make sure you have an essay planned for the likely questions you prefer. But don't bank too much on them coming up; have your other knowledge in reserve.

Revising

Most books advise you not to cram yourself full the night before. But lots of people do! If you can't sleep anyway, you may as well. The main thing is to stop worrying and just get on with it when you sit down and start the exam.

EXTRAS THAT OFTEN AREN'T COVERED

The importance of talking

At school most of us had to study in silence, and looking at a classmate's work or discussing it was called cheating. Nothing could be sillier. Talking about what you learn (especially to someone else who's also learning it) is absolutely invaluable. It is a way for your mind to organise what it's been given in its own way – an essential element of all learning. And discussion is the basis of the tutorial system in university education. Until you can explain something to someone else, you can't be sure you've learned it yourself. So, if you have a friend or family member who can stand it, make a point of explaining what you've learned to them; of telling them what you're going to put in your essay; of showing them how to do whatever skill you've just mastered. And co-operate with fellow students if you have any! Make agreements to read each other's essays and notes, even to take turns to take notes of lectures or broadcasts, so that one of you can concentrate on watching and the other on writing. Then write them up together. It's not cheating!

Learning a skill

If you're learning a skill – that is, teaching your body to do things to something else, like working a machine or making things, you may not be able to practise at home because the equipment isn't there – not many people have lathes or road rollers in the back yard!

But you can still practise by using your imagination and your friends.

- Imagine yourself doing the job you're learning. Picture yourself going through all the procedures. If there's something you find hard, imagine yourself doing it easily.

- Explain what you've learned to someone else. Show them, by making all the movements in the air, or, using the cooker as the machine you're learning to use. Describe the bits you find difficult or don't understand. Talking them through often solves the problems.

ADULT REALITIES

A place to study

Most books on learning and studying advise you to start by getting yourself somewhere warm and quiet to write in. But for many of us it's almost impossible. If you have children, getting somewhere quiet can mean that they never see you. The other thing about it that's wrong is the assumption that people always study best in silence. There are different levels of concentration needed for different tasks. Lots of people can cope with some noise, some people prefer it; many students always have the radio on as they work; we know of one who could only concentrate while travelling on the underground; he did his work by travelling the whole length of the Piccadilly Line twice a week! The important thing is to decide what suits you.

Getting organised

This can become a way of avoiding getting started. If you spend long enough worrying about the details – silence, warmth, pen to hand, paper, books in neat piles – you'll never start. And even when you do, your mind is on your surroundings, not your work. You sit there thinking of yourself sitting there studying; you seem to be reading but when you reach the end of the chapter, you don't know what it said.

Breaks

The other wrong assumption is that everyone sits still at studying for long periods at a time. People behave quite differently from one another. Short interruptions are okay! They give you a breather, a chance to see the family; time for your mind to work without strain. Visits to the toilet are a great help to many; you may come back feeling more relaxed and with fresh, clean ideas! Baths do the same. Planning your study time in short periods is also a good way of proving yourself – you can aim to do a particular item, complete it, then have a break. If you force yourself to study when you don't want to, you won't be learning effectively.

Danger – student at work!

Despite all we've said so far, you *will* need some peace and quiet. And you will have to work out how many hours a week you should be doing, to see if you can fit them in. If not, something will have to go. Most people can't study, decorate their home, play with the baby, watch TV, go to football, the pub, see friends, make love, do a job, run a household ... all at once.

Ideally you should have several blocks of time spread over the week – if you're a regular person, always at the same time, if not, arranged week by week. If you get behind, or you're only on a short course, or it's just before an exam, you can try a short intensive burst (a week or so!) when you cut out everything else. But that sort of thing can't go on for long. It causes nervous breakdowns and breaks up families. There are also more subtle family problems. A lot of people turn to study when they want to make some kind of change in themselves, or can sense one coming anyway. The family may not like it. They may prefer the mother or father, wife or husband they've always known. Becoming a student probably isn't the reason for the change, it's the result of it. But husbands, wives or children, wondering what's happening to the family, may not see it in that way.

WOMAN, 35, DOING SOCIAL WORK TRAINING
My second essay I failed, but that was entirely my own fault. When I say it was my own fault, going on a course meant a big upheaval in my family and my marriage, and I was getting an awful lot of hassle from my husband: jealousy, being excluded. I was under a great deal of pressure, and I think it went to my head a little bit, the freedom. Anyway, when I knew that I'd failed it – it's not unusual apparently – what happens then is that you get a tutorial immediately – a private tutorial, and help to rewrite it. I've been exceptionally lucky in my tutor, she's bothered to talk to my husband, saying you're not the only ones going through this, she and her husband went through it.

Hangovers
Don't be surprised if, when it's all over, you feel rather flat and empty. You may have had high hopes for your course: that it would make you feel cleverer, get you a job, change your life. And it might have done all those, but you still feel you're the same person; the change is perhaps rather less dramatic than you'd hoped. Or perhaps some of your expectations haven't happened.

It often takes time to see the point of what you've done, perhaps weeks or even years.

COURSES TO HELP WITH STUDYING

Study skill courses
More and more courses these days include something on study skills. There are also special courses to help you if you want to return to study and are a bit worried about it; some of these are discussed in *18 Adult routes*, *19 Starting again* and *20 Basics*. The Open University recognises this problem by offering new students preparatory packages before they start. There are also a number of correspondence courses available on the subject (see *26 Learning by post*).

Any courses
In all adult education, tutors say that what it's really about is developing self-confidence – so in the last resort, you are probably learning to learn by doing it, whatever the course, whatever the subject, whatever the level. Don't let worrying about it stop you – you only find out by trying. If in serious doubt try a short course, or a part-time course, as a taster before committing yourself.

WOMAN, 34, DOING AN A-LEVEL
I'm very uncertain about myself. I went to a secondary modern school and I was put off going further. I thought that if I tried doing an A-level to see where I stood, if I was successful I might try for another and take it from there.

BOOKS ON STUDYING

There are many books on studying available; go to your library or bookshop and have a browse. Here are a few that are useful.

Read better, read faster, De Leeuw, Penguin 1965
Learn how to study, Derek Rowntree, Macdonald and Co Publishers Ltd, 1976
Speed reading, Tony Buzan, David and Charles, 1977
How to study, Harry Maddox, Pan Information, 1982
Mastering study skills, Richard Freeman, Macmillan, 1982

NEC Study skills series
The National Extension College has produced a set of booklets on studying.

★ **WRITE TO** National Extension College, 18 Brooklands Avenue, Cambridge CB2 2HN. Tel: (0223) 316644. Ask for information on study skills.

3 Studying with children

Fitting in with school times | *Child care facilities*

WOMAN, 26
I did a TOPS clerk/book-keeping course when my youngest child was two and the older ones were six and seven. The two year old was in the state nursery and the older ones were at school – a 15 year old collected them and looked after them until I got home. I was lucky. I am a single parent so I had more chance of getting into a nursery. But I had to be prepared to do all the housework in the evening, cope with small children and do my homework as well. You need to be organised.

FITTING IN WITH SCHOOL TIMES

Many courses are full-time which may mean 9 am to 5 pm or even longer. Some JTS courses fall into this category. Other courses don't require such extended hours, and many are available part-time, but part-time could still mean 9 am to 4 pm which may be less useful than 10 am to 3 pm spread over more days. JTS courses are becoming increasingly varied. For example some now include an element of open learning (see *17 Flexible learning*).

Others are in modular form which could provide greater flexibility. Not many JTS courses leave school holidays free; in fact there is a move by MSC to encourage local colleges to put courses on in the holidays. You will often have a lot of homework or study to do outside lectures as well. You may not need to attend many lectures on a full-time higher education course and then it's only for thirty weeks a year. Colleges have longer holidays than schools, but they don't usually have half-term breaks. Some places like Hatfield Polytechnic and Queens College Glasgow do realise that some of their students are parents, and organise the length of day accordingly on some of their courses.

You could do something that fits in with your children, while they are at school or in bed, like a correspondence course, but it's a solitary form of study. Many people who have been looking after children full-time for some years want to get out and meet people as much as they want to study. You may have more time when children are younger; they go to bed early, don't yet have friends around and don't need help with homework.

Distance learning developments such as the Open University and other flexible study methods (described in *17 Flexible learning*) probably combine maximum flexibility with a chance to see other people from time to time. And courses which explore different careers or ways of returning to study (such as New Opportunities for Women, described in *19 Starting again*) are usually run from 10 am to 3 pm.

A book that will help you choose courses that fit in with school times, as well as those providing creche facilities, is due to be published in Spring 1987. It lists all courses and contacts that are useful for women returning to work and study.

★ **LOOK AT** *Women returners network directory* by Ruth Michaels, published by Longman, at about £5.95.

CHILD CARE FACILITIES

At the college

A number of colleges have a creche or playgroup attached to them, sometimes with priority for students, but child care facilities are often one of the first things to be cut at times like the present. A survey carried out in 1980 identified only 146 colleges with regular facilities for child care: 72 in higher education, 32 in FE colleges and 42 in adult education institutions. They may run all week or just for a few hours. Remember many colleges have buildings in several places and the playgroup may be in only one of them.

You will have to check with the college concerned. Even if the college you are interested in does have child care facilities, there may be a limited number of places available or there may be a waiting list. They may have some method of giving priority to certain students – so do ask well in advance. The *Gazetteer* at the end of the book gives information about child care provision for people attending adult education classes in some local education authorities.

Some of the newer provision has more extensive and imaginative child care. Some of the women's workshops described in *6 Women*, have not only child care facilities but also transport to collect children from school.

Outside the college

Since all child care facilities have to be registered with the local social services department, it should be able to tell you what other facilities there are near the college. The Pre-School Playgroups Association (PPA) may also be able to tell you of local playgroups.

★ **ASK** PPA, 61/63 Kings Cross Road, London WC1X 9LL. Tel: (01) 833 0991.

★ **ASK** Scottish Pre-Schools Playgroups (SCOPE), 16 Sandyford Place, Glasgow G3 7NB. Tel: (041) 221 4148/9.

★ **ASK** Northern Ireland PPA, 11 Wellington Park, Belfast BT9 6DJ. Tel: (0232) 662825.

Child-minders

Child-minders have to be registered with the local social services department so if you are thinking about using somebody to look after children while studying, do check whether they are registered. There are two useful leaflets on child-minding and child-minders:

★ **SEND FOR** *So you want to find a child-minder* and *So you want to be a child-minder*, free with SAE for first copy, 5p each for further copies (available while stocks last) from: The National Childminding Association, 8 Masons Hill,

Bromley, Kent BR2 9EY. It also publishes a more comprehensive leaflet *I need a child minder*, price 30p plus p&p or an A4 SAE. It gives more detailed information for parents, including questions worth considering.

Single parents

The position of single parents can be even more difficult though in some areas you will be given some priority with child care facilities. Two useful organisations are:

National Council for One Parent Families

Primarily an advisory and information agency and a pressure group concerned with lone parenthood. Advice is given on a wide range of subjects affecting single parents including welfare benefits, legal rights, child care and employment. It publishes leaflets and booklets useful to single parents. The library provides an information service about one parent families for students and researchers.

★ **ASK** National Council for One Parent Families, 255 Kentish Town Road, London NW5 2LX. Tel: (01) 267 1361.

Gingerbread

A self-help organisation with local groups all over the country which provide moral and practical help to single parents. There are a few formal day-care arrangements in some areas, but in most cases any child care arrangements would be made through informal contacts within the local group.

It publishes two relevant leaflets, *Daycare* which gives information about sources of day care available and *Further education and how it affects your supplementary benefit*. You can get them from the London office who can also put you in touch with local groups. The local group in Bradford has started a self-help educational project, *GingerALE*. It runs free courses for single parents, usually one day a week for six to ten weeks, though some courses run continuously. Things covered include health education, DIY, racism awareness, welfare rights, matrimonial law, literacy and basic skills. It also provides information and counselling for single parents wanting to go back into education.

★ **ASK** Gingerbread, 35 Wellington Street, London WC2 7BN. Tel: (01) 240 0953. GingerALE, Gingerbread Centre, 45 Darley Street, Bradford BD1 3HN. Tel: (0274) 720564.

4 Job change and development

Changing job
Education and training
Fellowships
New ways of working
Books

CHANGING JOB

It is becoming increasingly normal for us to change job several times during our working lives for a number of reasons:

- some industries are declining and employing fewer people in total
- other industries are developing and growing – such as the computer industry, videos, laser technology and so on
- times of recession mean that firms close and fewer people are employed
- mechanisation, automation and now computerisation mean that fewer people are needed to do a job than was the case a few years ago
- changes in society mean that people have different expectations and are now happier to change jobs than they might have been a few years ago
- and so on.

You may be changing job because:

- you're fed up with the one you've got
- you need to change job to get promotion
- you've been made redundant
- you've suffered illness or accident
- or for a number of other reasons.

Equally, you may stay in the same job but need to retrain as your job changes.

WOMAN, 29, RECENTLY RETRAINED AS A TOURIST GUIDE

I'd got as far as I could go in careers work without going into management – the choice was either to go into management, take an administrative job which I didn't feel would suit me, or to make a sideways move and I didn't see the point of that. It wasn't that I didn't like it, it was more that I needed a change and I wanted a job that would give me the freedom not to have to work to a regular pattern.

I did a six-month course run by the London Tourist Board, technically a part-time course but in reality it's very hard to pass the course unless you are full-time for at least half of the six months, I would say. In fact I gave up work two months after the beginning of the course; I had two months where I was working and studying, and then four months where I was studying full-time. I got the London Tourist Board Blue Badge qualification.

Job change and unemployment

Because of the huge growth of unemployment, lots of schemes have sprung up to help unemployed people find new jobs. Much of what they do is useful to anyone who wants a new start – even if they don't *have* to change jobs. Such schemes often start by getting you to look at yourself, examine your strengths and weaknesses, skills and knowledge and work out how to use these in different ways. Schemes specially for people without work are described in *5 Out of work*.

EDUCATION, TRAINING AND JOB CHANGE

Education and training are great aids to the process of job change and so the whole of this book is relevant. Some of the things you can use education for include:

- learning a new skill that you can use as the basis for a new trade or profession
- updating an existing skill, learning how your skills can be developed using new technology or other new methods
- gaining extra skills to enhance those you already have (eg reading and writing, marketing, computing, management, languages)
- gaining a qualification to legitimise skills you already possess (eg going on a welding course in order to get the necessary insurance certificate that would allow you to be employed on certain jobs)
- trying out or testing a new field to see whether you will like it
- giving yourself space to think about your future and the options available.

And there are many others.

Any education or training may be relevant – it depends how you use it.

Computer-aided guidance

In the Leeds area Lifeskills Associates offer do-it-yourself careers guidance using *Career-builder*. This is a computer-assisted interactive career development programme. You book time on a two hourly session basis.

★ **WRITE TO** Lifeskills Associates, Clarendon Chambers, 51 Clarendon Road, Leeds LS2 9PJ. Tel: (0532) 467128.

Full-time courses

Money is clearly the biggest problem in doing a full-time course, especially if you have been used to a good income. There are three types of course for which you can usually get a grant:

- higher education – but only if you haven't done it already
- the Job Training Scheme also offers a range of courses; many are full-time and in some cases allowances may be paid
- adult residential colleges.

Even if you get a grant, things can still be tight. Some people use their savings, some manage to get bank loans, some live off their partners, some work part-time. It is undoubtedly difficult but don't give up without trying.

Part-time courses

Part-time courses are more attractive than full-time courses to many people and there are many types available.

Distance learning is a type of provision that is growing, in particular for the updating of skills – some of the opportunities such as the Open Tech are described in *17 Flexible learning*. Short courses provide another type of updating training that is widely used and that is being actively encouraged by the government through its PICKUP scheme (described in *33 Training at work*). Almost every type of education or training is available in a part-time version, though part-time degree courses are only beginning to be widespread.

Part-time study combined with paid work is usually hard, but on the other hand employers will often contribute to the cost and the things you learn may have immediate relevance to your work.

FELLOWSHIPS

A number of organisations provide funds to allow people to take a break for travel or study in mid-career. Each has different objectives, but they usually advertise in relevant newspapers. They are competitive – many apply, only a few succeed – but they can provide a good way of creating your own career development. Two examples:

The Arkleton Trust which awards two fellowships of up to six months each year, for people in mid-career concerned with rural development. Proposals should reach the trust by 1 May each year.

It has also set up the Bernard Conyers Fund Rural Communications Fellowship to encourage individuals or small organisations to disseminate information, findings or ideas related to rural development with priority given to material relating to the Third World, the links between Europe and the Third World, or the lessons Europe can learn from Third World experience.

★ **WRITE TO** The Administrator, The Arkleton Trust, Enstone, Oxford OX7 4HH. Tel: (01) 584 9315.

Winston Churchill Memorial Trust which awards a number of travel fellowships in different fields each year.

★ **WRITE TO** Winston Churchill Memorial Trust, 15 Queen's Gate Terrace, London SW7 5PR. Tel: (01) 584 9315. Applications close each year on 31 October.

To find the names of other such trusts:

★ **LOOK AT** *The grants directory* published by Macmillan, which you should find in the public library.

NEW WAYS OF WORKING

In recent years a number of different ways of working have become more common and in many instances facilitate job change. In these cases the change of job and the education may be closely inter-linked.

Job sharing
This means taking one job and dividing it between two people. It can be a successful way of working part-time if you can find someone to share with, and if your employer is willing.

New Ways to Work
New Ways to Work, a small charity, promotes flexible working arrangements: job sharing in particular. If you live or work in the Greater London area their computerised register aims to match you with a partner seeking similar work and costs £2 to waged people and 50p to the unwaged. They may also be able to give you local contacts in some other parts of the country. They publish several booklets and factsheets covering various aspects of job sharing and in particular *Guide for employers* and *A factsheet for employees*.

★ **WRITE TO** New Ways to Work, 347A Upper Street, London N1 0PD. Tel: (01) 226 4026.

Self employment
See *35 Training for self employment*.

BOOKS ON CAREER CHANGE

The *What else* series published by COIC provides a lot of useful ideas about career development. Current titles include:
What else can a secretary do? £2.50 plus 50p p&p
What can a teacher do except teach? £1.95 plus 30p
What else can a housewife do? £1.95 plus 30p
What can a nurse do? £1.95 plus 30p
What else can you do? £2.50 plus 50p

Other useful COIC books are:
Occupations '87 £15.00 plus £1.90 p&p
Working it out £ 1.00 plus 30p
Job ideas £ 3.50 plus 50p

★ **WRITE TO** COIC, Sales Department, MSC, Moorfoot, Sheffield S1 4PQ. Tel: (0742) 704563. Orders for books to the value of up to £15 should be sent to MSC, Department CW, ISCO 5, The Paddock, Frizinghall, Bradford BD9 4HD. Payment must accompany order; cheques should be made out to MSC.

Other sources:

Branching out: a workbook for early retirement
Build your own rainbow – a workbook for career and life management. By Barrie Hopson and Mike Scally.
Published by Lifeskills Accociates (address above).

What colour is your parachute?
UK edition by Richard Nelson-Bolles with added material by Tom Snow.
Published by Ten Speed, 1985.

5 Out of work

Education and training
What can you do?
Money
Specially for the unemployed
Other sources of help

EDUCATION AND TRAINING

Unemployment is an unpleasant experience – but it can also be an opportunity to do new things that you previously wanted to do, and couldn't. Education and training provide one way of doing new things. Whether they are appropriate for you depends on what you want – if you're not sure, see *1 Advice and help*.

Education and training can give you the chance to:

- learn new skills
- update existing skills and knowledge
- gain confidence
- get new contacts, and access to a new set of people who may be useful (for finding work or developing new interests)
- keep occupied – help you to stop yourself getting depressed
- show you've been using your time well when you apply for jobs
- spend your time in a pleasant way – it can be enjoyable.

WHAT CAN YOU DO?

Almost everything in the book is available to you. A few courses are mainly for people at work – but because of the growth of unemployment, lots of schemes have sprung up to help unemployed people find new jobs and learn new skills. Much of what they do is useful to anyone who wants a new start. Such schemes often start by getting you to look at yourself, examine your strengths and weaknesses, skills and knowledge, and work out how to use these differently.

Some types of education or training are especially suitable because:

- you get paid while you do them – such as higher education or adult residential colleges (described in *24 Training for a new job*, *21 Adult residential colleges* and *22 Getting a degree*)
- they're flexible – you don't have to attend at fixed times to complete the course, so you can continue even if you find a job (described in *17 Flexible learning*)
- you're worried about your basic maths or writing – there are many opportunities to work on these skills (described in *20 Basics*); basic education is also often very flexible in approach
- you are young and unemployed – the Youth Training Scheme offers many opportunities for work and training (described in *7 School leavers*).

MONEY

If you're unemployed, you're not earning. You've usually got to be available for work in order to draw unemployment or supplementary benefit. If you go on a course, even a part-time course, you might be considered not available for work.

The 21 hours rule

Unless you are a single parent or someone who is not required to sign on as available for work in order to get supplementary benefit (eg because of age or disability), you cannot study full-time and claim supplementary benefit.

But you can claim supplementary benefit and study providing it is part-time and you carry on signing on as available for work. This means that you would have to be prepared to leave the course immediately a job vacancy occurred. The supplementary benefits regulations and their interpretation are confusing and it is not possible to say with any certainty what constitutes 'part-time study'. If it is less than 21 hours a week there is a good chance of getting benefit. If it is less than 12 hours a week there is no risk of losing either supplementary benefit or child benefit. Before starting on a course you have to have been available for work for three months, during which time you can only study for 12 hours without risk of loss of benefit. If in doubt, get advice from a student welfare officer if your college has one, from the Citizens' Advice Bureau or from your local Educational Guidance Service for Adults. There is more about the 21 hours rule in *39 Money: what for, where from.*

JTS – the Job Training Scheme

The Job Training Scheme (JTS), a successor to the Training Opportunities Scheme (TOPS), provides a choice of training for unemployed people. It can add to the skills they already have or develop the new skills that local employers particularly need. Opportunities in the technical and new technology fields are particular features of the training offered. Most training is full-time and in some cases allowances may be available. The training schemes are open to people over the age of 18 (see *7 School leavers* if you are under 18) who are unemployed on the day the course starts – and you must have been away from full-time education for at least two years.

JTS includes special provision for disabled people – for example, individual training with an employer for between four weeks and a year, after which the disabled person is normally employed for at least a short period.

★ **ASK** at your local Jobcentre.

Higher education

If you go on a full-time degree level course and haven't done one before you should be eligible for a local authority grant (described in *40 LEA grants*).

Adult residential colleges

These courses carry a government bursary. The colleges concerned will provide the necessary information about the awards.

The Open University

If you have been unemployed for six weeks or more when your fees become due, the Open University may be able to waive most of the fee. You should first apply to your local authority for assistance with fees. If they turn you down, you can then ask the OU to waive the fees. Details of the scheme are available from OU regional offices (listed in *23 The Open University*). If you are suffering financial hardship, you may be able to get fees paid from the student assistance fund. To find out if you are eligible contact your OU regional office.

Fees

If you get a local authority grant to go on a course your fees are usually paid for you as well. If you just go along and enrol at your local college however, you will have fees to pay and they can be quite high. Some colleges and local authorities have a policy of *no fees* or *reduced fees* for people who are registered unemployed. Others don't have a policy about it but you can still ask to have your fees waived. It may be straightforward or complicated – for example, you may sometimes have to write a letter applying to have your fees waived – it's still worth asking. The policy about fees for unemployed people in adult or further education classes in each LEA is described in the *Gazetteer: places to study*.

SPECIALLY FOR THE UNEMPLOYED

Special courses

Many colleges and adult education centres have courses for unemployed people which may be to teach you new skills, to help you develop ideas about new jobs and fields of work or just to help you cope with unemployment. There are many of these and, often being short courses, they are put on at short notice so it is not possible to list them here. Information should be available at your local college, library, advice centre or unemployment centre.

REPLAN

A programme which has encouraged local authorities and others to set up courses for unemployed people.

★ **WRITE TO** REPLAN, c/o NIACE, 19b de Montfort Street, Leicester LE1 7GE.

★ **ASK** your regional REPLAN field officer about opportunites in your area.

Replan field officers

Janet Mokades, NIACE Office, Regional Advisory Council for Further Education, Tavistock House South, Tavistock Square, London WC1H 9LR.

David Parker, 108c Stokes Croft, Bristol B31 3RU.

Sue Waddington and Kay Driver, NIACE Office, 47 New Walk, Leicester LE1 6TE.

Pat Gale, NIACE Office, Northern Council for Further Education, 5 Grosvenor Villas, Grosvenor Road, Newcastle Upon Tyne NE2 2RU.

Margaret Purdy, NIACE Office, Welsh Joint Education Committee, 4th Floor, Aribee House, Greyfriars Road, Cardiff CF1 3AE.

Jane Cowell, NIACE Office, North Western Regional Advisory Council for Further Education, The Town Hall, Walkden Road, Worsley, Manchester M28 4QE.

TUC unemployed workers' centres

The TUC and trades unions through local trades councils have established over 210 centres for the unemployed. All offer advice on welfare benefits and many offer social and recreational facilities and opportunities for education. Users are often involved in their management.

To find out if there is one in your area, or to help get one started, contact your trade union, the local trades council, or the TUC regional office (addresses listed in *32 Trade union education*).

Voluntary agencies

There are a variety of drop-in and self-help schemes operating through the work of voluntary bodies, frequently through local councils for voluntary service.

★ **ASK** your Citizens' Advice Bureau or library.

The Job Change Project

It offers advice and support to groups and agencies concerned with unemployment and runs a programme of workshops for people who work in unemployment centres or are involved in self-help groups. There is also a national development worker, available to offer advice on setting up a self-help group, finding premises, negotiating leases, advertising and management.

★ **ASK** Job Change Project, 318 Summer Lane, Birmingham B19 3RL. Tel: (021) 359 6596.

For redundant managers

Organisations like the British Institute of Management offer courses for redundant managers and professional staff. They tend to cost more; but firms may pay for them as part of a redundancy settlement. The BIM have published a useful book:

★ **LOOK AT** *Guidelines for the redundant manager*, Sue Webb, from Professional Publishing Ltd, 7 Swallow Place, off Princes Street, London W1R 8AB. Tel: (01) 409 3322.

Professional and Executive Recruitment

PER has set up a Job and Career Change Programme to help unemployed managers and professional staff to get new jobs. The programme operates on a part-time basis over a maximum of four months. It offers access to expert advice, workshops and a jobsearch base with telephone and secretarial facilities.

★ **ASK** the local PER office, Jobcentre or Job Club.

OTHER SOURCES OF HELP

Don't forget the Education Guidance Services for Adults in *1 Advice and help*.

★ **LOOK AT** *The unemployment handbook* and *Nice work if you can get it*. Both by Guy Dauncey and available from the National Extension College, 18 Brooklands Avenue, Cambridge CB2 2HN. Tel: (0223) 316644.

6 Women

The problem
Sex discrimination
Women-only courses
Management and professional courses
Technology and technical skills
Return to work or study
Women into business
Women's studies
Women's organisations

THE PROBLEM

The hard fact is that this country spends much more of its money on the education of men than on that of women. Equality will not be realised until the education system fully recognises that women have babies, look after children and care for old people; that many women seek a career when they are 30 and so want to make a new start – something that used to be regarded as exceptional. Though things are changing now, it is still hard for women to get the services they undoubtedly want from the education system. The problem is partly unwillingness to arrange courses to suit the convenience of mothers, but attitudes have a lot to do with it too. To get what they want, women often have to be more determined and more persistent than men.

SEX DISCRIMINATION

It is unlawful to discriminate against anyone because of their sex. No education or training opportunity should be denied to you because of your sex, whether you're a man or a woman. But apart from formal discrimination, the system works against women indirectly too. For example:

- Women may not be told about training opportunities traditionally used by men, eg engineering courses.
- Women with children are asked whether they'll miss time on a course because of their children being ill (something men are never asked)
- Many courses are not available on a part-time basis so parents (usually, but not always, women) with children to look after find it difficult to attend
- The hours courses run may not be very helpful. A starting time of 9.30 am is quite different from 9 am if you've children to get to school first.

Overcoming sex discrimination

The law is on your side and the Equal Opportunities Commission (EOC) exists to help you fight sex discrimination (there is a separate EOC for Northern Ireland). If you think you have been the victim of sex discrimination they want to hear from you. The EOC publishes several guides to the Sex Discrimination Act. *A catalogue of free publications* lists these guides and other relevant publications; ask to be put on the mailing list for their magazine *Equality now*.

★ **ASK** The Equal Opportunities Commission, Overseas House, Quay Street, Manchester M3 3HN. Tel: (061) 833 9244, or the Equal Opportunities Commission for Northern Ireland, Chamber of Commerce House, 22 Great Victoria Street, Belfast BT2 7BA. Tel: (0232) 242752.

WOMAN, 33, NOW A UNIVERSITY GRADUATE
I was 24. I'd been a secretary since leaving school at 15. I wanted to go to university. I had no qualifications at all. They gave me a hard time. I felt they laughed at me – 'who does she think she is?'. My interviews were all about my motivation – not my ability. They didn't take me seriously – they kept throwing at me the idea that I was doing it as a substitute for my husband, since my marriage had broken up. It made me angry because it wasn't true. I was told I had to do O-levels, but I didn't want to. It would have taken years. I didn't believe it and I was right, I did my A-levels straight away and then went to university.

Legal discrimination
Having said this, there are some courses and facilities for women or men only. It is still legal to employ men only for some jobs: coal-mining (underground jobs), the armed services, ministers of religion, deep-sea fishing and firms employing fewer than six people are exempt from the Sex Discrimination Act. So, training for these jobs can also be restricted to men.

It is illegal in education or training to discriminate in favour of women or men unless:

- it's a course to prepare women for jobs that are traditionally men's jobs
- the course has been 'designated' by the Secretary of State for Employment
- it was a single-sex establishment before the Act came into force
- it is a course of physical education (whether a yoga group once a week or full-time course to train PE teachers)
- it is a private club – that should cover many self-help groups.

Using these exemptions, a number of courses have been, and are being set up to encourage women to use education to the full. You can use all the opportunities described throughout the book but many women prefer to use women-only courses, colleges and facilities, and courses set up for this represent what is often called *affirmative action*, also sometimes called *positive discrimination*.

So this chapter describes some courses which have been specifically and exclusively designed to meet the needs of women. Many offer better than average child-care facilities.

The Woman Returners Network
WRN exists to promote and encourage opportunities for women in education and training. They produce a *Women returners directory* which lists opportunities on a county by county basis of courses with contacts and relevant local information. They are also setting up local networks.

★ **LOOK AT** *Women returning to learning,* Enid and Edward Hutchinson, available for £9.95 from the National Extension College, 18 Brooklands Avenue, Cambridge CB2 2HN.

WOMEN-ONLY COURSES

This selection is intended to provide an idea of the range of courses and providers now emerging. Addresses are given in the *Gazetteer*.

Single-sex colleges

There are still a few single-sex colleges for women in higher education mainly at Cambridge (Lucy Cavendish College, New Hall and Newnham), Oxford (St Hilda's and Somerville), and Durham (Trevelyan and St Mary's). Lucy Cavendish College, Cambridge, is for women over the age of 25 only. Duncraig Castle College in the Highland region of Scotland is a domestic science and catering college for young women.

Hatfield Polytechnic

This polytechnic provides a good example of what can be achieved by designated institutions. It runs a range of courses: New Opportunities for Women, Accountancy Plus for Women, and Marketing for Women. These last two are EEC sponsored; unemployed women over the age of 25 are eligible and if accepted have their fees paid and receive a training allowance. They also run a part-time day degree course and a polyprep course but these are not exclusively for women.

Hillcroft College

This is the only one of the eight adult residential colleges which is for women only. It runs one- and two-year courses for women over the age of 21 who may lack qualifications. It is described more fully in *21 Adult residential colleges*.

WOMAN, 43, STUDENT AT HILLCROFT COLLEGE

When I first thought about it I thought 'ugh' and then I thought more about it. I knew about trade union courses where often you are the only woman with 17 men. They think you are there as a bed-warmer. It takes you days to convince them that you are there as a shop steward. At college I knew I'd have the pressure of returning to studying. I didn't want the battle to be accepted as equal, as well. Here, there is a strong identification that we are all women.

Bradford and Ilkley Community College

Encourages women to apply for all their courses and in particular for areas that have traditionally only been studied by men, such as engineering. They also have a range of introductory women-only courses in some areas of science and technology, and publish a leaflet listing them.

MANAGEMENT AND PROFESSIONAL COURSES

Henley Management College
Although designated, they do not run separate courses for women. They do offer some scholarships each year (to women already in management and those hoping to return to it) on their eight-week General Management course and on the 18-month modular MBA.

★ **WRITE TO** Henley, The Management College, Greenlands, Henley-on-Thames, Oxon RG9 3AU. Tel: (0491) 571454.

Industrial Society/*Cosmopolitan*
The Industrial Society runs one-off conferences, evening sessions and workshops and courses in various parts of the country for women at a professional or supervisory level. They also run a residential course (The Pepperell Development Course) and three courses in conjunction with *Cosmopolitan* magazine (The Saturday Development Course, Personal Marketing and Setting Up Your Own Business).

★ **ASK** Juliet Relph, Administrator for Women's Courses, The Industrial Society, Robert Hyde House, 48 Bryanston Square, London W1H 7LN. Tel: (01) 262 2401.

Engineering Employers West Midlands Association
Run twelve-week women and management courses; an appreciation of management principles, techniques and practices.

★ **ASK** Engineering Employers West Midlands Association, St James House, Frederick Road, Edgbaston, Birmingham B15 1JJ. Tel: (021) 455 9797.

Open University – Women into Management
Starting in September 1987 the Open University will be offering a Women into Management course, funded by MSC.

★ **WRITE TO** Rosemary Smith, WIM, Open Business School, Walton Hall, Milton Keynes MK7 6AA.

TECHNOLOGY AND TECHNICAL SKILLS

Women-only training workshops
Over the past two years a number of training workshops run by women for women have been set up. Funding is mainly from the European Social Fund, local councils and in one or two cases, the MSC. They offer training in skills such as carpentry and joinery, electronics and microcomputing, to women over 25. Courses are full or part-time and most give a training allowance. They all provide child care facilities and give priority to women who are unemployed, have disabilities, are single parents or who are from ethnic minorities.

This list includes many training workshops, but as this is a growth area there may be more. Let us know if there is one in your area.

England

Avon

Bristol Women's Workshop, Totterdown Centre, 144 Wells Road, Totterdown, Bristol BS4 2AC. Tel: (0272) 711672.
Ask for: Janet Davies.
Offers: Basic woodwork classes.

Buckinghamshire

Milton Keynes Women and Work, The Bakehouse, 6 Church Street, Wolverton, Milton Keynes, Bucks MK2 5JN.

Cambridgeshire

Cambridge Women's Resource Centre, 7c Station Road, Cambridge CB1 2JB. Tel: (0223) 321148.
Ask for: Mo Laird.
Offers: a range of part-time courses, including carpentry, DIY, information for work, video production. Also offers many full-time courses and a variety of non-vocational/recreational courses – the subjects for these vary from term to term, so do get in touch for more information. Computer and video courses are free; other courses are priced on a sliding scale depending on what women feel they can afford. All courses have free child-care facilities. The centre also offers a resources and information service as well as a meeting place and social centre for women.

Cleveland

Middlesbrough Women's Training Centre, 4th Floor, Sun Alliance House, Albert Road, Middlesbrough. Tel: (0642) 244223.

LONDON – GREATER

Haringey

Haringey Women's Training and Education Centre, Lordship Lane, London N17. Tel: (01) 801 6233.
Offers: three courses, one full-time and two part-time. The full-time course in computing and electronics offers places to 30 students who receive a grant which varies according to individual circumstances (approx £65 a week). Part-time courses offer 15 places each for construction including plumbing, carpentry, electronics and a science technician taster course. Child-minding fees are paid by the centre. A child-care co-ordinator helps arrange child-care places.

LONDON – INNER

Camden

Kentish Town Women's Workshop, 169 Malden Road, London NW5. Tel: (01) 267 0688.
Ask for: Shahida Guereshi
Offers: a wide range of part-time courses including sewing, cultural cooking, writing groups, girls groups, older mother's groups, tarot, car maintenance, assertion training, drama, New Opportunities for Women, South Asian studies, writing and various other activities. Courses last from six to ten weeks and fees are minimal. They also have an alternative health clinic offering reflexology, massage, and acupuncture for which fees are on a sliding scale depending on circumstances. The centre offers a comprehensive child-care facility including creche, after-school collection, holiday schemes. Times and days of courses are flexible. The centre responds to the needs of students.

Lambeth

Lambeth Women's Workshop, Unit C22, Park Hall Trading Estate, Marteli Road, West Norwood, London SE21 8EA. Tel: (01) 670 0339.
Open: two days per week.

Offers: four part-time courses a year in basic carpentry, each course lasting four months. Trainees receive a small travelling allowance (£4.00 per week) and training allowance (£6.25 per week). There is also a child-care allowance (£8.00 per week) paid to trainees who have children under five as there are no facilities at the workshop for child-care.

Women's Motor Mechanic Workshop Ltd, Bay 4R, 1/3 Brixton Road, London SW9 6DE. Tel: (01) 582 2574.
Ask for: Jane Freeston or Angela Norman.
Offers: six-month part-time courses in car mechanics to prepare women for further training or work at semi-skilled level. Priority for places is given to ex-prisoners, black and ethnic minority women, single parent women and those with no previous vocational training. Students must live within Greater London. Fares, child-care costs and book allowances are paid.

Lewisham

Lewisham Women's Training Centre Ltd, 78b Blackheath Hills, London SE10.

Southwark

Southwark Women's Workshop, 164/180 Union Street, London SE1. Tel: (01) 261 0575.
Ask for: Val Fineman, child-care co-ordinator.
Offers: full-time training course for the trade in carpentry and joinery, to women aged from 18 to 58 who live in Southwark. Well-equipped workshop with specially designed facilities for disabled women. Instructors are also trained to teach deaf women. Trainees receive a training allowance which varies according to circumstances (approximately £58 per week) plus all child-care fees.

MANCHESTER – METROPOLITAN DISTRICTS

Women's Skill Centre Group, Mancoda, 12 Moseley Street, Manchester M2 3AQ.

MERSEYSIDE – LIVERPOOL

Women's Technology Training Ltd, Hardman Street, Liverpool.
Ask for: Claire Dove

MIDLANDS

Birmingham Women's Workshops, Unit 65, George Street, Balsall Heath, Birmingham B12.

Nottinghamshire

Nottingham Women's Training Centre, High Pavement, Nottingham NG1 1HN. Tel: (0602) 586236.

YORKSHIRE

Leeds

East Leeds Women's Workshop, 161 Harehills Lane, Leeds 8. Tel: (0532) 499031.
Ask for: Brenda Jones.
Offers: free courses in carpentry and joinery full-time over six months or in electronics and microcomputing part-time over twelve months. Child-care facilities available.

High Technology Training Centre, 38 Sweet Street, Leeds LS11 9AJ. Tel: (0532) 435511.
Ask for: Linda Vaughan or Maggie McCool.
Offers: one-year full-time courses in electronics and computing, one course for the 18 to 25 age group, one for women over 25. Priority is given to women who live in South Leeds who are long-term unemployed, or single parents, or disabled, or from ethnic minorities. Courses include three months' work experience. Trainees receive £45 per week. There is substantial child-care provision.

Icom Women's Linkup, 14 George Street, Leeds. Tel: (0532) 432474.

Sheffield

Women's Technology Training Workshop, TruTech, Commerce Street, Sheffield S1 4LE. Tel: (0742) 756297.

Ask for: Dr Wendy Miller, co-ordinator.

Offers: two one-year part-time courses in microelectronics and microcomputing. Priority is given to women with no formal qualifications. Trainees receive an expenses allowance. There is no creche but a child-care worker arranges child-minding places and there is some financial help fees. The centre is heavily oversubscribed. This year there were 800 applicants for 40 places.

WALES

Glamorgan

South Glamorgan Women's Workshops Ltd, Edena House, East Canal Wharf, Cardiff. Tel: (0222) 493351.

Ask for: Barbara Castle or Carol Collins..

Offers: two parallel one-year, part-time courses in basic electronics and computing. The workshop pays trainees a travel allowance and offers a free creche for pre-school children. Priority for places is given to women who would not be able to get on any other course. The courses are geared to jobs in electronics and computing or as pre-entry to further training.

Other training centres

Women-only Skillcentre courses

A small number of these courses have been run around the country. They are designed to give women a taste of a range of craft skills such as carpentry, bricklaying or plumbing. The aim is to give trainees basic skills and enable them to identify their particular aptitudes. The women are then able to apply for a full skill training course in a chosen trade, but must satisfy normal entry requirements.

Camden Training Centre

This is not a women-only centre but offers six courses for women only:

- Introductory building, 12 weeks, part-time, lunch and fees paid
- Carpentry and joinery, 26 weeks, full-time
- Microelectronics, 26 weeks, full-time
- Business technology, 20 weeks, full-time
- Return to work, 6 weeks, full and part-time
- Self employment, 12 weeks, full-time

Training allowances are paid on all full-time courses, and free child care (with the centre's nursery for under 5s and childminders for others up to 12 years). In addition there are various mixed courses they are keen for women to apply for. There is more information about this centre in *29 Local councils*.

Women's Computer Centre

Part of a national women and computing network. It provides an opportunity for women to gain confidence through introductory ten-week and other courses. The centre in London should be able to put you in contact with others.

★ **ASK** Women's Computer Centre, Wesley House, Wild Court, London WC2. Tel: (01) 430 0112.

★ **LOOK AT** *Teaching computing to women: a resource pack*, by Mary Jennings and Robyn Smits, available for £7.95 from the National Extension College, 18 Brooklands Avenue, Cambridge CB2 2HN.

College courses

Polytechnic of the South Bank
Runs a BTEC HNC course in electronics for women only, in the Department of Electrical and Electronic Engineering.

South East London College
Runs an information technology and electronics course for women leading to a BTEC certificate, and a part-time day course, 'Introduction to Computing' which lasts 18 weeks.

The Open University – Women in Technology
This programme is for qualified women engineers who left work for family reasons and now want to return. Some courses enable qualified women technologists to broaden or update their previous knowledge. Other courses are designed to encourage women into technological areas by giving them basic technical knowledge. The programme is also intended to promote confidence and skills in career planning. It is part of the Associate Student Programme, and includes a residential weekend Return to Study course at Loughborough University, and a summer school. There are bursaries available from the MSC to cover course fees and travelling expenses for the weekend course and summer school.

★ **ASK** Ailsa Swarbrick, Project Coordinator, or Rosie Atkins, Project Counsellor, Women in Technology, The Open University, Yorkshire Regional Office, Fairfax House, Merrion Street, Leeds LS2 8JU. Tel: (0532) 444431.

RETURN TO WORK OR STUDY

There are many part-time courses advertised as being for women. They have names like New Opportunities for Women (NOW), Fresh Start, Fresh Horizons, Gateway. Some look at work and study opportunities, eg NOW courses (normally 10 am to 3 pm once a week for ten weeks with a creche). Some are study skills courses, some GCE courses. There are also refresher courses, especially in secretarial skills. Make sure you know what the course is before you enrol – the names can be misleading. They are an important development and more appear each year.

★ **ASK** your local education guidance service for adults, college, adult education centre, WEA, extra-mural department or ask the library or Citizens' Advice Bureau. Some of these courses are also listed in *19 Starting again.*

★ **LOOK AT** *Women returning to learning*, by Enid and Edward Hutchinson, available for £9.95 from the National Extension College, 18 Brooklands Avenue, Cambridge CB2 2HN. Tel: (0223) 316644.

Wider Opportunities for Women (WOW)

WOW courses are run by the Manpower Services Commission as part of its Wider Opportunities Training Programme. The courses are for women who wish to return to work after an absence from the labour market for domestic reasons. They are designed to help the women identify what type of work or training they want, to update job-hunting skills, to replace obsolete job skills and to rebuild lost confidence. Courses may be full or part-time, and in some cases a training allowance may be paid in addition to expenses. Information about the availability of courses can be obtained from the local Jobcentre.

YWCA

Runs short courses of several kinds aiming to develop potential and self confidence – for the unemployed, women at work and young women in traditionally male jobs. These are run by the further education department at the national headquarters. There are also many regional courses on offer, eg Breakaway, run in London and the South East (a two-day course offering information about education, training, voluntary opportunities and self employment), Horizons, in the North West (a week's residential course which includes communications skills and other aspects of personal development).

★ **ASK** Further Education Officer, YWCA National Offices, Clarendon House, 52 Cornmarket Street, Oxford OX1 3EJ. Tel: (0865) 726110.

WOMEN INTO BUSINESS

A training programme aimed specifically at women who want to run their own businesses has been set up by Mid-Wales Development. Run at four different locations, it offers a course lasting three to four months covering the basic business mechanics and the skills needed to form and develop a business idea.

★ **ASK** Anne Morris, Women into Business Co-ordinator, Mid-Wales Development, Ladywell House, Newtown, Powys SY16 1JB. Tel: (0686) 26965.

WOMEN'S STUDIES

This can involve looking at the role of women in society, past and present, and women's contributions to literature, art, music and so on. A number of higher education institutions run courses or house collections of relevant literature.

Libraries

City of London Polytechnic
Houses the Fawcett Library, the major resource for the history of feminism and women in general. It operates on a subscription basis.

★ **ASK** Catherine Ireland, Fawcett Librarian, Calcutta House, Old Castle Street, London E1 7NT. Tel: (01) 283 1030.

Girton College Library
Contains a special collection on women's education and suffrage. Visit by appointment only. It is not a browsing collection.

★ **ASK** Girton College Library, Cambridge CB3 0JG. Tel: (0223) 338970.

★ **ASK** the Feminist Library and Information Centre, Hungerford House, Victoria Embankment, London WC2N 6PA. Tel: (01) 930 0715.

The Feminist Archive
This is a library and museum to identify, preserve and produce women's work. It documents the development of the women's liberation movement and maintains national and international contacts for exchange of material and information.

★ **ASK** Feminist Archive, University of Bath, Claverton Down, Bath BA2 7AY. Tel: (0225) 826826 ext 5249.

Courses

The University of Kent at Canterbury
Runs a postgraduate (MA) course in women's studies.

The Polytechnic of Central London
Runs a Diploma in Women's Studies course.

There are also a substantial number of LEA and WEA part-time classes, but a large amount of this sort of education is done informally through women's groups. Many of these can be found in the directory listed in *42 Things to study: women's studies*, by contacting organsations listed under 'Women only centres' (see below) or by looking at the small ads in *Spare rib*.

Correspondence courses
National Extension College
Produces a home study pack for women called *Equality for some* and a women's studies resource pack in conjunction with the WEA. This is produced for teachers but would be a useful resource if you are for instance running a self-help study group.

★ **WRITE TO** National Extension College, 18 Brooklands Avenue, Cambridge CB2 2HN. Tel: (0223) 316644.

The Open University
Is running a course called *The changing experience of women* as a second level course, lasting a year. It can be taken as part of a degree or on its own. For more information look at *23 The Open University*.

Publications

WEA Women's studies newsletter
Published twice a year in May and November. Subscription £1.60 for two issues.

★ **WRITE TO** WEA National Office, 9 Upper Berkeley Street, London W1H 8BY. Tel: (01) 402 5608.

More information

A network is being set up for women studying or teaching women's studies in adult or higher education. To join the mailing list:

★ **WRITE TO** Joanna de Groot, Department of History, York University, Heslington, York YO1 5DD enclosing £2.

WOMEN'S ORGANISATIONS

Women-only centres

There are now several centres designed to provide a meeting place and space exclusively for women. Some offer informal workshops on topics such as assertiveness training, dance, drama, health awareness etc. One centre, as well as providing a space for meetings, offers an information service by post or telephone.

★ **ASK** A Woman's Place, Hungerford House, Victoria Embankment, London WC2N 6PA. Tel: (01) 836 6081.

★ **VISIT** Sisterwrite, 190 Upper Street, London N1. Tel: (01) 226 9782. A feminist bookshop.

★ **LOOK AT** *Spare rib* (and other magazines produced by and for women). They frequently list courses and informal consciousness-raising groups in the small ads. They also run a monthly young women's page.

Women's work groups

There are now over two dozen groups set up by women in various occupations. In general, they aim to provide mutual support for women to help them explore their position in their industry, and to provide practical help.

Women in Manual Trades

An organisation based in London with contacts in large cities which offers support to women working in traditionally male jobs. WIMT puts out a monthly newsletter, rents out videos, offers talks in schools, publishes a comprehensive listing of training courses for women in manual and technical trades, and has a list of tradeswomen who are in business.

★ **ASK** Women in Manual Trades, 52/54 Featherstone Street, London EC1. Tel: (01) 251 9192.

For information about voluntary organisations and women's groups generally:

★ **ASK** the Voluntary Organisations Unit at the Equal Opportunities Commission.

★ **LOOK AT** *Women and training news*, a free newsletter with information about all aspects of training for women. It is available from Women and Training, GLOSCAT, Oxstalls Lane, Gloucester GL2 9HW. Tel: (0452) 426836/7/8.

Women's Institutes and Townswomen's Guilds
Have a long tradition of self-help in education. Membership is open to women of all ages. Activities include talks, home economics and craft demonstrations, music, drama, public affairs and international activities. Many WIs organise classes in villages and the 71 federations arrange day schools and classes. Training is offered for judges and demonstrators and instructors of crafts and home economics, and correspondence courses are provided in a variety of craft subjects. Many classes are run in conjunction with local adult education services. Drama producers' examinations and speech training are available from NFWI. The National Federation also offers training and opportunities for the training of adult education tutors. The WI also has its own residential college for its members.

★ **ASK** National Federation of Women's Institutes of England, Wales, the Channel Islands and the Isle of Man, 39 Eccleston Street, London SW19 9NT. Tel: (01) 730 7212.

Denman College, Marcham, Abingdon, Oxfordshire OX13 6NW. Tel: (0865) 391219 and 391425. Prospectus available but details also available through your local WI. Contact the Denman Representative or the Voluntary Education Co-ordinator.

Similar opportunities are offered by the following organisations.

★ **ASK** Scottish Women's Rural Institute, 42 Heriot Row, Edinburgh EH3 6ES. Tel: (031) 225 1724.

★ **ASK** Women's Institutes of Northern Ireland, 209 Upper Lisburn Road, Belfast BT10 0LL. Tel: (0232) 625506.

★ **ASK** National Union of Townswomen's Guilds, Chamber of Commerce House, 75 Harbourne Road, Edgbaston, Birmingham B15 3DA. Tel: (021) 455 6216.

National Housewives Register
There are now over 1200 local groups in this self-help women's organisation. Local groups, which are basically discussion groups, meet and plan their own programmes. To find a local group:

★ **WRITE TO** The National Office, National Housewives Register, 245 Warwick Road, Solihull, West Midlands B92 7AH. Tel: (021) 706 1101.

National Advisory Centre on Careers for Women
Advice service covering educational choices, career changes, retraining and part-time work; appointment necessary. Publishes a useful booklet, *Returners*, which describes a number of career possibilities and the specific training needed. Also runs an annual careers course.

★ **ASK** National Advisory Centre on Careers for Women, Drayton House, 30 Gordon Street, London WC1H OAX. Tel: (01) 380 0117.

7 School leavers

BEFORE YOU START

Opportunities for education or training vary depending on where you live, and are changing all the time. This chapter is a general outline of the opportunities available for school leavers everywhere; check out how it all applies in your area. Many other things in the rest of the book could also apply to you, so look through it.

Get advice locally

The careers service have the best local information on opportunities for school leavers. Use this chapter so that you'll know what to ask for. It always helps if you have some ideas yourself. You can also get information from books and leaflets at the careers office and sometimes from the library, from your local radio station or Radio 1 or TV.

WHAT IS THE CHOICE?

There are basically six choices:

- try to get a job
- get education or training
- join a YTS scheme
- make yourself useful for no pay (but you may save some money)
- set up in business on your own
- do nothing much for a while.

Whichever you choose, remember there won't be so many opportunities for free education and training after your 18th birthday (19th in some areas).

DECISION POINTS

Education or work?

There are still jobs – and most people still work. It is harder, especially for young people, and in some areas it's particularly difficult. But there's no need any more to look for a job just because you've done badly at school. That used to be true, but nowadays there are plenty of opportunities for further education for people who didn't get on well at school, whatever the reason. If you really want a job, our advice would be to have a go. You can always come back to education if you are unlucky. If you are not sure, you can use the education system as a way of taking your time, and improving your chances of a job later anyway. You may just want a change from school – a job is not the only way to get that.

But remember that you might not be eligible for a Youth Training Scheme place if you do something else first.

Stay on at school or leave?

Stay on if:

- you're happy
- it's a good school, and you're doing okay
- you can't study what you want somewhere else
- the alternatives will cost too much.

Otherwise, leave!

What does further education offer?

Sixth form college

Really a school for sixth formers only. The idea is that if all the local schools send their fifth formers to one place, there can be better facilities and more choices. They only exist in some areas but if your school feeds into a sixth form college you'll be able to find out about it from school. Sixth form colleges are part of the school system; if you want a complete break from school try further education.

Further education (FE) colleges

There are hundreds of FE colleges. They are described in *16 Further education, adult education*. All the FE colleges in the country are listed in the *Gazetteer* – so you can check easily which ones are near to where you live.

Colleges of further education normally offer GCSE/GCE/SCE courses and courses that train you in skills needed for a particular job (vocational courses). There are also specialist colleges (eg for art, agriculture, building). They are open to anyone of 16 or over, and usually have adult students too. They do full-time and part-time courses.

Tertiary colleges

They are further education colleges that also do all the sixth-form work for an area and probably adult education as well. If that is the system where you live, you may have no choice. They already exist in some counties (eg Devon, Somerset, Lancashire, Derbyshire, Gwent, Richmond – but not in Scotland) and are likely to appear in many other places in the next few years.

And that's not all...

There are a lot of other things available, many of which are described in the *Providers* section of this book. Some of these cost money – such as private FE and private secretarial colleges (described in *34 The private sector*).

What to study?

Academic subjects
GCSE, GCE (O-levels and A-levels) and in Scotland SCE (Ordinary, Standard and Higher Grade) are still the main, recognised general qualifications. They are useful for getting into higher education (HE) – that is getting a degree or similar qualification – and for many jobs. You can do them at school or at college.

Vocational subjects
That is, specific training for jobs usually leading to a qualification. You can study some of these at a local college (typing, catering etc). For some you usually get a job first, then get day release (eg engineering and building). This part of the system is changing – you will probably do this type of training through YTS.

Pre-vocational courses
These courses are getting more and more common. They are run in colleges of further education and in schools. They include a mixture of project work, practical work and work experience and they give you a chance to try different sorts of work. A course may offer you several sorts of work (eg building, engineering, work with children, catering) or concentrate on just one.

A national pre-vocational course is the CPVE (Certificate of Pre-vocational Education) run by the PVE Joint Board (BTEC/CGLI). CPVE is offered in both schools and colleges for one year for 16 year olds. It allows young people to plan their own studies by choosing areas which interest them most from business, production, distribution, technical services and services to people. It specifically helps young people to develop the skills and knowledge which they need to prepare them for work and further education. Completion of the CPVE means having a national qualification which includes a record of individual learning experience and personal success to show to colleges and employers.

Scotland
Qualifications in Scotland have been reorganised. You can build up a course from modules in different subjects, leading to a SCOTVEC qualification.

Qualifications
If you want to know more about the main qualifications, look at *41 Qualifications*. To find out what there is, and how you can study it, go and ask at the local colleges. If you want to see a full list of every course in the country:

★ **LOOK AT** *The directory of further education* (see *Booklist*).

If you want an idea of what to study look at *42 Things to study*.

YOUTH TRAINING SCHEME (YTS)

If you don't want to stay in full-time education but would like to learn some skills go to the careers office or Jobcentre and ask about YTS. It exists everywhere and includes many different types of training. The basic rules are:

- if you are a 16 year old school leaver you are entitled to 104 weeks on a scheme. If you haven't got a job with your company you'll get a training allowance of £28.50 a week for the first 52 weeks, then £35.00 a week for the second 52 weeks. You will also get help with your travel costs.

- if you are a 17 year old school leaver you are entitled to 52 weeks on the scheme. You'll receive £28.50 for the first 13 weeks, then £35 for 39 weeks
- if you have a job with your company you'll get a full wage.

All schemes include training. It doesn't matter how badly you did at school; this is a good opportunity to start again. What schemes there are will vary locally, so you will have to get local advice. Some employers advertise their own YTS vacancies in the local paper or in shop windows, and many will inform the careers office or the organisations that run the schemes.

Who runs YTS?

The Manpower Services Commission (MSC) is the body responsible for YTS – there is more information about the MSC in *24 Training for a new job*. In Northern Ireland, training courses are run by the Department of Economic Development and are called the Youth Training Programme (YTP).

What does YTS offer?

A number of things:

- high quality training in different kinds of work
- training for a group of jobs such as office work, community work, engineering, distribution, work in the new technologies etc
- at least ten weeks off-the-job training or further education spread over two years
- a chance to learn new things both at work and in everyday life
- help and advice to give you a better chance when looking and applying for future jobs
- a vocational qualification
- a certificate to show what you have achieved.

Information Technology Centres (ITECs)

175 Centres have been established by the MSC and the Department of Trade and Industry to provide young unemployed people with training in electronics, computing and basic information technology skills. Trainees (supported by YTS allowances) get experience of assembling computers and repairing programmes as well as developing keyboard skills and gaining work experience on placements with local employers. In some areas workshops produce marketable products and many centres also cater for adult education in information technology-related activities, often using flexible open-access means of delivery.

Community Industry

This is a scheme set up in 1972 by the National Association of Youth Clubs. It provides about 7000 temporary employment places for young people aged up to 19, in workshops and projects of community benefit. The scheme, which is funded by the Department of Employment, offers post-YTS provision for young people who are recruited through the careers service or by Jobcentres. People on Community Industry are paid on a national wage scale ranging from £29.70 at 16 to £43.90 at 19 years of age.

TECHNOLOGY AND COMPUTING

National Computing Centre (NCC) Threshold scheme

Another scheme in which you get paid £30 per week for ten months doing computing work and training. Open to any unemployed school leaver aged 17 and under 20; you do not need qualifications, though you have to pass some tests. Threshold schemes operate in colleges of FE or commercial organisations.

★ **WRITE TO** The Administrator, NCC, Oxford Road, Manchester M1 7ED. Tel: (061) 228 6633, or

★ **LOOK AT** the section on Information Technology Centres (ITECs) in the *Youth Training Scheme* section of this chapter.

ADVICE

Careers offices are there to give you advice. Use them. You can also get advice from anyone providing education (people at colleges, school careers teachers etc), but no one is absolutely objective – and anyway, *they* may not think you need what *you* think you need. Shop around – ask more than one person. And use the 'network' eg did some of your mates go to FE college last year? What was it like? Go and see for yourself. Also look at *1 Advice and help*.

FINANCE

As a general rule, full-time education should be free until you're 18, but you don't normally get paid for it. If you leave school and study at college, you'll probably have to pay for books, paper, exam fees etc. You may have to pay course fees as well when you're 18 – which might mean hundreds of pounds a year. It varies a lot from LEA to LEA, so check.

Grants

You probabaly won't get a grant for most FE courses though local authorities can make discretionary awards. You only have the right to a manditory grant for higher education (see *22 Getting a degree*). If you need advice, ask the college and, if necessary, try the education office as well. Grants are explained in more detail in *40 LEA grants*.

If your parents are very hard up you may be able to get a maintenance grant from your local authority to help with the costs of books and travel. If you think you may be eligible ask your LEA.

The 21 hour rule

You can only claim supplementary benefit and study full-time if you are estranged from your parents, have a child or are disabled. But you can claim and study in some circumstances if you are available for work. This means that you must sign on and be prepared to leave the course immediately should a job vacancy come up. The rules are complicated so contact the student welfare officer in your college or an advice centre before making a claim at the DHSS.

Broadly, the present situation is that you can claim benefit and study if:

- the course has 21 hours or less of classroom and supervised study a week
- you are prepared to leave the course if a suitable vacancy is offered
- you have been unemployed and in receipt of benefit for the three months before starting the course; this qualifying period does not apply if you have been on a YTS scheme.

During the three-month qualifying period, you can study on a course as long as it is not full-time. A course of 12 hours and under is unlikely to be considered full-time. After three months you can study up to 21 hours on a different course (eg studying different subjects or the same subjects at a higher level). It is complicated, so take advice.

TRAINING AT WORK

Many jobs also involve training – apprenticeships and YTS give you time at college. Some industries provide in-service training and possibly the opportunity for day release. You should learn about them when you get the job. Ask the employer; you can also get information from some industrial training boards which are described in *33 Training at work*, and from those industries which have their own careers advisory services.

HIGHER EDUCATION

Carrying on in education and working for a degree has not been included in this chapter. See *22 Getting a degree*. If you want to know more:

★ **LOOK AT** *The student book*.

YOUR BEST BET

If you're not sure of which course of action to take, go and ask for vocational guidance from the careers office. Any course should be useful and whatever course you do, you can change your mind. You are not taking an oath, you are not committed for life (though beware of changing your mind half way through a degree course – you could find it leads to money problems).

It will be normal during your life to retrain several times. Find a course that will help you to pursue a decision you have already made, or one that is as broad as possible, for flexibility of choice later. For that you need good communication skills (reading, writing, persuading, etc) and good basic maths. And there *are* courses for those things, with qualifications, mainly from City & Guilds and RSA. Ask the local college. After that, anything is good experience and any skill can be useful. If someone on a building course decides to be a bank clerk, at least they will be able to fix their own drainpipes!

8 Age

No one is too old to learn
What's available
Money
More information
Education is a two-way process

No one can really say how old you have to be to become elderly. It seems to depend on what you do and where you are, as well as how you feel. Judges retire much older than most of us, politicians are still 'young' at 50. You're too old to start in medicine after 35 and too old to start as a ballet dancer by the time you're 15. Many people begin to feel old when they retire or when someone close dies, leaving them alone. But it can also be a wonderful opportunity to spread your wings and do things that were never possible before.

WOMAN, 70
When my husband died, I was stricken. We'd spent the first years of his retirement together working in our garden. I hadn't thought about myself much. But since then I've travelled all over Britain and I've made friends. I'm learning pottery and I teach an Asian lady how to speak English. I'm so busy, I'm never at home.

NO ONE IS TOO OLD TO LEARN

One of the harmful effects of compulsory schooling is that so many people think you're too old to learn once you've left school. That's a mistake. Learning gets easier as you get older. True, a time arrives when it takes longer to learn new things. But it's also easier to make sense of them because you have so much more experience and knowledge to connect things to. So you gain on the swings what you lose on the roundabouts. Experience shows that even the very old are able to learn new things. And keeping mentally active has beneficial physical and psychological effects. Too many people believe learning in old age is impossible. So the opportunity is not offered. When it is, it's eagerly accepted.

Your purposes also change with age. People over retirement age have more leisure time, so there's no need to think about training for a job or getting qualified; some do, for amusement and satisfaction, and because some voluntary work also involves training. Recent trends in adult education suggest that more and more attention is being directed towards the elderly.

Separate or with others?

There is no agreement about whether education for elderly people should be separate from other provision. On the one hand, studying together can let older people draw on common experience for support, and share their worries about trying something new. On the other, people in mixed age groups can learn a lot from one another and an older person in a class often makes a major impact. There is almost certainly no right answer – you will have to choose according to what you prefer yourself and what is available in your area. Most of the opportunities listed in the book are open to older people and if they're not, it will say so. So the bulk of this chapter looks at special provision for older people.

Forum on the Rights of Elderly People to Education (FREE)
This group brings together organisations and individuals wishing to promote education for older people, and produces a quarterly bulletin giving details of initiatives, research and publications. It organises occasional discussion forums.

★ **WRITE TO** Dianne Norton, Co-ordinator, Forum on the Rights of Elderly People to Education, Age Concern England, Bernard Sunley House, 60 Pitcairn Road, Mitcham, Surrey CR4 3LL. Tel: (01) 640 5431.

WHAT'S AVAILABLE?

Most adult education and training is (in theory) open to all ages.

Access to *training* for jobs is affected by your chances of finding work after it. The Job Training Scheme may only be open to you if you can demonstrate that you have got a good chance of finding work; for example, you're unlikely to get a job as a newly trained fitter when you're over 50, acceptance over the age of 35 for physiotherapy is unusual, though not forbidden, and so on. But there seems to be no equivalent reason why anyone should be denied access to *education* because of age. In practice some places will be more open than others.

Adult and further education
In most areas there are some separate courses specially for the elderly provided by FE colleges, the adult education service, the WEA and other agencies. There may be courses to help you keep fit, like *Keep fit for over 50s* and *Keep fit for over 60s* in Cardiff. Or they may be intensive study, such as *Learning in later life* at the Polytechnic of North London which runs one day a week between 10 am and 4 pm for three ten-week terms (but you can join in just for a term if you want). Or there may be crafts courses at an adult education centre. There could be more. Why not approach your local FE college, adult education centre or WEA branch? If they don't have what you want, ask them to start it.

The Open University
Around seven percent of all OU students are over the age of 60. Besides taking degree courses, they enrol for courses as associate students studying undergraduate courses but not actually taking a full degree, or they follow one of several short courses.

These now include *Planning retirement*. This particular package has been produced in collaboration with the Pre-Retirement Association, the Health Education Council and the Scottish Health Education Group. It can be used by people in their own homes to plan ahead or by groups of people who want to discuss the topics together. It is divided into four sections which look at the various issues to consider at different stages of retirement planning. *Taking stock* suggests ways to tackle the change from work to retirement and there is a whole section devoted to the changes which happen after retirement, while *Looking ahead* is the self-explanatory title of the last part.

There is also a *Health and retirement pack* of fifteen looseleaf topic leaflets drawn from *Planning retirement* with a particular focus on health.

The OU will put any of its students in touch with local co-ordinators who will advise on setting up self-help groups of students following the same courses.

★ **ASK** your Open University Regional Office (addresses listed in *23 The Open University*).

Radio and TV

Channel 4 has two programmes designed to meet the needs of older people. *Years ahead* is a magazine programme, which includes practical information on educational opportunities, benefits, health etc. *Ten million* concentrates on older people as consumers. Both programmes have substantial back-up material, available from PO Box 4000, London W3 6XJ or Glasgow G12 9JA or Belfast BT2 7FE.

All channels offer back-up material for many of their programmes if you are interested in finding out more. For example:

★ **LOOK AT** *Years ahead – getting the most out of retirement*, published by Ward Lock in conjunction with Channel 4.

For more information on how to use radio and TV look at *25 Radio and TV*.

Pre-retirement courses

Run all over Britain, some for employees of particular firms, others open to all. They deal with things such as what to do with your leisure, cookery for one or two, organisations for the elderly. For example Ford Motor Company runs a wide range of courses for its employees in Essex and elsewhere, and there is an increasing emphasis on mid-life courses. Information and advice can be had from your LEA, the WEA, library or adult education advice service or the nearest organisation federated to the Pre-Retirement Association in Scotland.

★ **LOOK AT** *Pre-retirement courses in Scotland: a directory and commentary*, from Age Concern Scotland (address below).

The Pre-Retirement Association

Helps organisations provide pre-retirement education for employees and operates an information and advisory service on retirement. Individual membership is presently £15 for associate members, £30 for full (professional) members, and £30 for overseas membership. It includes a subscription to *Choice*, a magazine for retirement planning.

★ **WRITE TO** The Pre-Retirement Association of Great Britain and Northern Ireland, 19 Undine Street, Tooting, London SW17 8PP. Tel: (01) 767 3225.

★ **WRITE TO** Retirement Association of Northern Ireland, 25a University Road, Belfast BT7 1NA. Tel: (0232) 221324.

MAN, 71
I was a railway porter. When I retired, I thought, 'Right, this is it', and I was determined to have a good time. I go to college a lot – I like studying and the meals in the refectory are cheap. I get into most of the classes I want at half price. I'm on a few committees and things, and I help out where I can at the Student Union and with the adult literacy scheme. Oh, and I've learned to speak Russian because I'm going over there next year for a fortnight's holiday.

The University of the Third Age (U3A)
More than 100 centres throughout the country are now organising 'mutual aid' learning groups. Some are connected to educational institutions, others are not. U3A aims to involve older people in teaching, organising and research, as well as learning, to make education available in people's homes and local communities and mobilize the personal resources of this generation. For a manual on setting up new groups or addresses of local groups, send an SAE:

★ **WRITE TO** The Executive Secretary, U3A, 6 Parkside Gardens, London SW19 5EY.

MONEY

Most LEAs do make some concession over fees for adult education classes for pensioners – most of these are listed in the *Gazetteer*. This is more likely to be true for non-vocational classes. A few offer completely free classes. Because the rate charged for adult education classes varies dramatically between areas the amount a pensioner is asked to pay must be checked locally, but the information in the *Gazetteer* will be a useful guide. In an increasing number of LEAs concessions are available only when specially asked for. For full-time higher education anyone who obtains a place, no matter what their age, is eligible for a grant if they haven't done such a course before.

Early retirement reading

★ **LOOK AT** *Branching out: a workbook for early retirement* by Maggie Smith. This offers exercises to help you review your life, manage change and develop new interests. It also deals with health and financial issues. Available from Lifeskills Associates, Clarendon Chambers, 51 Clarendon Road, Leeds LS2 9PJ. Tel: (0532) 467128.

MORE INFORMATION

Age Concern
Has over 1300 local groups, many listed in the phone book under Age Concern, or Old People's Welfare Association. A few run courses using retired experts.

Try local branches for advice. Nationally, Age Concern promotes increased education opportunities in a wide variety of situations, often through FREE (see above). If you can't find them in the phone book, try the library or Citizens' Advice Bureau, or:

★ **LOOK AT** *Social services yearbook.*

★ **WRITE TO** Age Concern, Bernard Sunley House, 60 Pitcairn Road, Mitcham, Surrey CR4 3LL. Tel: (01) 640 5431. Age Concern Wales, 1 Park Grove, Cardiff. Tel: (0222) 371821. Age Concern Scotland, 33 Castle Street, Edinburgh 2. Tel: (031) 225 5000. Age Concern Northern Ireland, 6 Lower Crescent, Belfast BT7 1NR. Tel: (0232) 245729.

Help the Aged

The largest fund-raising and campaigning organisation working for the elderly. You may be interested in the monthly newspaper *Yours* (subscription £5.50 a year). It has a readers' advisory service which can help you with any problem, including education.

The work of the Help the Aged Education Department is also relevant. In particular, two publications are useful to adult learners:

★ **LOOK AT** *The time of your life,* published by Help the Aged with the Health Education Council, 1986, revised fifth edition, 96 pages, £4.50 including p&p. This is a handbook for retirement and covers a wide variety of topics, including leisure and education.

★ **LOOK AT** *Have you heard?*, published by Help the Aged Education Department, April 1981. This pamphlet is written for the pre-retirement field and introduces the idea of volunteering to a general audience. 20 pages, 80p.

In addition, the Education Department is a contributor to *FREE* and plays an active role in furthering educational opportunities for older people. The department produces educational materials for schools, colleges and adult groups. Of particular interest: *Recall*, three sets of tape slide sequences covering 1900 to the present day, to help old people reflect on their experiences. For more information, to obtain the publications listed, or a free publications list:

★ **WRITE TO** Help the Aged Education Department, 16/18 St James' Walk, London EC1R OBE. Tel: (01) 253 0253.

EDUCATION IS A TWO-WAY PROCESS

Opportunities are available for retired people to involve themselves, and use their skills, to help youngsters, both in school and in the community.

★ **ASK** Pensioners Link, 17 Balfe Street, London N1 9EB. Tel: (01) 278 5501. Activities in the Greater London area only.

★ **ASK** Community Service Volunteers, 237 Pentonville Road, London N1 9NJ. Tel: (01) 278 6601. Projects in various areas.

Or why not try offering your services to a local school?

9 Ethnic minorities

The issues
Positive action in education and training
Ethnic minority organised schemes
Sources of information and advice

THE ISSUES

Although modern Britain is a multi-racial society it does not have racial equality. The discrimination and disadvantage faced by black people in terms of education and training have three main sources:

- The discrimination (often indirect and unconscious) operated by organisations which provide essential services and employment opportunities
- An absence of appropriate educational and training opportunities for black people themselves which will enable them to take full advantage of employment and service provision
- The present recession and its disproportionate effect on ethnic minority adults, many of whom had been employed in a limited range of industries, particularly vulnerable in a recession.

WEST INDIAN WOMAN, 48
I went to the interview for the nursery nurses course. I had to go 30 miles in three buses – I was a bit late. When I came in, I could see they were thinking 'Typical West Indian, always late'. They gave me a test – asked me things like 'What happened on 1 July 1945?' and 'When was Mount Everest climbed?' or something. I couldn't remember – I'd been in the West Indies until 1968. She told me they only had 15 places, and I couldn't have one. But in our town, hundreds of black kids are left in private nurseries – there are no qualified black nursery nurses at all. I've been promised a job if I can qualify.

INDIAN MAN, 46
I have worked for this company for 22 years. I came to Britain in 1962 when I was 21 and this was my first job. I've worked in every department here and know every job. I have been a chargehand since 1976 and I applied for a foreman's job in 1982 in the moulding section. The works manager and the other managers gave me an interview but they turned me down. Since then, I've applied five times for a foreman's job, they interview me each time but turn me down. Last time they gave the job to John Stanley – he only came here in 1977 and I taught him everything he knows about moulding. They tell me I haven't got the right skills to be a foreman, but they don't tell me what the skills are. And there are no black foremen in any of the other departments either!

POSITIVE ACTION IN EDUCATION AND TRAINING

Positive action is the name sometimes given to policies and provision designed to overcome the disadvantage and discrimination faced by ethnic minority adults. Under the 1976 Race Relations Act, an act of racial discrimination is illegal. It means that you should never be excluded from anything because of your race, colour or creed. Indirect discrimination is also illegal – it means you can't be excluded because of something which doesn't seem to be due to race, but you know is. All the opportunities in this book are available to people from ethnic minorities. Some examples of positive action in education and training are:

- courses to help ethnic minority adults get jobs
- courses to develop basic education and skills
- Access courses to higher and further education.

Help in getting jobs

Within the MSC's Wider Opportunities Training Programme are initiatives aimed particularly at the ethnic minority unemployed. The courses combine practical or workshop training with classes.

Developing basic education and skills

It is being increasingly recognised that English language is only one of the basic education skills that ethnic minority adults need to possess, and that maths, technical drawing, basic science and other practical skills are an essential aspect of basic education. Part-time courses are widely available through a range of establishments, some of which are linked to workshops or practical skills units, for example in adult, community or further education. Whilst colleges and adult education services differ widely in their provision for ethnic minorities, it should be increasingly possible for students to get the help they need with English language and literacy whilst enrolling on the course of their choice.

Courses to improve basic skills, reading, writing and spoken English are provided in a number of ways:

- Adult education provides classes or tuition in reading and writing and in English as a second language in all parts of the country, often free, and nearly always cheaper than other courses. How basic education is organised in your area is explained in the *Gazetteer*.
- For people who work, Industrial Language Units provide a range of training aimed at improving your language and communication skills at work. Teaching is designed to meet your own needs and the needs of the workplace and can include improved job access and effectiveness and the promotion of equal opportunities. There is no cost to trainees for tuition. The main units providing this type of teaching are listed in *33 Training at work*. To find out more at work, ask your trade union shop steward or your employer.
- There are some courses in the MSC's Job Training Scheme specifically for speakers of English as a second language. Other JTS courses are open to ethnic minorities who speak enough English to be able to follow the course.

Access to higher education

Access courses are a way of getting into higher education and the professions for people who may not have been to school in Britain and do not have O- or A-levels.

They are mainly for people from ethnic minorities, and are often linked to courses for training in teaching/social work and youth/community work at particular universities and polytechnics. For a list of courses see *18 Adult routes.*

EXAMPLES

Project Fullemploy

Project Fullemploy has training centres in London, Birmingham, Bradford, Bristol, Manchester and Sandwell where they run training and advice programmes mainly in basic office skills, retailing and self-employment, and an Access programme leading to a business studies degree.

The majority of courses are intended for unemployed young adults but two centres also offer YTS programmes for school leavers. People from ethnic minorities are particularly welcome though the courses are open to anyone.

Fullemploy has a long established relationship with many employers to whom they now also offer equal opportunities training. Fullemploy trainees continue to have a high success rate in finding employment and setting up small businesses.

★ **ASK** Project Fullemploy, Central Office, 102 Park Village East, London NW1 3SP. Tel: (01) 387 1222.

Afro-Caribbean and Asian management course

The Engineering Employers West Midlands Association runs a 12-week course which gives an appreciation of management principles, techniques and practices.

★ **ASK** Engineering Employers West Midlands Association, Management Training Centre, St James House, Frederick Road, Edgbaston, Birmingham B15 1JJ. Tel: (021) 455 9797.

Scheme for young black solicitors

It is often difficult for young qualified solicitors from ethnic minority groups to obtain their articles, and there are plans to establish a scheme to help them become articled clerks in a law centre in combination with private practice.

★ **WRITE TO** The Law Centres Federation, Duchess House, Warren Street, London W1.

Training for change

Lancashire Industrial Language Training Unit offers a countywide training scheme for ethnic minority unemployed. The scheme is funded by MSC under the Wider Opportunities Training Programme and aims to help ethnic minorities retrain for a range of jobs or further training. It involves both full and part-time provision, run in collaboration with employers, colleges and training agencies.

★ **ASK** R Munns, Lancashire Industrial Language Training Unit, 54/56 Blackburn Road, Accrington, Lancashire BB5 1LE. Tel: (0254) 393316.

Linked skills
In some places the need for English language support in order to attend mainstream classes has led to the development of 'linked skills' classes which act as a bridge between language-based classes and content-based classes. For example, women wishing to attend an adult education computer familiarisation course or typing, in Sheaf Valley Adult Education Division, can attend 'linked skills' classes in preparation, where they learn the specialised vocabulary and some of the initial skills needed.

Women hoping to do the one-year Women's Technology Training Workshop course can attend a preparatory bridging course in Porter Valley Adult Education Division.

Access
A foundation course for black students is run at Granville College, Sheffield, to prepare students for entry to Sheffield City Polytechnic degree courses. The Access course is for people over 21, who are from one of Sheffield's black communities, who do not have the formal entry qualifications, and who wish to do a degree in applied social studies, education, housing studies or public administration.

ETHNIC MINORITY ORGANISED SCHEMES

Local authorities, MSC, and central government have all been concerned to help ethnic minority communities to organise and develop their own schemes in the field of education, training and enterprise.

Black self-help schemes are increasing. Some of them welcome outsiders, some don't. Some work in traditional arts and crafts; some are religious or political; some involve education, some don't. TUBE (Trade Union and Basic Education Project), Manchester, works mainly with groups who have limited resources. They are particularly interested in working on issues relevant to trade unionists and ethnic minorities, such as unemployment, redundancy, racism and race relations.

★ **ASK** Trade Union and Basic Education Project, Workers Educational Association (NW District), 2nd Floor, 769 Stockport Road, Levenshulme, Manchester, M19 3DL. Tel: (061) 224 7014.

The Commission for Racial Equality (CRE)
CRE publishes lists of ethnic minority organisations, which include self-help education schemes.

★ **SEND FOR** the list covering your area from CRE (see below).

Grants may be available through your local CRC to help self-help educational projects.

SOURCES OF INFORMATION AND ADVICE

The Commission for Racial Equality (CRE)
CRE exists to help enforce the law and overcome discrimination. It supports local Community Relations Councils (CRCs) which help with any problem met by people from minority groups. Some CRCs have an education officer. If you think you have been a victim of discrimination, contact your local CRC first (see below). If they can't help you, you can try the CRE itself. You can also fight through the courts on your own.

★ **SEND FOR** *Racial discrimination: a guide to the Race Relations Act 1976*, free from the CRE, Elliot House, 10/12 Allington Street, London SW1E 5EH. Tel: (01) 828 7022. Ask also for their publications list.

There are also recently appointed Development Officers funded by the Manpower Services Commission, attached to your local CRC, local authority or regional CRE office. These officers have been appointed specifically to encourage black young people to participate in the Job Training Scheme, and to provide a link between JTS managing agencies and local communities.

★ **ASK** your CRE Regional Office or your local CRC.

Commission for Racial Equality (CRE) Regional Offices

Birmingham
CRE, Alpha Tower, 11th floor, Suffolk Street, Queensway, Birmingham B1 1TT. Tel: (021) 632 44544.

Leeds
CRE, Yorkshire Bank Chambers, 1st Floor, Infirmary Street, Leeds LS1 2JT. Tel: (0532) 434413/4.

Leicester
CRE, Haymarket House, 4th Floor, Haymarket Shopping Centre, Leicester, LE1 3YG. Tel: (0533) 517852.

Manchester
CRE, Maybrook House, 5th Floor, 40 Blackfriars Street, Manchester. M3 2EG. Tel: (061) 831 7782/7788.

COMMUNITY RELATIONS COUNCILS

There are Community Relations Councils in most towns, and some are involved in educational projects. They are also likely to know of local self-help initiatives. You will find them in the local phone book. For an up-to-date list:

★ **WRITE TO** The Commission for Racial Equality (address above).

★ **LOOK AT** *The social services yearbook.*

10 Disability

What's available
The education system itself
Government training
Money
Specific disabilities
Help and information

WHAT'S AVAILABLE

This chapter is no more than a brief survey. There are more and more schemes aimed at disabled people; many are described here. But disabled people are not excluded from *any* opportunities in the book, at least in theory.

In practice, some colleges may worry about their lack of facilities, or the fact that they can't give any extra support that may be needed. Others are putting great effort into making their facilities more open, with new lifts, ramps, wide doorways, special toilets etc. We can't give a complete list here but the key question is – has the college got someone with responsibility for disabled students? If so, they're more likely to be helpful and welcoming. If a college that didn't used to accept disabled students offers you a place, check they have thought about your needs and whether *they* can cope. The choice you have is:

- use a normal college course, with whatever extra help may be available from the college, the local authority, the MSC and voluntary organisations
- use flexible education schemes aimed at *all* mature students, which enable you to work at home
- do a special course for disabled people, perhaps run by the MSC or one of the specialist colleges or organisations that exist.

THE EDUCATION SYSTEM ITSELF

Colleges of further and higher education

The prospectuses for individual colleges of further education, polytechnics and universities often make brief statements, a few colleges issue leaflets, describing their provision for disabled students. Some colleges of further education may run courses allowing disabled students to 'bridge' on to ordinary courses once they have built up their study skills. The colleges may also, in some instances, provide personal care help, while other severely disabled students can use Community Service Volunteer help. Write directly to the college you are interested in, explaining the nature of your disability and asking what facilities they could provide. If you go for interview, make sure they show you round so you can judge for yourself. If your local college isn't helpful, contact the National Bureau for Handicapped Students (NBHS).

Some regional advisory councils (London, the Home Counties, East Anglia and the East Midlands) publish books listing colleges in their region that provide for disabled people. For addresses see *16 Further education, adult education.*

Flexible schemes

There is a growing number of education schemes aimed at mature students working at home. They're explained elsewhere in the book and include:

- correspondence courses (described in *26 Learning by post*)
- distance learning schemes (described in *17 Flexible learning*)
- getting a home tutor – someone who comes to teach you in your own home, often provided by basic education schemes (described in *20 Basics*)
- the Open University (described in *23 The Open University*)
- books and other learning approaches you can use by yourself (described in *36 Teach yourself systems*)
- broadcasting (described in *25 Radio and TV*).

The Open University

The OU has a specialist adviser for students with disabilities:

★ **WRITE TO** The Adviser for Disabled Students, Office for Students with Disabilities, Walton Hall, Milton Keynes MK7 6AA. Tel: (0908) 74066.

The OU Students Association also helps disabled students very actively. A fund exists to provide financial help with study-related costs in approved cases and to provide and loan specialist equipment to enable those otherwise unable to do so, to study effectively. Where possible, ancillary support is also provided, sometimes including helpers for summer schools.

★ **WRITE TO** OUSA, Open University, PO Box 397, Walton Hall, Milton Keynes MK7 6BE. Tel: (0908) 652094 or answerphone (0908) 652198.

Hereward College of Further Education, Coventry

Hereward College is a national residential college administered by the City of Coventry LEA. It is purpose-built for physically disabled students and offers accommodation with full personal care and nursing provision. Formal conditions of entry are not specified but candidates of average ability levels and above can benefit from the range of courses similar to that found in mainstream further education. Foundation studies include the Certificate in Pre-Vocational Education; GCSE and A- and O-level subjects are offered and a variety of vocational courses include B/TEC National Diploma in Business Studies and B/TEC and C&G Certificate in Computer Aided Engineering. An Open-Learning Centre specialises in Open-Tech materials. The college aims to ensure that even the most severely physically disabled students have access to mainstream curricula and courses through the provision of appropriate technological, study and counselling support. Through its Access Centre, the college offers short communication aids assessment courses lasting between one and three days according to individual student needs. As well as accepting residential students, the college offers places to non-resident day, full and part-time students. Application forms from the college admissions officer.

★ **WRITE TO** Hereward College of Further Education, Bramston Crescent, Tile Hill Lane, Coventry CV4 9SW. Tel: (0203) 461231.

GOVERNMENT TRAINING

Government training is geared to the needs of disabled people. Ask at your nearest Jobcentre for details of what is available in the system. The disablement resettlement officer (DRO) will be able to tell you. Government schemes cost the trainee nothing, some pay allowances (see *24 Train for a new job*). The MSC trains about 4000 disabled people a year through JTS and about 8070 receive training alongside able-bodied people in Skillscentres, colleges or on employers' premises. For disabled people the standard rules on eligibility can be relaxed. YTS offers training and work experience for up to two years for 16 and 17 year old school leavers (see *7 School leavers*) and there are special arrangements for disabled young people. Ask the DRO for details.

Residential colleges

The MSC also supports four residential colleges for disabled people. They're all comfortable and pleasant places. Nurses and other medical staff are available.

Courses vary in length, and where appropriate extensions can be granted. Students can take exams and get recognised qualifications. The choice is good – from basics to technical or clerical work, and they're always looking for new things to try out and introduce.

Finchale Training College
Offers: business studies, computer studies, keyboard and communication skills including word-processing and audio-typing, domestic service engineering with electronic module, assistant quantity surveyor's training, bench joinery, horticulture, electronic servicing, electronic office machinery servicing, watch and clock repairs, production workshop engineering skills.
More information: Finchale Training College, Durham DH1 5RX. Tel: (0385) 62634.

Portland Training College for the Disabled
Offers: business studies, keyboard and communication skills, computer studies, electro/mechanical craft, horticulture, industrial electronics, watch and clock repairs, literacy/numeracy courses, basic work skills (preparatory), multipurpose skills (preparatory for adults). Other facilities include:

- further education for the handicapped school leaver, including life and social skills and independent living, and preparation for vocational training
- an assessment/development centre offering individual programmes including education, communication and training towards purposeful pursuit of life
- sheltered employment providing opportunities for both resident and non-resident severely handicapped employees.

More Information: Portland Training College for the Disabled, Harlow Wood, Nottingham Road, Mansfield, Nottingham NG18 4TJ. Tel: (0623) 792141/2.

Queen Elizabeth's Training College
Offers: business studies – basic office skills, book-keeping, commerce, accounting, copy/audio typing, shorthand or speedwriting, reception (general), telephone/switchboard operating, word-processing, bench joinery, electric arc

welding, engineering draughtsmanship, gardening, electronic wiring for slow learners, domestic appliances servicing, spray painting, industrial sewing machining (two courses – one for slow learners), pre-vocational assessment, computer programming.
More information: Queen Elizabeth's Training College, Leatherhead, Surrey KT22 OBN. Tel: (037284) 2204.

St Loyes College for Training the Disabled for Commerce and Industry
Offers: commercial skills comprising typing, audio-typing, word processing, shorthand, record keeping (manual and computer), principles of accounts, use of office machinery, reception duties, telephone and automatic switchboard usage supplemented by business studies, English and communication skills, business calculations and other office skills and practices. Vocational training is also offered in watch and clock repairs, electronics production techniques, food preparation and cookery, storekeeping, horticulture, joinery, light precision engineering, light electro-mechanical fitting, engineering inspection and electronics servicing.
More information: St Loyes College for Training the Disabled for Commerce and Industry, Fairfield House, Topsham Road, Exeter, Devon EX2 6EP. Tel: (0392) 55428. Contact chief instructor (commercial) or chief instructor (technical) or make applications through local Jobcentres.

MAN, 42, WAITING TO GO ON A COURSE
I applied to go on a course for instrument maintenance. They told me 'about March' and I kept ringing through every three weeks to see when they were opening the course. When they said 'come in' I went down with a virus infection which left me deaf – by the time I recovered, the course was closed again.

I've been trying for electronics – took the test, went for the interview where they hold the course. There was 13 recommended to go through but only nine went on the course and unfortunately they took them first come first served and I was out. They said they would put me down, top of the list for the next course, but that's in ten months time, that's an awful long time to wait. So now I'm trying to get one at St Loyes in Exeter which is the handicapped school. It starts in June so I've applied to go there. The course is almost identical, it's a residential college as well.

Employment rehabilitation centres (ERCs)
There are 27 ERCs; they offer disabled people the chance to think about suitable work or training. First you're given a number of different tests, then you're given the chance to try different kinds of work, perhaps for a few days at a time. There are specialists who try to assess which type of work suits you best.

Courses usually last seven to eight weeks, though they can be shorter or longer but not more than 26 weeks. You get an allowance while you're there. Two of the centres enable you to live in during the course.

★ **ASK** for Leaflet EPL 86 (see below).

On-the-job training
The MSC runs a scheme called Individual Training Throughout with employers. Skilled or semi-skilled work is arranged on an individual basis with an employer on condition that they employ you for at least six months afterwards.

★ **ASK** for the leaflet *All that counts is ability* (see below).

Sheltered employment and training
Severely handicapped people can be employed at sheltered workshops run by local authorities or by voluntary bodies, or by Remploy Ltd. If training is needed first, it's done through on-the-job training (as above) and the trainee gets training wages. To qualify you need to be *registered disabled.*

Registered disabled
The Register of Disabled Persons, established by the Disabled Persons (Employment) Act 1944, is kept by the MSC at local Jobcentres. Registration is open to disabled people who already have jobs, as well as those who are unemployed, and carries a number of benefits. Most types of assistance provided by the MSC are available to both registered and non-registered disabled people. However, the provisions of the quota, designated employment and sheltered employment schemes apply only to registered disabled people. Also, only registered disabled people are eligible for assistance under the MSC's *Special aids to employment* and *Assistance with fares to work* schemes. The advantages of registration will, therefore, depend on individual circumstances. A leaflet about registration, DPL 1, is available from Jobcentres and employment offices.

More information
Leaflets to ask for at the Jobcentre:

The disabled persons register
Residential training colleges for the disabled
How your employment rehabilitation centre can help you
Employment rehabilitation allowances
Aids and adaptations
Assistance with fares to work
Into work
Sheltered employment and you
All that counts is ability.

For all government training for disabled people:

★ **ASK** the DRO, who is there to help you if you have an employment problem.

MONEY

LEA grants
There should be no problems about getting a grant for higher education, but if you need one for ordinary further education, it may be harder. Social workers, the college itself, or the NBHS can all help with appeals to the LEA.

All LEAs can give an extra payment to disabled students of up to £540 a year on top of their grant for extra expenses caused by the disability. There is more about grants in the section *Money*.

Job Training Scheme
JTS trainees may be able to get allowances for some courses, and you should enquire at your Jobcentre. There are extras for disabled people:

- you may get an allowance for a part-time course if you can't do a full-time one
- you may get sponsorship for longer than one year if your employment prospects after a course are improved
- there are special grants to help disabled professionals.

Help with money
There are a number of other organisations that can give grants to disabled people for various purposes. For example:

- the Open University Students Association has its own charity Open University Students Educational Trust (known as OUSET) which can assist in approved cases with loans or grants towards OU study-related costs. Applications can be received at any time, and should be addressed to The Secretary to the Trust, OUSET, OUSA, Open University, PO Box 397, Walton Hall, Milton Keynes MK7 6BE. Tel: (0908) 652094
- if you're doing a correspondence course with the National Extension College consult their student services advisor
- the Snowdon Award Scheme and the COMET Scheme can provide help with microcomputers – details are available from the NBHS. If you're registered blind, the Royal National Institute for the Blind (RNIB) can help with a grant for further or higher education studies.

Here are some organisations that can help you sort out who to approach:
- National Bureau for Handicapped Students
- National Union of Students
- Disablement Income Group.

Their addresses are all given below.

Disability rights handbook
A goldmine of information on income, benefits and services for disabled people. It is updated every year and includes sections on all the different benefits and services available, including those to do with education and training. For full details, see *Books and leaflets* below.

PROVISION FOR SPECIFIC DISABILITIES

Many voluntary organisations exist to help people with particular disabilities, or to help disabled people with their careers, education and employment. This is a short list of some of the ones which can help with education problems.

The blind

The Royal National Institute for the Blind (*RNIB*)
The RNIB runs a number of courses and colleges. It can provide information about these and provide advice about courses and finance for blind adult students. It also publishes an *Information directory*. For more information and advice:

★ **ASK** Careers and HE Adviser, Royal National Institute for the Blind, 224 Great Portland Street, London W1N 6AA. Tel: (01) 388 1266.

Colleges and courses
RNIB Commercial Training College, London (includes computer programming).
Royal Blind School, Edinburgh.
RNIB North London School of Physiotherapy, London.
Royal National College for the Visually Handicapped, Hereford. The only independent FE college specifically for people with visual handicaps.
London College of Furniture, piano-tuning courses.

The RNIB has close contact with all these colleges and courses and can be approached for information, advice and help.

Adult literacy
The RNIB through its Adult Literacy Steering Group (including representation from RNIB and the Partially Sighted Society) has appointed an adult literacy co-ordinator to develop a national service for integrating visually handicapped adults into adult basic education. The co-ordinator's responsibilities include liaison with mainstream adult education institutes and further education colleges and centres. The co-ordinator's role is also peripatetic in providing material resources in braille, moon, large print and tapes and maintaining student/tutor contact. A range of materials is currently on sale and an order form can be obtained from the address below. The co-ordinator will also provide a low vision aid assessment service.

★ **ASK** Adult Literacy Co-ordinator (RNIB), Mark Braithwaite, RNIB Commercial Training College, 5 Pembridge Place, London W2 4XB. Tel: (01) 229 6673.

Other facilities

National Library for the Blind, 35 Great Smith Street, London SW1P 3BU. Tel: (01) 222 2725.
British Talking Book Service, Mount Pleasant, Alperton, Wembley, Middlesex HA0 1RR. Tel: (01) 903 6666.

The deaf

The Royal National Institute for the Deaf (*RNID*)
The RNID is an important central reference point, especially for technical information. RNID also has a list of further education courses for deaf people.

★ **ASK** the Royal National Institute for the Deaf, 105 Gower Street, London WC1 6AH. Tel: (01) 387 8033.

Colleges
Facilities are available in a number of areas to support hearing impaired students in normal further education.

City Lit Centre for the Deaf runs classes for deaf adults and those who work, or wish to work, with deaf people. A wide range of adult education is provided for deaf people, including English and maths, computer literacy, lip-reading, typing, crafts etc. There is also speech therapy. Advice is offered to hearing impaired students on further and higher education opportunities, and a new course, *Turning point* for over 21 year olds, aims to provide an opportunity to return to study for those wanting to change jobs or go on to more advanced study.

★ **ASK** City Lit Centre for the Deaf (and Speech Therapy Unit), Keeley House, Keeley Street, London WC2B 4BA. Tel: (01) 430 0548.

For a list of courses that have been taken by hearing impaired students:

★ **SEND FOR** *Directory of courses,* from Chris Green, High Peak College, Harper Hill, Buxton, Derbyshire FK17 9JZ. Tel: (0298) 2806.

The mentally handicapped

MENCAP: Royal Society for Mentally Handicapped Children and Adults
MENCAP has seven divisional offices covering England, Wales and Northern Ireland which provide support, advice, counselling and information to people with mental handicaps and their families.

Each division has an educational adviser who will provide information, counselling and advice to parents on education – in particular on points of law.

MENCAP runs three educational training establishments which provide a two year course for school-leavers who are mentally handicapped, covering social, independence and vocational skills training. The educational advisers provide support and follow-up for all trainees attending the establishments.

★ **ASK** MENCAP, 123 Golden Lane, London EC1 0RT. Tel: (01) 253 9433.

Adult training centres
Training centres and workshops for mentally handicapped people are run by local authority social services departments in all areas. They are listed in the *Social services yearbook* (see *Booklist*). The work they do varies and may include unskilled assembly work or may concentrate on crafts – woodwork, metalwork, domestic work – which include a greater element of education. Most centres provide some education, some more than others; it is provided by either the centre itself or the local education authority. Trainees are paid an attendance allowance and transport is provided.

Hospitals
In the past, mentally handicapped adults tended to find themselves in special hospitals. Many were dumps for unwanted people. However, some have

education programmes aimed at giving independence. There is also a trend for mentally handicapped adults to live in the community, at home or in smaller residential homes, where adult education classes are often provided.

Further education
More and more FE colleges offer courses specifically for the mentally handicapped and those with mild learning difficulties. Many colleges can cater for students of low ability on ordinary general education and work preparation courses (some are MSC funded). It's worth asking.

HELP AND INFORMATION

The National Bureau For Handicapped Students (NBHS)
Helps disabled people in education. Their services include:

- giving information/advice to students with disabilities
- advising colleges on how best to make provision for students with special educational needs
- staff development
- producing publications which are designed to meet the needs of disabled students in F/HE, their parents, and those working with them
- organising conferences/seminars/courses
- producing a journal *Educare*
- carrying out research
- regional groups.

★ **LOOK AT** *Compendium of post-16 education* (*COPE*), which gives detailed information about residential training colleges for young people.

Applying to higher education: some notes for disabled students, their parents and advisers (single copy free to handicapped students).

Deaf students in college (single copy free to handicapped students).
Blind and partially sighted students in college (single copy free to handicapped students).

Occupational information – a supplement for disabled students (single copy free to handicapped students but a charge of 50p is made for postage).

A full publications list is available from NBHS. For up-to-date, informed advice:

★ **ASK** National Bureau for Handicapped Students, 336 Brixton Road, London SW9 7AA. Tel: (01) 274 0565.

The Royal Association for Disability and Rehabilitation (RADAR)
RADAR has an education and training bureau which will help you, if all else fails, with anything – from basics to astrophysics. It provides correspondence courses and home tuition (the latter in London only). They are also interested to hear if anyone is refused education on account of disability. They produce two journals: *Contact* (quarterly) and *Bulletin* (monthly newsletter). There is also a comprehensive and useful publications list.

★ **ASK** RADAR, 25 Mortimer Street, London W1N 8AB. Tel: (01) 637 5400.

Other organisations

Talking Books for the Handicapped (National Listening Library), 12 Lant Street, London SE1 1QR. Tel: (01) 407 9417. Annual subscription £15.00. Over 1000 books available.

The Disabled Living Foundation, 380 Harrow Road, London. Tel: (01) 602 2491. Information service on aids and services. They also have samples available to try.

Disablement Income Group (*DIG*), Attlee House, 28 Commercial Street, London E1 6LR. Tel: (01) 247 6877.

National Union of Students, 1 Holloway Road, London N7 6LJ. Tel: (01) 272 8900.

Spastics Society, Park Crescent, London W1N 4EQ. Tel: (01) 636 5020.

Northern Ireland Council for the Handicapped, 2 Annadale Avenue, Belfast BT7 3JH. Ask for: The Information Officer.

Scottish Centre for the Tuition of the Disabled, Queen Margaret College, 36 Clerwood Terrace, Edinburgh EH12 8TS. Tel: (031) 339 8111.

Line 81, Broadcasting Support Services, PO Box 7, London W3 6XJ. Tel: (01) 992 5522. A service providing an additional source of information for disabled people.

Education Guidance Services for Adults often have useful information about how disabled people have been received in education locally, should know what's available in the area and should be able to help in cases of difficulty. They are described and listed in *1 Advice and help*.

Books and leaflets

Compass – direction finder for disabled people. Useful source of addresses and contacts; currently being updated. Available from DIG, Attlee House, 28 Commercial Street, London E1 6LR.

The wheelchair child, Philippa Russell, a Condor Book, Souvenir Press (E and A) Ltd, 1984, paperback (especially the chapter *Leaving school: education and work problems*).

Directory for the disabled: a handbook of information and opportunities for the disabled and handicapped, compiled by Ann Darnborough and Derek Kinrade, published by Woodhead Faulkner in association with RADAR. 3rd edition, 1981, available from RADAR (see above). Currently being updated.

Disability rights handbook for 1984, published by Disability Alliance, 25 Denmark Street, London WC2A 8NJ. Tel: (01) 240 0806.

Employers' guide to disability, edited by Melvyn Kettle and Bert Massie, 1982, RADAR. An excellent guide to different disabilities including relevant sources of extra help and information for each one. Loose leaf format so it can be updated.

Blind and partially sighted students in college, by the RNIB and NBHS, available free from the RNIB (address above).

The disabled student in higher education, R Holmes and F Aprahamian, Open University Press.

11 Travellers

DISCRIMINATION

People who don't live in one place continuously (gypsies, circus and fairground people, seamen) are at a disadvantage when it comes to education. Gypsies, the largest such group in the country, may suffer the additional problem of having had little education as children.

Although travellers have the same rights as other people, it is not always easy to exercise them if there is a hostile local attitude. If you feel that you are being discriminated against, contact your local education authority or the Department of Education and Science or one of the organisations listed below.

THE LOCAL EDUCATION AUTHORITY

Local education authorities vary in their provision. Some are making efforts to provide facilities; many now employ advisory teachers to work with travellers. They are good people to talk to for help in getting the provision you need.

Your children's school

Your children's school may be a good place to ask for help with your own education. Some primary and secondary schools are called *community schools* and many of these run courses for parents as well as children.

READING AND WRITING

Nearly all areas provide help with learning to read and write, usually free. A teacher may come to see you at your stopping place, or at a drop-in centre (see *20 Basics*). Some areas provide basic education especially for travellers. The Write Here Adult Literacy Drop-In Centre in Sheffield works specifically with travellers, and combines literacy with welfare rights advice and under 5s work, in an informal setting.; in the central region of Scotland they have a pack to help with filling in forms, a women's group and *Traveller tales,* a newsletter which includes travellers' writing as well as general information. For a mailing list:

★ **ASK** Teacher-in-charge, Travellers, Cannongrange Teachers Centre, Main Street, Stenhousemuir FK5 3BQ.

OTHER FLEXIBLE EDUCATION

See *17 Flexible learning* and *26 Learning by post*. Facilities exist at:

Bradford
Mandi Farrar, Roadside Stop, Austral House, 51 Well Street, Bradford BD1 5PS. Tel: (0274) 726737.

Kent
Anne Kesteven, Tutor-in-Charge, Coldharbour Education Project for Travellers, Aylesford Adult Education Centre, Teapot Lane, Aylesford, Kent. Tel: (0622) 79144.
Julie Hetherington, Co-ordinator, Sittingbourne Travellers Project, Adult Studies Centre, Sittingbourne College, College Road, Sittingbourne, Kent ME10 1LF. Tel: (0795) 25124.

London
Penny Roberts, Co-ordinator for Adult Literacy with Travellers, ILEA, Language and Literacy Unit, 1 Gerridge Street, London SE1 7QT. Tel: (01) 633 0053.

Sheffield
Write Here Drop-In Centre, 697 Attercliffe Road, Sheffield S9 3RE. Tel (0742) 444377.

Correspondence courses need you to have a holding address but some of the organisations listed below could help.

GETTING A GRANT

For a grant you can use the address of the college you hope to attend and apply to the LEA in which the college is situated.

USEFUL READING

The traveller's handbook, (a guide to the law affecting gypsies) by Bill Forrester, 1985, Interchange Books, London. ISBN 0948309–00–8

USEFUL ORGANISATIONS

Advisory Committee for Education of Romany and Other Travellers (*ACERT*), Mary Ward Centre, 42 Queen Square, London WC1N 3AJ. Tel: (01) 831 7079. Has published *Swann report & travellers*. Chapter 16 is on Traveller education. *A report on designation* and an *Information booklet* (free).

National Gypsy Education Council, Donald Kenrick, 61 Blenheim Crescent, London W11. Tel: (01) 727 2916. Publishes *Traveller education*, see below.

The Romany Guild, an organisation run by gypsies for gypsies. Office Tel: (01) 558 7303 or write to The Caravan Site, 50/56 Temple Mills Lane, London E15 2ER. Ask for: Tom Lee. For education, 204 Church Road, Hanwell, London W7. Tel: (01) 579 5108. Ask for: Elsie Fisher.

Romanestan Publications, 22 North End, Warley, Brentwood, Essex CM14 5LA. Tel: (0277) 219491. Sell *Traveller education* and other material about and by travellers, and in Romany. Send for their regularly updated publications list.

National Association of Teachers of Travellers, c/o Broad Lanes, Bilston, Wolverhampton. WV14 0SB. Tel: (0902) 405091.

12 In prison and after

Into prison
Out of prison
Some useful organisations

INTO PRISON

If you're new to it, the first couple of days of a prison sentence may seem a bit strange, and it will take a little time to settle in to the new routine. When you arrive, you're seen by six or seven different departments; you spend much of your time hanging around in queues or in your cell, and the rest rushing about. You may not realise that one of the people you've seen is the education officer, and that if you said 'yes' to whatever he or she asked you, you're probably 'on' classes. But even if you didn't, go back and see the education officer later. They are there to help and can lay on anything from basics to postgraduate degree work. And the prison is legally obliged to give every encouragement to anyone who could benefit from education.

Prison education service

Every prison has an education department. They all run part-time courses; some bigger ones are open all day long and offer full-time courses. There is full-time education for young offenders up to school leaving age.

There's usually a good mixture of subjects: art, soft toys and other crafts are popular because you can make presents for friends and family; basic education is quite a big attraction; languages, discussion groups, GCSEs and A-levels, keep fit, weight training and vocational training are all on offer. Talking it over doesn't mean you have to commit yourself; but if there's something you really want to do which isn't available at your prison, the education officer might be able to help you get moved to somewhere else. And basic education has been on offer in prisons for longer than anywhere else. If nothing else, it's an excellent alternative to being 'banged up', and many educators believe that people often start successful educational careers in that way.

Young offenders

Since May 1983 all young offenders who receive a custodial sentence will serve it in either a Detention Centre (DC) or a Youth Custody Centre (YCC) (formerly borstal). All trainees in YCCs have to attend a minimum of two hours a week on day classes (or the equivalent). The subjects for these classes are 'work related' or concerned with life and social skills. Trainees who need more education are given the opportunity to attend the day and/or evening classes on a voluntary basis. In DCs attendance on evening classes is compulsory and trainees with special needs can attend the daytime classes.

Learning by post in prison
You can do correspondence courses in prison. Most of them are 'programmed texts' where the subject is broken up into short, simple steps. But you can also ask about other types of course, for example some places do Open University courses.

Correspondence courses seem attractive to prisoners in the early part of their sentence because the Home Office helps to pay for them. But they are often left unfinished; perhaps because learning alone is even more lonely in prison than outside. Often the courses chosen are very vocational; though it seems like a good idea at first, once you start it becomes rather remote. These types of course are described more fully in *17 Flexible learning, 23 The Open University* and *26 Learning by post*.

Library services
All prisons have a library. There have been big improvements in many recently. They are a branch of the local public library so should send in a visiting librarian regularly who can order books from the public library system.

Training for jobs
Most prisons have industrial training in their workshops. But you don't have much choice about what you do. Some prisons have really good facilities for learning a trade; if you're not in one, you can apply to the governor and ask to be transferred. The courses (vocational training courses) are usually recognised, so you get a qualification out of them. There are also Construction Industry Training courses – a scheme of full-time training in bricklaying, plumbing, plastering, painting and decorating etc. Ask your education officer.

OUT OF PRISON

Being an ex-con isn't as much of a disadvantage for getting into education or training as it is for getting jobs. Almost every opportunity in this book is open to you. The only thing that may cause problems is your release date. You may be too late to enrol, and have to wait several months. If you're doing basics (reading, writing, maths) and want to carry on, ask your prison teacher to fix it. If you have difficulty getting accepted on a course, get your probation officer to approach colleges or the adult education service on your behalf. The education officer will give you general advice about courses available outside the prison.

SOME USEFUL ORGANISATIONS

NACRO
A voluntary organisation that provides an education advisory service giving advice on all education and training matters, including entry to further education, and runs a number of basic education day centres and Youth Training Scheme projects throughout the country. The day centres also offer educational advice to people not attending their own courses, and the services are available to offenders and ex-offenders, whether in prison or not.

NACRO may tell you about:

- their 17 educational day centres offering tuition in a full range of basic education activities including things like literacy, maths, art, office skills, basic computing, domestic skills
- education projects and services run by other people

★ **ASK** NACRO Education Advisory Service, 2 Hulme Street, Manchester M1 5QA. Tel: (061) 236 2604.

NACRO Education Day Centres

England

Essex

Basildon, c/o Essex Probation Service, 2nd Floor, Essex House, Cherrydown, Basildon, Essex. Tel: (0268) 24043.

London – Inner

North London Education Project, 16 Nevill Road, London Nl6 8SR. Tel: (01) 241 1049.

Manchester – Greater

Manchester, 2 Hulme Street, Manchester M1 5QA. Tel: (061) 236 2604.

Wigan, 2nd Floor, Victoria Building, 36/44 King Street, Wigan. Tel: (0942) 41090.

Merseyside

Liverpool, Whitechapel Project, St Francis Xavier Nursery School, Langsdale Street, Liverpool L3 8DX. Tel: (051) 207 7617.

Knowsley, 88 Liverpool Road, Huyton, Knowsley, Liverpool L36 3RF. Tel: (051) 480 3100.

Tyne and Wear

Newcastle, 18 Westmorland Road, Newcastle-upon-Tyne NE1 4EG. Tel: (091) 261 8872.

Sunderland, l6/17 Nile Street, Sunderland SR1 1EY. Tel: (0783) 655041.

West Midlands

Birmingham, BURRA Project, 395 Soho Road, Handsworth, Birmingham B2l 9SS. Tel: (021) 523 8026.

Sandwell, 23/24 Essex Flats, York Road, Rowley Regis, West Midlands B65 0TX. Tel: (021) 561 5610.

Yorkshire

Bradford, 46–48 Westgate, Bradford 1. Tel: (0274) 736055. PO Box 6, Bradford BD1 1LB. Tel: (0274) 733l65 ext 52/5/6.

Sheffield, 2nd Floor, Hallam House, Fitzallen Square, Sheffield 1. Tel: (0742) 753986.

Two new basic skills training centres will be opened in Bolton and Warrington this year; ask a local probation officer or the NACRO Education Advisory Service for details.

Wales

Gwent

Newport, 6–8 Chepstow Road, Newport, Gwent. Tel: (0633) 52500.

Mid Glamorgan

Pontypridd, 22 Gelliwastad Road, Pontypridd, Mid Glamorgan. Tel: (0443) 404036.

West Glamorgan

Swansea, The YMCA, Kingsway, Swansea, West Glamorgan. Tel: (0792) 473 726/701.

SACRO

The counterpart of NACRO for Scotland. As well as information and advice services and a range of help and support facilities, SACRO have day centres in

Glasgow and Edinburgh and in Glasgow they run Onward Workshop – a furniture reclamation workshop to get ex-offenders back into work habits. SACRO also have accommodation for ex-offenders, in both Glasgow and Dundee. The day centres provide a range of recreational activities, education and skill training. They also have information about other relevant local provision.

★ **ASK** SACRO Central, c/o Central Region Social Work Department, Grangemouth. Tel: (0324) 464876. SACRO Lothian, Epworth Halls, 25 Nicholson Square, Edinburgh. Tel: (031) 668 1091. SACRO Strathclyde, 218/220 Renfrew Street, Glasgow. Tel: (041) 332 1763. SACRO Tayside, 5 West Bell Street, Dundee DD1 1EX. Tel: (0382) 23445. National Office: SACRO, 53 George Street, Edinburgh EH2 2ET. Tel: (031) 226 4222.

NIACRO

NIACRO Education Service runs courses from Headquarters and a number of out-centres in Belfast and around Northern Ireland. Types of courses include basic education, literacy and numeracy, sports and driving lessons. Their Bursaries Scheme provides financial assistance for people studying certain courses which are not eligible for normal grants.

★ **ASK** NIACRO, 22 Adelaide Street, Belfast BT2 8GD. Tel: (0232) 20157.

APEX Trust

The APEX Trust is a registered charity providing advice, specialised training and educational facilities to ex-offenders and others facing particular difficulties in the job market.

It seeks to get jobs for ex-offenders and acts as a training and advisory service to people working with them (such as probation officers and social workers).

APEX Employment Resource Centres are in operation throughout London and in various parts of the country, providing pre-employment training, advice on job-search techniques, training in basic skills needed for work or further formal training, a job placement service and opportunities for volunteering.

APEX also runs a number of Community Programme Schemes in the north of England, specialising in helping ex-offenders, particularly drug misusers.

★ **ASK** APEX Trust, 31/33 Clapham Road, London SW9 0JE. Tel: (01) 582 3171.

Also there are two units offering educational guidance and support to prisoners in penal institutions in Kent, whether you live in or out of the county, and also for inmates of other establishments who will be returning to Kent.

★ **ASK** Gabrielle Wilson, Unit Co-ordinator for East Kent, Kent Unit for the Education and Guidance of Ex-offenders (KUEGO), College of Technology, New Dover Road, Canterbury CT1 3AJ. Tel: (0227) 454398.

★ **ASK** Judith Cressey, Unit Co-ordinator for West Kent, Kent Unit for the Education and Guidance of Ex-Offenders, Mid-Kent College of Higher and Further Education, Oakwood Park, Maidstone ME16 8AQ. Tel: (0622) 687735.

13 Overseas students

What's on offer?
Things to know
Helpful organisations
Helpful books

WHAT'S ON OFFER?

Nearly all the full-time education described in this book is open to overseas students. But it is getting harder to use; people from overseas may feel they are less welcome than they were a few years ago.

As most of what you can do is described somewhere else in the book, the information is mentioned briefly here and you are referred to the relevant chapters. And do look at the lists of books and organisations that can help you.

The public sector

Universities, polytechnics, HE and FE colleges and adult residential colleges all accept overseas students. The fees are much higher than for UK or EEC residents.

Eaton Hall International

This is the only public sector college specifically for overseas students. It is a residential college run by Nottinghamshire County Council. Courses include professional training for a wide range of subjects, and English language.

The private sector

Heavily used by overseas students. If you want to be sure you're not being exploited, contact organisations which try to monitor standards, such as The Association for Recognised English Language Teaching Establishments in Britain (ARELS-FELCO) and the Conference for Independent Further Education. These and other such organisations are decribed more fully in *34 The private sector*.

Correspondence colleges

You can study with a British correspondence college without coming here, but not with the Open University which requires bona fide UK residence. Many foreign students do correspondence courses at the same time as college ones, in the same subject. They find it provides a back-up. For a list of correspondence colleges and how to choose one, look at *26 Learning by post*.

THINGS TO KNOW

Getting into Britain

For holiday courses in English as a foreign language, there's no problem. It's only difficult if you're staying for more than three months. A letter from your college saying you have a place for up to one year, on a course taking 15 hours per week or more day-time study should get you in. But you still have to prove you have enough money to live on. So you must get accepted by the college *before* you come, and obtain entry clearance from the British High Commission or Embassy in your own country to save difficulties at immigration. When you do finally get to Britain, you may have to report to the police regularly.

Qualifications

If you want to know what your qualification is worth in Britain, the British Council provides a useful service.

★ **ASK** The National Academic Recognition Information Centre (NARIC) for the United Kingdom, British Council, 10 Spring Gardens, London SW1A 2BN.

Grants

No one gets a grant from a British local education authority (LEA) unless they have been *ordinarily resident* for three years before the 1 September of the year the course begins, and their purpose for being in the UK during that time has *not at any time* been wholly or mainly that of receiving full-time education. Ordinarily resident means being in the UK for a continued and settled purpose including education. However, the second condition means that most overseas students will not be eligible for a grant. The same conditions apply to fees, so most overseas students will not qualify for the home student rate of fee either. The only exceptions to this are:

- refugees (see below)
- EEC nationals ordinarily resident in the EEC for three years before the 1st September of the year the course begins, but not if they have been living there wholly or mainly for the purpose of receiving full-time education
- those admitted for settlement who have not had the right of abode at or before the beginning of the three-year period before 1 September of the year the course begins
- students on reciprocal exchange agreements.

For detailed information on grants and fees:

★ **ASK** The United Kingdom Council for Overseas Student Affairs (UKCOSA), see below for address.

Refugees

Those granted refugee status in the UK should be treated as UK residents. This is particularly important as it means that you don't pay overseas students' fees and should be eligible for grants. Students with refugee status granted by other countries will be treated like other overseas students. The World University Service offers an educational advisory service to refugees in the UK.

★ **ASK** World University Service (UK), 20/21 Compton Terrace, London N1 2UN. Tel: (01) 226 6747.

HELPFUL ORGANISATIONS

The United Kingdom Council for Overseas Student Affairs (*UKCOSA*), 60 Westbourne Grove, London, W2 5FG. Tel: (01) 229 9268/9.

The British Council, 10 Spring Gardens, London SW1A 2BN. Tel: (01) 930 8466; 28 Park Place, Cardiff CF1 3QE. Tel: (0222) 97346/7/8/9; 3 Bruntsfield Crescent, Edinburgh EH10 4HD. Tel: (031) 447 4716; 1 Chlorine Gardens, Belfast BT9 5DJ. Tel: (0232) 666611/666706.

International Students House, 229 Great Portland Street, London W1. Tel: (01) 636 9472.

National Union of Students, Nelson Mandela House, 461 Holloway Road, London N7 6JL. Tel: (01) 272 8900.

Central Bureau for Educational Visits and Exchanges, Seymour House, Seymour Mews, London W1H 9PE. Tel: (01) 486 5101; 3 Bruntsfield Crescent, Edinburgh EH10 4HD. Tel: (031) 447 8024; 16 Malone Road, Belfast BT9 5BN. Tel: (0232) 664418/9.

As well as helping British people study overseas, it provides help for overseas students in Britain. In particular it publishes *Young visitors to Britain* every year in English, French, Spanish, German and Italian. This publication lists a large number of study and holiday opportunities in Britain. Also *Working holidays*.

Educational establishments
Many higher education institutions have overseas students societies run by and for students of different nationalities. Some are political, others cultural, but they should all provide support and help.

HELPFUL BOOKS

Higher education in the United Kingdom 1986–88, a handbook for students from overseas and their advisors. British Council and the Association of Commonwealth Universities, Longmans.

Courses of special interest to overseas students, 1978. Available from NELPCO, c/o North East London Polytechnic, Romford Road, Stratford, London E15 4LZ. Tel: (01) 590 7722 ext 4181.

14 Studying abroad

WHY STUDY ABROAD?

It's quite normal to spend part of your life abroad, working or studying. People working in big companies frequently spend time abroad; academics often teach and study abroad; students in higher education often go abroad during their vacations and sometimes as part of their course. But the world is *your* oyster too, and if you are thinking of major changes in your life (change of job, beginning to do a course) most of the world is open to you.

THE MAIN PROBLEMS

Language

Things are weighted in your favour if you speak English because many countries use English as their main language and many use English for some of their teaching in higher education, even if it's not their *lingua franca*. However, you won't get the most benefit out of a stay abroad if you can't speak the local language. So if you're taking the trouble to go abroad, it's worth learning the language. You can start before you go but using the language in the country concerned is the best way of learning it fast. If you've time, go there for a holiday first, both to practise the language and to get a feel of the country. For more information on learning languages look at *42 Things to study: languages*.

Immigration

Each country has different rules about what you have to do before you can visit, live, work or study there.

★ **ASK** the Embassy or High Commission of that country. These are mostly in London.

Money

This is of course the main problem. You'll need money to get there, to live on and for course fees. British LEAs and the MSC will not pay your expenses overseas, so you'll have to find:

- a country that costs little to live in, that you can get to cheaply, that provides cheap or free courses. That may still seem expensive but if you are in the situation of having to pay for yourself for a course in Britain, you could find it much cheaper abroad

- private finance from your employer, a bank loan or an educational charity (described in *39 Money: What for, where from*)
- a scheme that pays for a period overseas such as the Winston Churchill Travelling Fellowships. They are usually advertised in the national dailypress.

Health
This is important as health care overseas can be very expensive. Some countries do have reciprocal arrangements with Britain allowing you free health care.

★ **ASK** your local office of the DHSS, if you're going for a short stay. For longer stays, contact: DHSS, Overseas Contributions 3, Newcastle-upon-Tyne NE98 1YX. Tel: (091) 285 7111.

OF PARTICULAR INTEREST

There are a number of possibilities to look out for.

College courses
Some British colleges do provide opportunities for overseas study, though it's still unusual apart from degree courses in foreign languages.

The EEC
One of the advantages of being part of the EEC is that you can not only work in all the other eleven countries (France, Italy, West Germany, Holland, Belgium, Luxembourg, Denmark, Ireland, Greece, Spain, Portugal) on the same basis as their nationals, but also study there. EEC nationals (apart from Greeks) living in Britain have the right to be treated the same as UK residents for fees, grants and government training and the same *should* apply the other way too, though we still don't have a lot of information about how that works in practice. If you have such experience, please let us know!

American universities
American and Canadian universities advertise in the British press. They have the advantage not only of teaching in English but also of having a much more flexible course structure – you could do part of a course here and then continue it in North America. Though you will have to pay, some say they offer bursaries. For more information about universities in the USA:

★ **WRITE TO** The American University Bureau, c/o CLC, 213/215 Tottenham Court Road, PO Box 4US, London W1. Tel: (01) 580 0163.

MORE INFORMATION

The Central Bureau for Educational Visits and Exchanges
Exists to help people wanting to study overseas and could be a good place to start if you want information or contacts. They also publish a number of useful booklets.

★ **LOOK AT** *Adventure and discovery*, an annual guide to thousands of learning opportunities abroad.

★ **LOOK AT** *Volunteer work*, a directory of organisations recruiting volunteers for projects in the UK and in 153 countries worldwide.

★ **WRITE TO** The Central Bureau for Educational Visits and Exchanges, Seymour Mews House, Seymour Mews, London W1H 9PE. Tel: (01) 486 5101; 3 Bruntsfield Crescent, Edinburgh EH10 4HD. Tel: (031) 447 8024; 16 Malone Road, Belfast BT9 5BN. Tel: (0232) 664418/9.

The British Council

Has an office in 82 countries and most of them have libraries. There is also an information department and library in London.

★ **LOOK AT** *Scholarships abroad.* It lists over 300 scholarships offered to British students by overseas governments, a number of bursaries and lots of useful information.

★ **WRITE TO** The British Council, 10 Spring Gardens, London SW1A 2BN. Tel: (01) 930 8466; 3 Bruntsfield Crescent, Edinburgh EH10 4HD. Tel: (031) 447 4716; 1 Chlorine Gardens, Belfast BT9 5DJ. Tel: (0232) 666706; 28 Park Place, Cardiff CF1 3QE. Tel: (0222) 397346/7/8/9.

Other useful publications

Higher education in the European community: a student handbook published by HMSO for the European Communities.

UNESCO study abroad, Vol. 24, 1983–6, published by HMSO for UNESCO.

PROVIDERS

15 Some notes about the system

WHAT DO THE NAMES MEAN?

The terms used to describe education for people who have left school are many and bewildering. Adult education might easily be taken to mean any education for adults, but it is often used to describe particular kinds only, such as evening classes at various local centres, or weekend courses. Further education is sometimes used to mean education for people who have left school and want to go further but it tends more often to be used to describe education in colleges of further education – often vocational training for young people who have just left school or for technicians. To confuse it further, some areas have both further education colleges and adult education colleges, others have one set of colleges to do both sorts of work.

Then there is community education, the term used in Scotland for informal local activities involving adult education and youth work. Elsewhere it may be just another name for adult education or a far more informal type of education which may not use classrooms at all.

You have to find out what is available in your area, regardless of what it is called.

WHO RUNS IT?

Local education authorities

In Britain, central government has never provided much education. It says what should be done, pays for much of it and checks what is being done. Actual provision is largely left to local government; the part of the local council that provides it is called the local education authority (LEA). In Scotland, the polytechnics and colleges of education are centrally funded by the Scottish Education Department and this is reflected in their title – central institutions.

At present the LEAs are:

- In England and Wales – County Councils, Metropolitan District Councils, Outer London Boroughs and the Inner London Education Authority (ILEA) for Central London
- In Scotland – Regional Councils
- In Northern Ireland – Local Education and Library Boards appointed by the Department of Education for Northern Ireland.

Since public education is locally organised, it varies considerably from area to area. We have provided a summary of how it is organised in each area in the

Gazetteer. To find out more, use the contacts listed there, use the educational guidance service for adults listed in *1 Advice and help*, or use the public library.

For a list of all LEAs in the country, including names of their professional staff, adult and further education advisers, subject advisers and so on:

★ **LOOK AT** *The education yearbook* (see *Booklist*).

Manpower Services Commission (MSC)
The MSC is a nationwide organisation. It supports an enormous number of courses at Skillcentres, FE colleges, polytechnics, training centres, universities and even schools. It trains school leavers through the Youth Training Scheme (described in *7 School leavers*) and people aged 19 and over through the Job Training Scheme and many other programmes.

The Commission itself and its area boards are made up of people nominated by government, industry and the trade unions. It is not accountable to local government – parliamentary questions about the MSC are answered by the Secretary of State for Employment.

The MSC's work does not extend to Northern Ireland where the equivalent work is done through the Department of Economic Development. Key addresses are listed in *24 Training for a new job*.

Health authorities
The district health authorities (health boards in Scotland) deal with nurse education, occupational therapy and other medical services. Many have health education officers who may do some work with the public.

Social service departments
These are part of local government like the LEAs and deal with adult training centres, sheltered workshops and other facilities for disabled people. For addresses and names of both district health authorities and social service departments:

★ **LOOK AT** *The social services yearbook* (see *Booklist*).

Public services
The police, fire service and prison service run their own colleges but they're restricted to their own staff.

Universities
Funded mainly by government through the Universities Grants Committee (UGC) but not accountable financially.

Voluntary organisations
May run education or training as part of their wider work. Examples are the YWCA, Women's Institutes, trade unions and organisations formed to provide education such as the WEA. Since these are organisations which you may join as a member, you can participate in decisions about their work.

Private training organisations
This means organisations that provide education or training as a business, not for the general public at public expense. The person using it pays for it. For some things it is easier to get what you need.

There is more information about this type of provision in *26 Learning by post* and *34 The private sector*.

If you want to know if anyone looks at the quality of their work, you can ask these questions:

- are they registered with any body that monitors standards (eg the British Council)?
- are they a registered charity?
- are they grant-aided (by the DES, SED, an LEA, any other public body)?
- does the MSC sponsor any of their work?
- do their courses lead to recognised qualifications?

WHAT IS A COLLEGE?

The word 'college' really means 'a place where people read together'. There are many different kinds: colleges of further education, technology, art, education, agriculture; community colleges, village colleges; colleges of higher education; correspondence colleges; private colleges (often advertised on buses, on the underground and in the small ads); professional bodies (like the College of Physicians); private schools (like Eton College); university colleges (Goldsmiths' College, London; New College, Oxford) which are parts of a university.

Even if someone goes to a place of learning that isn't called by that name, they may say 'I'm going to college'. Anyone can start one – you can invite a few people to your house, show them your holiday slides and call yourself 'The College of Vacation Studies'! The word itself tells you very little.

COMPLAINTS AND SUGGESTIONS

LEA provision
Who you talk to depends on what you want. If it's to do with problems of study, choice of courses or subjects, then talk to the teachers; if you want a grant ask in the local education offices; if you want changes in the way education is organised locally, or you want things provided for adults that aren't, ask your local councillor. The education guidance services for adults listed in *1 Advice and help* should be able to help you work out how to make a complaint, request or suggestion.

Teachers, lecturers, tutors
In general they see it as part of their job to talk with students, sort out problems, help with decision making. If you're having a problem because you don't get on with the teacher, you should still speak to him or her about the problem first, if you can. If that's impossible, there may be someone else you can talk to like a course tutor or organiser or, if you're lucky, a college counsellor. If there's a serious problem you can go to the teacher's boss, usually a head of department.

The college itself will have a principal or director – the bigger the college the more people there will be in the hierarchy whom you can approach.

As a last resort you can go to the chief education officer, and ultimately the local council chief executive, or for Scottish General Institutions, to the SED.

LEA officials
Will decide things according to the rules, but the rules aren't always clear and there are many exceptions open to interpretation. Rules can also be broken so don't be put off by an initial rebuff. The higher you go, the more power people have to break the rules for you.

Local councillors and MPs
Decisions are usually made not by the full council (though they have to agree major policies) but by the education committee, sometimes in practice by a further education sub-committee. Your local county councillor may not be a member of these committees but can certainly talk to other councillors who are.

Your councillor can take up individual matters on your behalf if you feel you can't make sense of the system.

Your MP, though nothing officially to do with local government, may still take up matters on your behalf, know who to talk to, how to get things done.

The ombudsman
If there seems to be a case of maladministration (the authority breaking its own rules) your MP can refer it to the ombudsman. There's a separate one for local government who must be approached through your local councillor. They're not used a great deal in educational matters, but education is part of their job.

College governors
Each college has a governing body made up of councillors, representatives of local interests, college staff and students. They are responsible for the work of the college.

Manpower Services Commission
Not nearly so open, as it's directly responsible to neither local nor central government – it's semi-autonomous. Although that means it can do things very quickly, and does, it can also be very closed to pressure from the public. Its organisation is complex; for training matters go to the local area office of the TD; if someone else is responsible, they will tell you. If you want action, the area manager is the person to get things done. As a last resort, go to your MP.

Private organisations
They may be members of bodies set up to monitor standards. If their advertising is misleading you can complain to the local consumer protection department, or the Advertising Standards Authority. Otherwise, you depend on their integrity.

GETTING IN – SOME GENERAL POINTS

- Higher education courses (universities, polytechnics, colleges of higher education, Scottish central institutions) are organised in academic years which usually run from September to July (the main exception is the Open University which runs from January to December). You start at the beginning of the academic year. You're supposed to apply nearly a year ahead.

- Further education courses have the same academic year, but you often have to go and queue on 'enrolment days'. It's sometimes possible to book places in advance. Ask.
- Government training courses admit you as soon as a place becomes available, which could be any time of year. So apply any time.
- Basic education is usually supplied when you want it, though there's sometimes a wait of a few weeks and it's not usually available in the summer as many providers work the academic year.
- Correspondence courses start once you've sent them the money.
- Private colleges often have courses starting every few weeks, so you can choose when you want to start.

But many organisations don't work the way they're officially supposed to, and more and more places are organising courses that work in more flexible ways (see *17 Flexible learning*).

GETTING IN – CRACKING THE SYSTEM

Receptionists

Most organisations offering courses are fairly large. The person you first talk to will nearly always have several bosses, so if you don't like what he or she says you may get a different answer from upstairs, or you may not. Receptionists are never responsible for admitting students, so don't be put off by them; they'll usually give you the official version not the alternatives, indeed may not know about the alternatives and may not even have heard about the course you want, particularly if it's new or different.

Procedures

Getting in usually involves most of these steps:

- filling in an application form
- sometimes by a certain date
- often having an interview (or more than one)
- showing that you have a minimum qualification or passing some kind of test – which may be one where you tick boxes or it may demand some writing
- giving a reference(s)
- going through an enrolment procedure – which will probably include paying all or part of the fee.

The specific procedures for particular places are described in the relevant chapters, but you should not always take them at face value, eg universities may accept students at the last minute to take up places that have become vacant; and they may be prepared to take you without the usual O- and A-levels if you can convince them that they should. You can even be over qualified!

Presenting yourself

If you have no qualifications, or too few, you can still get into a lot of places. Mature students are becoming more and more acceptable, because people working in education realise that they are often keener, appreciate the courses more and contribute a great deal to the life of the college. So when you fill in the application form or go to an interview, try and be what they want!
Characteristics they'll look for are:

- seriousness of purpose (recent attendance at other courses is something looked for)
- tolerance of others (especially the young if it's not an adults-only course)
- determination to take advantage of this chance
- ability to benefit from the course.

If it's not absolutely clear on the form that you are an adult, attach a letter saying what you've done before.

MATURE ENTRANT TO UNIVERSITY

I needed to retrain. My first attempt was the year before I applied to university – I enquired about teacher training and was told to go and get my A-levels first. This was difficult while I was doing a responsible job, so I didn't. A friend suggested I try the local university as they took mature students. I wrote to the head of department explaining what I wanted to do and asking what I'd need to be able to apply. They asked me for an interview and spent most of their time trying to discourage me but said 'yes, we'll accept you now'. I still had to apply through UCCA but they'd already given me an unconditional offer of a place.

---

16 Further education, adult education

Further education | *What is FE like?*
More information | *Adult education*

Local education authorities are the main providers of education in Britain. The biggest part of the education they provide for people who have left school is further education (FE) and adult education (AE). The *Gazetteer* lists all the LEAs in the country, all their further education colleges, and describes their arrangements for adult education.

The main distinctions between FE and AE are:

- FE offers full-time and substantial part-time courses (up to 21 hours per week) or lots of part-time day and evening courses for particular exams. Most FE courses lead to some exam or accreditation, and this determines what's offered. You can do GCEs though there is often an emphasis on technical, commercial and vocational subjects. However, the range of subjects is enormous.
- AE offers mainly part-time courses, perhaps 2 to 4 hours per week or sometimes 1 to 12. There are many different kinds – some are recreational, some vocational, some prepare you for exams.

FURTHER EDUCATION

There are several hundred colleges of further education in Britain run by LEAs. They often go under other names. Further education provides the bulk of education below degree level for anyone over 16 who has left school. Colleges offer a very large range of courses, many of which are geared to qualifications. They sometimes offer work at degree level as well and there is no clear dividing line between further and higher education or between further and adult education. To make it easier to deal with, degree level studies are discussed in *22 Getting a degree: higher education*, and this chapter deals with the basics of further education, including adult education.

What colleges are called

A variety of names, all of which mean more or less the same thing:

- College of Further Education
- FE College
- College of Technology
- Technical College
- . . . College (eg Barnfield College)
- College of Commerce
- Tertiary College

These differences reflect their origins. You can only find out what a particular college does by asking it. The term 'further education' also sometimes includes adult education classes run outside colleges (see below).

Colleges and institutes of higher education
They are usually amalgamations of colleges, or colleges of education that have expanded their work by adding other courses (see *22 Getting a Degree*). But some also offer the normal fare of an FE college (eg Doncaster Metropolitan Institute of Higher Education).

Polytechnics
These are usually large educational institutions providing mainly higher education and meeting national and regional requirements, although they also serve their local community and make some provision at non-degree level.

College of education
A college mainly used for training teachers – many have been closed or amalgamated with colleges of higher education or polytechnics.

Community colleges
These can be further education colleges which have broadened out to include adult and community education (eg Bradford and Ilkley Community College). Often they are schools which also do some adult education work. In some counties (eg Cambridgeshire, Leicestershire) the secondary schools are called community colleges to emphasise that they are there to serve the whole community, and so are used for other things (they may house the local library, evening classes, swimming pool and so on). In some LEAs they have taken the idea to its logical conclusion – adults can go back to school to study if they want to. This may be a well developed scheme, as in Leicestershire, or just an informal arrangement. But it's increasingly possible in many places. The entries for LEAs in the *Gazetteer* note any such formal arrangements that we know of.

What do FE colleges offer?

- They offer a wide range of courses leading to many qualifications ranging from general education (English, maths, languages, science, social science etc) to training for jobs (engineering, catering, hairdressing, business studies etc).
- They run many courses for enjoyment or recreation and courses for particular groups, like elderly or disabled people.
- They offer courses at a wide range of levels (from below GCE/GCSE to degree level).
- They cater for people of all ages who have left school. However, some deal mainly with people in the 16 to 19 age range especially in areas where there is separate well-established provision for adult education.
- They often follow an academic year of at least 36 to 38 weeks from September to June – though some courses may be shorter or longer, at weekends or in the summer. The college year keeps growing, so some colleges now have courses running throughout the year.

- Because of their size, and the variety of people who work in them, they can be receptive to new ideas and needs, and are often the places where new developments occur. It's worth asking!
- They are good places to ask if you are looking for a qualification locally.
- They are usually organised into departments (which may be called something else!) specialising in one or two types of work: art, engineering, building, business studies, nursing, catering etc.
- Major qualifications offered include GCE O- and A-levels, the new GCSE, regional examining bodies and City and Guilds craft courses, BTEC courses, secretarial qualifications such as RSA, London Chamber of Commerce and others and in Scotland the new 16 to 18 qualifications and SCOTVEC courses. These are all described in *41 Qualifications*. There are others as well and some colleges offer their own certificates or diplomas for some courses.
- Courses may be offered full time or part time; day or evening; by day release, block release, or by sandwich courses. Increasingly they are offering open learning and other non-traditional courses as well – this is described in more detail in *17 Flexible learning*.
- They are increasingly offering short courses to help people update their skills – an initiative that is being encouraged by the PICKUP programme (see below).

Some subjects with special provision

Some subjects are special in that they may be studied in specialist colleges offering only the one subject either at degree level, non-degree level or both. There are a number of colleges of agriculture or horticulture, nautical studies, art or building, run as LEA colleges, as central institutions in Scotland or as independent colleges. The public sector subject specialist colleges are listed with other colleges in the *Gazetteer*.

42 Things to study picks out some subjects with special arrangements such as a centralised form of application or specialist college; for details of all courses in FE and HE colleges and polytechnics:

★ **LOOK AT** CRAC *Directory of further education* (see *Booklist*).

MAN, 33

I'm building a harpsichord. I wanted to see if there was a course anywhere where I could learn to tune it. I looked in the CRAC Directory of further education *and found that there was one course, at the London College of Furniture.*

Sources of information

Your LEA: ask the further education department or you local Education Guidance Service.

The Regional Advisory Councils

The Regional Advisory Councils for Further Education (and ILEA, the Scottish Education Department and the Department of Education for Northern Ireland), publish lists of further education courses in their areas.

Inner London

Inner London Education Authority, The County Hall, London SE1 7PB. Tel: (01) 633–1066. Publishes *Floodlight*, a guide to part-time day and evening classes. Obtainable from bookstalls in the London area, price £1 including p&p. Also lists giving details of most courses in Inner London, available free from Room 77 at the above address.

South East England

Regional Advisory Council for Further Education, London and South-Eastern Region, Tavistock House South, Tavistock Square, London WC1H 9LR. Tel: (01) 388 0027. Covers Greater London, Buckinghamshire, East Sussex, Hertfordshire, Kent, Surrey, South and West Essex. Publishes *Index of courses*, £1.75. Also publishes subject course guides covering art and design, business and management, construction, engineering, food and catering, science. Also publishes, on behalf of all the Regional Advisory Councils a guide to advanced courses in further and higher education throughout the country – *Compendium of advanced courses in colleges of further and higher education*, £3.25 (for 1987/88 edition published September 1987). This covers degree, BTEC, HND and equivalent level full-time and sandwich courses.

Southern England

Southern Regional Council for Further Education, 26 Bath Road, Reading RG1 6NT. Tel (0734) 52120 and 52193.

South West England

Regional Council for Further Education for the South West, Wessex Lodge, 11/13 Billetfield, Taunton, Somerset TA1 3NN. Tel: (0823) 85491 (From April 1987, 335481). Publishes *Further and higher education in the South West, a directory of courses*, £2.00.

West Midlands

West Midlands Advisory Council for Further Education, Norfolk House, Smallbrook Queensway, Birmingham B5 4NB. Tel: (021) 643 8924. Publishes *Directory of institutions and courses in higher and further education*, £2.35 plus 44p p&p.

East Midlands

East Midland Further Education Council, Robins Wood House, Robins Wood Road, Aspley, Nottingham NG8 3NH. Tel: (0602) 293291. Publishes *Directory of courses in further education in the East Midlands*, £1.90 plus postage (1987–1988 edition will be £2.00 plus postage).

East Anglia

East Anglian Regional Advisory Council for Further Education, 2 Looms Lane, Bury St Edmunds, Suffolk IP33 1HE. Tel: (0284) 64977. Publishes *Directory of courses of further and higher education in maintained colleges in the region*, £2.00.

Yorkshire and Humberside

Yorkshire and Humberside Association for Further and Higher Education, Bowling Green Terrace, Leeds LS11 9SX. Tel: (0532) 440751. Publishes *Directory of courses in further education*, £2.00.

North West England

North Western Regional Advisory Council for Further Education, incorporating the Union of Lancashire and Cheshire Institutes, Town Hall, Walkden Road, Worsley, Manchester M28 4QE. Tel: (061) 702 8700. Publishes *Directory of further education courses*, £1.00.

Northern England

Northern Council for Further Education, 5 Grosvenor Villas, Grosvenor Road, Newcastle-upon-Tyne NE2 2RU. Tel: (091) 281 3242. Publishes *Guide to further education courses in the region*, free.

ALSO

Wales

Welsh Joint Education Committee, 245 Western Avenue, Cardiff CF5 2YX. Tel: (0222) 561231. Publishes *Directory of establishments and courses for technical, agricultural and art education in Wales*, £2.50 plus postage.

Scotland

Scottish Education Department, Room 3/04, New St Andrews House, Edinburgh EH1 3SY. Tel: (031) 556 8400 ext 4158. Publishes *Directory of day courses, free.*

Northern Ireland

Department of Education, Rathgael House, Balloo Road, Bangor, Co. Down BT19 2PR. Tel: (0247) 66311. Publishes *Directory of vocational courses in N Ireland*, free.

Other directories

For the most comprehensive list of FE courses in the whole country:

★ **LOOK AT** CRAC *Directory of further education* (see *Booklist*).

PICKUP

The government's PICKUP programme encourages short courses to help adults update their skills. Regional development agents have also been appointed to help colleges identify the educational needs of people working in local industries. There is more information about PICKUP in *33 Training at work*.

WHAT IS FE LIKE ?

Although the biggest part of FE is general and vocational education for 16 to 19 year olds, much of it sponsored by the Manpower Services Commision, there are thousands of people over 19 using it. For example, in Inner London, 50% of students in colleges are over the age of 19. Some of them are doing courses that are specially designed for adults; many of them are not. In fact, it's very hard to tell what is meant by an 'adult' course in many parts of FE, though some courses are designed for an exclusively adult market (eg PICKUP).

Nineteen is an important age; after 19 (in some cases 18) you have to pay which is expensive these days. For example, a full-time GCE, or BTEC course may cost over £300, and you may have to pay it in one lump at the beginning. So it's not common for adults over 19 to do full-time courses because you won't usually get a grant (unlike when you do a degree). Most adults use FE part-time, or take courses of up to 21 hours per week (without losing benefit if you're unemployed). But there are some 'concessionary' fees – it's worth asking.

People between the ages of 16 and 19 usually don't pay fees, and stand some chance of getting a grant for full-time study. It varies a lot though, so there are no guarantees. Arrangements for people in this age group are explained more fully in *7 School leavers* and grants in *40 LEA grants*.

For young people

FE has a long tradition of being 'different from school'. For school leavers used to a lot of discipline it can seem very free and easy. It's up to you to get the best out of it. There are no punishments; if you don't do any work or if you mess about someone will eventually suggest that you leave. Other than that, your fate is in your own hands. There are opportunities to join in running things outside the classroom; everyone is in the student union so if you're interested you can help organise discos, sports and things like that. Some colleges, including those in London, have Student Services Officers and Careers Service Officers and many also have counselling staff.

For over 19s

As well as all the traditional courses, it is noticeable that nowadays there are a lot of new courses aimed at making it easier for all people to use further education. They include:

- GCE/GCSE courses for mature students (new GCSE options for adults are being developed for 1988)
- skills courses in particular subjects (eg typing, bookkeeping – often funded as part of JTS)
- courses with flexible hours and methods of study (see *17 Flexible learning*)
- courses to provide alternatives for adults to the traditional routes (like GCE/GCSE) whether to higher education or to other training opportunities via such things as Access courses (see *18 Adult routes*)
- such courses may have been set up for particular groups such as women, or ethnic minorities or may be designed to open up the system for adults in general courses to help people return to study or work after a break such as NOW (New Opportunities for Women) courses (see *19 Starting again: returning to study*)
- some provide basic education and in particular, many MSC funded courses are located in FE colleges (see *20 Basics*)
- courses to assist unemployed people to maintain or develop skills and to sustain employability.

Is it for you?

If you want to do a GCE/GCSE course, learn a skill, or get back to study, to be realistic, the local college is local and that may well be the most important thing.

Many students do get a lot out of traditionally-run courses just because they mix with other students of all ages. On the other hand, if you don't like that idea, look at the next four chapters, and see the range of new ways in which FE is being offered to make it more open to people who want it to fit in with their adult lives.

COURSE TUTOR – MATURE STUDENTS' GCE COURSE

We try to breed success. It's not really a separate course. Having a course tutor is the key to it – adult students start off with a daunting timetable but I suggest they do a bit at a time – they're often astonished that they can. We give intensive support where necessary to try and head off problems. Many adults have an unreal view of attainment – feeling 80% is poor, not realising 40% is a pass.

STUDENT ON SAME COURSE

I much prefer a mixed age group. I've been in both. At first they treat you with suspicion, then they accept you. I have the added embarrassment of studying alongside my children's classmates. But I'm going to have to work in a mixed age group eventually and I think this helps both. I like studying in a class situation and I find my studying benefits my children. My little one complains because she is the only one without homework.

ADULT STUDENT IN AN ORDINARY FE CLASS
I did A-levels in an ordinary full-time class. It was better than doing it by the mature students' scheme because they were all women on that course – and I got a lot out of mixing and just being a student. I learnt more from the other students than from the course.

ADULT EDUCATION

The adult education service may be linked closely with further education, with youth and community work or it may be run totally separately. This varies between LEAs – you will find a description of how it is organised in your local area in the *Gazetteer*.

The main difference between adult, continuing or community education and further education is that classes for adults are usually part time. Adult education classes take a number of forms:

- the traditional evening class (once a week for one or two hours, often in a local school)
- day time classes (mainly in places where there are special adult education facilities)
- classes in FE colleges run alongside provision for younger people
- all day courses (such as a whole day Saturday school)
- short residential courses (many LEAs have special colleges running them)
- study trips (sometimes abroad)
- summer schools (sometimes for the whole family)
- classes in hospitals, old people's homes, social services centres etc
- roll on/roll off basic education where you can start any time you like, and it may be in a small group, or individual tuition
- programmes for unemployed adults (some courses are available through the REPLAN programme, see *Useful organisations* below).

How it's organised

It is organised in a wide variety of ways. Here are some examples although you will certainly find others.

- A free standing Adult Education Service, based on institutes of adult education (eg Kirklees) or community education services (eg Leeds and Barnsley).
- A network of adult education organisers based at a school or other centre, responsible for organising classes throughout the area, taught mostly by part-time tutors.
- Special adult institutes (as in Inner London) or adult colleges. These may employ a number of full-time teaching staff.
- Short term residential colleges which offer courses for people in the area (though sometimes open to people from further afield as well). These are listed in the *Gazetteer*.

- A teacher or youth worker in a school with additional responsibility for running classes for adults.
- A department responsible for adult education in an FE college.
- A 'detached' adult education worker or 'outreach' worker who works with people in the community in their own homes and in other places away from centres and classes (eg West Sussex, Southwark, Birmingham, Central Region and Strathclyde in Scotland).
- Basic education (classes in reading, writing, basic maths, English for second language speakers) is often organised separately, with its own organiser, and with special arrangements for joining etc. But in other respects it is part of the adult education network of provision.

Although most organisers and some teaching staff will be full-time, most teaching in adult education is done by part-time staff who may do lots of other part-time teaching, or may equally teach in addition to another main occupation.

There is also a lot of adult education provided by higher education institutions (such as university extra-mural or adult education departments), the WEA and other voluntary bodies (eg Women's Institutes, Townswomen's Guilds etc) (see *More information* below).

What can you study?

There is always a large demand for the old favourites: languages, yoga, crafts, cooking, keep fit, local history and so on. But adult education also responds to changing needs and changing demands so programmes usually include courses like self-defence for women, black studies, welfare rights, computing, fresh start, health studies, food studies, return to learn and so on. It is often organised in smaller units than FE and as a result can be more responsive to local demands and needs. Check with your local service to see the range of opportunities available, or to suggest a course which you would like.

MORE INFORMATION ABOUT ADULT EDUCATION

Elsewhere in the book

In practice everything in the book can be seen as part of adult education. For more information about the areas traditionally called 'adult education', look at:

- the *Gazetteer*, to tell you how it's organised in your area
- 28 The WEA
- 27 Leisure classes: part-time, weekends, holidays
- 20 Basics.

Many areas also have a local Educational Advice or Guidance Service (there is one in each Inner London borough). See *1 Advice and help* and also below.

Useful organisations

The Educational Centres Association (*ECA*)

ECA is a voluntary body which aims to promote adult education and works as a partnership between organisers, teachers and students. Over 150 adult centres are affiliated. They publish a lot of useful leaflets and booklets, organise conferences and meetings.

★ **ASK** The ECA, Chequer Centre, Chequer Street, Bunhill Row, London EC1Y 8PL. Tel: (01) 251 4158. General Secretary: Dominic Delahunt.

Community Education Association
An organisation for anyone interested in lifelong learning. Can be contacted through the Community Education Development Centre.

★ **ASK** CEA, c/o CEDC, Briton Road, Coventry CV2 4LF. Tel: (0203) 440814.

National Institute of Adult Continuing Education (NIACE)
The main body concerned with adult continuing education in England and Wales. Runs conferences and publishes material for professional adult educators, including a useful *Year book of adult continuing education* and a twice yearly directory of residential courses. Undertakes research and development in all aspects of education for adults. Incorporates the Unit for the Development of Adult Continuing Education (UDACE) and the Unit for the development of adult unemployed programmes (REPLAN). Specific developments in Wales are fostered by the Wales Committee of NIACE.

★ **ASK** NIACE, 19b De Montfort Street, Leicester LE1 7GE. Tel: (0533) 551451.

Scottish Institute of Adult and Continuing Education (SIACE)
A similar body concerned with adult and continuing education in Scotland. Has individual as well as organisational membership. Produces a number of useful publications including *The Scottish handbook of adult and continuing education 1986,* £3.25*;* and *The Scottish journal of adult education*, published twice a year, £4.50 per year or £2.50 per issue.

★ **ASK** SIACE, 30 Rutland Square, Edinburgh EH1 2BW. Tel: (031) 229 0331.

Northern Ireland Adult Education Association
An association to promote the cause of adult education and to bring together providers and users of the adult education services in Northern Ireland.

★ **WRITE TO** Honorary Secretary, Northern Ireland Adult Education Association, c/o 42 Northland Road, Londonderry BT48 7ND.

The Association for Recurrent Education

★ **WRITE TO** Roger Mercer, Secretary of ARE, Department of Education Management, Sheffield City Polytechnic, 30 Collegiate Crescent, Sheffield S10 2BP. Tel: (0742) 665274.

The National Association of Educational Guidance Services.

★ **WRITE TO** Judy Alloway, Secretary NAEGS, Education Guidance for Adults, Hatfield Polytechnic, PO Box 109, Hatfield AL10 9AB

17 Flexible learning

FLEXIBLE STUDY METHODS

One of the big developments over the last few years has been the growth of flexible study methods in further and adult education. They are called things like Distance Learning or Open Learning, or by the name of particular schemes like Flexistudy or Learning by Appointment. It's also spreading in higher education, with the Open University, and increasingly in universities and polytechnics.

What all these schemes have in common is that you do your studying when you can fit it in. They often use correspondence material but you also get help and support from a tutor as well as other facilities. Traditional correspondence courses are described in *26 Learning by post*.

This is the field in which the use of new technology is having a great impact. Open learning is increasingly involving the use of:

- broadcasting
- computers
- video and audio tapes and discs
- other audio-visual aids
- combinations of all these.

The growth of the MSC's Open Tech has brought a lot more money to the development of this sort of learning (see below), and an enormous growth in the number and range of distance learning facilities.

FLEXISTUDY

One of the key developments which influenced the spread of open learning. Developed by the National Extension College in conjunction with Barnet College, it is a way of using distance learning with local tutorial support.

Flexistudy is usually based at FE colleges and adult centres. The centre buys correspondence course units from the National Extension College and sends them to you itself. You enrol for the course at the centre and have a tutor there who marks your work. You can see him or her regularly (you arrange how often) and can telephone for extra help. There are meetings and seminars from time to time, but you don't have to go. You take as long as you like; you are not expected to do a minimum amount each week; you pace yourself.

Flexistudy is now a registered trade name owned by the National Extension College. Some colleges have similar schemes but use different materials and call their scheme something different.

What's it like?
Each scheme is different.

SHOP ASSISTANT, 20s, BARNET COLLEGE
I came to do another course and couldn't get in because of numbers. I just wanted something to do in my spare time. I got on quite well last year doing O-levels. I'm doing A-levels now. It's just a bit difficult to contact the tutor. I do the work in the evening, and then I have to ring in the day which is difficult because I work. I usually come in to see the tutor on my half day, about once a month.

TRAIN DRIVER, 20s, BARNET COLLEGE
I saw it in the local paper. I hope to go to university. Because of my irregular shifts I couldn't do regular study. It's better than an ordinary correspondence course because of the tutor support. The politics and government course is very clear – in the way it's laid out. It makes revision easy. Sociology is more difficult; I need a lot of extra tutor support. It's a long time since I studied. I wish there had been more student interaction – but it's not always possible – that's the nature of flexistudy.

More information
Centres offering flexistudy are in the list below. Or, for an up-to-the-minute list:

★ **WRITE TO** Pat Gouldstone, National Extension College, 18 Brooklands Avenue, Cambridge CB2 2HN. Tel: (0223) 316644.

SOME OTHER APPROACHES

BTEC open learning schemes
The Business and Technician Education Council (BTEC) (see *41 Qualifications*) has arranged for some centres to offer distance learning schemes for BTEC courses. Some are by correspondence and some by directed private study.

The courses involved cover:

- mechanical and production engineering
- electrical engineering, electronic engineering
- general engineering
- marine engineering
- process technology
- refrigeration and air conditioning
- lift technology
- science
- communications engineering
- telecommunications
- building studies
- distribution studies
- business and finance
- financial sector studies, public administration
- accounting technicians

- hotel catering and institutional management
- printing
- computer technology.

Approved centres are included in the list below. They may not necessarily offer all courses every year.

Some correspondence colleges also offer BTEC courses: Metropolitan College, Institute of Grocery Distribution and NALGO. See *26 Learning by post.*

Over thirty centres offer the Telecommunications External Student Scheme, mainly to employees of British Telecom, though some offer it to others.

For more information about BTEC open learning:

★ **ASK** BTEC, Central House, Upper Woburn Place, London WC1H 0HH.

★ **WRITE TO** The Secretary, The Coordinating Committee for Distance Learning Schemes for Vocational Further Education, 22 Great King Street, Edinburgh EH3 6QH. Tel: (031) 557 4555.

SCOTVEC – distance learning

SCOTVEC will, at national certificate level, accept candidates who have studied by means of open learning, where the arrangements have been approved between the centre providing the support for the open learning and the council. At HNC and HND levels special arrangements have to be made between the centre and SCOTVEC and at present only a limited experiment is on offer in the highlands and islands.

Scottish Telecommunications Board employees can follow the Board's scheme leading to the SCOTVEC certificate in electrical and electronic engineering.

College of the Sea

A department of the Marine Society (the oldest maritime charity in the world), the College of the Sea offers correspondence courses to those at sea, on oil rigs and in the lighthouse sevice. Also offers a book loan service to students who have a permanent address in the UK, and will supply books, cassettes and hobby kits. Produces a quarterly magazine *The seafarer*. Offers a huge range of general courses (GCSEs and A-levels, basic education, bookkeeping, merchant navy studies etc). Where courses are not offered, advice on other facilities is given, for example on Department of Trade qualifications.

★ **WRITE TO** College of the Sea, 202 Lambeth Road, London SE1 7JW. Tel: (01) 261 9535.

Department of Trade qualifications

About a dozen colleges do the DOT qualifications; some offer all or part in correspondence courses. For advice and up-to-date information contact the College of the Sea.

FLEXIBLE LEARNING WORKSHOPS

Many further education colleges and some others, are offering flexible learning workshops (called by a variety of names) to make their courses easier to use. The best known is probably at Bradford and Ilkley Community College where a maths workshop has been operating for a number of years (see below). You can go along and register to study whatever level you want, at times to suit you, for as long as you choose. If you register with the college to do GCSE or A-level maths you could also find yourself studying in the workshop. The method works well; students often prefer it to traditional classes. There are also workshops in communication skills and information technology and others are planned. planned.

There are many other examples all over the UK such as the Flexastudy system at Redditch College, for advanced professional qualifications in business and management subjects, and the languages workshop at Blackpool College. Those we know are listed below as Workshops, but keep your eyes open locally.

Bradford and Ilkley Community College

The college offers a wide range of alternative provisions including open learning workshops in maths, communication skills and information technology as well as more conventionally structured programmes such as return to learn and MS certificate.

A substantial amount of the study is vocationally based. There is a NEBS centre; an industrial sewing course as a provision within the district and in-house work in factories and industries.

★ **ASK FOR** Mr W Green, Vice Principal, Director of Resources, Bradford and Ilkley College, Great Horton Road, Bradford BD7 1AY. Tel: (0274) 753111.

Doncaster Assisted Private Study

Doncaster Institute of Higher Education has responded to the needs of the quarrying industry with an impressive 'directed private study' scheme. Employers like their quarry managers to be qualified, but find it hard to release them to attend college courses. So the Institute runs an Assisted Private Study unit (known as DAPS). They produce and run their own correspondence courses, which prepare students for the professional examination of the Institute of Quarrying. It takes three years, and involves four weekend courses per year as well as the correspondence units. You can start in the second year if you have the right qualifications. There are no formal entry requirements. If you have no qualifications or haven't studied for a long time it's a good idea to apply early (January/March) and have an interview. They will advise you as to whether you should do any preliminary work before the course starts in September.

South West London College Directed Private Study (DPS Scheme)

A well established method of study comprising a linked oral and correspondence system, specifically designed for students on shift work or working irregular hours, who cannot get to a college regularly. It is a blend of face-to-face tuition and personal study directed and monitored by post. Courses lead to BTEC, HNC and Institute of Chartered Secretaries and Administrators qualifications. All students must be over 18 years of age.

Learning by appointment

Some colleges invite people to come in and teach themselves, using books and programmed texts. The emphasis is on the teaching materials, which are written to allow students to work on their own. For example, at Glenrothes and Buckhaven Technical College in Fife, the student (after a trial study session) books a study place, equipment and materials in advance. When you arrive to study, everything is ready for you to start work right away. The materials cover a wide range of things – external exams, languages, basic computer programming and so on. Ask at your local FE college whether they have a learning by appointment scheme. If the receptionist doesn't seem to know what you mean, ask to speak to the librarian. Because this sort of teaching starts from the teaching materials, learning by appointment is often based in departments or centres that specialise in educational technology and are increasingly developing into open learning workshops (see above).

THE OPEN TECH

The Open Tech is a major initiative from the Manpower Services Commission. Unlike the Open University, it is not establishing one large central institution but is providing part of the funds to encourage a whole range of open learning developments all over the country. It has about 140 projects under way in colleges, firms and other organisations; most are operational projects, a small number are support projects (such as MARIS – below). The intention is that in the end, these projects will all be able to continue without special central funding. The area of study covered is technician and supervisory management level; it is not intended that there should be any overlap with existing provision.

★ **WRITE TO** The Open Tech Unit, Manpower Services Commission, Moorfoot, Sheffield S1 4PQ. Tel: (0742) 700996.

★ **WRITE TO** Open Tech (Northern Ireland), c/o Swinson House, Glenmount Road, Church Road, Newtownabbey BT36 7LH.

How the projects work

Each project recruits its own students and is likely to be already involved in training for the field concerned. Courses use teaching methods such as:

- a package of audio tapes, slides and text
- a video with text
- interactive video discs
- computer based training (as at Austin-Rover)
- video text with telephone tutorials (as at Leith Nautical College)
- the Humberside Refrigeration Project which sends students parts of fridges, and provides telephone tutorials or simply the printed word.

Regional Delivery Systems

There are now 13 of these (some have more than one site). They provide a service to employers and individuals who want to use open learning materials. They may offer all or some of these:

- help with selecting material
- support while working through it
- advice on where to go when you finish.

There are changes expected in the way they are run in 1987, but do get in touch. The Regional Delivery Systems are at:

Bedfordshire, Cambridgeshire, Hertfordshire and Milton Keynes
Midtech Open Learning, Midtech Project Office, Skillcentre, Pixmore Avenue, Letchworth, Herts SG6 4AS. Tel: (0462) 671113.

Cheshire
Cheshire Open Tech Project, Hall 9, Padgate Campus, Fernhead, Warrington WA2 0DB. Tel: (0925) 818244.

Devon
Devon Open Tech, Suite 3, Renslade House, Bonhay Road, Exeter EX4 1BY. Tel: (0392) 52258.

Dyfed, South and West Wales
Dyfed County Council, Education Department, Pibwrlwyd, Carmarthen, Dyfed SA31 2NH. Tel: (0267) 233333 ext 4512/4534.

Essex, Suffolk and Norfolk
EASTEK, 32a High Street, Hadleigh, Ipswich IP7 5AP. Tel: (0473) 823400.

Gwent
Gwent LEA, Allt-yr-yn Avenue, Newport, Gwent NP1 5XA. Tel: (0633) 51525.

Hereford, Worcester and Powys
Hereford/Worcs/Powys Open Tech Project, Henwick House, Henwick Grove, Worcester WR2 6AJ. Tel: (0905) 429836.

Mid and North Wales
Mid and North Wales Training Group Ltd, Castle Works, Hendomen, Montgomery, Powys SY15 6EZ. Tel: (068 681) 670/681.

North East England
North East Open Learning Network, 3rd Floor, Erick House, Princess Square, Newcastle upon Tyne NE1 8ER. Tel: (091) 261 4072.

North Wales
North East Wales Institute of Higher Education, Connah's Quay, Deeside, Clwyd CH5 4BR. Tel: (0244) 817531.

North of Scotland
North of Scotland Open Tech Unit, HIDB Offices, 62 High Street, Invergordon, Scotland IV18 0DH. Tel: (0349) 853337.

Staffordshire
Staffordshire OL Delivery System, North Staffs Polytechnic, Beaconside, Stafford ST18 0AD. Tel: (0785) 52331 ext 306.

Tayside
TAYTEC Ltd, 6 North Isla Street, Dundee DD1 4UF. Tel: (0382) 819815.

Practical training facilities

A number of centres have been set up where people using open learning can get 'hands on' experience to reinforce their distance learning. These are at Accrington, Dudley, Tyne and Wear, Chatham, Liverpool, Swindon, Plymouth, Watford, Leeds, Glenrothes and Gwent. In some cases these will be open 24 hours a day, seven days a week.
Practical training facilities are at

Devon
Tamar Tech, Plymouth Skillcentre, Strode Road, Plympton, Devon PL7 4BG. Tel: (0752) 335921.

Dorset
Dorset Microsystems Centre, 2nd Floor, Norwich Union House, Lansdowne, Bournemouth BH1 3NG. Tel: (0202) 26349.

Hertfordshire
Watford College, Hempstead Road, Watford, Herts WD1 3EZ. Tel: (0923) 41211.

Kent
Mid Kent College, Horsted, Maidstone Road, Chatham, Kent ME5 9JQ. Tel: (0634) 41001 ext 235.

Lancashire
East Lancs Tech Unit, Accrington and Rossendale College, Sandy Lane, Accrington BB5 2AW. Tel: (0254) 31392.

Manchester
National Computing Centre, Microsystems Admin Unit, Bracken House, Charles Street, Manchester M1 7BD. Tel: (061) 273 5173.

Merseyside
Riversdale College of Technology, Riversdale Road, Liverpool L19 3QP. Tel: (051) 427 1227.

Scotland
Flexitec, Dowanhill, 74 Victoria Crescent Road, Glasgow G12 9JN. Tel: (041) 357 0340.
Flexitec, Hill Park Education Centre, Bannackburn, Stirling. Tel: (0786) 816552.
Flexitec, Lang Lee Centre, Marigold Drive, Galashiels. Tel: (0896) 56512.
Computer Assisted Training Services, 9–10 Flemington Road, Queensway Estate, Glenrothes KY7 5QW. Tel: (0592) 759447.

Tyne and Wear
Washington Micro Technology Centre, Armstrong House, Armstrong Road, District 2, Washington, Tyne and Wear. Tel: (091) 417 8517.

Wales
Open Learning Unit, Faculty of Engineering and Science, Gwent College of Higher Education, Allt-yr-yn Avenue, Newport, Gwent NP1 5XA. Tel: (0633) 51525.

West Midlands
Dudley Open Access Centre, The Broadway, Dudley, West Midlands DY1 4AS. Tel: (0384) 237940.

Wiltshire
Swindon Technology Unit, The College, Regent Circus, Swindon, Wiltshire SW1 1PT. Tel: (0793) 616178.

Yorkshire – South
Sheffield Skillcentre, Richmond Park Road, Sheffield S13 8HT. Tel: (0742) 446471.

Yorkshire – West
EDMC, Hennymoor House, 7–11 Manor Row, Bradford BD1 4QY. Tel: (0274) 733766.
West Yorkshire Microsystems Centre, Leeds Polytechnic, Queenswood House, Beckett Park, Leeds LS6 3QS.

MARIS-NET

This is an Open Tech funded information project which has established a computer based information system listing over 7,000 distance learning materials. It is currently free and is intended for colleges and training departments to be able to identify distance learning resources that are already in existence.

★ **ASK** MARIS-NET, Bank House, 1 St Mary's Street, Ely, Cambridgeshire CB7 4ER or MARIS-NET, Dowanhill, 74 Victoria Crescent Road, Glasgow G12 9JN. Tel: (041) 334 9314.

The Open College

This is a new initiative which brings together broadcasters, educationalists and sponsors to provide vocational education and training. See *25 Radio and TV*.

More Information

★ **ASK** The Open Tech Unit, Room W601, Manpower Services Commission, Moorfoot, Sheffield S1 4PQ. Tel: (0742) 704996.

CENTRES OFFERING FLEXIBLE STUDY

Main addresses of colleges listed can be found in the *Gazetteer* (see those marked with DL – for distance learning). An address is only given in this list if the course is running at a different centre.

England

Avon

City of Bath Technical College. Flexistudy. Ask for: John Manley or Alan Mackie.
Brunel Technical College. BTEC units. Ask for: Mr S Rabone or Mr D Streatfield.
Filton Technical College. Ask for Ian Barker. Flexastudy scheme. Ask for: Department of Business Studies and Management.
South Bristol Technical College. Flexistudy. Ask for: Joan Schrecher.

Bedfordshire

Bedford College of Higher Education. Mid-Tech (Open Learning) in arrange of subjects. Ask for: Mrs B Payne on (0272) 45151.
Challney Community College, Luton. Flexistudy. Ask for: Mr W S Oliver.
Cranfield Institute of Technology. Open Tech Scheme.
Dunstable College. Fonalang. DL Mid-tech Open Learning. Ask for: Mr Ian Hunter.
Lea Manor Community College, Luton. Flexistudy. Ask for: J J Andel.
Luton College of Higher Education. Flexistudy and Open Tech Scheme. Ask for: Mr N G Wellings. Special Adult Learning Programmes. Distance learning. Ask for: Judith Robinson.

Berkshire

Bracknell College. Business flexistudy. Ask for: Mr P C Cheape.
College of Estate Management. Specialist higher education. Ask for: Elizabeth Moir.
Reading College of Technology. Flexistudy, BTEC telecommunications. Ask for: Mr L Head. Robotics and automation Open Tech/ORT course. Ask for: Mr B Bumford.
Slough College of Higher Education. Ask for: The Registrar.

Buckinghamshire

Amersham College of Further Education, Art and Design. Ask for: Mr Sidell.

Aylesbury College of Further Education and Agriculture. Flexistudy. Ask for: Mr Winget.

Buckinghamshire College of Higher Education. Home Learning Service. Ask for: Brian Maunder. Tel: (0494) 38266 (24 hours).

Milton Keynes College, Bletchley Campus. BTEC and GCSEs. Ask for: Lee Knapp.

Cambridgeshire

Bottisham Village College. Flexistudy. Ask for: the tutor, Mr Edwards.

Cambridgeshire College of Arts and Technology. Open Tech Scheme. Ask for: Katherine Bull.

Cambridge College of Further Education. Open Tech Scheme. Ask for: Mrs P Savage. Home Tel: (0223) 313836.

Isle College. Homestudy. Ask for: Mr P Clow.

Peterborough Regional College. Flexistudy, NALGO, Open Tech Scheme for Institute of Fire Engineers. Communications workshop. Ask for: Terry Chatter/David Wynne.

Cheshire

Macclesfield College of Further Education. Distance learning in computer studies. Open learning in a wide range of subjects. Ask for: Mr F D Graham.

Mid-Cheshire College of Further Education. Flexistudy – a wide range of opportunities in English (M Daniels); sciences (Mrs D Richardson); business studies, (J Ellis); basics (J D Chappell); Ask for: person in brackets.

North Cheshire College. Distance Learning. Open Tech. Ask for: Mr Ian Taylor. Tel: (0925) 818244.

South Cheshire College. Flexistudy. Ask for: Mike Kasklowski.

South Trafford College of Further Education. Flexistudy. Ask for: P J Buchanan.

West Cheshire College of Further Education. Open Tech. Ask for: Mr J Vasey.

Cleveland

Brotton Further Education Centre. Flexistudy. Ask for: Mr M A Elliott.

Cleveland Technical College. Flexistudy. Ask for: Dr W King.

Hartlepool College of Further Education. Flexistudy. Ask for: Mark Taylor.

Longlands College of Further Education. Flexistudy. Ask for: Alan Wilby or Mrs Austin.

Redcar Further Education Centre. Ask for: P H Suttle.

Stockton-Billingham Technical College. Distance Learning. Ask for: Mr S Hetherington.

Cornwall

Callington/Launceston Centre. Distance learning. Ask for: Mrs Abel.

Carrick Adult Education Centre. Homestudy. Ask for: Mrs Spargo.

Cornwall College of Further and Higher Education. Flexistudy. Ask for: David Ager.

Restormel Adult Continuing Education Centre. Flexistudy and Homestudy. Ask for: G S Birkby or Mrs Weightman.

Cumbria

Carlisle Technical College. Flexistudy. Ask for: Dr Bernard Priest.

West Cumbria College. Open learning in conjunction with MSC. Ask for: Mrs Faulder.

Derbyshire

Chesterfield College of Technology and Arts. Ask for: Mr M J Hewitt, Head of Student Services (ext 205).

Derby College of Further Education. BTEC. Flexistudy. Ask for: Norman Hockley.

High Peak College of Further Education. Open access course. Ask for: Stuart Graham.

South East Derbyshire College. Flexistudy. Ask for: Pamela Ashley.

Devon

Bideford Community College. Flexistudy. Ask for: Mr Nigel Melville.

Devon Open Tech. Flexistudy. Ask for: Mr C Greenwood.

East Devon College of Further Education. Flexistudy. Ask for: Ron Yates.

Exeter College. BTEC. Flexistudy. Ask for: Phil Hobbs. Open Tech. Ask for: Raj Sharma.

North Devon College. Open Tech. Ask for: Graham Martin.

Plymouth College of Art and Design. Open Tech, photography. Ask for: A C Mears.

Plymouth College of Further Education. Flexistudy. Ask for: M E Frost. BTEC, Open Tech microelectronics and telecommunications. Ask for: Mr E H Farrar (0752) 264730, or Mr J Carr (0752) 264762.
Sidmouth College. Flexistudy. Ask for: T Hamilton.
St Clare's Adult Education Centre. Flexistudy. Ask for: Mr D W Tinkler.
Seale-Hayne College. Farm Business Management. Ask for: Mr N F Warren.
South Devon College of Arts and Technology. Flexistudy. Ask for: Mrs A Gaywood.

Dorset
Bournemouth and Poole College of Further Education. Flexistudy. Ask for: Mr A G Udall.
Weymouth College. Flexistudy. Ask for: Mr S Mauger or Mr M Dadds.

Durham
Darlington College of Technology. Flexistudy. Ask for: Mr S Morgan.
New College, Durham. Flexistudy. Ask for: Mrs Wendy Jones.
Peterlee College. Flexistudy. Ask for: Miss Pat Smith.

Essex
Braintree College of Further Education. Flexistudy. Ask for: Mrs M Starkey
Chelmsford College of Further Education. Distance learning science speciality. Ask for: Dr Allan Evans.
Colchester Institute. BTEC. Flexistudy. Ask for: Mr L Weeks.
Essex University. Ask for: Mr J M Bowles, Director of Continuing Education.
Harlow College. Flexistudy, Nalgo Open Learning. Ask for: the Principal, Ms Jane Ford.
Loughton College of Further Education. Flexistudy, Nalgo Open Learning. Ask for: Mr K Gardner.
Southend College of Technology. Open learning. Ask for: Barry Hendry.
Thurrock Technical College. Flexistudy. Ask for: Mr A P Spiers (ext 226).

Gloucestershire
Gloucestershire College of Arts & Technology. Ask for: D Gibbard.
Mid-Gloucestershire Technical College. Open Learning. Ask for: Ms Marion Cartwright.
Royal Forest of Dean College. Flexistudy. Ask for: Sue Kear.

Hampshire
Basingstoke Adult Education Centre. Flexistudy. Ask for: Malcolm Kaill.
Basingstoke Technical College. Ask for: Dave Leharne.
Bournemouth and Poole College of Further Education. Flexistudy. Ask for: T Udall.
College of Maritime Studies. Distance learning. Ask for: David Barwell or Captain Roger Harding.
Cricklade College. Flexistudy/Open Learning. Ask for: Mrs P Horner.
Eastleigh College of Further Education. Flexistudy. Ask for: Mr C Robinson.
Farnborough College of Technology. Telecommunications. Ask for: Mr G M Cornell.
Highbury College of Technology. Flexistudy. BTEC. Ask for: Mr S Reid.
Portsmouth College of Art Design and Further Education. Flexistudy. Ask for: Dr K Rodgers.
Southampton Institute of Higher Education. Distance learning.
Southampton Technical College. Distance learning.
South Downs College of Further Education. Open Learning. Flexistudy. Ask for: Dr Mary Ottaway.
Southampton Open Learning Centre. Flexistudy. Ask for: David Chapman.
The Tertiary College, Fareham. Flexistudy. Ask for: Angus Reid.

Hereford and Worcester
Evesham College of Further Education. Flexistudy. Ask for: Mrs A L Scaiff.
Herefordshire College of Agriculture. Distance learning. Ask for: Mr R Garnett.
Herefordshire College of Art and Design. Open learning. Ask for: John Clark.
Herefordshire Technical College. Flexistudy. Ask for: Dr S Morgan.
Kidderminster College of Further Education. Flexistudy. Ask for: Jill Edwards.
Pershore College of Horticulture. Open learning. Ask for: Mr S W Wilkinson.
North Worcestershire College. Flexistudy. Ask for: Mr R Williams.
Redditch College. BTEC, Flexastudy. Ask for: Mr A A V Marsh.

Worcester Technical College. Flexistudy. Ask for: Mr M Wilson.
Worcestershire College of Agriculture. Open Tech. Ask for: Mr T A Adcock.

Hertfordshire

Cassio College. Open Tech project and Open Learning centre planned. Ask for: I M Strachan.
de Havilland College. Open Tech project planned. Ask for: K Staple.
East Herts College. Open Tech project. Ask for: Miss M Ashby.
North Herts College. Flexistudy. Ask for: Eugene Gavin.
St Albans College. Learning by Appointment. Ask for: Barrie Mort.
Stevenage College. Distance Learning. Ask for: R Gomm.
Ware College. Open Tech project. Ask for: J Grisbrooke.
Watford College. BTEC. Ask for: Mrs Jackie Tanner.

Humberside

East Yorkshire College of Further Education. Ask for: Jeremy Skinner.
Grimsby College of Technology. BTEC. Ask for: Mr T Leadbeater. GCEs. Ask for: Mr M Carson.
Humberside College of Higher Education. Open Tech. Ask for: Mr C Whitfield. Open College (part-time only).

Isle of Wight

Isle of Wight College of Arts and Technology. Flexistudy. Ask for: M Rutland.

Kent

Canterbury College of Technology. A wide provision of open learning courses; programmes will be devised to suit specific needs of students and employers. Ask for: Mark Stacey.
Maidstone Training Centre. Flexistudy. Ask for: Major H B Bingham.
Merchant Navy College. BTEC.
Mid-Kent College of Higher and Further Education. Oakwood Park, Tonbridge Road, Maidstone ME16 8AQ. Tel: (0622) 56531. Flexistudy. Ask for: Peter Elsmore.
Sittingbourne College Adult Studies Centre. Flexistudy. Ask for: Vanessa Ehman.
South Kent College of Technology. Flexistudy. Ask for: Mike Robins.

Lancashire

Accrington and Rossendale College. BTEC Mechanical Engineering, Open Tech Unit footwear. Ask for: Mr F Jones.
Blackburn College. Flexistudy. Ask for: Stuart Brooks.
Blackpool and the Fylde College of Further and Higher Education. Wordshop Flexible language learning scheme. Includes Fleetwood Nautical Campus. Distance learning in seamanship, navigation. Ask for: Mr P Shaw.
Nelson and Colne College. Distance Learning. Drop-In Skillcentre. Ask for: Derek Crossland.
Runshaw Tertiary College. Distance Learning. Ask for: Gaye Houghton.

Leicestershire

Brockington College. Brockington Open Learning and Flexi Study – Brockolflex. Ask for: Mr I T Watts.
Grantham College of Further Education. Ask for: Mr B R Phillips.
Hinckley College of Further Education. Flexistudy, Nalgo Open Learning, Open Tech for the knitted textile industry. Ask for: C A Heard.
Loughborough Technical College. Distance learning.
Melton Mowbray College of Further Education. Distance learning. Ask for: Mr R A Flúde.
South Fields College of Further Education. Open learning, BTEC construction. Ask for: K Roberts.
Wigston College of Further Education. Flexistudy, phonolang. Ask for: Mr D Harris.

Lincolnshire

Boston College of Further Education. Flexistudy. Open learning. Ask for: Dr John Glazier.
Lincoln College of Technology. Flexistudy. Distance learning. Ask for: Mrs Blackburn.

LONDON – GREATER

Barking

Barking College of Technology. Ask for: Mrs P Rowe.

Barnet

Barnet College of Further Education. Wood Street site. Ask for: Nancy Cowley. Russell Lane site. Ask for: Carol Elliott.
Hendon College of Further Education. Business Studies. Ask for: Mr C Langley (ext 234).

Brent

Willesden College of Technology. Institute of motor industry membership. Ask for: G H Haggar.

Bromley

Bromley College of Technology. Ask for: Mr P Bolton.
Orpington College of Further Education. Flexistudy. Ask for: Mr A C Sweetland.

Croydon

Coombe Cliff Adult Education Centre. Computing.
Croydon College. Adult training. Ask for: Mr Trill.
South Norwood Adult Education Centre. Flexistudy. Ask for: Anne Leaky.

Ealing

Acton Technical College.

Enfield

Capel Manor Horticultural and Environmental Centre. Open Tech in horticulture and countryside recreation. Ask for: Peter Stott.
Enfield College. Ask for: Mr C J Baldwin.

Harrow

Harrow College of Higher Education. Open learning Business and Management. B/TEC post-experience. Ask for: Dr Dennis Whitmore.

Havering

Havering Technical College. Open learning. Ask for: R Tansley.

Hillingdon

Brunel University. Management studies; project management. Ask for: Mrs Robbie Friendship. Tel: (0491) 571454.
London Bible College. Diploma certificate in religious studies. Extension Department. Ask for: Miss M Anders.
Uxbridge Technical College. Open Access. Ask for: R Broadbent.

Hounslow

Cranford Community School. Flexistudy. Ask for: Derek Lysight-Jones.
Merton Institute of Adult Education. Flexistudy.

Newham

Newham Community College. Ask for: Roy McLean or Pam Peers.

Redbridge

Redbridge Technical College. Flexistudy. Ask for: John Sillis.

Waltham Forest

Walthamstow Adult Education Centre. Flexistudy. Ask for: Rosemary Stille.
YMCA National College. Youth and community work training.

LONDON – INNER

Brixton College. Ask for: Ann Follows.
City and East London College. Open Learning, Flexistudy.
Holborn Law Tutors. Law (various levels).
Institute of Education, University of London. Education in developing countries. Ask for: Mrs Rajagopalan.

Kingsway-Princeton College. Learning by appointment and flexistudy. Ask for: John Johnson.
New Central for Adult Education (formerly The City Lit Centre for Adult Studies). Open Study. Ask for: Philip Mercer or Jane Ansell.
Open College of South London. Flexistudy. Ask for: Julian Brightman.
Paddington College. Flexistudy. Ask for: Roger Deats.
Roehampton Institute of Higher Education. Ask for: Christopher Jarman.
South Bank Polytechnic. Languages and corrosion technology courses; many more planned. Ask for: J Semple or C Wakefield.
South London College. Fleximaths. Ask for: Phil Walters
Southwark College. Flexistudy. Ask for: Ishmael Onan (maths), Jim Ray (physics), Robin Moody (chemistry), Jan Broughton or Steve Flowerday (biology).

MANCHESTER – METROPOLITAN DISTRICTS

Bolton

Bolton Metropolitan College. Various schemes. Ask for: Mr P Stewart.

Bury

Bury College of Adult Education. Open learning. Ask for: Kevin Brady.

Manchester

Abraham Moss Centre. Flexistudy. Ask for: Mr John Buckley.
Basic Skills Unit, South Manchester Community College,The Birtles Centre. Ask for: Alan Winn. Open learning workshops. Ask for: the open learning coordinator.
Manchester College of Adult Education. Independent study. Flexible study planned.
North Hulme Centre. Open learning, access to learning for adults. Ask for: Brenda Cox.
North Manchester College, Moston Centre. BTEC scheme.
North Manchester College, Abraham Moss Centre. Ask for: John Buckley.
South Manchester Community College, Fielden Park Centre. Open Learning Workshop. Ask for: Ruth Jones.
Withington Centre for Community Education. Ask for: Beth Wilson.

Oldham

Oldham Industrial Language Training Unit. Distance learning planned. Ask for: K Adams.

Tameside

Tameside College of Technology. Flexistudy. Ask for: G Crawshaw.

Wigan

Leigh College. Flexistudy. Ask for: Mrs M E O'Leary.

MERSEYSIDE

Knowsley

Kirkby College of Further Education. Ask for: Mike Belshaw.
Knowsley Adult Education Centre. Distance learning. Ask for: Barbara Fletcher.
Knowsley Central Tertiary College. Distance Learning. Ask for: Tom Rowbottom.

Liverpool

Sandown College. Flexistudy. Ask for: Frederica Hayes.
The South Mersey College. Riversdale Campus. Ask for: Peter Pickering.

St Helens

St Helens College. Computing.

Wirral

Wirral Metropolitan College, Withens Lane Site and Carlett Park Site. Flexistudy, Learnaway. Ask for: D W Hill.

Norfolk

Norfolk College of Arts and Technology. Distance learning. Ask for: Ian Swinburn, ext 312.
Norwich City College of Further and Higher Education. Distance Learning. Ask for: Mrs C Williams.

Northamptonshire

Nene College. BTEC, British Telecom and Construction Industry Training Board. Ask for: D Willis. Language Tapes for Business. Ask for: J Whistler.
Tresham College. Open learning. Ask for: Mr Hindley.

Northumberland

Northumberland Technical College. Correspondence Supporting Service. Ask for: College Librarian.
Open Door Basic Skills/Open Learning Unit. Queen Elizabeth High School. Ask for: David Halpin.

Nottinghamshire

Arnold and Carlton College of Further Education. Flexistudy. Ask for: J Gannon.
Broxtowe College of Further Education. Flexistudy. Ask for: Head of Department of General Education.
Clarendon College of Further Education. Tele lang courses. Ask for: Mr Roddam.
Eaton Hall International. Distance learning.
Newark Technical College. Flexistudy. Ask for: P Tallon.
North Nottinghamshire College of Further Education. Flexistudy. Ask for: G E Atkins.
People's College of Further Education. Distance learning. Ask for: M Stringer.
South Nottinghamshire College of Further Education. Flexistudy. Ask for: Bernard Jarvis.
West Nottinghamshire College of Further Education. Home Study. Ask for: A P Davis.

Oxfordshire

Abingdon College of Further Education. Open Learning, languages and office skills. Flexistudy. Mathematics planned. Ask for: Mr Owen Reed.
Henley, The Management College. Distance learning.
North Oxfordshire Technical College and School of Art. Flexistudy. Ask for: Mr Little.
Oxford College of Further Education. Languages, telecommunications, computing.
Oxford Polytechnic, Faculty of Education Studies. Flexistudy. Ask for: P E Martin.
South Oxfordshire Technical College. Flexistudy. Ask for: Mr Craghill.
West Oxfordshire Technical College. Flexistudy. Ask for: David Evans.

Shropshire

Bridgnorth and Shropshire College of Further Education. Flexistudy. Ask for: Tim Wilcox.
Gateway Education and Arts Centre. Second Chance, Distance Leaarning. Ask for: Angela Fricker.
Shrewsbury College of Arts and Technology. Flexistudy. Ask for: Mr N T N Cole, ext 62.
Telford College of Arts and Technology. Phonalang course. Ask for: A Gosling. Open Tech engineering project planned. Ask for: R Overton.

Somerset

Bridgewater College. Flexistudy. Ask for: Ken Brown.
Wellington Community Education Centre. Flexistudy. Ask for: R Chatfield.
West Somerset School Community Education. Flexistudy. Ask for: B Woodger.
Yeovil College. Flexistudy. Ask for: Allen R Parrott.

Staffordshire

Burton-upon-Trent Technical College. Open Learning. Flexistudy. Ask for: Tony Fenwick.
Cauldon College of Further and Higher Education. Open Learning. Many subjects. Ask for: Mrs A Bowes, Mrs Beaumont or Mr Bloor.
Leek College of Further Education and School of Art. Distance learning. Ask for: D Graham.
Stafford College of Further Education. BTEC, distance learning project for hotel and catering industry. Ask for: A J Coleman.

Staffordshire College of Agriculture. Distance learning.
Stoke on Trent Technical College. Open Learning, Flexistudy. BTEC Continuing Education. Ask for: Jeff Kent or Mike McNeal.
Tamworth College of Further Education. Ask for: Mr D C Robinson.

Suffolk

Lowestoft College of Further Education. Open learning. Ask for: Malcolm Brown or Colin Snook.
Otley College of Agriculture and Horticulture. Distance learning.
Suffolk College of Further and Higher Education. Flexistudy. Ask for: Mr R Ades.
West Suffolk College of Further Education. Open Learning, agricultural engineering mechanics. Ask for: John Sharpe.

Surrey

Brooklands Technical College. Flexistudy. Ask for: Mr Cockerham.
East Surrey College. Flexistudy. Ask for: Mrs DB Clarke. Open Learning and Adult Training. Ask for: AW Parsons. Aviation Studies. Ask for: G Allan.
Guildford County College of Technology. Distance learning. Ask for: Ms S May.
Mole Valley Adult Education Institute. Flexistudy. Ask for: Ian Hewes.
North East Surrey College of Technology. Flexistudy. Ask for: Mrs Ellen Wright.
University of Surrey. Distance Learning. Ask for: Professor L R B Elton.

Sussex – East

Brighton College of Technology. BTEC, telecommunications.
Hastings College of Arts and Technology. Flexistudy. Ask for: J R Longfield or B W Larkin.

Sussex – West

Chichester College of Technology. Flexistudy. Ask for: Peter Bailey.
Crawley College of Technology. Open Learning planned. Ask for: A Ekins.
Forest Community School. Flexistudy. Ask for: Mrs M Arbon.
Northbrook College, Design plus Technology. Distance learning.

TYNE AND WEAR

Gateshead

Gateshead Technical College. BTEC units, Open Tech courses planned. Flexistudy. Ask for: Mrs L Darwin.

Newcastle-upon-Tyne

Heaton Education Centre. Open Learning. Ask for: Doreen McCarthy.
Newcastle College of Arts and Technology. BTEC. Flexistudy. Ask for: Mrs D C Ambrose.
Newcastle Polytechnic/Newcastle College of Arts and Technology. Open learning access centre (091) 232 6230. Statistics for librarians course.

North Tyneside

North Tyneside College of Further Education. Open Learning and Flexistudy. Ask for: S Reed or F Pattison.

South Tyneside

South Tyneside College. BTEC.

Sunderland

Monkwearmouth College of Further Education. Flexistudy. Ask for: Anne Tweddle
Sunderland Polytechnic, Sunderland Open Learning Access Centre. Ask for: Gordon Wainwright.
Wearside College of Further Education. Flexistudy. Ask for: Alan Owen.

WEST MIDLANDS – METROPOLITAN DISTRICTS

Birmingham

Bournville College of Further Education. Ask for: Ms Sadie Walton.
City of Birmingham Polytechnic. Town planning course.
Garretts Green Technical College. Flexistudy. Resource Unit – Birmingham Open Tech Scheme. Ask for: J W Standing.

Hall Green Technical College. Ask for: Colin Fussell.
Handworth Technical College. Ask for: Bob Kay.

Coventry

Coventry Technical College. Open learning. Ask for: Roger D'Albertson.
Henley College of Further Education. Home Study. Ask for: A Thomson. Flexistudy. Ask for: J L Fisher.
Stoke Park School and Community College. Flexistudy. Ask for: Chris Marks.
Tile Hill College of Further Education. Home study in business studies. Ask for: I Gibbs. GCE A- levels. Ask for: M H Rippon.

Dudley

Dudley College of Technology. Open Access/Flexistudy. Ask for: Karen Evans.

Sandwell

Sandwelll College of Further and Higher Education. BTEC, Open Learning. Flexistudy. Ask for: Mr G L Richardson.

Solihull

Solihull College of Technology. Flexistudy. Ask for: Ken Williams.

Wolverhampton

Wulfrun College of Further Education. Flexistudy. Ask for: Marion Reeves.

Warwickshire

East Warwickshire College of Further Education. Flexistudy. Ask for: A Leahy.
North Warwickshire College of Technology and Art. Distance Learning. Ask for: Paul Simpson.

Wiltshire

Chippenham Technical College. Flexistudy. Ask for: David Cornwell.
Salisbury College of Technology. Distance learning. Ask for: S Dear
Swindon College, Swindon. Open Learning Centre. Ask for: I J Wallis.
Trowbridge Technical College. Flexistudy. Ask for: Jeff Osborn.

Yorkshire – North

Craven College of Adult Education. OWTLET – various open learning schemes. Tel: (0423) 524659. Ask for: Mrs Warren.
Harrogate College of Arts and Technology. OWTLET. Tel: (0423) 524659. Ask for: Mr Taylor.
Scarborough Technical College. OWTLET. Tel: (0423) 524659. Ask for: P Ingham.

YORKSHIRE – METROPOLITAN DISTRICTS

Barnsley

Barnsley College of Technology. Flexistudy. Ask for: A Cox or R Cohen.

Bradford

Bradford and Ilkley Community College. A very comprehensive range of services.
Keighley Technical College. Flexistudy. Ask for: V Richards.

Calderdale

Percival Whitley College of Further Education. Flexistudy. Ask for: John Ogden.

Doncaster

Doncaster Metropolitan Institute of Higher Education. Assisted private study, quarrying. Ask for: M J Arthur.

Kirklees

Dewsbury College. Open Learning. Ask for: G Shoesmith.
Huddersfield Technical College. Open Learning. Ask for: K Mellor.

Leeds

Airedale and Wharfedale College of Further Education. Flexistudy. Ask for: Mrs L Foxcroft. Open Learning. Ask for: Clive Moule.
Joseph Priestley Institute of Further Education. Flexistudy. Ask for: Lynne Foxcroft.

Leeds College of Building. Open Learning. Ask for: B F Noble, M Sergent.
Park Lane College of Further Education. Flexistudy. GCSE/A-level, business and professional courses.
Swarthmore Centre. Flexistudy. Ask for: Pam Cole.

Rotherham
Rockingham College of Further Education. Flexistudy. Ask for: Mrs B Laird.

Sheffield
Granville College. Ask for: J Edwards.
Sheffield Educational Information Service for Adults. Ask for: Frank Lipman.
Sheffield City Polytechnic. Distance Learning. Ask for: K Searstone.
Stannington College. BTEC Telecommunications course.
Stocksbridge College. Flexistudy. Ask for: Ms D R Jones.

Wakefield
Bretton Hall College. Distance Learning. Ask for: Don Sissons.
Wakefield District College. Wide range of open learning courses. Ask for: Gwen Harris

WALES

Clwyd
North East Wales Institute of Higher Education. Flexistudy. Ask for: Tom Wright.

Dyfed
Aberystwyth University College of Wales. Distance Learning. Welsh medium external degree course. Ask for: Cynfael Lake.
Carmarthenshire College of Technology and Art. Open Tech. Ask for: the Principal.
College of Librarianship. Masters degree in management of librarianship and information studies.
Dyfed Open Tech. Flexistudy, Open Tech. Ask for: Ron Harvey.

Gwent
Crosskeys College. Flexistudy. Ask for: Mr Bevan. Open Learning. Ask for: Mr Llewellyn. Tel: (0495) 272233.
Ebbw Vale College of Further Education. Open Learning. Ask for: V Waters.
Gwent College of Higher Education. Open Tech, plant engineering, energy management. Ask for: L Oelmann.
Newport College of Further Education. External Student Scheme for Telecommunications, BTEC course. Ask for: W K Whitehill. Distance Learning. Ask for: G S Llewellyn.
Pontypool College. Distance/Open Learning. Ask for: R Mustard.
Usk College of Agriculture. Distance Learning. Ask for: David Norgate.

Gwynned
Coleg Meirionnydd. Flexistudy, Open Tech. Ask for: Bryn Williams.

Mid-Glamorgan
Aberdare College of Further Education. Distance Learning.
Bridgend College of Technology. Distance Learning, supervisory studies, planned. Ask for: T M Pugh.
Pontypridd Technical College. BTEC Flexistudy. Ask for: Mr Herbert.

Powys
Montgomery College of Further Education. Flexistudy. Ask for: Bernard Wakeley.
Radnor College of Further Education. Distance Learning business studies. Ask for: Mr Penny.

South Glamorgan
Adult Basic Education Centre. Flexistudy. Ask for: Pam Griffiths.
Rumney College of Technology. Flexistudy. Ask for: J Knight.

West Glamorgan

Afan College. Open learning. Ask for: Don Taylor.

Gorseinon College of Further Education. Distance Learning. Ask for: D N Davies.

SCOTLAND

Borders

Border College of Further Education. Flexistudy. Ask for: Robin Mason.

Central

Clackmannan College of Further Education. Ask for: Ron Marshall.

Falkirk College of Technology. Open Learning. Ask for: Stuart Dean.

Dumfries and Galloway

Dumfries and Galloway College of Technology. Open learning. Ask for: Roseanne Graham.

Fife

Glenrothes and Buckhaven Technical College. Learning by Appointment, Flexistudy. Open Tech, various subjects, planned. Ask for: Head of Department of Educational Services.

Kirkaldy College of Technology. Distance and Open Learning, electrical and electronic engineering, building. Ask for: I Davidson, H Clelland, P Kennedy.

Lauder Technical College. Distance learning planned. Ask for: Michael Morris.

Grampian

Aberdeen College of Commerce. Open Learning. Ask for: A R Dale.

Aberdeen College of Education. In-service teacher's courses.

Aberdeen Technical College. Open learning fishing, transport and telecommunications. Ask for: G Goolnik.

Banff and Buchan College of Further Education. Distance Learning planned.

Moray College of Further Education. SCOTVEC scheme. Distance Learning. Ask for: Stewart Chalmers.

Highland

Inverness College of Further and Higher Education. SCOTVEC Business Studies. Ask for: I Gordon. Distance Learning. Ask for: Ms A Parker. Hairdressing. Ask for: Mr H Wood, Electronics. Ask for: Mr W Dawson.

Thurso Technical College. Local based open learning (includes Scottish National Certificate modules), Flexistudy and distance learning. Open Tech (RSE in Road Competence; NEBSS certificate). Ask for: Mrs Allison Smith.

Lothian

Edinburgh Walk-In Numeracy Centre. Home Study Packs, planned. Ask for: Laure Paterson.

Esk Valley College. Open Learning. Ask for: R Bain or Stanley Nisbet.

Heriot Watt University. Higher Education – degree courses, Distance Learning.

Leith Nautical College. Open Tech, instrumentation and control systems, the handling of hazardous cargoes, stability for semi-submersible wrecks. Ask for: John Ford.

Napier College. Learning by Appointment. Ask for: Dr F Percival.

Stevenson College of Further Education. Flexistudy. Ask for: J Dalziel.

Telford College of Further Education. Open Learning/Flexistudy: Ask for: T Davies. Open Tech, large programme aimed at the oil industry. Ask for: John Thomson.

West Lothian College of Further Education. Open learning. Ask for: Mr A Henderson.

Orkneys

Orkney Education Department. Flexistudy. Ask for: Mr Drever.

Roxburghshire

Borders College of Further Education. Flexistudy. Ask for: N S McLeish.

Shetland Islands

Lerwick Further Education Centre. Distance Learning. Ask for: A Miller.

Strathclyde

Argyll Community Education. Home study courses.
Ayr College. Open learning. Ask for: Mr Kilgour.
Cambuslang College. Distance learning. Ask for: Gordon Robbins.
James Watt College. Distance Learning. Ask for: Maryanna Kay.
Jordanhill College of Education. Diploma in Educational Technology.
Motherwell College. Open learning. Ask for: Mary Burns.
Springburn College. Garage management, marketing. Ask for: Mr Dolan. Refrigeration and air conditioning. Ask for: Mr Muir.
Strathclyde University. Distance Learning, Masters of Business Administration: Ask for: John Martin. Pharmacy refresher. Ask for: Dr J Johnson.

Tayside

Angus Technical College. Open Learning. Flexistudy. Ask for: M J Finn.
Duncan of Jordanstone College of Art. Scottish elements of the Royal Town Planning Institute/ Open University examinations. Ask for: Dr Hugh Begg.
Dundee College of Education. Postgraduate diploma in educational technology. Ask for: Dr Mainwaring.
Perth College of Further Education. Open learning. Ask for: A Cowper.

Western Isles

Lews Castle College. Distance Learning. Ask for: the Principal.

NORTHERN IRELAND

Ballymena

Ballymena Technical College. Distance Learning. Ask for: D Elliott.

Banbridge

Banbridge College of Further Education. Flexistudy. Ask for: Miss B Gaffney.

Bangor

North Down College of Further Education. Flexistudy. Ask for: Mr Burns.

Belfast

Belfast College of Technology. Distance learning.

Dungannon

Dungannon Further Education College. Planned. Ask for: G McCague.

Enniskillen

Fermanagh College of Further Education. Open Tech. Flexistudy. Ask for: J Maxwell.

Lisburn

Lisburn College of Further Education. Computer Studies. Ask for: D Currie.

Londonderry

North West College of Technology. Flexistudy. Ask for: Patrick Breslin.

CHANNEL ISLANDS

Jersey

Highlands College. Distance Learning, Ask for: B G Wilson.

MORE INFORMATION

There is an annual directory of flexible study opportunities in Scotland:

★ **SEND FOR** *A directory of open learning opportunities in Scotland 1986*, free from Scottish Council for Educational Technology, Dowanhill, 74 Victoria Crescent Road, Glasgow G12 9JN. Tel: (041) 334 9314.

18 Adult routes

Alternatives to A-level
Fresh horizons
Access courses
Polymaths, polyphysics
List of courses

ALTERNATIVES TO A-LEVELS

The most common traditional route to post-school study is through the various school leaving exams such as GCE O- and A-levels, GCSE, and Scottish Certificates. These are the entry route to higher education and many occupations and professions. (See also *41 Qualifications*). These exams were mainly designed for people aged 16 to 19 in full-time education and many people find them inflexible and inappropriate in content for adults.

A number of courses spcifically for adults have been set up. Different approaches have been used but they have some common characteristics:

- they have no entry qualifications (though they may ask you to write an essay or attend an interview before accepting you)
- they emphasise study skills (efficient reading, essay writing, note taking etc)
- they often include a lot of individual counselling (everyone's at a different level so this is important)
- most of them are one-year courses, though some are longer
- they may be full-time or part-time
- some aim at particular groups or fields of study, others are wider in scope.

These courses are becoming more acceptable as entry qualifications to degree level studies for mature students; some lead in to particular courses. They may also be an end in themselves. The different approaches described include:

- Fresh Horizons and other similar courses aimed mainly at women
- Access courses designed to open up opportunities for ethnic minorities
- Various courses to provide a more accesible route for adults in general
- Open College schemes
- Polymaths and polyphysics to encourage adults into maths or physics.

Many courses combine a number of these elements and do not necessarily fit neatly into one category. But they all have the same overall purpose.

FRESH HORIZONS

The City Literary Institute in London (City Lit) was the pioneer of this type of course. The City Lit Fresh Horizons course covers learning how to learn, thinking about what you can do, and studying new subjects. It can be full-time or part-time (day or evening). The part-time day course is designed especially for women with children, the hours matching school hours – 10 am to 3 pm; there is a chance of a discretionary grant for a full-time course. It has a good reputation and is widely accepted for entry to higher education.

★ **LOOK AT** *Learning later*, Enid and Edward Hutchinson, Routledge and Kegan Paul, 1979.

ACCESS COURSES

These courses, also called higher education preparatory courses, were originally set up in London, Birmingham, Bradford, Leicester and Manchester as part of a Department of Education and Science scheme to encourage people from ethnic minorities without formal qualifications to train for teaching, social work and other professions. In some cases LEA discretionary grants are available. The number of these courses has grown enormously in the last couple of years.

These courses can be full-time or part-time and take one or two years. They are usually set up by a college in conjunction with a university or polytechnic. The higher education institution involved generally accepts the access course as an entry qualification to certain courses, and in some cases reserves places for people coming from the access course, providing entry qualifications are met.

ADULT FOUNDATION COURSES

An alternative approach to the Access course is the Adult Foundation Course, being set up in a number of colleges especially in London. They are similar to Access courses but are different in that they do not prepare students for one profession or for a particular higher education course and are therefore intended to provide a foundation for a number of further courses or careers. Examples are at City and East London College and at Newham Community College.

OPEN COLLEGE SCHEMES

A number of open college schemes have been set up, the first was in the North West of England. But the term has been used for all sorts of courses, some not very different from traditional courses. Some schemes (eg Birmingham Return to Learn) have some characteristics of open college schemes without using the name. The more developed versions are described below.

Open College Federation of the North West

Ten years ago a group of further and adult education colleges in Lancashire and Cumbria pioneered a whole set of courses designed specially for adults. Originally developed by Nelson and Colne College in conjuction with Lancashire Polytechnic, Lancaster University, the colleges of higher education associated with the University and four local education authorities, there are now thirteen colleges of further and adult education involved. They offer:

- courses in a wide range of subjects designed specially for adults
- no entry qualifications or prior experience needed – some courses where you start from the beginning
- low cost

- a qualification if you want, acceptable for entry to a range of universities, polytechnics and colleges and to some professional institutions
- courses that you can do for pleasure as well
- a 'mature' approach
- courses that are available part-time, evenings
- a faster route than doing GCSEs and A-levels from the beginning.

The courses are at two stages – A and B. If you want a complete preparation for HE you do four A units and two B units (though people who already have some qualifications may not need to follow the whole course). Two B units are worth a A-level for HE entrance. You can enrol in September and February.

Distance learning variants of certain units are currently being prepared.

A units: Everyone is encouraged to study two introductory courses (study techniques and methods of enquiry) to help learn to study. You choose two more from courses like: a modern language, politics and economics, introduction to literature, man in the environment, introduction to the physical sciences, engineering, introduction to religious studies, geography, women's studies, drama and others. A units take 50 hours and cost £17.25 (1986/87 prices).

B units: Courses such as history and culture of Britain, modern language, electronic business studies, people in organisations, music, art, computing, English, natural sciences, maths, geography. B units last a full year (100 hours) and cost £34.50 (1986/87 prices) plus an exam fee.

Not all the units are available at the same time or at all the colleges involved.

What does it lead to?

Stage A: Informal assessment of individual units leading to Stage A certificate.

Stage B: A letter of credit for individual Stage B units and a certificate if the full course is completed.

Complete course: an Open College Certificate. This is accepted by Lancaster University and Lancashire Polytechnic as meeting the entry requirements for degree courses. Open College students have been accepted by a wide range of other universities, colleges and professional associations.

Since the mid 1970s, over 6,000 adults have taken Open College courses; over 300 have decided to take degrees and equivalent courses in institutions of higher education. Over 100 of these have already graduated in various subjects.

Recognition of Open College as an A-level equivalent has now been accorded by a wide range of institutions of higher education, professional bodies, Civil Service Commission and Joint Matriculation Board.

MAN, LATE 20s

I went to a secondary modern. I had a real inferiority complex at the start. You lack confidence in your own ability. Academic qualifications are something 'they' do. I couldn't afford to take A-levels. This course is ideal. I've now been accepted by two universities for next year. I've done it with eighteen months' part-time study.

Open College of South London (OCSL)
The first Open College network to be set up in London. It was established in 1983 to improve access to education for adults without formal qualifications, whether in further, adult or higher education. Member institutions are:

- Brixton College
- Clapham-Battersea Adult Education Institute
- Lambeth Adult Education Institute
- Morley College
- South Bank Polytechnic
- Southwark College
- Southwark Adult Education Institute
- South London College
- South Thames College
- South West London College
- Vauxhall College
- Westminster College
- Woolwich College.

Open College leaflets provide information about courses of special importance to adults returning to study such as Access courses, return to learning courses (see *19 Starting again*), foundation courses, flexible learning opportunities (see *17 Flexible learning*), basic education (see *20 Basics*) and new technology courses.

Contact the Open College for advice and information about any of these courses. The Open College welcomes applications from disabled people and can provide information about facilities at member institutions. Students enrolled on Open College courses are entitled to an Open College Student Card. This card will give access to library, sports and social facilities at all member institutions.

If you live in the South London area and want help finding the right course:

★ **ASK** Open College of South London, Manor House, 58 Clapham Common North Side, London SW4 9RZ. Tel: (01) 228 2015.

Other London Open Colleges
Other Open College schemes are being developed in London. They are likely to be based at the Polytechnic of North London, City of London Polytechnic and Polytechnic of Central London.

Manchester Open College Federation
Set up in 1981 by Manchester Education Committee, MOCF is a federation of education and training providers now operating across Greater Manchester and beyond. MOCF is an accreditation body; it does not provide courses. Two areas of work are accredited. First, courses and learning activities are accreditied by approving and registering their design and organisation in direct consultation with staff involved. Second, people's achievement on these courses and learning activities are accredited and MOCF credits awarded on successful completion of course and learning requirements.

50 hours of work, including private study at home, gains one credit. Credits are accumulated and recorded in an individual Study Passport by MOCF certificates. There are four levels of credit:

Level 1: for people wishing to improve basic skills and confidence in English, maths, computers, practical coping activities and English as a second language.

Level 2: for people building on experience and extending into other areas including practical job training and voluntary community activities.

Level 3: for people moving on to deeper study of a specialist subject including training for paid and voluntary work.

Level 4: for courses and training programmes enabling people to seek access to university and polytechnic courses, professional and community work training.

There are 600 courses registered with MOCF in 60 colleges and centres; over 6,000 students are involved. 100 Access-type courses are registered in 13 institutions. Open Learning and Open Tech activities in Manchester can be accredited by MOCF.

MOCF is negotiating with similar Open Colleges in Liverpool, Sheffield, West Yorkshire, South, Central and North London, and the Open College of the North West for a national system of credit transfer.

For details of MOCF courses contact your local College, Study Centre or Community Education Organiser. For further information, write to MOCF giving your study or training interest, where you live, and/or work, and your personal aims and ambitions for education, training or voluntary community activities.

★ **ASK** Rosemary Fleetwood, Manchester Open College Federation, Manchester Polytechnic, All Saints, Manchester M15 6BH.

Other schemes

Similar schemes operate in Birmingham (the Return to Learn Scheme), the North East of England (the Northumbria Consortium Scheme), Staffordshire (Open College) and Humberside. Each works in different ways so ask at one of the colleges in the list below.

POLYMATHS, POLYPHYSICS

Polymaths

A specially designed maths course for adults. Originally a way of getting people to A-level standard in maths to prepare them for a polytechnic maths degree. Many people use it as a maths course without going on to do a degree. To begin, you usually need a standard in maths of about O-level.

There are five books designed for the course which include assessments. There is no exam at the end – assessment is continuous. It is accepted by the CNAA for entry to maths degree courses and by some universities, and its acceptability is spreading. Originally taught in polytechnics, it's now increasingly offered in FE colleges.

The scheme is administered nationally by the Institute of Mathematics and its Applications. The colleges listed have run polymaths; but courses don't run if there is insufficient demand, so the list at the end of the chapter is only a general guide. For up-to-date information about local colleges offering polymaths:

★ **WRITE TO** The Secretary and Registrar, Institute of Mathematics and Its Applications, Maitland House, Warrior Square, Southend-on-Sea, Essex SS1 2JY. Tel: (0702) 612177.

Pre-polymaths

Some colleges offer pre-polymaths courses for people who aren't up to the necessary standard to start a polymaths course. These are sometimes called tri-maths. They are usually for one evening a week for ten weeks and have a specially written text. If you don't feel ready for an A-level standard course, ask one of the colleges doing polymaths whether they offer any other courses to prepare for it. If you're not up to that standard – think about basic numeracy (see *20 Basics*). There are many other introductory or start again maths courses all over the country, too many to list here, so ask your local colleges.

Polyphysics

Similar to polymaths, this is a special course for adults which aims to get you up to A-level standard, with the possibility of going on to a degree course. There are no formal entry requirements. There are seven course books specially written by a group from ten polytechnics.

The colleges listed at the end of the chapter have run polyphysics but if you want to know whether there is one locally, you should ask the physics or science department at your nearest polytechnic.

LIST OF COURSES

Higher education preparatory courses

This list includes access courses, other higher education preparatory courses and open college schemes. Some courses are specifically aimed at ethnic minorities, but they do not always say so. All the courses listed here are likely to be supportive to adult students. All courses we know of are listed, but there may be others. Some may be planned and not run; ask the college for more information. Main addresses of colleges listed can be found in the *Gazetteer*. An address is only given in this list if the course is running at a different centre.

England

Avon

City of Bath Technical College
One year, 21 hours per week courses available leading to entry for BEd (Hons).

Filton Technical College
Access: Preparation for higher education. Part-time, one year, linked to applied social studies courses, Bristol University.
Ask for: C Burgess or D Williams.

South Bristol Technical College
One day per week, 36 week courses leading to polytechnic degree courses.
Ask for: Dr Angela Cattell.

Cheshire
Mid Cheshire College of Further Education
Gateway course.
Ask for: M W Daniels.

North Cheshire College
Level 4 access courses for entry to higher education. One day per week, between 10 and 30 weeks, in conjunction with Manchester Open College Federation.

Cumbria
Carlisle Technical College
Open College of the North West.
Ask for: Dr B Priest.

West Cumbria College
Access course – psychology, sociology, history, English literature, combined studies in conjunction with Preston Polytechnic.
Ask for: Anne Topolor.

Derbyshire
Chesterfied College of Technology and Arts
Access courses – social sciences, creative design, science and technology, linked with Northern College. Guaranteed interviews at Sheffield Polytechnic.
Ask for: Student Services.

Derbyshire College of Higher Education
Gateway and Pathway courses; can be used for entgry to full time BEd or BCS (combined studies).
Ask for: Dr John Hey.

High Peak College of Further Education
Access for degree study; part-time, one evening per week, emphasis on history and politics.
Ask for: Mike Jones.

Devon
Dartington College of Arts
One year, two days per week courses in arts.
Ask for: Mary Collins.

East Devon College of Further Education
Return to study. Full-time, one year, linked to BA courses at Rolle College. Accepted by Exeter University.
Ask for: Mr R Sutcliffe.

Rolle College
One year, three days per week, leading to entry for higher educaion in social sciences and humanities.
Ask for: Robert Gee.

Durham
New College
One year full-time general course for mature students, leading to further study in the subject of the student's choice.
Ask for: Carole Sweet.

Essex
Chelmsford College of Further Education
Essex Access Scheme for entry to HE in Essex colleges.
Ask for: Christine Maher (county co-ordinator). Tel: (0245) 267222 or (0375) 371621.

Harlow College
Ask for: Christine Maher at Chelmsford (see above).

Colchester Institute
Open course. Part-time, two years, linked to science and maths courses at Essex University.
Ask for: Dr J A Knight.

Gloucestershire
College of St Paul and St Mary
BEd preparatory course. Full-time, one year. Successful students have automatic right of entry to college BEd course.
Ask for: K Mason.

Hampshire
The Teritary College, Fareham
Access course in 20th century studies leading to degree entry in humanities or social sciences.

Southampton Technical College (in conjunction with the College of HE)
Leading to entry to either BEd in primary education or BA in combined studies. Part-time, under 14 hours pw.
Ask for: David Hibbs.

Humberside
Beverley College of Further Education
Higher education foundation course. Planned. Being developed with Humberside College of Higher Education for entry to its courses.
Ask for: Mrs M Dunn.

Grimsby College of Technology
Higher education foundation course. Planned. Being developed with Humberside College of Higher Education for entry to its courses.
Ask for: Mr M Bagley.

Hull College of Further Education
Higher education foundation course in conjunction with Humberside College of FE.
Ask for: Mrs C Andrew.

North Lindsey College of Technology
Higher education foundation course. Part-time, daytime, one year. Linked to courses at Humberside College of Higher Education.
Ask for: Mr P Fretwell.

Kent
University of Kent at Canterbury
Access: various courses in humanities and social services.
Ask for: N C Riding, School of Continuing Education.

Lancashire
Most of the colleges in Lancashire participate in the Open College Federation of the North West. Special links with Lancaster University and Lancashire Polytechnic degree courses.
Accrington and Rossendale College. Ask for: Margot Clarke.
Blackburn College. Ask for: John Jackson.
Blackpool and Fylde College of Further and Higher Education. Ask for: Dave Swan.
Burnley College. Ask for: Joe McCafferty.
Lancaster and Morecambe College of Further Education. Ask for: Michael Swarbrick.
Lancaster College of Adult Education. Ask for: Sheilagh Wainwright.
Nelson and Colne College. Ask for: Jakes Makin.
W R Tuson College. Ask for: Terry Thompson.

Lancashire Polytechnic
Foundation courses in science and technology.
Ask for: Pam Ackroyd.

Pre-degree course.
Ask for: Lynne Thompson

LONDON – GREATER

Barnet
Barnet College of Further Education
Courses planned from September 1987.

Brent
Kilburn Polytechnic
Return to study. Proposed course. Linked to institutional management, librarianship and modern studies courses at Polytechnic of North London.

Croydon
Coombe Cliff Adult Education Centre
Preparatory courses for Open University towards 4 main foundations; social science, maths, science and technology, humanities.
Ask for: Terry George.

Ealing
Acton Technical College
Access to higher education: BSc, HND in applied physics and science at Kingston Polytechnic; HND in science, technology and engineering at Slough College of FE. Youth and community course leads to Diploma in youth and community; BEd access for primary and secondary (planned) at Kingston Polytechnic. Access to business studies (BA/HND) planned.

Ealing College of Higher Education
Fresh Start. Part-time, one year. Linked to own higher education courses.
Ask for: B Govett.

Enfield
Enfield College
Access course in humanities, linked with Middlesex Polytechnic, from Sept 1987.

Haringey
Haringey College of Further Education
Access course. Planned. Discussions with Middlesex Polytechnic on access links.

Tottenham College of Technology
Access course. Part-time day and evenings, two years. Leading to degree courses at Middlesex Polytechnic in BA sociology or BA humanities.
Ask for: B Buchan.

Harrow
Elm Park College
Access to science planned for September 1987.

Greenhill College
Access to social sciences planned for September 1987.

Harrow College of Further Education
Preparatory BA social science Access course. Part-time, day, one year. Linked to social science degree courses at Middlesex Polytechnic and the Polytechnic of Central London.
Ask for: Bob Vesey.

Weald College of Further Education
Access to science planned for September 1987

Merton
Merton College
Access course for entry to Kingston Polytechnic degrees.
Ask for: D Preece and M Bernard.

Newham

Access by independent study; part-time, 1 year, day or evenings. Linked to Dip HE in School for Independent Study at North East London Polytechnic.

Ask for: Paul Edwards.

Foundation course in art and design, 1 year full time.

Ask for: Peter Jones.

Higher education foundation Course; 2 years 15 hours per week.

Ask for: Barry Pilboro.

Waltham Forest

Waltham Forest College

Two full-time courses preparing for social sciences and BEd degrees; part-time cultural studies and humanities.

LONDON – INNER

Avery Hill College (Thames Polytechnic)

Open routes course. Run in conjunction with South Greenwich Adult Education Institute.

Ask for: Lee Rogers.

Brixton College

Access to the BEd degree. Full-time, one year. Succesful students have right of entry to BEd (Primary) at South Bank Polytechnic.

Ask for: Ian Hadley.

Access course in electronics/electrical engineering. Full-time, one year. Links with B/TEC and BSc courses at South Bank Polytechnic.

Ask for: Roy Lansdowne or T Ruthen.

Evening Access course in social science. Part-time, evenings, four terms. Successful students have right of entry to BSc social science course at South Bank Polytechnic.

Ask for: Ian Hadley.

Access to the Certificate of Qualification in Social Work. Full-time, one year. Designed especially for ethnic minorities. Leads to CQSW course at West London Institute of Higher Education.

Ask for: Hugh Dale.

Access to nursing.

Ask for: P Chapman.

City and East London College

Social work foundation course. Full-time, one year. Designed for students of Afro-Caribbean or Asian origin, with some bilngual support. Students must be over 20. Successful students have right of entry to Diploma in Social Work at the Polytechnic of North London.

Ask for: Ms V Rosen.

Special Access in business studies. Full-time. Designed for students of Afro-Caribbean origin. Successful students have right of entry to HND or BA business studies courses at the Polytechnic of North London.

Ask for: J Menzies.

BEd preparatory course. Either full-time, one year (course designed for students of Afro-Caribbean origin) or part-time four terms. Successful students have right of entry to BEd at the Polytechnic of North London.

Ask for: Ms R Pitt.

BEd preparatory course. Full-time, one year course especially for students of Bangladeshi origin. Course provides for students of English as a second language. Linked to BEd (Primary) course at Avery Hill College – students taught one day a week at Avery Hill College.

Ask for: A P U Bagchi.

BA comparative studies preparatory course. Full-time, one year. Automatic entry to comparative studies/social studies courses at Essex University for successful students.

Ask for: C Neal.

BA social studies preparatory course. Part-time, evenings, four terms starting after Easter. Linked to social studies courses at Essex University.

Ask for: C Neal.

City Lit
Fresh horizons. Full-time (20 hours a week), part-time day and evening. Pioneering course, started 1966. No links to HE institution but well known. Early application advisable.
Ask for: Janette Jeffries or Liz Ahrends.

Hackney College
Access to BEd degree. Full-time, one year. Two courses – primary education and youth and community. Linked to degrees at Avery Hill College – students taught there one day a week.
Ask for: David Drake.
Access to maths degree. Linked to City of London Polytechnic.
Ask for: Tony Fisher.
Access to higher education.
Ask for: Chris Shingler.

Hammersmith and West London College
Return to study (science) part-time, one year. Linked to physical and biological science courses at Birkbeck College. Return to study (humanities).part-time, one year. Linked to humanities courses at the Polytechnic of North London.

Kingsway-Princeton College
Access in science and mathematics. Full-time, one year. Linked to BSc (maths and science) and HND courses at the Polytechnic of North London.
Ask for: L Lindsay.
Access in humanities. Part-time, evenings, one year. Linked to BA (humanities) course at the Polytechnic of North London.
Ask for: Norman Carey or Pete Vines.
Access in law. Full-time, one year. Linked to BA (law) courses at Polytechnic of Central London and Polytechnic of North London.
Ask for: Margaret Haynes.
Foundation course in social and community work. Full-time, one year. Course designed for students of Caribbean origin. Linked to social work courses at the Polytechnic of North London and the Polytechnic of Central London.
Ask for: G Wilkes.

Paddington College
Access: humanities and social sciences course. Full-time or part-time. Not linked to any specific HE institution.
Ask for: Drew Burns.
Access computing. Full-time, one year. Linked to BSc or HND computing studies courses at the Polytechnic of Central London.
Ask for: Ms J Geary.
Access: mechanical engineering. Full-time, linked to BEng, HND, in computer assisted engineering.
Ask for: Drew Burns.
Access science. Full-time, one year. Linked to BSc or DipHE modular science courses at the Polytechnic of Central London.
Ask for: Ms L Redmond.
Access to BEd. Full-time, one year. Linked to BEd (General) course at Middlesex Polytechnic.
Ask for: Drew Burns.

South Bank Polytechnic. Course designed especially for students from ethnic minorities.
Ask for: Ray Tregear and John Agyemang.
Access to diploma in office administration. Part-time, day time, one year. Linked to diploma course at the City of London Polytechnic. Course designed especially for mature women.
Ask for: Claire Durkin.

South East London College
Pre-BEd course. Full-time, one year. Designed for Afro-Carribean students. Linked to London University BEd (Primary) degree at Goldsmiths' College. Secondary schools course planned.
Ask for: C Hodson.

Pre-BEd course. Full-time, one year. Linked to BEd (craft, design and technology) course at Avery Hill College, (Thames Polytechnic) where students are taught one day a week.
Ask for: C Hodson.

South London College
Food studies Access course. Tower Bridge Site. Full-time, one year. Linked to various related courses at the South Bank Polytechnic and the Polytechnic of North London.
Ask for: John Arris and Mike Osborne.
Business studies Access course. Part-time, evenings, three terms with September start, Knights Hill site. Linked to BA (business studies) course at the South Bank Polytechnic.
Ask for: Robert Webb or Ian Hatchard.
Health, biology and the environment Access course, Tower Bridge site; part-time day, 1 year. Linked to degree/HND courses at South Bank Polytechnic.
Ask for: John Arris or Judy Fairlie.
Engineering Access, Knights Hill site. Part-time day, 1 year; Linked to HND courses at South Bank Polytechnic.
Ask for: Colin Hovers or Mr Withan.
Social administration Access, Knights Hill site; part-time day, 1 year, linked to degree courses at Goldsmiths' College, University of London.
Ask for: Rob Webb or Helen George.

South Thames College.
Access to BEd course. Full-time, one year. Linked to BEd (youth and community) course at Roehampton Institute of Higher Education.
Ask for: Ms V Hudson.
Access to BEd (*science*) *course*. Part-time, four terms. Designed with ethnic minority students in mind. Linked to BEd degree at Kingston Polytechnic.
Ask for: R A Anghileri.

Southwark College
Access (*social science*) *course*. Full-time, one year. Linked to BSc (social science) course at the South Bank Polytechnic .
Ask for: Linda Reaich and Penny Allen.
Access (*maths, science and computing*) *courses*. Full-time, one year. Linked to various courses at City of London Polytechnic and the South Bank Polytechnic .
Ask for: Laurie Lenheim, Kay Singleton or Doug Williams.
Languages with international studies Access. Part-time, day time, one year. Linked to BA or B/TEC Higher Diploma courses at the South Bank Polytechnic
Ask for: Cynthia Dixon.
Access course in humanities. Part-time, day and/or evenings, one or two years. Successful students have right of entry to BA humanities course at Thames Polytechnic.
Ask for: Mike Jutsum.
Polystudy. Part-time, day time, one year. Course in humanities and social science, linked to South Bank Polytechnic.
Ask for: Mike Jutsum.

Thames Polytechnic (*incorporating Avery Hill College*).
Polystudy. Part-time, day time and evening. Successful completion of four units would normally give access to Thames Polytechnic BA degrees in humanities or sociology, and BEd degrees in primary or physical education.
Ask for: Pam Linn or Tony Hendrey, Continuing Education Unit.

University of London
Goldsmiths' College
Access English literature; 2 year, part-time. mature students only. Leads to Intermediate Certificate.
Ask for: Dr Linden Peach.
Access social sciences (psychology, sociology, social anthropology, social policy and administration).

Ask for: Dr Linden Peach.
Access law and science courses (planned).

Vauxhall College of Building and Further Education
Access to the Faculty of the Built Environment. Full-time, one year. Linked to various courses in the faculty at the Polytechnic of the South Bank.
Ask for: Tony Goldman.
Law Access course. Full-time, one year. Linked to BA (law) course, at the Polytechnic of the South Bank. Course designed especially for students from ethnic minorities.
Ask for: Ray Tregear or John Agyemang.
Access to diploma in office administration. Part-time, one-year. Linked to diploma course at the City of London Polytechnic. Course designed especially for mature women.
Ask for: Claire Durkin.

Westminster College
Access to BEd (home economics) course. Full-time, one year. Linked to course at the South Bank Polytechnic.
Ask for: Mrs Dick.

Woolwich College
Access to BEd. Full-time, one year. Linked to BEd at Avery Hill College where students are taught one day a week.
Ask for: Mr Collins and Ms Jenvy.
Science Access. Full-time, one year. Linked to BSc course at Thames Polytechnic.
Ask for: Steve Lockett.

MANCHESTER – METROPOLITAN DISTRICTS

Manchester Open College Federation. Full explanation earlier in the chapter.

Manchester

Manchester Business School
Access course leading to business administration; part-time, 1 day per week.
Ask for: Graduate Programme Department.

North Hulme Community Education Centre
Access course. Full-time, one year. Designed for ethnic minority students. Special links to courses at Manchester Polytechnic.
Ask for: Ms Nyala Vaughan. Tel: (061) 226 0319.

North Manchester College, Abraham Moss Centre
Access course. Full-time. Linked to course at Manchester Polytechnic.
Ask for: R Hardy

South Manchester Community College, Fielden Park Site
Threshold course. Full-time, one year. Leads to JMB mature matriculation exam for entry to Manchester University.
Ask for: M Taylor, A Davidge and Mrs A Kearney.
Gateway course. Part-time, one or two years. Course preparing for DipHE entry.
Ask for: M Taylor, A Davidge and Mrs A Kearney.
Access course. Preparation for higher education courses in social/welfare work.
Ask for: M Taylor, A Davidge and Mrs A Kearney.

Oldham

Oldham College of Technology
Access course. Manchester Open College Federation course for intending DipHE students.

Rochdale

Rochdale College of Art
Full and part-time courses leading to BA in art and design .

MERSEYSIDE

Knowsley

Kirkby College of Further Education

Open College Federation of the North West. Special links to Lancaster University and Lancashire Polytechnic.

Ask for: Mike Belshaw.

Liverpool

Childwall Hall College of Further Education

Access to higher education. Full-time, one year or part-time, up to four years. JMB validation.

Ask for: Ann Lees.

Sandown College of Further Education (including Old Swan)

Inner city Access to higher education. Full-time, one year. Jointly run course designed especially for black students from inner Liverpool. Liverpool Polytechnic and Liverpool University have reserved some places on social science departments' courses under mature entry schemes.

Ask for: Mr E Conway, Liverpool Education Authority, 73 Canning Street, Liverpool 8 7NW. Tel: (051) 708 6650.

Sefton

Southport College of Art and Technology

Open College Federation of the North West. Special links with Lancaster University and Lancashire Polytechnic.

Ask for: Charles Losasso.

Wirral

Wirral Metropolitan College, Carlett Park site

Second chance; pilot access courses in English, history and social sciences, leading to BA.

Norfolk

Norfolk College of Arts and Technology

Open access course combines history, English, sociology and history of art. Recognised for entry by University of East Anglia.

Ask for: Dr Paul Richards.

Northumberland

Northumberland Technical College

Higher education foundation course. Planned part-time courses linking to Newcastle Polytechnic as part of Northumbria Consortium Scheme.

Ask for: L Agar.

Nottinghamshire

Clarendon College of Further Education

Gateway course (integrated studies). Part-time, two years. Linking to courses at Trent Polytechnic.

Ask for: Alan Field.

North Nottinghamshire College of Further Education

Higher education access course.

Ask for: Mr T G Waddle.

People's College of Further Education

Gateway course (science and mathematics). Part-time, two years. Linking to courses at Trent Polytechnic. O-levels required.

Ask for: Tony Hall.

Shropshire

Telford College of Art and Technology

Access modern studies incorporates study skills, British economic and social history, Modern English literature and economic perspectives; partnered with North Staffs. Polytechnic.

Ask for: Alan Gosling or Martin Park.

Somerset
Yeovil College
OU Prep courses; an Access tutor group; feeds adults into apprpriate HE courses.

Staffordshire
Cannock Chase College.
Open college course. Possible new course in September 1987.

Stoke-on-Trent
Cauldon College of Further & higher Education
Access humanities and social studies courses; linked with North Staffs Ploytechnic.

Newcastle-under-Lyme College
Open college course. Possible new course.

Stafford College of Further Education
Open college course. Part-time, two years. Linking to BA courses in modern studies, literature and history at North Staffordshire Polytechnic.
Ask for: J Bastable.

Stoke-on-Trent Technical College
Open college course. Link with degrees at North Staffordshire Polytechnic.
Ask for: Philip Davies.

Suffolk
Lowestoft College of Further Education
Access to BTEC courses in electronics, fibre optics and PLC.
Ask for: Industrial Liaison Unit.

Otley College of Agriculture and Horticulture
Access to diploma or degree level courses.

Surrey
Guildford County College of Technology
Access course. Planned course.
Ask for: Dr Haydon.

West Surrey College of Art and Design
Pre-degree courses, mainly for entry to own humanities degree programme. Pre-diploma course planned Autumn 1987.

TYNE AND WEAR – METROPOLITAN DISTRICTS

Gateshead
Gateshead Technical College
Higher education foundation course. Part-time, one to three years. Linking to various areas of study at Newcastle Polytechnic. Part of Northumbria Consortium Scheme.
Ask for: Mrs L Darwin.

Newcastle upon Tyne
Newcastle College of Arts and Technology
Higher education foundation course. Part-time, one to three years. Linking to various areas of study at Newcastle Polytechnic. Part of Northumbria Consortium Scheme.
Ask for: Neil Sharpe.

South Tyneside
South Tyneside College
Certificate in foundation studies. Part-time, day time, one year. Linking to BEd and other courses at Sunderland Polytechnic.

Sunderland
Monkwearmouth College of Further Education
Certificate in foundation studies. Part-time, day time or evenings, one year. Linking to BEd and

WEST MIDLANDS – METROPOLITAN BOROUGHS

Birmingham

Return to learn scheme. An integrated scheme involving various colleges and institutes. Part-time, a three stage modular scheme offering alternatives for adults. Special links to City of Birmingham Polytechnic courses.

Ask for: R Goy at Matthew Boulton Technical College, Scheme Co-ordinator.

Return to learn courses are offered by the following colleges:

The Brasshouse Centre
Brooklyn Technical College
Erdington and Kingstanding Adult Education Institutes
Hodge Hill Adult Education Centre
Matthew Boulton Technical College
Sparkbrook Area Adult Education
Sutton Coldfield College of Further Education
Yardley Area Office

Bournville College of Further Education
New way. Part-time, evening, two years. Course designed with ethnic minority students in mind. Linking to City of Birmingham Polytechnic courses especially in education and social work.
Ask for: Mrs Ann Owen.

Matthew Bolton Technical College
Mature students' alternative admissions scheme. Part-time, one year. Linking to City of Birmingham Polytechnic BEd course on which successful students normally gain a place.
Ask for: Mr Stukey.

Coventry

Tile Hill College of Further Education
Open Access to higher education. Full-time, one year. Linking to BEd, humanities, social science or law courses at Coventry (Lanchester) Polytechnic and Warwick University.
Ask for: Noel Harte.

Warwick University
Ask for: John Hogan.

Dudley

Dudley College of Technology
Access course. Part-time course linked to Wolverhampton Polytechnic.
Ask for: Derek Underhill or David Andrews.

Sandwell

Sandwell College of Further and Higher Education
Access to BEd course. Full-time, one year. Linked to West Midlands College of Higher Education (students go there one day a week).
Ask for: Mr S J Russell. Tel: (021) 558 4121 ext 583.

Solihull

Solihull College of Technology
Access course. Full-time, one year. Linked to arts and social science studies at City of Birmingham Polytechnic and Coventry (Lanchester) Polytechnic.
Ask for: Tim Cross.

Sutton Coldfield

Sutton Coldfield College of Further Education
Mature students' alternative admissions scheme. Part-time, one year. Linking to City of Birmingham Polytechnic BEd course on which successful students normally gain a place.
Ask for: Mr Dolley.

Walsall

Walsall College of Technology

Mature students' alternative admissions course. Full- or part-time, time, one or two years. Linked to Wolverhampton Polytechnic.

Ask for: Mike Lomax or Martin Huggins.

Wolverhampton

Wulfrun College of Further Education

Access linked with Wolverhampton Polytechnic. Ethnic minorities and women given priority.

Warwickshire

North Warwickshire College of Technology and Art

Access courses. For students of 21 and over, part-time. In art, social science, humanities. *Ask for:* Phyllis Hyde. In science and technology. *Ask for:* Fred Cattell. In life sciences. *Ask for:* Carol McLaughlin.

YORKSHIRE – METROPOLITAN DISTRICTS

Barnsley

Barnsley College of Technology

Certificate of preparation for higher education.

Ask for: R Cohen and A Cox.

Bradford

Bradford and Ilkley Community College

Mature students' certificate. Social sciences and humanaities. Part-time (seven hours a week), two years. Accredited by JMB. Linked to higher education .

Business studies certificate for mature students;. Part-time (nine hours per week), one year. Prepares for HNC and HND.

Direct Access course for graduates from the Indian subcontinent. Part-time (15 hours per week), one year. Preparation for BEd and PGCE.

Keighley Technical College

General education for mature students. Full-time, one year or part-time and flexible study. Linked to Bradford and Ilkley Community College higher education courses.

Ask for: Mr J Bewick.

Leeds

Park Lane College of Further Education

Mature matriculation course. Part-time, day time one year. Wide range of HE courses in various institutions. Preparation for the JMB mature matriculation exam. Foundation year also available. Part time evening: Pre-degree study skills for candidates for the JMB mature matriculation exam.

Ask for: Mrs R P Garrick or Mrs M O Leiper.

Rotherham

Rother Valley College of Further Education

Access business studies and social sciences for degree entry.

Ask for: Hazel Baxter.

Rotherham College of Arts and Technology

Pre-degree Access course. Full-time or part-time, one year. Linked to social studies, psychology or humanities at Doncaster Metropolitan Institute of Higher Education and Sheffield Polytechnic.

Sheffield

Norton/Woodseats Adult Education Division – Rowlinson Campus

Higher education preparation course. Part-time. Links with Sheffield Polytechnic.

Ask for: Richard Pinder.

Shirecliffe College
Alternative to A-level course. Full-time, one-year. Linking to various courses at Sheffield Polytechnic.
Ask for: Peter Reed.

Stocksbridge College
Preparatory course in politics and contemporary history. Linked to Salford University degree course.
Ask for: Dr N Sellars.
Foundation course – applied social studies. Gives exemption from first year of Sheffield Polytechnic courses.
Ask for: Dr P Duff.

SCOTLAND

Grampian
Aberdeen University
Higher education Access course, one or two years.
Ask for: Dr Melvin Dalgarno.

Strathclyde
Clydebank College
Strathclyde regional Access to higher education course. Designed for foreign students. Links with Glasgow and Strathclyde Universities.
Ask for: Ian Graham.

Glasgow University
Introduction to study for mature students. Part-time, two evenings a week, 26 weeks. Study skills and two subjects from a list of eleven arts, language and social science subjects. May be considered for entry to Glasgow University courses in arts, divinity, law and social science. Part-time degrees in MA arts subjects.
Ask for: Enrolment Secretary, Department of Adult and Continuing Education, 57/61 Oakfield Avenue, Glasgow G1LW. Tel: (041) 339–8855 ext 394.

NORTHERN IRELAND

University of Ulster, Belfast Campus, Magee Campus, Londonderry
Certificate in foundation studies for mature students. Full-time, one year and part-time, two years linked to social science and arts courses at the University of Ulster.
Ask for: Mr George Johnson.

Polymaths, pre-polymaths and polyphysics courses

England

Cleveland
Teesside Polytechnic. Polymaths. *Ask for:* Mr B Dummigan.

Devon
Plymouth Polytechnic. Polymaths. *Ask for:* B T C Patel.

Gloucestershire
Gloucestershire College of Arts and Technology, Park Campus, Cheltenham. Polymaths and trimaths. *Ask for:* C West.

Hampshire
Southampton Institute of Higher Education. Polymaths. *Ask for:* Mr D Moteane (ext 292).

Hertfordshire
Hatfield Polytechnic. Polyphysics. *Ask for:* Dr J A Shaw.

Lancashire
Preston Polytechnic. Polyphysics. *Ask for:* Dr E Webster, course leader.

LONDON – GREATER
Hounslow
West London Institute of Higher Education. Polymaths. *Ask for:* Mr Marratt.

LONDON – INNER
Greenwich
Thames Polytechnic (*incor. Avery Hill College*). Tel: (01) 854 2030. Polymaths. *Ask for:* D J Hunt.

Southwark
South Bank Polytechnic. Polyphysics. *Ask for:* A L Jones.
Southwark College. Polymaths. *Ask for:* the course tutor.

MANCHESTER – GREATER
Bolton
Bolton Institute of Higher Education. Polymaths. *Ask for:* Dr C W Lee.
Bolton Technical College. Pre-polymaths. *Ask for:* Mr S Russell.

Manchester
Manchester Polytechnic, Chester Street, Manchester M1 5GD. Tel: (061) 228 6171. Polymaths. Ask for: Mr P A Armstrong. Polyphysics. Ask for: Mr Ratcliffe.

Wigan
Wigan College of Technology. Polymaths. *Ask for:* S S Cotton. Pre-polymaths. *Ask for:* Mr Crompton.

MERSEYSIDE
Liverpool
Liverpool Polytechnic. Polymaths.

Staffordshire
North Staffordshire Polytechnic. Polyphysics. *Ask for:* Mrs J E Ball.

TYNE AND WEAR
Newcastle-upon-Tyne
Newcastle-upon-Tyne Polytechnic. Polymaths. *Ask for:* Mr R S Symonds.

Sunderland
Wearside College of Further Education. Pre-polymaths. *Ask for:* D Duffew.

WEST MIDLANDS
Birmingham
City of Birmingham Polytechnic. Polymaths. *Ask for:* Dr M Mortimer.

Coventry
Coventry (*Lanchester*) *Polytechnic*. Polymaths. *Ask for:* Nigel Steele.

YORKSHIRE
Sheffield
Rowlinson Adult Education Centre. Pre-polymaths. *Ask for:* Mr J Etchell.
Sheffield City Polytechnic. Polymaths. *Ask for:* Miss A C Baker.

19 Starting again: returning to study

Some approaches *New opportunities courses*

The courses in the previous chapter are designed to be used instead of A-levels or Scottish Highers if you are trying to get into higher education as well as to help you return to study.

There are hundreds of other courses, short and long, which are designed to help you start studying again or prepare for a return to work. They can also be useful in helping you to get accepted for higher education – all applications to HE from adults are helped by evidence of recent study.

There are a number of approaches used. Some are mentioned in *18 Adult routes*. Basic education (see *20 Basics*) may be a better starting point if you feel worried about reading or writing. There are hundreds of courses to prepare people for the Open University – the local OU regional office will tell you what's available locally.

There are many more, but it's difficult to give a useful list because they're starting up all the time and their titles (Return to Learning, Fresh Start, New Opportunities, Second Chances etc) may cover anything from a six-week introduction to study course to a full-time GCE course.

SOME APPROACHES

New opportunities courses

Usually one day a week for ten weeks, 10 am to 3 pm with child care facilities, though the format does vary from place to place. Most include a mixture of study skills, a close look at career opportunities, individual counselling, and group discussions. The idea is to help students explore possibilities and boost their confidence enough to take advantage of them. Some of these are New Opportunities for Women (NOW) courses – only open to women.

Fresh start courses

These are run in many different ways. For example the course in Richmond provides a choice – one day a week, Tuesday or Wednesday 9.30 am to 2.45 pm or Saturday 9.15 am to 1.45 pm for 30 weeks. Course fee £30.

Making experience count

A new approach being tried in a few places. It is based on self-assessment. During the course students are helped to analyse past experience and present it in such a way as to make sense to other people such as prospective employers. It seeks to demonstrate the value of experience as an alternative to formal qualifications.

How to find out more

Ask whoever offers education to adults in your area. Courses may be run by the LEA in an FE or adult college, by the WEA, in a polytechnic, university extramural department or elsewhere. Shorter ones should be advertised in your local library or in college prospectuses.

The Women Returners Network

This exists to help women returning to study both with a directory and an informal network for support. For more information, see *6 Women*, and

★ **LOOK AT** *Women returners directory* (see *Booklist*).

WOMAN, 35

I was beginning to vegetate: for ten years I was home, and suddenly I got this urge to go back to work again, but things have changed. I went on a WOW course. It was really based on getting your confidence back. It did help a lot – it gave me an insight into what jobs were available and everything. Now I go out to work I'm a lot happier, a lot more confident and not so worried about things at all.

NEW OPPORTUNITIES COURSES

NOW courses (or courses like the ones described above) have run or are running at the places listed below. They're hard to track down, so if you find one, or are running one that is not listed, please let us know! Main addresses of colleges listed can be found in the *Gazetteer*. An address is only given in this list if the course is running at a different centre.

England

Avon
Bristol Polytechnic. Women Returners course. Ask for: Peggy Henning.
City of Bath Technical College. Ask for: J Manley.

Bedfordshire
Elstow Craft Centre, Bedford. NOW. Ask for: Sally Freer.

Berkshire
Bracknell College, (Woodley Centre), Woodley Hill House, Eastcourt Avenue, Earley, Reading RG6 1HH. Tel: (0734) 61621. Second Career course. Ask for: Mr Cardy.

Cambridgeshire
SCOPE (Second Chance Opportunities for Education for Women). 10-week course run in Cambridge. Phone: Alice Zeitlyn. Tel: (0223) 357395.

Cornwall
Cornwall College of Further and Higher Education. Ask for: Mrs S Freeborn.

Cumbria
West Cumbria College. Ask for: Ms Penny Chadwick or Mandy Shephard.

Durham
New College. Ask for: Carole Sweet.
University of Durham. Ask for: Ben Knights, Department of Adult and Continuing Education.

Hampshire

Fareham Adult Education Centre. New Horizons.

University of Southampton. Second Chance for Women course. Ask for: Jane Thompson, Department of Adult Education. Return to study courses. Ask for: Maureen Barraclough, Department of Adult Education.

Hertfordshire

Dacorum College. Fresh Horizons. Ask for: Hazel Ward.

Hatfield Polytechnic. Ask for: Mrs R G Michaels. Also Polyprep course.

St Albans College. Restart. Ask for: Di Wallsgrove.

Humberside

Hull University, Department of Adult and Continuing Education. Tel: (0482) 465414. Ask for: Ms Rosa Brown.

Kent

Ashford Adult Education Centre. Ask for: Barbara Ford.

Medway Adult Education Centre. Ask for: Anna Reisenberger.

South Kent Adult Education Service. Fresh Start course.

Tunbridge Wells Adult Education Centre. Ask for: Barbara Feistner.

University of Kent at Canterbury. Access Courses. Ask for: A Harrison, School of Continuing Education.

Lancashire

Edge Hill College of Higher Education. NOW. Ask for: Mr G W Barrett.

Lancashire Polytechnic. NOW. Ask for: Tony Goddard.

Nelson and Colne College. Ask for: Brenda Dyer.

LONDON – GREATER

Croydon

Coombe Cliff Adult Education Centre. Back on Course. Ask for: Terry George.

Hillingdon

Uxbridge Technical College. Ask for: Enid Tobin.

Hounslow

Cranford Community School. Ask for: Jean Kelly.

Merton

Merton Institute of Adult Education. Fresh Start course. Ask for: Mary Bernardi.

Richmond

Richmond Adult and Community College, Clifden Road, Twickenham TW1 4LT. Tel: (01) 891 5907. Fresh Start course. Ask for: Pauline Nashashibi.

LONDON – INNER

Camden

Kentish Town Women's Workshop. NOW course. Ask for: Jackie Donaldson.

City

City University. NOW course. Ask for: Dr Stella Parker. Return to Study. Ask for: Brigitte Flock.

Islington

Polytechnic of North London. Ask for: Sandra Ashman at the Access Continuing Education Centre.

Southwark

Morley College. Fresh Start programme. Ask for: Judy Craven.

Southwark Institute.

Wandsworth
Clapham/Battersea Adult Education Institute. New Horizons course. Run by the basic education department – does not accept anybody with O-levels.

Westminster
Paddington College. Moving on and Fresh Opportunities courses. Ask for: Carol Burgess.

MANCHESTER – GREATER
Bury
Whitefield Centre. Further Opportunities for Women course.

Manchester
College of Adult Education. Fresh Horizons course. Ask for: David Chaytor.

Wigan
Drop-in-Centre, Wigan College of Technology, Orchard Street, Wigan WN1 3SW. Tel: (0942) 38695. NOW course.
Leigh College. Ask for: Tricia Wood.

MERSEYSIDE
Liverpool
Sandown College. Ask for: Trevor Low.
South Mersey College of Further Education. Ask for: Ann Lees.

Wirral
Conway Education Centre.
Wirral Metropolitan College. Carlett Park and Wallasey sites. Ask for: Mrs R Evans.

TYNE AND WEAR
Newcastle-upon-Tyne
The University of Newcastle-upon-Tyne, Centre for Continuing Education. Tel: (091) 232 8511 ext 2792.

North Tyneside
Adult Education Centre, Hawkeys Lane. Ask for: Caroline Beech or Sheena Dennison.

Sunderland
Wearside College of Further Education. Ask for: A Owen.

YORKSHIRE – SOUTH
Sheffield
Sheffield City Polytechnic. Ask for: Mrs M Monteith.

YORKSHIRE – WEST
Leeds
Leeds University Adult Education Department. Ask for: Jean Gardiner.
Park Lane College of Further Education. Return to Study (for men and women). Includes basic English, maths, study skills and counselling. Day time 8 hours per week, 10 weeks. Evening 2 hours per week, 10 weeks.
Swarthmore Education Centre. Fresh Start course. Ask for: Pamela Cole.

Wales

West Glamorgan
Bryn House Adult Education Centre.

Scotland

Fife

Lauder Technical College. Women's Studies. Ask for: Michael Morris.

Highland

Thurso Technical College. Ask for: Mrs Hughes or Mr Kinnaird.

Lothian

Edinburgh University, Department of Extra-Mural Studies, 11 Buccleuch Place, Edinburgh EH8 9JT. Tel: (031) 667 1011 ext 6246. Ask for: Mrs Mona Macdonald.

Tayside

Dundee University, Extra-Mural Department.

Northern Ireland

Newtownabbey

University of Ulster, Newtownabbey Campus. NOW course.

WOMAN, 32

I decided it would be more of a challenge to leave work and go to college and do A-levels and try and go to university. Everybody said to me 'you'll never do it – you haven't the brains' and that was the biggest motivation of all, not really the desire to study. I wanted to prove that I could do it. I ended up with an A, a B and a D and from there I went to university to do a degree in social administration and sociology.

---

20 Basics – reading, writing, maths and spoken English

BASIC EDUCATION FOR ADULTS

Until a few years ago, any adult who couldn't read, write, speak English or do basic maths could get almost no help from the education system. All that's now changed; basic education opportunities exist nearly everywhere in Britain, often free and usually cheaper than other courses. It's one of the most open and welcoming areas of the education system as far as adults are concerned. Every LEA provides some basic education as part of its adult and further education work and there are voluntary schemes in many areas offering help.

What's it like?
Often very good. Much of the basic education work being done is really exciting, both for the tutors and students. This is because it is based on your needs and wants, not what a teacher thinks you should want. It is also often very informal. It is probably the part of education that is least like school.

MAN, 40
With my first tutor, I did mostly reading. Then I went to a group as well. We worked on our own. The tutor helped us in turn. The people were very friendly and we had a good chat. I got more done with my own tutor, but gained a lot of confidence seeing other people learning to read. I learnt I wasn't the only one.

WHO'S IT FOR?

It is for anyone
- who can't read or write
- who has difficulty with spelling
- who can write but isn't confident about writing
- who can't do arithmetic or basic maths
- who can't speak English very well but does live in Britain
- who feels uncertain about any part of their basic education and wants a chance to polish it up
- who wants to start learning again but is worried about joining a class.

This sort of education tries to help people by boosting their confidence, helping them find out they can learn, getting them learning, so that they can use all the other education that's available if they want to.

WOMAN, 33
I went along to my daughter's school for a parents' meeting. We were talking about reading and someome said she was going to classes for it! I thought, that's what I need! I never realised I could do that – I mean, I thought I'd finished with education. She's going to take me along for a look, next week. I might as well give it a try!

How basic is basic?
Basic is a misleading term – it doesn't just mean absolute beginners, though it does include them too. What is included varies from place to place; some places are offering 'post-basic' education which may be courses that provide a bridge to GCSEs, to other adult education classes, or lead to an exam (see below).

WOMAN, 35
I'd been out of work for a long time and my confidence was at a low as it is when you're at home. I went on the course and I don't think I'll ever make a mathematician, but it made me realise that I wasn't as bad as I thought I was. I still make spelling errors, but so do lots of people. It is not because I can't spell, it's because I'm writing at quite a fast pace and I miss things out, but before I went on that course I didn't like people to watch me.

WHAT'S ON OFFER?

In almost every area you can get help with reading and writing. Most places also offer basic maths; in areas where there are a lot of non-English speaking people, there's also help with learning to speak English. There are also a number of interesting new projects which offer help on a drop-in basis with virtually anything from filling in forms to helping you help your children at school.

Where's it done?
You usually learn in a class, a small group, or just by yourself – sometimes with a volunteer tutor. It may be for a couple of hours a week or it could be more. It's partly up to you, but it also depends on what is available. It may be free or you may have to pay something.

It's usually done in colleges, adult education centres, evening institutes, at work, at home, at a volunteer tutor's home or anywhere else (even in the pub!), or in a drop-in centre.

MAN, 23, LEARNING MATHS
My tutor is great. We're both interested in the same things – hi fi! He knows things about it I don't; I know things he doesn't. My maths is going on alright. It's the basic stuff. I can do take aways now. I'm working on my tables and multiplication; long division is quite difficult. I tell him if I don't understand and he says, 'Well, we'll try another way'. While I work something out, he goes and makes some coffee.

TV and radio
There are a lot of useful programmes. The most famous – *On the move* - is over now, but it has been followed by others on all channels. All of them have some form of printed back-up and some have a referral service (see below). There are other programmes coming along all the time and most are repeated; for example, in the autumn of 1986 Channel 4 started a new series, *Write on*, to help people to develop their writing skills, at all levels. There is a workbook as well, called *Write on*. And the BBC's series *Switch on to English*, to help with improving spoken English, also had an accompanying book, with help in different languages. If you want to know how to find out what's coming look at *25 Radio and TV*.

★ **WRITE TO** The Adult Literacy and Basic Skills Unit, PO Box 213, London WC1V 7ET, for *Write on*, £1.50, and *Switch on to English*.

Student writing
One of the exciting aspects of basic education is the amount of student writing that has been published, often on a self-help basis. The student-written newspaper *Write first time* produced a list of books written by adult literacy and basic education students. For a copy of the list:

★ **WRITE TO** The Adult Literacy and Basic Skills Unit (ALBSU), Kingsbourne House, 229–231 High Holborn, London WC1V 7ET.

IF YOU'RE 16–18 YEARS OLD

You can still use the basic education chances in this chapter. In fact, adult literacy is a great way to carry on education after you leave school. You'll be amazed at how different it is. You're with other adults; you're a respected member of the group and your needs are what count. In the adult literacy world, all the teachers know that if they don't do a good job, their students will walk out. It makes a big difference! But there are also a lot of other things you could think about.

Further education (FE)
The whole range of opportunities in further education is developing rapidly and is described in more detail in *7 School leavers*.

A lot of FE colleges are now running courses specially for people who leave school, can't get a job and don't feel ready for GCSEs and A-levels. They have names like basis for choice, foundation courses, prevocational courses, coping with unemployment – all sorts of things. They're not usually called basic education though they should cover a lot of the same things. Some of them lead to a qualification, usually a certificate that says what you have learned and what an employer can expect of you.

These are often awarded by the City and Guilds, the Royal Society of Arts and the Regional Examining Bodies and BTEC (see *41 Qualifications*). Many of these courses will be absorbed in the new Certificate of Prevocational Education; in Scotland these courses have been reorganised under the 16–18 Action Plan.

If you want to do such a course, you should contact your local FE college. These are described in *16 Further education, adult education*. To find out which are near to where you live, look at the *Gazetteer*.

If you have a handicap
Most basic education schemes will do their best to help you. If you are disabled, for example, they may be able to arrange for a tutor to visit you at home; or will suggest a centre where access is easy. If you have a hearing problem, there may be help available. For those with a sight problem, there is advice available from the Royal National Institute for the Blind (RNIB).

★ **ASK** The Adult Literacy Co-ordinator, RNIB, RNIB Commercial Training College, 5 Pembridge Place, London W2 4XB. Tel: (01) 229 6673.

CAN YOU GET A QUALIFICATION?

One or two organisations offer qualifications to basic education students. The Royal Society of Arts (RSA) offers a Certificate of Continuing Education. The qualification is given for course work, and you also do a project. There's no actual exam; the examiner comes and talks it all over with you in a very friendly and informal way. You don't fail, but you can see the examiner more than once and you can take as long or as short a time as you like. There are also qualifications in both basic English and maths, which are done by taking an ordinary exam, offered by organisations like City and Guilds and RSA. The main bodies offering such exams are described in *41 Qualifications*. If you would like such a qualification, ask the tutor in charge of local basic education classes.

MAN, 35
When I came to the class, I was really nervous. I wasn't sure if I wanted to do it or not. I hated English at school, and always failed all the exams. But this has really changed my attitude. I really enjoyed meeting the examiner; I knew my work was good and now I'm determined to do GCSE. I feel at last I've laid to rest the ghost of my crummy education.

NATIONAL STUDENTS ASSOCIATION

A number of students in adult literacy schemes have got together to form the National Students Association which has now attracted funding from ALBSU and has a National Coordinator, Kathy Turner. The Association aims to increase student involvement in the running of their schemes and act as a means of mutual support. It does not cost anything to be a member.

★ **WRITE TO** The National Students Association, 41 Hamilton Square, Birkenhead, Merseyside. Tel: (051) 647 8456.

WHERE TO ASK FOR HELP WITH BASICS

For adult literacy, basic maths, spoken English
Find out who your local organiser is – you could ask at the library, local college or adult education centre. The list at the end of this chapter may be a good starting point. The *Gazetteer* explains how basic education is organised in each area and what it costs. You could also use the local educational guidance service for adults if one exists; they will be well informed about basic education provision locally. In Northern Ireland, contact the central referral service (below) first.

Referral services
If you still can't find the right person, you can contact one of the national referral points listed below who will pass your name on to someone locally, probably the LEA, possibly a voluntary scheme or the WEA.

England and Wales
The Adult Literacy and Basic Skills Unit (ALBSU), Kingsbourne House, 229–231 High Holborn, London WC1V 7ET.

Scotland
Network Scotland Ltd, 74 Victoria Crescent Road, Glasgow G12 9JQ. Tel: (041) 357 1774.

Northern Ireland
Reading and Writing Help Service (Northern Ireland), Room 208, Bryson House, 28 Bedford Street, Belfast BT2 7FE. Tel: (0232) 322488.

For spoken English at work
Ask your trade union representative or your employer direct. If you don't feel like doing that, contact the National Centre for Industrial Language Training, The Havelock Centre, Havelock Road, Southall, Middlesex UB2 4NZ. Tel: (01) 571 2241. There are local units as well and these are listed in *33 Training at work*.

Drop-in centres
There is a growing number of places which offer help as and when you want it. You just arrive, tell them what your problem is and they try and help you. Quite a few places are happy if you drop in, even though they don't call

themselves drop-in centres. If you want to know if there is one in your area, keep your eyes open since they should be quite good at local publicity, or ask your local organiser. The Citizens' Advice Bureau, the library or the local educational guidance service for adults may also know.

Main addresses of drop-in centres listed here can be found in the *Gazetteer*.

England

Berkshire
Reading Adult College. The Key Ring. Ask for: Jean Turton. Tel: (0734) 589900 ext 28.

Durham
Derwentside College. Drop-In Basic Education. Ask for: Jim McCaffery.

LONDON – GREATER
Newham
Newham Parents Centre. Ask for: Ray Phillips.

London – Inner
The Bookplace – Peckham. Ask for: Rosey Frazer.
Hammersmith Neighbourhood Literacy Scheme. Ask for: Phyllis Thompson.
Walk-in-Numeracy. Ask for: Joan O'Hagen.

MANCHESTER – GREATER
Wigan
Wigan College of Technology. Drop-In Centre.

MERSEYSIDE
Wirral
Conway Education Centre. Drop-in Centre. Ask for: Bet Plumbe.
Wirral Metropolitan College, Withens Lane Site.

Northumberland
Open Door Basic Skills/Open Learning Unit. Ask for: Mary Hall.

YORKSHIRE – WEST
Calderdale
The Education Shop. Ask for: Tony Lilley.

Leeds
Drop-in Education and Advice Centre.

Scotland

Lothian
Edinburgh Walk-in-Numeracy Centre. Ask for: Ros Richardson.

21 Adult residential colleges

ADULT RESIDENTIAL COLLEGES

The eight long-term adult resiedential colleges are a long-established method of returning to study for adults, as an end in itself or as preparation for higher education. The first was established in 1899; the latest has recently been started. The education they offer is academic and of a very high quality.

For information on other residential courses and leisure activities, see *27 Leisure classes; part-time, weekend, holidays*.

How they work

They have a number of things in common and we describe their general characteristics before giving details of each of the individual colleges.

- They offer what is quite clearly education and not training.
- They are residential (though limited non-residence is availabler at some).
- They offer one and two-year full-time courses, with some shorter ones.
- None of them demand formal entry qualifications. Normally selection is by interview; you usually have to give names of referees; you may have to write an essay.
- Most of them offer a qualification that satisfies higher education entrance requirements. They may also be suitable for entry to some professions.
- They are all recognised and grant-aided by the Department of Education and Science (DES), the Scottish Education Department (SED), or by the Welsh Office Education Department.
- Financial support is available in the form of an Adult Education State Bursary from the DES (in England), the SED (in Scotland) or the Welsh Office in Wales. Applicants resident in Scotland or Northern Ireland should apply respectively to the SED or the Department of Education, Northern Ireland. You have to be resident in Britain for three years to be eligible. If you are offered a place you will be given a form with which to apply for such a grant – you can't apply for one without having been offered a place first.
- The grants cover fees, residence and maintenance and dependents allowances.
- Most have other bursaries available as well – for details see each prospectus.
- The courses offered are mainly in humanities and social sciences. Some of the colleges are also concerned with industrial relations and trade union studies.
- The teaching is geared to the learning needs of each student; there are regular individual or small group tutorials with lectures and seminars and a lot of individual study. Essay writing is an important element.
- Terms are usually September to December, January to Easter, Easter to June.
- Overseas students, in limited numbers, are accepted by all. Fees are higher

than for UK students. Application is normally through the Ministry of Education in the applicant's country, or the British Council.

THE INDIVIDUAL COLLEGES

Coleg Harlech

Courses
Two-year courses leading to University of Wales Diploma in General Studies, recognised as satisfying British university entrance requirements. A few students can take one-year courses leading to college certificate. Internal exams only.

Subjects
Include English literature, history, economics, industrial relations, philosophy, politics, sociology, psychology, Welsh studies, Welsh language and literature, Llenyddiaeth Cymraeg.

Entry requirements
Minimum age 21. Entry is by interview alone. At least two referees. Final date for application 7 March of the year in which you wish to enter.

Notes
Men and women. About 140 students. College has its own audio-visual centre, theatre and squash courts. Residence in study bedrooms and hall of residence (or occasionally in lodgings). Also provides short residential summer schools.

★ **WRITE TO** The Registrar, Coleg Harlech, Harlech, Gwynedd LL46 2PU. Tel: (0766) 780363.

Co-operative College

Courses
One-year course in Policy Studies, January to December.

Subjects
Communication, numeracy and organisation skills. Case studies, study visits. Economic, social, financial management, and development policies.

Entry requirements
Enquiries and applications are welcome throughout the year. Applicants are expected to undertake a nine-week project in the summer period which will be of value to themselves, their colleagues and the community.-

Notes
They welcome applications from people who are 'non-academic' but have contributed to the well-being of the community. Eight study bedrooms can accommodate students in wheelchairs. Other courses are for officials from Third World countries, postgraduate trainee managers and employees of co-operatives.

★ **WRITE TO** The Director of Studies, Co-operative College, Stanford Hall, Loughborough, Leicestershire. LE12 5QR. Tel: (050982) 2333.

Fircroft College

Courses
One-year course in Liberal Studies. No final qualification or examination. Two-year part-time courses compatible with the 21 hour rule.

Subjects
Economics, politics, industrial relations, sociology, social anthropology, literature, philosophy, peace studies, mathematics.

Entry requirements
Minimum age 20, but no upper age limit. Three referees. Entry by essay and interview.

Notes
Fifty residential places; some in single study bedrooms, some in twin rooms, and a few non-residential. One study bedroom for a student in a wheelchair. It is part of Selly Oak Colleges (800 students, 50 nationalities) with many recreational and sporting facilities. Students can use the University library.

★ **WRITE TO** The Bursar, Fircroft College, Bristol Road, Selly Oak, Birmingham B29 6LH. Tel: (021) 472 0116.

Hillcroft College

Courses
One and two-year modular courses. Two-year course leads to CNAA Certificate, recognised for entry to professional and degree courses. Students select a flexible integrated package of four study areas. The social studies option, mainly for careers in social work and allied professions, includes four months' practical work and one year's community involvement.

Subjects
Art history, computer studies, drama, economics, literature, history, mathematics, numeracy, political ideas, psychology, study skills, social policy, social survey methods, sociology.

Entry requirements
Minimum age 21. Two referees. Interview and written excercise. Applications by 30 April. Short residential courses: July and September. Extensive short course programme open to full-time and part-time students.

Notes
Women only. Mainly residential (single study bedrooms) but some day students. Seventy full-time students per year.

★ **WRITE TO** The Secretary (AE), Hillcroft College, South Bank, Surbiton, Surrey KT6 6DF. Tel: (01) 399 2688.

Newbattle Abbey Adult College

Courses
One-year course in two subjects, leading to optional examinations. Two-year course leading to Diploma in Liberal Studies (recognised by Scottish universities and some English universities for university entrance).

Subjects
History, government, political theory, English literature, philosophy, sociology, economics, trade union studies, general studies, French.

Entry requirements
Applicants for two-year course must submit an essay. Interview. Two referees. Early application advised.

Notes
Only residential adult college in Scotland. Accommodation for 75 students in single and double study bedrooms. Remedial English provision available.

★ **WRITE TO** The College Secretary, Newbattle Abbey College, Dalkeith, Midlothian. Tel: (031) 663 1921.

Northern College

Courses
One and two-year courses leading to the award of the College's Certificate and Diploma respectively in Trade Union and Industrial Studies, Social and Community Studies and Liberal and Gateway Studies. One hundred and ten student places – over one third are reserved for students taking part in short courses of between one weekend and five weeks in a variety of different areas.

Subjects
All courses cover a number of basic disciplines and study skills. These include: history, sociology, economics, English literature, political thought, law, industrial relations, trade union studies, media studies, welfare state and community organisation, and a choice of optional subjects.

Entry requirements
Admission to one and two-year courses by interview. Minimum age usually 21.

Notes
Founded in 1978 by the LEAs of South Yorkshire, it has a strong local commitment. Accommodation in single and double study bedrooms. Limited child-care facilities available for children aged two and a half to five years.

★ **WRITE TO** The Senior Administrator, Northern College, Wentworth Castle, Stainborough, Barnsley, South Yorkshire S75 3ET. Tel: (0226) 285426.

Plater College

Courses
Two-year courses lead to Special Diploma in Social Administration or Social

Studies. This can be endorsed for supervised social work training and may give access to one-year courses leading to Certificate of Qualification in Social Work, Diplomas in Ethics and Social Studies or Theology and Social Studies.

One-year courses leading to the College Certificate in Social Studies for Parish Visitors, or the College Certificate in Social Ethics.

All students follow a College certificate course in theology and ethics and there are optional courses in statistics and in mathematics for economists.

Entry requirements
Minimum age 21. As well as two referees, reference will be asked from a parish priest. Although this is a Catholic college, applications from other practising Christians are welcomed. Essay. Interview.

Notes
Catholic workers' college. Both sexes. 80 students.

★ **WRITE TO** The Tutor for Admissions, Plater College, Pullens Lane, Oxford OX3 0DT. Tel: (0865) 67626.

Ruskin College

Courses
Two-year diploma course in one of labour studies, literature, development studies, history, social studies; students may take an individual programme of study leading to a Certificate of Studies with or without formal assessment.

Two-year Diploma in Applied Social Studies recognised by Central Council for Education and Training in Social Work. Includes supervised practical work. Pre-course placement with an appropriate agency may be required.

Facilities also available for study of French, German, or Spanish.

Entry requirements
Minimum age 20 (25 for Diploma in Applied Social Studies). 1,000 to 2,000 word essay. Interview. Applications by 31 January.

Notes
Approximately 180 students. A few non-resident 'external' students. Also four flats and two houses for married students and their families – usually reserved for second-year students.

★ **WRITE TO** The General Secretary, Ruskin College, Oxford OX1 2HE. Tel: (0865) 54331 for a prospectus and particulars of scholarships and admissions.

22 Getting a degree: higher education

HIGHER EDUCATION

Higher education leads mainly to degrees (BA, MA, BSc, LLB etc and also the DipHE). For more on these, see *41 Qualifications*. This chapter seeks to show how some providers cope with adults. All are listed; for full details

★ **LOOK AT** *The student book* (see *Booklist*).

What we don't include

We have not fully covered a number of specialist fields:

- in-service BEd degrees for serving teachers
- postgraduate degrees, diplomas or certificates
- all 'degree equivalent' courses in performing arts
- professional qualifications equivalent to first degrees
- the diploma in higher education.

HE is an adult experience as the teaching approach assumes maturity in the students. During the last twenty years, there has been a vast expansion to cope with increased demands from school leavers. Because good A-levels are the mark of a successful school pupil HE institutions have come to rely on these as a way of selecting from many thousands of school leavers. HE is competitive, proud of it, and interested in high standards. They want successful people as students. Often, adults returning to education have not been successful at school.

HE is becoming more welcoming to adults, with or without A-levels (though some places are distinctly unhelpful to older people, and some courses, like medicine, have age limits). The ultimate example of openess is the creation of the Open University which lets anyone in on a first come first served basis.

Higher education and adults

All higher education institutions are open to adults – it's just that some are more welcoming than others. Some take this as far as having special schemes which allow for the particular difficulties adults face. Since universities are self-governing each one has its own policy; but all places offering CNAA degrees have the automatic right to admit unqualified mature students to those courses. They may welcome adults in a number of ways.

- With special entrance schemes. The normal way into HE is through O- and A-levels. Other qualifications are often taken as being equivalent (including many professional and technical ones). Or you may do an HE preparatory course (described in *18 Adult routes*). They may set you their own exam, or let you in on the strength of an interview alone, because of your experience.
- Some places provide child care facilities.
- Some places provide accommodation for married students – many HE institutions have their own living accommodation and they may reserve some for married students.
- Many places run part-time or evening degree courses.
- There are some courses designed for adults. One example is at North East London Polytechnic where you can design your own course.

But remember, all HE is run in big organisations. Even if they have a special policy, the first person you speak to may not know about it, so persist. When it comes to it you may well want to go to the place nearest to you, but it is noticeable that where colleges do have special arrangements, people travel considerable distances to go to them in preference to other more local colleges. It is not unusual for people to study away from home in HE. Most degree courses are full-time and last for three years (four in Scotland). Some are part-time and take longer and there are also sandwich degrees which combine study in college with blocks of work – usually in industry.

Is it for you?

If you are returning to education, HE is worth considering first without worrying about GCSEs and A-levels or Scottish Highers as you have a right to get a grant to study for a first degree. (Be careful of all the catches – see *40 LEA grants*.) If you don't think you could cope straight away, you could try:

- an HE preparatory course (described in *18 Adult routes*)
- a course at an adult residential college (see *21 Adult residential colleges*)
- GCSEs and A-levels at a college of FE
- distance learning (described in *17 Flexible learning*) or a correspondence course (see *26 Learning by post*).

Where can you do a degree?

There are six main types of place providing higher education:

- Universities – there are 44 in Britain which receive public money. They award their own qualifications and are the oldest established providers of HE.
- The Open University – one of the 44 but special – you study their courses at home. See *23 The Open University*.
- Polytechnics – there are 30 of these in England and Wales. They are run by local education authorities and usually award CNAA degrees.
- Colleges and institutes of higher education – these are comparatively new, and have usually been formed by the merger or development of teacher training colleges with other colleges. However, many are still being merged or closed. Their degrees are either from the CNAA or a neighbouring university.

- Central institutions – there are 11. They provide most of the advanced full-time courses in Scotland outside universities and are directly funded by the Scottish Education Department. Their degrees are from the CNAA or a neighbouring university.
- A few surviving teacher training colleges, the private University of Buckingham, a few FE colleges and other places offer degree level studies.

THE CNAA

The Council for National Academic Awards (CNAA) is a central body that awards degrees and other qualifications to people who have studied in polytechnics, colleges of higher education and other places. CNAA degrees are specially attractive to adults for a number of reasons.

Getting in

You can start them without any formal entry qualifications. All the colleges offering them are allowed to admit you if, in the college's opinion, you could benefit from the course. Most of them look for some sort of qualification, or evidence that you've done some recent studying, perhaps a preparatory course. Technical courses (eg maths) usually require previous study of the subject. You must have O-level English and maths (or an acceptable equivalent) to do a BEd (teacher training) course.

Moving around

Higher education is the part of the education system which has got furthest with credit transfer. That can mean several things:

- recognising one qualification as equal to another for entry to a course
- letting you *not* do part of a course because of a qualification you already have
- starting a course in one place, then moving somewhere else and having what you did in the first place counted in the second.

The CNAA allows many colleges teaching for its qualifications to make transfer arrangements, though the individual college makes decisions about individual cases; eg you can usually do the two-year DipHE in one place and do the final degree year somewhere else. Because so many polytechnics and colleges teach for CNAA degrees, it's easier to transfer credits between them than between universities, a point worth noting if you're likely to have to move while studying. For details of Open University credit transfers see *23 The Open University*. See also *41 Qualifications*.

Modular courses

During 1986 the CNAA established a Credit Accumulation and Transfer Scheme (CATS). This aims to provide additional flexible educational opportunities for students in both university and public sector higher education. CATS offers an advisory service for individual students on the credit rating of their qualifications and work experience in order to facilitate their admission, with exemption where appropriate, to existing courses both at undergraduate and postgraduate level. In addition it offers the opportunity for students to construct a tailor-made programme of studies leading to a CNAA award. A fee of £25 is charged where an assessment interview is considered appropriate.

★ **ASK** the CATS Unit at the CNAA (address below).

Some degrees are made up of several free standing courses called modules. You get credits for each one completed. To earn your degree you have to build up the right number of credits. (You may only be able to study certain combinations of modules.) The OU is the most developed example of this approach. Several CNAA approved modular courses have also been established; a good example is Oxford Polytechnic (see below).

Part-time degree courses

There are a lot of CNAA part-time degree courses, in all subject areas. For details of CNAA degrees:

★ **SEND FOR** *Directory of first degree courses* and *Opportunities in higher education for mature students*. Both are free, from Publications Officer, CNAA, 344/345 Grays Inn Road, London WC1X 8BP. Tel: (01) 278 4411.

UNIVERSITIES

The only HE institutions which are not linked to LEAs. They get their money direct from central government. They have more freedom to decide what they are going to do and how to do it, are quite often a lot richer than other types of colleges, and award their own degrees. Usually you have to live in or near the university you are studying at and may have to attend a minimum number of lectures, seminars and tutorials. The holidays are long (about six months of the year) but you are expected to work on your own during that time (though some people don't). The long holidays are a good time to get a part-time job. To find out what each university offers:

★ **SEND FOR** The prospectus from any university you are interested in.

UCCA

The Universities Central Council on Admissions is the central place to apply for most first-degree full-time courses in universities in the United Kingdom. The exceptions are the Open University, University of Buckingham and Cranfield Institute of Technology. For a list of most universities, their addresses, courses and how to apply:

★ **SEND FOR** *How to apply for admission to a university*, free from UCCA, PO Box 28, Cheltenham, Gloucester GL50 1HY.

For a good guide to what to study and where to study it:

★ **LOOK AT** *The student book* (see *Booklist*).

How can universities be more open?
Every university listed in the *Compendium of university entrance requirements* (it should be in your local library) has some kind of special policy towards mature entrants without the usual qualifications. For particular courses (especially science) you may need to have studied particular subjects before. Do check.

Most want you to show evidence of recent study, suggesting that any HE preparatory course might help you get into any university. Because universities have the widest choice of applicants, they can get what they consider the 'best' students – those with the best exam results. But there is a growing realisaton that mature students may be of a high standard even without the qualifications.

You may choose a university because you live nearby (though universities *don't* usually have policies favouring local people) or for some other reason. Ask about their likely attitude before you make your UCCA application. Don't just ask the admissions tutor or registrar. Get the prospectus and write to the head of the department concerned, asking if you could have a chat about your situation. Whatever happens, you will still have to put in your UCCA application later.

UNIVERSITY TEACHER
I came out of the RAF, worked in a stereo shop, wanted to study music, but hadn't any qualifications though I could play several instruments and composed things. I didn't know what to do. Somebody said just go and ask. I did. I went, talked, played my compositions and got accepted. Now I'm a university teacher.

Even if you are qualified they may not accept you and they probably won't tell you why – so be prepared for disappointments.

How some universities deal with adults
Universities with mature student entry, working with open college access schemes are coded MS in the *Gazetteer* and the list at the end of this chapter.

The JMB universities
Birmingham, Leeds, Liverpool, Manchester and Sheffield Universities and University of Manchester Institute of Science and Technology (UMIST) are members of the Joint Matriculation Board (JMB). These universities and the colleges whose degrees they validate may accept unqualified mature students through their mature students entry exam. Even if you pass, they still consider you rather carefully, but it's a move towards more openness. They have produced a leaflet describing the scheme:

★ **SEND FOR** *21+ Returning to learning* free from The Secretary, Joint Matriculation Board, Manchester M15 6EU.

University of East Anglia
Seems to welcome mature students and offer a lot of choice of subjects. It accepts professional qualifications for entry, and welcomes applications from people without qualifications who can show evidence of recent study.

University of Essex
Is always glad to receive applications from mature students who are usually asked to submit some written work or take a special exam if they don't have normal qualifications. It recently offered a place to a student from the Open College of the North West and takes students from the access course at City and East London College.

University of Hull
Mature entrants can be admitted in special circumstances. It's up to the individual department. But it also accepts a lot of non-GCE qualifications for entry, including SRN, and has a reputation for friendliness.

University of Keele
Usually interviews mature applicants if they have attended a systematic course of study in the last three years (by contrast, only a small proportion of other applicants are interviewed). Four-year course includes general foundation year. Three-year course also offered.

University of Kent at Canterbury
Has a clear policy of welcoming mature students and also, unusually, local students. The continuing education department is participating in a scheme with local adult education centres to provide alternative routes for adult students.

University of Lancaster
Asks you to submit written work, like evidence of recent study. Involved in setting up the Open College Federation of the North West (see *18 Adult routes*), and has opened up its lecture programmes to members of the public.

University of Sussex
Has a long standing special entry system, involving written work, interviews and evidence of recent study.

Lucy Cavendish College
The Cambridge college for mature women – willing to consider applicants with other qualifications equivalent to A-level.

The University of Ulster
Runs its own preparatory course at the Magee Campus, Londonderry.

The University of Glasgow
Runs its own preparatory course for adults.

London University
Has a long history of catering for mature students. Birkbeck College and Goldsmiths' College offer part-time degrees in the evenings. The University also offers external degrees.

Birkbeck College
Specialises in courses for part-time and evening students doing first and higher degrees. Always on the look-out for new ideas. They do accept mature students without GCEs who have other qualifications (diplomas, degrees, HND, HNC, professional qualifications) or who can show evidence of mature age study. Part-time students attend two to four evenings a week, from 6 to 9 pm. (See *Gazetteer – Colleges of London University*.)

Goldsmiths' College
Offers a number of part-time degrees and diplomas in the evening. Accepts mature students from ethnic minorities who have done the preparatory course at South East London College. Also looking at distance learning for adults, and unlike most university colleges does a wide range of non-degree courses and qualifications, and has an active adult education programme in the area. (See *Gazetteer – Colleges of London University*.)

London University external degrees
The oldest way of getting a degree part-time. They are a bit cheaper than the Open University but are quite different in several ways. They prefer you to have A-levels so it's harder to get in. They offer single subject degrees, not modular ones like the OU. There are programmes in law, economics, management, arts, music and divinity. You organise your study for yourself; you can get a correspondence course from one of the correspondence colleges (see *26 Learning by post*). There is an advisory service to help external students.

★ **WRITE TO** The Secretary for External Students, University of London, Senate House, Malet Street, London WC1E 7HU. Tel: (01) 636 8000. Ask for *First degrees and diplomas for external students: general information.*

But do try any university.

Occasional students
Many universities will allow people to attend some courses and sit in on lectures without registering for a degree. This is geared to people from overseas but many will allow UK residents to do the same. How much they charge, what they'll let you attend and entry requirements vary enormously. Lancaster University has decided to open most of its lectures to the public. It is indicated in the list at the end of the chapter where such schemes exist.

POLYTECHNICS

The polytechnics offer many courses similar to those of universities, but there are some differences: they have a stronger bias towards training for jobs; most of their degrees are awarded by the CNAA; their holidays are slightly shorter; their entry requirements are slightly lower; LEAs pay for them directly – they are not so independent; some offer the Diploma in Higher Education (DipHE); a lot have part-time courses. For the adult, they offer a more flexible approach, especially if you live nearby. They have also developed some interesting schemes for adults like polymaths and polyphysics (see *18 Adult routes*).

Application

A new central application procedure has been established: this excludes art and design and teacher training.

The system has been set up by the Committee of Directors of Polytechnics and is known as Polytechnics Central Admissions Scheme (PCAS). It covers first-degrees and DipHE courses.

There is also a Polytechnic Clearing Scheme. Vacancies are displayed on computer via the Times Network System and on Prestel.

★ **WRITE TO** PCAS, PO Box 67, Cheltenham, Gloucester GL50 3AP.

For a list of most polytechnics and their courses:

★ **LOOK AT** *Polytechnic courses*, Lund Humphries, for the Committee of Directors of Polytechnics.

★ **LOOK AT** *The student book* (see *Booklist*).

Some more open polytechnics

Hatfield Polytechnic

Very welcoming to mature students – looks sympathetically at any non-standard qualifications or experience. Also has a wide ranging set of services aimed at adults called the Continuing Education Programme. Includes:

- Part-time degrees and diplomas and postgraduate courses. A wider range than usual, normally one afternoon and two evenings a week, but can be negotiated.
- BA Contemporary Studies: a part-time day degree or degree with honours; 10 am to 3 pm for a maximum of three days a week, leading to a degree or a degree with honours in four years depending on the rate of study chosen.
- Associate Students – study one or more units from the degree or diploma programme. They don't do the whole course – just the unit they want.
- A kind of 'Open Door' policy, letting people into courses for interest as well as qualifications. (You can take the exams if you want to; if you pass you get a credit towards a degree.) Attendance is usually two to three hours a week.
- Non-degree part-time programmes: usually lead to a national qualification.
- Shortened Day Courses – for students with home commitments – 10 am to 3 pm for BA contemporary studies, NOW and Polyprep.
- New Opportunities for Women (NOW) – a guide to opportunities for mature women wanting to start or come back to a career.
- Polyprep – a short course to prepare you for a return to study; study skills, essay writing etc. Two days a week for eight weeks, it's run three times a year. Also part two, leading to a certificate.

North East London Polytechnic

Their most dramatic innovation is the Diploma in Higher Education by Independent Study. Available full- or part-time. It's special because they are more interested in motivation and whether you're likely to benefit than in previous education. On the course you can also brush up on your reading, writing and study skills if they're a bit rusty. All eligible applicants are invited for interview. You devise your own programme of study. In your first term, you write a 'statement' which is the basis of your course. It describes:

- where have I been? (experience of education and work up to now)
- where am I now? (what strengths and weaknesses do I have?)
- where do I want to go to? (what level do I want to reach?)
- how am I going to get there? (what do I have to do to become the person I want to be? What skills do I need? What programmes of study should I have?)
- how will I know if I have arrived? (what should be the level of my achievement?)

If you're not sure what to do, you're encouraged to tour the Polytechnic, to help you choose. You negotiate your own supervisor who is a specialist in your subject area, and your own access to the resources and the courses of the whole of the rest of the Polytechnic.

Oxford Polytechnic
Though they don't bend over backwards to admit mature students without qualifications, they offer one of the most flexible courses available which is particularly suitable for adults. It's a 'mixed mode' degree. Not just full-time or part-time, you can do a mixture: one term part-time, one term full-time, as required. It's also a modular degree: you choose two fields from a large number of subjects, choose modules within the fields plus a few floating modules too according to your interests. You build up credits towards a general degree. You can't take unlimited time to complete your degree but you have a lot of flexibility and choice about pace and your own individual course of study.

London polytechnics
All the London polytechnics are becoming actively involved in provision for adults. Most have links to access courses (see *18 Adult routes*). They are involved in the setting up of the open colleges in London (the Polytechnic of the South Bank is the basis of the Open College of the South Bank), and have had a variety of other initiatives – a short course unit at the Polytechnic of Central London, an active Continuing Education Unit at Thames Polytechnic and so on.

Try any polytechnic; all over the country they are becoming involved in similar initiatives.

COLLEGES AND INSTITUTES OF HE

The newest higher education institutions. Usually smaller than polytechnics and universities; they offer a wide choice of courses. Some are LEA colleges, 21 are independent; some of those are colleges of education. They often offer courses below degree level; most offer CNAA degrees (though some prepare you for a local university degree); many offer the DipHE. They have the lowest admittance requirements and are often very supportive places to study. You apply to them direct except for subjects with central application procedures (see *42 Things to study*).

For a list of all the colleges and institutes of higher education:

★ **LOOK AT** *The colleges and institutes of higher education.* £1.00 from Mr G Mann, Standing Conference of Principals and Directors of Colleges and Institutes in Higher Education, Edge Hill College of Higher Education, Ormskirk, Lancashire L39 4QP. Tel: (0695) 75171.

★ **LOOK AT** *The student book* (see *Booklist*).

★ **LOOK AT** *Compendium of advanced courses in colleges of further and higher education,* £3.00 from the Regional Advisory Council for London and South Eastern Region, Tavistock House South, Tavistock Square, London WC1H 9LR. Tel: (01) 388 0027.

Some more Open Colleges of HE

Bulmershe College
Of special interest is its unique link with the Open University. It means that OU students can do some Bulmershe courses (not in the OU programme) and Bulmershe students can do some OU courses. The courses tend to be practical ones you can't do with the Open University like art, film, drama, sport, recreation and leisure and music. Students who have done the courses are, on the whole, delighted with them. It seems to be a way of getting the best of two worlds – belonging to a small college community and working independently as part of the vast OU operation.

BULMERSHE STUDENT
With the OU, there's little discussion with the tutors – most of the discussion is remedial. Here, you can actually talk about work before you do it. You know where you're going. Within the OU you're working in the dark. This is quite a luxury.

Bradford and Ilkley Community College
A college of higher education that caters for a very wide range of needs. Everything from learning to speak, read and write, to degree level work. The staff are very welcoming to adult students, and anxious to bring them in. Particularly interesting are:

Mature Students' Certificate Course
This is a drop-in group for mothers and toddlers (or any other one who needs to drop in). It is not a course, but it can become one if anyone wants it to. It can lead to a diploma in higher education, mainly concerned with problems of urban, industrial and multi-cultural society.

SCOTLAND

As indicated earlier, the situation in Scotland is somewhat different. There is a very useful publication which describes the approach to admission of mature students in all 28 colleges and universities in Scotland which admit degree students:

★ **SEND FOR** *A mature applicant's guide to Scottish degree courses*, produced by Fife Careers Service, Fife House, North Street, Glenrothes KY7 5LT. Tel: (0592) 754411.

★ **SEND FOR** *Scottish universities entrance guide* (£1.50), Scottish Universities Council on Entrance, Kinnessburn, Kennedy Gardens, St Andrews KY16 9DR.

For a list of the Central Institutions and their courses:

★ **SEND FOR** *The handbook of the Scottish Central Institutions*, available from the Publications Officer, Paisley College of Technology, High Street, Paisley PA1 2BE.

MORE INFORMATION

Higher Education Information Service (HEIS)
The Service provides free information about opportunities in higher and some professional education throughout the UK. The main objective of the service is to help individuals identify opportunities open to them at all institutions.

Courses covered are at first degree, Diploma of Higher Education and BTEC Higher Diploma levels. Course details such as length, structure and entry requirements are given. The use of a computer enables up-to-the-minute information to be retrieved readily and used as the basis for answering enquiries about undergraduate courses.

The information service is available throughout the year. The HEIS library contains prospectuses for every university, polytechnic and further education college in the UK.

Each summer, in collaboration with *The observer*, HEIS provides prospective students with a computerised list of undergraduate vacancies on courses at all institutions of higher education outside the university sector. For full details of the Centre's services:

★ **WRITE TO** Head of Information Centre, HEIS, Middlesex Polytechnic, 114 Chase Side, London N14 5PN. Tel: (01) 886 6599.

Educational Counselling and Credit Transfer Information Service (ECCTIS)
ECCTIS is a national computerised information service which holds details of all degree courses in the country. There is more information about its coverage in *1 Advice and help* and *40 Qualifications*.

Because there is a very wide range of higher education opportunities in the UK, the ECCTIS information bank is large. To make best use of the enquiry service it is advisable to make your enquiry as precise as possible; generalised replies can produce several hundred answers about 'appropriate' courses – far too much information for any enquirer to handle sensibly.

To avoid this information overkill, ECCTIS like enquirers to specify four things:

- subject areas (preferably narrowed down, eg to mechanical engineering rather than just engineering), both subjects in any enquiry about joint degrees
- level of study, ie postgraduate or first degree etc
- mode of study, ie full-time or part-time, sandwich courses or distance learning
- where you want to study, ie anywhere in the UK, in a particular town or region, preferences between university, polytechnic or college of HE.

For more information:

★ **ASK** ECCTIS, PO Box 88, Walton Hall, Milton Keynes MK7 6DI Tel: (0908) 368921.

TEACHER TRAINING

Teacher training takes place in polytechnics, colleges of higher education and colleges of education. Applications are made centrally. Teacher training courses normally expect you to have O- and A-levels, but as BEd courses usually lead to CNAA degrees there is provision for unqualified adults to be admitted. However, all entrants to teaching must have O-level English language and maths (or equivalent), so you'll need these before you start. Also anyone over 45 is unlikely to be accepted unless offering subjects where teachers are in short supply. There are courses which are acceptable alternatives, for students over 25 who are going on to do a BEd. For more information about teacher training:

★ **ASK** The Central Register and Clearing House, 3 Crawford Place, London W1H 2BN.

For all teacher training courses in Scotland:

★ **ASK** Advisory Service on Entry to Teaching, 5 Royal Terrace, Edinburgh EH7 5AF. Tel: (031) 556 0072.

For all teacher training courses in Northern Ireland:

★ **SEND FOR** *Courses of initial full-time teacher training provided by universities and colleges in Northern Ireland*, from Department of Education for Northern Ireland, Rathgael House, Balloo Road, Bangor, Co Down BT19 2PR. Tel: (0247) 66311.

To check if your existing qualifications allow you to teach in England and Wales:

★ **ASK** the DES, Mowden Hall, Staindrop Road, Darlington, Co Durham. Tel: (0325) 60155.

HIGHER DEGREES

All universities and polytechnics and some colleges of higher education offer higher degrees. There are different levels, and different ways of doing them but you usually have to have already done a first degree.

Taught courses: you follow a course and write a short thesis. Takes one to two years full time, longer part time. Usually leads to an MA or MSc.

Research degrees: by thesis alone. Takes from two years full time, three years part time for an MPhil, longer for a PhD.

For further details: write to the university, polytechnic or college that interests you. Ask for details of postgraduate studies. Say whether you want a taught course or a research degree and the subject area in which you are interested.

For CNAA postgraduate courses:

★ **SEND FOR** *Directory of postgraduate and postexperience courses*, free from CNAA, 344/354 Grays Inn Road, London WC1X 8BP. Tel: (01) 278 4411.

For a description of all postgraduate courses in the country:

★ **LOOK AT** *CRAC graduate studies*, Hobsons Limited, annual.

What about money?

Finance is likely to be the most difficult part of doing a full-time postgraduate degree – competition for grants is strong and there are age limits on many of them (see *39 Money: what for, where from*). If you're doing a part-time course, there is a good chance that your employer will help with your fees. Do ask.

DPhil DROPOUT

I did my first year without a grant, so I did all sorts of jobs from baby sitting to writing an encyclopaedia to keep going. Then I got a grant for three years. Just as I felt what I was writing was really good, I stopped. I was panicking because it was so depressing writing at home. I thought 'I'll never get an academic job and I'll never get another job either'. So I started working full-time with young people, and my thesis gradually drifted away. I keep telling myself I'll go back to it one day.

BUSINESS SCHOOLS

Postgraduate programmes (from short courses to PhD studies) in a wide range of business and management subjects, geared to the needs of executives. This is one area where you don't have to already have a first degree. Many universities have a business school but those in London and Manchester are free standing.

★ **ASK** London Business School, Sussex Place, Regents Park, London NW1 4SA. Tel: (01) 262 5050.

★ **ASK** Manchester Business School, Booth Street West, Manchester M15 6PB. Tel: (061) 273 8228.

PART-TIME DEGREE COURSES

We list these because they are so accessible to adults. Many are CNAA courses, though a number of universities have run, or are running part-time courses. For more information, write to the institution concerned. Addresses are listed in the *Gazetteer*.

England

Avon

Bristol Polytechnic. Biological sciences; business studies; electrical engineering; law; applied physics; special education; humanities.

Bedfordshire

Bedford College of Higher Education. Combined studies.
Luton College of Higher Education. Science.

Berkshire

Bulmershe College of Higher Education. BA combined studies; in-service BEd.
Reading University.

Cambridgeshire

Cambridgeshire College of Arts and Technology. Electronic engineering; geography; humanities/social studies.

Cheshire

Chester College. Combined studies; health and community studies. BA in health and community studies.
Crewe and Alsager College of Higher Education. Combined studies in BA and BSc; multidisciplinary.

Cleveland

Teesside Polytechnic. Chemistry; humanities; more courses planned.

Cornwall

Cornwall Education Centre. BEd for local teachers. Diplomas in maths and science.

Cumbria

West Cumbria College. English; law; computing; chemistry; physics; history; psychology; sociology; maths.

Devon

Plymouth Polytechnic. Mathematics; combined studies (science and social science); social policy and administration.

Derbyshire

Derbyshire College of Higher Education. In-service BEd.

Dorset

Dorset Institute of Higher Education. Business studies; business studies; computer aided engineering; catering administration; communication and media production; financial services; tourism studies.

Essex

Chelmsford College of Further Education. BTEC Higher Certificates; applied chemistry and medical laboratory sciences. Membership of Royal Society of Chemistry. Part 3 Association of Accounting Technicians.
Essex Institute of Higher Education. Law; mathematics; education; quantity surveying.

Gloucestershire

College of St Paul and St Mary. Choice of two subjects from: English; geography; history; religious studies.
Gloucestershire College of Arts and Technology. Computing; mathematics.

Hampshire

College of Maritime Studies. Nautical studies.
King Alfred's College. History with English.
La Sainte Union College of Higher Education. Modern languages and European studies.
Portsmouth Polytechnic. Politics.
Southampton Institute of Higher Education. Modern languages and European studies.

Hereford and Worcester

Kidderminster College of Further Education. Carpet and textile design only.

Worcester College of Higher Education. Courses for teachers: 6 weeks to 2 years. Diploma in higher education covering first two years of BA course.

Hertfordshire

Hatfield Polytechnic. Applied biology; applied chemistry; applied physics; computer science; contemporary studies; English with historical studies; humanities; mathematics.

Hertfordshire College of Art and Design. Fine art.

Humberside

Hull University. Law; regional and local history; social studies; theology; modern literary and historical studies; moral philosopy; classical studies; European art and civilization.

Humberside College of Higher Education. Applied biology; business studies; combined studies; humanities; secretarial studies; social studies; visual studies.

Kent

Canterbury Christ Church College. Arts and science.

Mid-Kent College of Higher and Further Education. Half day a week 3-year course leading to BEd.

University of Kent at Canterbury. German; women's studies; philosophy; English literature; local history; law; ecology; social sciences; theology; humanities; French.

Lancashire

Edge Hill College of Higher Education. History; geography; English; applied social science; urban policy and race relations.

Lancashire Polytechnic. Business studies; law; combined studies (humanities, sciences, social sciences); quantity surveying.

Lancaster University. Part-time degree at Part 1 (first year) level, also second and third years majors in independent study, humanities and social sciences course.

Nelson and Colne College. First year of Lancashire Polytechnic combined studies degree.

Leicestershire

Leicester Polytechnic. Applied physics; textile and knitwear technology; business studies; law; social sciences; surveying.

Leicester University. Combined arts; combined science; economic/social history; economics; geography; politics; sociology; applied sociology and some combinations of these.

Loughborough University of Technology. English; history.

LONDON – GREATER

Croydon

Croydon College. Law.

Spurgeons College. Theology.

Ealing

Ealing College of Higher Education. Business studies; humanities; law.

Enfield

Middlesex Polytechnic. Modular scheme; electronic engineering design and production; multidisciplinary social science; contemporary cultural studies; economics and geography; photographic media studies.

Harrow

Harrow College of Higher Education. Photographic media studies, multi-disciplinary.

Hounslow

West London Institute of Higher Education. Joint honours degrees from any two of the following: American studies; English; geography; history; religious studies.

Kingston-upon-Thames

Kingston Polytechnic. Aeronautical engineering; civil engineering; economics and politics; geography; languages; mechanical engineering; computer sciences; modern arts; music.

Richmond

Richmond-upon-Thames Tertiary College. BTEC Higher National Certificate in engineering and photographic studies.

Waltham Forest

North East London Polytechnic. Applied biology; architecture (only available to overseas students); archeological sciences; business studies; civil engineering; health studies; independent study; law; life sciences; mathematics; psychology; sociology.

LONDON – INNER

City of London Polytechnic. Business studies; metallurgy and materials.

Holborn Law Tutors. Law only.

London Business School. Business.

North London Polytechnic. Sociology; modern history; geography; English studies; combined studies (including two from the preceding subjects, plus: applied ecomonics; accounting; European literature studies; labour studies; women's studies; law; film studies); architecture; chemistry.

Polytechnic of Central London. Computing; social science; Arabic, Chinese, German or Russian; business studies; chiropody; law; photography.

South Bank Polytechnic. Building; business studies; civil engineering; chemical engineering; education; electrical and electronic engineering; environmental engineering; physics; mechanical engineering; social sciences; surveying; town planning.

Thames Polytechnic, incorporating Avery Hill College. Architecture; English studies; business studies; applied chemistry; applied biology; building surveying; civil engineering; computing science; electrical engineering; material science; estate management; mechanical engineering; quantity surveying; humanities; mathematics; statistics and computing.

University of London:

Birkbeck College. All courses available part-time.

Goldsmith's College. Religion; sociology; anthropology; psychology; mathematical studies; music; anthropology and psychology; anthropology and sociology (1988).

London School of Economics. Computing; geography; mathematics; social psychology; statistics.

St Martins School of Art. Fine art and critical studies.

MANCHESTER – METROPOLITAN DISTRICTS

Bolton

Bolton Institute of Higher Education. Humanities; mathematics; psychology.

Manchester

Manchester Polytechnic. Public administration; humanities; social studies; librarianship; applied chemistry; applied computing; combined studies; electronic engineering studies; business studies; engineering; law; physics; mathematics; nursing studies; polymer science and technology; psychology; manufacturing metallurgy; applied biological sciences.

Manchester University. Arts; nursing studies

UMIST. Some part-time MSc degrees offered.

Rochdale

Rochdale College of Art. Art and design.

Salford

University of Salford. Politics and contemporary history; sociology.

Stockport

Stockport College of Technology. Chemistry; HNC bridging course in chemistry.

MERSEYSIDE

Liverpool

Liverpool Institute of Higher Education. English environmental studies; geography; history; psychology.

Liverpool Polytechnic. Applied biology; business studies; electrical and electronic engineering; law; mathematics; mechanical engineering; quantity surveying; social studies.

Norfolk

University of East Anglia. History; history of art; sociology; philosophy; American studies; education.

Northamptonshire

Nene College. Health science.

Nottinghamshire

Trent Polytechnic. Applied chemistry; biological sciences; business studies; civil engineering; computer studies; engineering; humanities; law; modern European studies; quantity surveying; urban estate surveying.

University of Nottingham. Philosophy; politics; sociology; social administration; theology.

Oxfordshire

Oxford Polytechnic. Multi-disciplinary.

Staffordshire

North Staffordshire Polytechnic. Business studies; international studies; law; physics with electronics.

Surrey

North East Surrey College of Technology. Biological sciences; nursing studies.

Sussex – East

Brighton Polytechnic. Applied chemistry; business studies; combined studies (humanities); nursing studies.

Sussex – West

West Sussex Institute of Higher Education.

TYNE AND WEAR -METROPOLITAN DISTRICTS

Newcastle-upon-Tyne

Newcastle-upon-Tyne Polytechnic. Applied computing; business studies; applied chemistry; law; history of modern art; health studies; engineering technology; mathematics; physical electronics.

Newcastle-upon-Tyne University. Philosophy; religious studies.

Sunderland

Sunderland Polytechnic. Combined studies (Arts); engineering; materials science; science subjects; fine art; management studies.

WEST MIDLANDS – METROPOLITAN DISTRICTS

Birmingham

City of Birmingham Polytechnic. Business studies; electronic engineering; estate management; government; law; quantity surveying; mechanical engineering; economics; English language and literature.

University of Birmingham. Two-year part-time courses in English and theology lead to full-time or study for second year or BA course in these subjects.

Coventry

Coventry (Lanchester) Polytechnic. Applied economics; mathematics; modern studies in politics and history; engineering; applied social science; remedial health sciences; urban and regional planning.

Warwick University. Classical civilization; English and American literature; English and European literature; European studies; French studies; French and European literature; history. More courses planned from October 1987.

Sandwell

West Bromwich College of Commerce and Technology. Metals technology.

Wolverhampton

The Polytechnic of Wolverhampton. Applied chemistry; computer science; economics; applied sciences; biological sciences; business studies; humanities; industrial engineering; law; applied chemistry with computing; social and cultural studies; materials in manufacturing; building services engineering.

Yorkshire – North

College of Ripon and York St John. Combined studies BA or BSc course.
North Riding College – Scarborough. BEd.

YORKSHIRE – METROPOLITAN DISTRICTS

Bradford

Bradford Adult Education Centre (*Leeds University*). Humanities; economics and social studies.
Bradford and Ilkley Community College College. Humanities.
University of Bradford. Social studies.

Kirklees

Huddersfield Polytechnic. Business studies; humanities; education; social work; engineering (mechanical and electrical); chemistry; textiles; nursing; computing.

Leeds

Leeds Polytechnic. BA/BA (Hons) management and administration; combined studies; librarianship; social policy and administration; BSc (Hons) nursing studies; production engineering; BEd/BEd (Hons); LLB/LLB (Hons).
Leeds University. Humanities (planned).

Sheffield

Sheffield City Polytechnic. Applied chemistry; applied science; business studies; computer studies; engineering; English; fine art; metallurgy and microstructural engineering; public administration; social dimensions of health.

Wales

Dyfed

Aberystwyth University College of Wales. BA (external) through the medium of Welsh.
St David's University College, Lampeter. Arts subjects, all requests considered.

Mid Glamorgan

Polytechnic of Wales. Chemistry; civil engineering; computer studies; law; police studies.

Scotland

Central

Falkirk College of Technology. Engineering.
University of Stirling. BA and BSc courses. Students attend classes according to full-time study timetable. Also BA (educational studies).

Lothian

Heriot-Watt University. Business studies.
Napier College. Quantity surveying; business studies; life sciences.

Renfrewshire

Paisley College of Technology. Civil engineering.

Strathclyde

Glasgow College of Technology. Electrical engineering; mechanical engineering; social sciences.
Glasgow University. BSc and BD courses. MA in social sciences.
Jordanhill College of Education. Education only.
Strathclyde University. BA and BEd courses.

Tayside
Dundee College of Technology. Nursing; commerce.

Northern Ireland

Belfast
Belfast College of Technology.
Queens University of Belfast. BA general studies.

Londonderry/Jordanstown/Coleraine
University of Ulster. Advanced language studies; biological sciences; business studies; catering administration; combined humanities; education; engineering; hotel and tourism management; public sector administration; psychology; building; civil engineering, nursing.

WHERE CAN YOU DO A DEGREE?

This is a list of most of the colleges and universities where you can study at degree level, though not always for a degree. Some places deal with only one subject area, or clientele, and that is usually obvious from their title – some of them are indicated as well. Others are general colleges but may only offer degrees in a limited range of subjects. Other added information is:

- *CNAA* where CNAA is the degree awarding body
- *EM* where there is an extra-mural or continuing education department or short course unit
- *PT* where part-time degree studies are available – there is a list showing which subjects are available above
- *MS* where there is a special mature-student entry scheme – a formal procedure, not just a clause saying 'each student considered on merit'
- *Occ* where there are facilities for occasional students (see above) or for 'taster' courses
- *Credit transfer* if there is a formally negotiated credit transfer scheme with other places – that does not include all the facilities for continuation of a CNAA DipHE to degree level and transfers between CNAA courses.

The main college address is listed in the *Gazetteer*, but some courses may be run at a separate site. For more details:

★ **SEND FOR** their prospectus.

★ **LOOK AT** *The student book* (see *Booklist*).

Places where you can study for a degree

England

Avon
Bath College of Higher Education. CNAA.
Bath University. HE; MS; PTHE.
Bristol Polytechnic. CNAA.
Bristol University.
Trinity College – Bristol. MS entry scheme; Occ; CNAA; credit transfer (Oak Hill College and Spurgeon's College, London; London Bible College OU & CNAA Religious Studies Courses); theological studies only.

Bedfordshire

Bedford College of Higher Education. PT, combined studies; CNAA.
Cranfield Institute of Technology. MS entry scheme (postgrad only); Occ.
Luton College of Higher Education. CNAA; PT.

Berkshire

Bulmershe College of Higher Education. CNAA; credit transfer (OU); Occ; PT.
Reading University. MS entry scheme credit transfer (with Slough CHE, 1st year HND engineering to 2nd year BSc engineering).
Slough College of Higher Education. Credit transfer (1st year HND engineering to 2nd year BSc Eng. Reading University); CNAA.

Buckinghamshire

Buckinghamshire College of Higher Education - High Wycombe and Chalfont St Giles. CNAA.
The University of Buckingham. MS.

Cambridgeshire

Cambridgeshire College of Arts and Technology. CNAA; PT.
Cambridge University. EM.

Cheshire

Chester College. MS (JMB) entry scheme; multi-mode.
Crewe and Alsager College of Higher Education. CNAA; BA by independent study; PT; Occ.
North Cheshire College – Warrington. MS (JMB) scheme; BA combined studies, full time; EM; Occ.

Cleveland

Teesside Polytechnic – Middlesbrough. PT; CNAA; Occ.

Cornwall

Camborne School of Mines. CNAA; mining engineering and mineral process engineering only.
Cornwall College of Further and Higher Education – Redruth. CNAA, scientific and technical graphics only. Possible move to Falmouth College in 1987.
Falmouth School of Art. Fine art only; CNAA.

Cumbria

Charlotte Mason College of Education – Ambleside. Education only.
West Cumbria College. MS; CNAA; PT.

Derbyshire

Derbyshire College of Higher Education. MS gateway and pathway entry scheme; mainly mature students in certain courses; CNAA, University of Nottingham; PT.

Devon

College of St Mark and St John – Plymouth. CNAA, University of Exeter
Dartington College of Arts. Occ; CNAA; art in its social context; music and theatre.
Exeter College of Arts and Design. CNAA; line arts and graphic design; Occ (associate scheme).
Exeter University. EM; Occ; MS.
Plymouth Polytechnic. CNAA; PT; Occ; MS.
Rolle College – Exmouth. Credit transfer (with East Devon College of Further Education).
Royal Naval Engineering College. CNAA; engineering only; limited access for civilians.
Seale Hayne College. Agriculture only; CNAA.

Dorset

Dorset Institute of Higher Education – Poole. CNAA; PT; MS.

Durham

Durham University. EM; Occ; MS.

Essex

Colchester Institute. CNAA, music only.
Essex Institute of Higher Education. CNAA; PT; Occ.

Essex University. Occ; MS entry scheme; credit transfer (OU); HE prep course, City and East London College and Colchester Institute.

Gloucestershire

The College of St Paul and St Mary – Cheltenham. CNAA; PT; EM.
Gloucestershire College of Arts and Technology. CNAA; PT.
Royal Agricultural College – Cirencester.

Hampshire

The College of Maritime Studies – Southampton. Nautical science/engineering; PT.
Highbury College of Technology – Portsmouth. CNAA and BTEC HND; hotel and catering management only.
King Alfred's College – Winchester. CNAA; PT; Occ; credit transfer with Plymouth, Huddersfield and City of London Polytechnics.
La Sainte Union College of Higher Education – Southampton. PT; CNAA.
Portsmouth Polytechnic. CNAA; PT.
Southampton Institute of Higher Education. PT.
Southampton University. EM; PTHE.
Winchester School of Art. Foundation course validated by Southern Regional Council for FE, CNAA.

Hereford and Worcester

Kidderminster College of Further Education. CNAA; design of carpets and related textiles only.
Worcester College of Higher Education. Occ; CNAA; PT

Hertfordshire

Hatfield Polytechnic. MS entry scheme (some courses) and polyprep; CNAA; PT; Polyprep; associate students (Occ).
Hertfordshire College of Agriculture and Horticulture – St Albans. MS.
Hertfordshire College of Art and Design. HE; PT; fine art only.
Hertfordshire College of Higher Education – Watford. Occ; CNAA.
St Albans College - St Albans. PT; MS.
Watford College. CNAA; BSc printing and packaging technology only.

Humberside

Hull University. Credit transfer (OU and others); EM; PT; Occ; MS.
Humberside College of Higher Education. HE; CNAA; PT; MS accepts foundation certificate access from local further education colleges.

Kent

Canterbury Christ Church College. PTHE; MS.
Canterbury College of Art. CNAA; art, design and architecture.
Medway College of Design – Rochester. HE; MS; Occ.
University of Kent at Canterbury. PT; credit transfer (OU); EM; Occ.
Maidstone College of Art. CNAA; fine art and graphic design only.
Mid Kent College of Higher and Further Education. CNAA; PT.
Wye College, University of London.

Lancashire

Edge Hill College of Higher Education. Occ; PT; MS; participates in Open College scheme.
Lancashire Polytechnic. MS entry scheme; participates in Open College scheme; Occ; PT; EM; CNAA; credit transfer with OU and Edge Hill College.
Lancaster University. Credit transfer (OU); EM; PT; Occ; MS; participates in Open College scheme; independent study.
St Martin's College – Lancaster. EM; MS (Open College).

Leicestershire

Leicester Polytechnic. CNAA; PT; HE Prep course, Charles Keene College.
Leicester University. EM; MS; PT.
Loughborough College of Art and Design. Art and design only; CNAA.
Loughborough University of Technology. PT; EM.

Lincolnshire
Bishop Grosseteste College – Lincoln.

LONDON – GREATER
Barnet
Jews College. Occ; CNAA; Jewish studies Rabbinic education only.

Bexley
Rose Bruford College of Speech and Drama. CNAA (theatre arts only).

Bromley
Ravensbourne College of Design and Communication. CNAA.
Spurgeon's College. Theology only; mature students only; PT; CNAA.

Ealing
Ealing College of Higher Education. MS entry scheme (certain courses only); PT; Occ (certain courses only); CNAA.

Enfield
Middlesex Polytechnic. HE prep course, Paddington College; CNAA; credit transfer from OU; Occ; PT; MS.
Oak Hill College. Theology and pastoral studies; CNAA; Occ.

Harrow
Harrow College of Higher Education. CNAA; PT; HE MS prep course at Harrow College of Further Education.

Hillingdon
Brunel University. MS entry scheme; no arts faculty; EM.
London Bible College. BA and BA (Hons) Theology CNAA.

Hounslow
West London Institute of Higher Education. CNAA; EM; PT; MS.

Kingston upon Thames
Kingston Polytechnic. CNAA; PT.

Merton
Wimbledon School of Art. CNAA, BA (Hons) fine art (painting and sculpture); theatre and design MA and postgrad diploma in fine art print making; CNAA diploma in HE theatre wardrobe.

Richmond
St Mary's College. Teacher training and in-service courses PGCE, BEd; also BA and BSc for mature students; MS.

Waltham Forest
North East London Polytechnic. PT; EM; CNAA; independent study.

London – Inner:
Architectural Association School of Architecture. Architecture only.
Avery Hill College (Thames Polytechnic). CNAA; HE prep course, own and from City and East London College, Hackney College, South East London College, Woolwich College; credit transfer (Plymouth, Hatfield, North East London, and City of London Polytechnic and Open University).
The Byam Shaw School of Art. Fine art only.
Camberwell School of Art and Crafts. CNAA.
Central School of Art and Design. CNAA.
Central School of Speech and Drama. CNAA.
Centre for Clinical Communication Studies. BSc clinical communication studies only. MS.
Chelsea School of Art. BA graphics and fine art; CNAA.
City of London Polytechnic. PT; CNAA; HE prep courses, Southwark College and Tottenham College of Technology.

City University. EM; Occ.
Garnett College. MS entry scheme; mostly mature; CNAA.
Guildhall School of Music and Drama. Music and drama only.
Holborn Law Tutors. Law only; PT; Occ; London University LLB degrees; Bar examinations.
Laban Centre for Movement and Dance. CNAA; dance studies.
London Business School. PT; all mature students; no first degrees; business studies only.
London College of Music. Music only.
London College of Printing. CNAA; HE prep course in fashion and graphics from South Thames College.
London Contemporary Dance School. BA contemporary dance only.
London International Film School. Film only.
Polytechnic of Central London. PT; CNAA.
Polytechnic of North London. CNAA; PT; HE prep course, City and East London College; HE prep course, Kingsway-Princeton College.
South Bank Polytechnic. PT; CNAA; HE prep courses from Southwark College, Westminster College, Brixton College and through Open College, Roehampton Institute of Higher Education; MS entry scheme.
Royal Academy of Dramatic Art. Acting; stage management.
Royal Academy of Music. Music only.
Royal Academy Schools. Postgraduate courses only fine art, painting, sculpture.
Royal College of Art. Postgraduate courses only.
Royal College of Music. Music only.
St Martin's School of Art (*The London Institute*). CNAA.
Thames Polytechnic, incorporating Avery Hill College. PT; CNAA; HE prep courses; own polystudy course also Woolwich College and Southwark College.
Trinity College of Music. Music only.
University of London, Senate House, Malet Street, London WC1E 7HU. Tel: (01) 636 8000. Enquiries to individual colleges listed below; MS entry scheme; Occ; EM.
Birkbeck College (*London*). PT only.
Courtauld Institute of Art (*London*). History of art, conservation of paintings, wall paintings and textiles.
Goldsmith's College (*London*). MS entry scheme; EM; Occ; PT; CNAA; MS; HE Prep course.
South East London College.
Heythrop College (*London*). Theology.
Imperial College of Science and Technology (*London*). Occ; science; life sciences and management sciences; engineering and mining only.
Institute of Archaeology (*London*). Occ; archaeology and archaeological conservation only.
Institute of Education (*London*). Occ; DL.
King's College (*London*). Mainly science.
London School of Economics and Political Science (*London*). PT; Occ.
Queen Mary College (*London*).
Royal Veterinary College(*London*). BVet Med.
School of Oriental and African Studies (*London*). EM; Occ.
School of Slavonic and East European Studies (*London*). Occ.
The School of Pharmacy (*London*). BPhar and BSc in toxicology and pharmacology only.
University College (*London*). Occ.
Westfield College (*London*).
Charing Cross and Westminster Medical School.
King's College School of Medicine and Dentistry.
London Hospital Medical College.
Middlesex Hospital Medical School.
Royal Free Hospital School of Medicine.
St Bartholomew's Hospital Medical College.
St George's Hospital Medical School.
St Mary's Hospital Medical School. Credit transfer (Oxford and Cambridge Medical Schools).

United Medical & Dental Schools of Guy's and St Thomas's Hospitals. Credit Transfer (Oxford and Cambridge Medical Schools).

MANCHESTER – METROPOLITAN DISTRICTS

Bolton

Bolton Institute of Higher Education. PT; CNAA; MS only (education).

Manchester

De La Salle College. Occ; MS (JMB scheme).
Manchester Business School. No first degrees offered, all mature students.
Manchester Polytechnic. PT; CNAA; mainly mature (DipHE).
Manchester University. EM; MS (JMB scheme); PT; Occ.
Royal Northern College of Music. HE (music only).
University of Manchester Institute of Science and Technology. MS (JMB scheme); PT.

Rochdale

Rochdale College of Art. BA art and design PT.

Salford

The University of Salford. PT; CT with NE Wales Institute of Higher Education; MS from Stocksbridge College.

Stockport

Stockport College of Technology. PT; CNAA.

Wigan

Wigan College of Technology. Law only at degree level; CNAA.

MERSEYSIDE METROPOLITAN DISTRICTS

Liverpool

C F Mott Campus of Liverpool Polytechnic.
Liverpool Institute of Higher Education. HE; PT; MS (JMB scheme).
Liverpool Polytechnic. MS with access course scheme, from Childwell Hall College of Further Education, Sandown College, and Mable Fletcher Technical College. CNAA; PT; Polymaths provides direct entry to BSc and HND maths and computer studies.
Liverpool University. MS (JMB scheme) and access course; EM; Occ.

Norfolk

Norwich School of Art. BA (Hons) graphic design; BA (Honours fine art only); CNAA.
University of East Anglia – Norwich. PT; Occ.

Northamptonshire

Nene College – Northampton. MS entry scheme.

Nottinghamshire

Trent Polytechnic. College CNAA; PT; EM.
University of Nottingham. EM; MS (exam); PT.

Oxfordshire

Oxford Polytechnic. Occ; CNAA; PT.
Oxford University. EM.
University College Buckland.
Westminster College. CNAA.

Shropshire

Harper Adams Agricultural College – Newport. CNAA (agricultural technology only).

Staffordshire

Keele University. EM; Occ; MS.
North Staffordshire Polytechnic. CNAA; PT.

Surrey

North East Surrey College of Technology – Ewell. PT.
Royal Holloway and Bedford New College, University of London. MS entry scheme.
Surrey University. EM.
West Surrey College of Art and Design – Farnham. CNAA.

Sussex – East

Brighton Polytechnic. PT; EM; CNAA.
Sussex University. MS entry scheme.

Sussex – West

West Sussex Institute of Higher Education. HE; PTHE; MS; Occ; CNAA.

TYNE AND WEAR METROPOLITAN DISTRICTS

Newcastle-upon-Tyne

Newcastle-upon-Tyne Polytechnic. EM; CNAA; PT; MS from Newcastle College of Art and Technology and Gateshead Technical College.
Newcastle-upon-Tyne University. PT; EM; Occ.
St. Mary's College. CNAA.

Sunderland

Sunderland Polytechnic. Occ; PT; EM; CNAA; MS foundation course from Monkwearmouth College of Further Education and South Shields Marine and Technical College.

WEST MIDLANDS METROPOLITAN DISTRICTS

Birmingham

Aston University.
City of Birmingham Polytechnic. PT; CNAA; Occ; HE prep courses, Matthew Boulton Technical College, Bournville College of Further Education and Sutton Coldfield College of Further Education.
University of Birmingham. MS (JMB scheme) access course from Walsall College of Technology; EM; PT; HE prep course.
Newman College. MS (JMB scheme); MS from Matthew Boulton Technical College and Walsall College of Technology.
Westhill College. Mature only (community and youth work course) (church education course); MS (JMB scheme); HE prep courses, Matthew Boulton Technical College and Walsall College of Technology.

Coventry

Coventry (Lanchester) Polytechnic. PT; CNAA; MS from Tile Hill College of Further Education and North Warwickshire College of Technology and Art.
Warwick University. PT; CNAA; Occ; MS open access from Tile Hill College of Further Education; credit transfer (OU); EM.

Dudley

Stourbridge College of Technology and Art. CNAA (fine art and three dimensional design only).

Sandwell

West Bromwich College of Commerce and Technology. PT (metals technology only); CNAA.

Walsall

West Midlands College of Higher Education. CNAA; MS from Warley College of Technology.

Wolverhampton

The Polytechnic of Wolverhampton. PT; CNAA; Occ.

Wiltshire

Bath College of Higher Education (incorporating Bath Academy of Art). EM; CNAA.
Royal Military College of Science – Swindon. Some scholarships for civilians.

Yorkshire – North
College of Ripon and York St John. MS (JMB scheme); PT; Occ.
North Riding College – Scarborough. MS (JMB scheme); Occ.
York University. EM; Occ; (open courses); credit transfer with Open University.

YORKSHIRE – METROPOLITAN DISTRICTS

Bradford
Bradford Adult Education Centre. PT.
Bradford and Ilkley Community College. CNAA; EM; credit transfer (OU)(B/TEC Dips and Certs University of Bradford, and Huddersfield and Leeds Polytechnics); Occ; PT; own HE prep course; MS from Keighley Technical College, University of Bradford; PT.

Doncaster
Doncaster Metropolitan Institute of Higher Education. DipHE only MS entry scheme; CNAA.

Kirklees
Huddersfield Polytechnic. CNAA; PT.

Leeds
Leeds Polytechnic. CNAA; PT.
Leeds University. PT; MS (JMB scheme); EM; Occ.
Trinity and All Saints Colleges, (affiliated to Leeds University). MS (JMB scheme).

Sheffield
Sheffield City Polytechnic. PT; CNAA; EM; MS course from Rowlinson Campus Stocksbridge College, Rotherham College of Art and Technology, The Northern College, Shirecliffe; HE prep course; Barnsley College ofTechnology, North Nottingham College of Further Education.

Sheffield University. MS (JMB scheme); EM.

Wakefield
Bretton Hall College (Leeds University). PGCE; BA (Hons); BEd.

Wales

Clwyd
North East Wales Institute of Higher Education – Wrexham. Computer studies (Salford University); education BEd (Wales University); humanities BA (Wales Univ).

Dyfed
Aberystwyth University College of Wales. PT; EM.
College of Librarianship, Wales – Aberystwyth. CNAA.
St David's University College – Lampeter.
Trinity College – Carmarthen. Occ.

Gwent
Gwent College of Higher Education – Newport. CNAA (Wales University).

Gwynedd
Normal College – Bangor (Y Coleg Normal).
University College of North Wales – Bangor. EM.

Mid-Glamorgan
Polytechnic of Wales – Pontypridd. PT; Occ; CNAA.

South Glamorgan
South Glamorgan Institute of Higher Education – Cardiff. CNAA.
University of Wales Institute of Science and Technology – Cardiff.
Welsh College of Music and Drama.
University College, Cardiff. EM; Occ.
University of Wales College of Medicine – Cardiff.

West Glamorgan
University College of Swansea. EM.
West Glamorgan Institute of Higher Education – Swansea. CNAA (University of Wales).

Scotland

Borders
Scottish College of Textiles. CNAA; Occ.

Central
Falkirk College of Technology. Engineering.
University of Stirling. PT; EM; credit transfer (OU); Occ.

Fife
St Andrews University. Credit transfer; EM; Occ.

Grampian
Aberdeen College of Education.
Aberdeen University.
Robert Gordon's Institute of Technology – Aberdeen. CNAA.

Lothian
Dunfermline College of Physical Education. CNAA; physical education, recreation/leisure, sports coaching; community education, sport for the disabled, dance and movement.
Edinburgh College of Art.
Edinburgh University. MS (Faculties of Arts, Divinity, Law, Music and Social Sciences); PT; EM.
Heriot-Watt University – Edinburgh. EM; MS; Occ; PT.
Moray House College of Education. Distance Learning. Ask for: Mr HE Perfect.
Napier College – Edinburgh. CNAA; SCOTVEC, PT.
Queen Margaret College – Edinburgh. CNAA.

Strathclyde
Craigie College of Education. BEd; postgraduate study.
Glasgow College of Building and Printing. CNAA.
Glasgow College of Technology. CNAA; PT.
Glasgow School of Art. CNAA; art, design, architecture, planning (only).
Glasgow University. EM; PT; MS.
Jordanhill College of Education. CNAA; PT (education only).
Paisley College of Technology. CNAA; mainly science, engineering and social science.
The Queen's College – Glasgow. MS entry scheme (social work); CNAA.
Royal Scottish Academy of Music and Drama.
St Andrews College of Education.
Strathclyde University. EM; PT.

Tayside
Duncan of Jordanstone College of Art – Dundee. CNAA.
Dundee College of Education.
Dundee College of Technology. CNAA.
Dundee University. EM.

Northern Ireland

Belfast
Queen's University of Belfast. PT; EM; Occ; CT (OU planned).
Stranmillis College of Education. Education only.
St Mary's Colleges of Education. HE.

Coleraine
University of Ulster (Coleraine). EM; Occ; MS; HE prep course (at Magee campus).
University of Ulster (Jordanstown). PT; EM.

23 The Open University

A UNIVERSITY FOR ADULTS

The Open University is the only one set up especially for adults; you can get in without any qualifications. Its approach takes into account the problems adults have in returning to study; all students experience the same problems.

As well as taking students who want to study for degrees, it has developed a wide range of non-degree courses to cater for the education of the community. In every other way, it is completely different from other universities, in that:

- all the students are adults (ie 18 years or older)
- all but a few postgraduate students are part-time
- most of the work is distance learning – correspondence courses and broadcasts
- radio and TV programmes are used as well as some face-to-face tuition
- it has no minimum entry requirements; anyone resident in the UK can apply
- its academic year runs from February to November, not October to June
- you can spread your courses over many years, with breaks if you want.

Although it exists mainly for UK residents, there is a pilot associate student scheme for people living in Belgium and Luxembourg who can speak English. Residents in the Republic of Ireland can also take associate student courses.

WHAT COURSES CAN YOU DO?

First degrees

These are modular, combining different courses. Each one you complete successfully earns a full or half credit. Six make a degree, eight for honours.

Exemptions

You may be awarded some credits without studying by having other HE qualifications already (eg HNC). Each credit takes about nine months at 12 to 15 hours of work per week (sometimes longer). Though you have to complete each credit within a set time, you can take as long as you like to get the degree. It'll take anything from three to seven years for an honours degree, depending on your exemptions – four years minimum if you have no exemptions.

First you do a foundation course (you must usually take two during your degree) from a range in the arts, social sciences, maths, science or technology.

After that you can pick from 130 second, third and fourth level courses (including educational studies), until you get the credits you need. So you don't have to specialise in one subject; you can cover a very wide spectrum.

Higher degrees

You can study BPhil, MPhil or PhD full or part time internally (at Milton Keynes or Oxford) or externally part time.

These are all research degrees. Places are limited; demand is greater than supply. You can sometimes submit your work in Welsh.

The Open University also offers a programme of taught higher degrees of which the following are currently available:

- MSc in advanced education and research methods
- MA in literature
- MA in educational studies
- MSc in mathematics.

Continuing education courses

If you don't want a degree, you can take a single course or order a pack of self-standing materials. There are seven kinds:

- A programme of scientific and technical updating courses including two courses on microprocessor applications for managers and engineers (including one version for Women in Technology described in *6 Women*).
- In-service education for teachers eg advanced diploma in technology schools or the advanced diploma in educational management, and packs such as Children, Language and Literature.
- Health and social welfare, eg The Handicapped Person in the Community (training for professionals and volunteers). Also packs, eg Abuse in Families.
- Management education – a programme of courses for managers is run through the Open Business School. Courses like The Effective Manager are aimed at people in work; you can get a professional diploma in management.
- Personal and cultural education; short courses and packs in the arts and the history of ideas eg Looking at Paintings and The Changing Countryside.
- Most courses from the undergraduate programme.

Courses start at different times through the year. Packs are available at any time.

Community education courses

These deal with particular concerns or issues in the community. They include:

- Courses for parents such as The First Years of Life, The Pre-School Child, Childhood 5–10, Parents and Teenagers.
- Courses for consumers such as Energy in the Home and Work Choices.
- Courses about health such as Health Choices and Planning Retirement.
- Packs such as Racism in the Community.

Short courses are presented in the usual way though some are run jointly with other organisations (eg the PPA for The Pre-School Child).

Special enrolment procedures for short courses

The OU wants students. They welcome special arrangements, for example:

- Group enrolment. If several people want to study together, they can all join at once. Just send all the application forms in one envelope with a letter saying you want to enrol as a group. You'll be treated as a group for counselling, meetings and so on, and get a fee reduction (eg five for the price of four).
- Enrolling for several people if a group doesn't mind if most members don't get a qualification. One person can enrol, get the units, and everyone else can use them. Counsellors and tutors and the OU will try to co-operate.

If you want to talk to someone about these:

★ **ASK** the OU Regional Centre, address at the end of this chapter.

PREPARING FOR A DEGREE

Some colleges run preparatory courses for prospective OU students who are returning to study. The National Extension College has suitable correspondence courses and since 1985 the OU has provided its own preparatory packages for new students. The local OU Regional Centre will be happy to advise you about preparation and the courses available.

★ **ASK** for the Regional Enquiry Service.

Preparation is worthwhile; an OU degree is hard work. Most students need at least twelve hours a week for study – some find it is nearer twenty.

HOUSEWIFE WITH TWO CHILDREN

Doing the course was very, very hard. I had to do essays. I hadn't held a pen for years – since the children were born. All the programmes were at awkward times. When you're doing housework, you can talk to the children and see to their needs at the same time and involve them in it. When you're studying, you have to concentrate. I managed to get to a couple of tutorials. I'm glad I did it. It gave me confidence. In spite of all the difficulties it was the most rewarding piece of learning I've ever done. The learning was well structured – I never felt at sea. I always knew just where I was and what I needed to do. They also gave plenty of scope for individual work, and showed you how to go about it.

HOW IT'S DONE

There are four elements in a degree course.

The correspondence materials

Every student gets a big package at regular intervals, by post. It contains specially written booklets (course units), some notes, perhaps some experiments (with kits for science and technology courses), exercises and self-assessment tests (so you can make sure you've understood things). There are also some assignments which you send back to be marked. Some are questionnaires marked by computer, others are essays marked by tutors. There may also be tapes, records, slides or videos.

Broadcasts
At the beginning of the course, everyone gets a list of all the radio and TV programmes which relate to the course. Many programmes are broadcast twice and tapes and video tapes can be found at local study centres if you miss them. But the programmes are not usually essential; they're really to make the course more immediate, to give interesting examples of things to reinforce what you've already learnt, and to help you pace yourself.

Tutors, counsellors, study centres
There are more than 250 study centres around the country, usually in FE or HE colleges. They all have radio and TV, some have video recorders and other equipment, and most have computer terminals. Course tutors hold regular meetings of students; there are discussions, lectures and a chance to talk to fellow students. As there are many foundation course students, there will probably be a tutor at a study centre near you. For other level courses there are fewer students so the tutor may be some way away and it may be more difficult to attend tutorials. Each student may phone, write to and if necessary meet their tutor. They help if you're getting behind or finding things difficult. In areas such as Scotland, telephone tuition is readily available for students who are far away from a study centre.

Summer schools
Are one-week residential courses, probably at a university, where you'll have an extremely hard working time. They are meant to be a chance for students to feel the traditional university atmosphere, use the proper equipment (labs, university libraries etc) and meet fellow students and staff. Most people agree that summer schools succeed completely in all these things. Most first degree students will go to quite a few as about half the courses have summer schools – especially those in science and technology. Excusal from summer schools may be possible (eg for single parents) and it is possible to choose courses without summer schools after the (compulsory) foundation course.

HOW IT'S ASSESSED

Continuously
You don't get your degree purely on the strength of passing an exam. You are assessed continuously – your computer-marked and tutor-marked assignments are recorded on your file. Your assessments are combined with your final exam result – high marks can earn you a distinction.

By exam
There is a three-hour exam at a local centre at the end of each course which contributes to your total marks.

TRANSFERABILITY

Your existing qualifications may enable you to qualify for a degree by taking fewer courses, through credit exemptions (maximum of three).

If you have completed part of a CNAA degree or DipHE course or one or two years' study at the Universities of Belfast, Essex, Heriot-Watt, Hull, Kent, Lancaster, St Andrews, Salford, Southampton, Strathclyde, Sussex, Stirling, Ulster, Wales or York, and Trinity College Dublin, the OU may count that study towards a degree. It's called direct credit transfer.

For enquiries about credit exemptions and directly transferred credits:

★ **ASK** Advanced Standing Office, PO Box 80, Milton Keynes MK7 6AS.

WHAT IT COSTS

The cost of a full credit course is £152 (half as much for a half credit course). Summer schools cost £99 for the week, and for some courses set books may cost about £25. Because courses are part-time there are no mandatory grants; LEA help is patchy although many pay some or all of the cost of summer schools.

In addition, if you get an OU degree and then want to do a 'first degree' elsewhere, you forfeit your eligibility to a mandatory grant for that course – even if you paid all your OU fees from your own pocket!

Some employers are generous to employees who are OU students. Ask your personnel or training department. The OU has a special booklet to help employers decide whether to back its students.

To do a six credit BA course with three or four week-long summer schools (depending on the courses chosen), the University would charge, at 1986 prices, £1,310. An honours degree with eight credits would cost at least £1,790.

Students may pay course and summer school fees by installment. Course fees may be paid in two, three, four or six instalments; summer school fees in four.

The University is very sensitive about the cost of study and how this could put people off. Its advice is never to let money worries stop you from applying or registering, and there may be help from a specially earmarked fund of £500,000 for unemployed students.

HOW TO APPLY

First degree courses

As the OU year starts in February you must apply in the previous year, before October. It's first come first served so apply as early as possible.

★ **SEND FOR** *Guide for applicants for BA degrees*, from The Admissions Office, Open University, PO Box 48, Milton Keynes MK7 6AB. Tel: (0908) 74066.

Postgraduate courses

★ **SEND FOR** *Research degree prospectus,* from The Higher Degrees Office, Open University, PO Box 49, Milton Keynes MK7 6AD. Tel: (0908) 74066.

Continuing education courses

In addition to the undergraduate programme of courses, the University also offers a wide range of single courses and self-contained study packs which vary in length and format. For full details:

★ **SEND FOR** *Open opportunities,* from The Associate Student Central Office, Open University, PO Box 76, Milton Keynes MK7 6AN. Tel: (0908) 74066.

IS IT WORTH IT?

Are OU degrees as good as others?

The OU type of modular degree is getting more common. That means that employers and others are getting more used to people with a degree that shows they've worked hard for some years at several things instead of one or two things in greater depth. The OU degree is every bit as good as other kinds and may even be better as it takes great determination to get one. Most British universities and polytechnics accept OU credits for entry to later years of their own courses and also accept OU degrees for postgraduate study.

FE LECTURER

I worked for twenty years in the steelworks, did an OU degree in my spare time. It changed my life. I got a lecturing job with no other qualifications.

Students

They give a good indication of its worth. When you've done an OU degree, you're often hooked on it and keep on doing other OU courses for years.

THE OPEN UNIVERSITY STUDENTS' ASSOCIATION (OUSA)

Membership of the Students' Association includes all currently registered students of the University and does not carry a subscription.

The Association provides the support services necessary for the effective representation of students' views, both within the University and outside. It also offers help with educational and welfare problems, sponsors weekend schools, organises self-help study groups, encourages the formation of societies for special interest groups, operates a marketing service, and provides a range of social activities for its members and their families through its branches.

The governing body is the annual National Conference attended by representatives from all study centres and affiliated societies. A National Executive Committee has responsibility for implementing the policies determined by National Conference.

The Association's offices are located at the University's main campus.

★ **ASK** Open University Students' Association, PO Box 397, Walton House, Milton Keynes MK7 6BE. Tel: (0908) 652199 (answerphone (0908) 652190).

FURTHER INFORMATION

To buy OU publications

★ **WRITE TO** Open University Educational Enterprises Ltd, 12 Cofferidge Close, Stony Stratford, Milton Keynes MK11 1BY. Tel: (0908) 566744.

Other information

Contact your OU regional centre, ask for the Regional Enquiry Service.

OU regional centres

Region 01 London The Open University, London Region, Parsifal College, 527 Finchley Road, London NW3 7BG. Tel: (01) 794 0575. Area covered: Greater London.

Region 02 South The Open University, Southern Region, Foxcombe Hall, Boars Hill, Oxford OX1 5HR. Tel: (0865) 730731. Area covered: Berkshire, Buckinghamshire, Channel Islands, Dorset, Hampshire, Isle of Wight, Oxfordshire, part of Wiltshire.

Region 03 South West The Open University, South West Region, 41 Broad Street, Bristol BS1 2EP. Tel (0272) 299641. Area covered: Avon, Cornwall, Devon, Gloucestershire, Somerset, Scilly Isles, part of Wiltshire.

Region 04 West Midlands The Open University, West Midlands Region, St James House, 66 High Street, Harborne, Birmingham B17 9NB. Tel: (021) 426 1661. Area covered: Hereford and Worcester, Salop, part of Staffordshire, Warwickshire, West Midlands.

Region 05 East Midlands The Open University, East Midlands Region, The Octagon, 143 Derby Road, Nottingham NG7 1PH. Tel (0602) 473072. Area covered: Derbyshire, Leicestershire, Lincolnshire, Northamptonshire, Nottinghamshire, South Humberside, part of Staffordshire.

Region 06 East Anglia The Open University, East Anglia Region, Cintra House, 12 Hills Road, Cambridge CB2 1PF. Tel: (0223) 64721. Area covered: Bedfordshire, Cambridgeshire, Essex, Hertfordshire, Norfolk, Suffolk.

Region 07 Yorkshire The Open University, Yorkshire Region, Fairfax House, Merrion Street, Leeds LS2 8JU. Tel: (0532) 444431. Area covered: North Humberside, North Yorkshire, South Yorkshire, West Yorkshire.

Region 08 North West The Open University, North West Region, Chorlton House, 70 Manchester Road, Chorlton-cum-Hardy, Manchester M21 1PQ. Tel: (061) 861 9823. Area covered: Cheshire, part of Derbyshire, Isle of Man, Lancashire, Greater Manchester, Merseyside.

Region 09 North The Open University, North Region, Eldon House, Regent Centre, Gosforth, Newcastle-Upon-Tyne NE3 3PW. Tel: (091) 284 1611. Area covered: Cleveland, Cumbria, Durham, Northumberland, Tyne and Wear.

Region 10 Wales The Open University in Wales, 24 Cathedral Road, Cardiff CF1 9SA. Tel: (0222) 397911. Area covered: Wales.

Region 11 Scotland The Open University in Scotland, 60 Melville Street, Edinburgh EH3 7HF. Tel: (031) 226 3851. Area covered: Scotland.

Region 12 Northern Ireland The Open University in Northern Ireland, 40 University Road, Belfast BT7 1SU. Tel: (0232) 245025. Area covered: Northern Ireland.

Region 13 South East The Open University, South East Region, Wyvern House, 230/232 London Road, East Grinstead RH19 1LA. Tel: (0342) 27821. Area covered: Kent, Surrey, East Sussex, West Sussex.

You can also contact regional sub-offices for local advice and information.

Cumbria 2 Sandgate, Penrith CA1 17TP. Tel: (0768) 64720.
Cleveland 37 Harrow Road, Middlesborough TS5 5NT. Tel: (0642) 816227.
Glasgow 22 Royal Crescent, Glasgow C3. Tel: (041) 332 4364.
Plymouth 58/59 South Side Street, Plymouth PL1 2LA. Tel: (0752) 28321.
Winchester Medecroft, Sparkford Road, Winchester, Hants. Tel: (0962) 67969.

24 Training for a new job

MSC training
Restart
Job Training Schemes (JTS)
The New Job Training Scheme
Existing JTS
Criteria
Things you should know
Where courses are held
How to find out more
Other courses
Equal opportunities
VET regional and area offices
Skillcentres

MSC TRAINING

The Manpower Services Commission (MSC) supports a range of training and retraining schemes in Great Britain. In Northern Ireland the Department of Economic Development runs its own schemes.

More and more people are finding that the skills and knowledge they have are no longer needed, and don't get them jobs. Training designed to give new skills or update or upgrade existing ones is available everywhere in Britain and tries to meet local needs. There are also opportunities for training if you are thinking of setting up your own business.

RESTART

Restart offers advice and counselling to people who have been unemployed for a time. It also provides a one-week morale-boosting course where people can look at themselves and plan ahead. One aspect covers education and training opportunities; your Restart counsellor will be a useful source of advice and help about them.

JOB TRAINING SCHEMES (JTS)

There are two main schemes for people over 18 – the existing Job Training Scheme and the new one. The names may change over the next few months.

THE NEW JOB TRAINING SCHEME

A programme open to those who have been unemployed for six months or more. Trainees receive an average of six months' integrated vocational training and practical experience with an employer. Training starts with an assessment of individual needs and leads to the opportunity to gain a vocational qualification.

Trainees receive an allowance equivalent to their previous benefit entitlement plus 'passported' benefits, eg housing benefit.

ASK your Restart counsellor at your Jobcentre.

EXISTING JTS

Replaced TOPS (Training Opportunities Scheme). Courses are often directed at occupational areas where there are skill shortages, eg modern engineering or business computing. Traineees must be unemployed or willing to give up work for training. Courses may be full- or part-time and some use open learning.

The range of courses

This includes mechanical engineering, engineering fabrication, making and processing, electrical and electronic engineering, automotive and construction work, engineering science and technology, computer skills, hotel and catering, clerical and office skills, shorthand and typing, health and welfare work, service and selling occupations, and management services.

Payments

All trainees have fees paid. Those on full-time JTS courses (other than the new JTS) are usually paid a training allowance. Allowances are described in leaflet ATL14 available from your local Jobcentre, employment office, careers office or Vocational, Educational and Training Group (VET) area office.

The current rates and conditions of payment for people aged 19 and over are:

Personal allowance. This is normally £38.00 per week.

Adult dependant's allowance. If you are married or have a resident house-keeper taking care of children, you may receive, in addition to the personal allowance, an adult dependant's allowance of £24.70 per week. This is payable provided the adult in question does not earn more than £36.00 per week (take-home pay) or receive a maintenance allowance or benefit from public funds.

Expenses of training. You will generally get:

- a contribution towards your daily travelling expenses if they are over £4 per week
- a midday meal allowance of £3.55 per week
- a living-away-from-home allowance if you have to lodge away from home during training and are not provided with residential accommodation; this is £40.00 for each complete week of training – trainees getting this allowance cannot also receive allowances for daily or weekend travel
- a free credit of National Insurance contributions.

Other points

You may get allowances on full-time courses for books and equipment. On some courses you may be given a tool kit for your own use during and after the course – the tools of the trade. If you are disabled or under 19, different rates of allowances will apply. All are tax free.

Part-time courses

Some JTS courses are run part time on a fees-only basis; if you join these, you will not usually be paid an allowance, but reasonable travel costs will be met.

CRITERIA

Rules which apply to current JTS courses:

- length of course – no more than one year unless you are disabled. 'One year' means 50 consecutive weeks of training
- they must prepare you directly for a job without further training. MSC never supports courses which do not improve your prospects of finding work; this is a strong emphasis on areas where there's a shortage of skilled workers
- you can't have more than one year's training in three years, on this scheme and the Training for Enterprise Scheme (see below) taken together
- you must have been out of full-time education for a total of two years since the minimum school-leaving age.

Age limits

There is a minimum age limit of 18 unless you are disabled. There is no stated maximum. In practice MSC is more likely to train you if you can show that you're likely to get work afterwards in the job they've trained you for, and older candidates may find this more difficult.

Disabled people

If you are registered as disabled(or could be), entry is made easier through more relaxed rules.

THINGS YOU SHOULD KNOW

Attendance

Full-time courses generally require attendance five days a week, from around 9 am to 5 pm. If you miss time through illness, you'll need a sick note.

Termination

If you miss more than two weeks in a row for any reason, you could be 'terminated' if they feel you've fallen too far behind. You could also be terminated if it turns out that you are not really suitable for your chosen course, and are not benefitting from it. If you are terminated for bad behaviour you have to wait three years to go on another course. If there are other reasons, you can reapply immediately.

Assessment

All courses have an early assessment to see if you have settled down and are on the right course. If you're not they may help you find another one. There are regular assessments during the course.

WHERE COURSES ARE HELD

Normally in Skillcentres (run by the MSC itself), in colleges of further education (run by LEAs), or in private training centres. A few are in polytechnics or universities.

Skillcentres mainly offer skills training such as bricklaying, carpentry, machining, fitting, welding, sheet metalwork, vehicle repairs, plumbing, radio and TV repairs, typewriter repair, welding.

College courses mainly offer office and commercial skills like wordprocessing, shorthand, accounts, computer work or technician skills.

Other training organisations. Many MSC courses are now run by training companies, associations or groups, eg Chambers of Commerce, Group Training Associates.

HOW TO GET ON A COURSE

When you have identified a suitable course for which there are entry opportunities, arrangements will be made for you to take the necessary tests. You don't have to get everything right as there's a different pass mark for different courses. You will be told at once whether you've passed or failed.

There are some courses for which you have to do a second test (eg TV repair, computers and some others). It may be held at the college if it's a college-based course. Other courses do not require a test at all.

If you pass all the tests, you may go to a panel interview, where three or four people will decide whether you're suitable by asking questions about yourself and your aims. One thing they look for is whether you understand what it's like to work in the job you want to train for.

If you are accepted for training, you may have to join a waiting list, or you may be able to get on a course straight away. If you don't want to wait – think about a different course.

HOW TO FIND OUT MORE

MSC produces useful free leaflets. The main way to get these and more information is to go to a Jobcentre. They will go through the possibilities with you and help you choose a suitable course.

You could also contact your VET area office or talk to the people who run the courses. Some Skillcentres have an open day each week, when you can visit and look around. If you know of local courses, you should be able to speak to the staff who run them.

OTHER COURSES

Wider Opportunities Training Programme

The Wider Opportunities Training Programme helps unemployed people to maintain their employability and improve their prospects of competing for jobs and staying in work, by offering training opportunities geared to individual requirements as well as local labour market conditions.

Courses vary greatly in content and duration and are offered on a flexible, modular basis. Course content can include: assessment of existing skills, capabilities and training needs; short modules of work-related skills training, basic communication skills, new technology familiarisation; small business/self-employment training and the skills needed to find and retain employment.

The five main programmes are:

- for those with narrow and outdated skills: training and assessment in broad-based occupational skills
- for those needing general preparation for work: courses focusing on work-related literacy and numeracy, developing job-getting skills and enhancing occupational skills
- for speakers of English as a second language: work-related language training linked to instruction in occupational skills and jobseeking
- for women wishing to return to work: training to update skills and provide better knowledge of the labour market and the job finding process
- for participants in the Community Programme: work-related training taken on days when participants are not working on their CP projects.

Wider Opportunities training courses are delivered through a wide range of training providers. These include colleges of further education, employers and STAs. All unemployed people and those taking part in the Community Programme are eligible. Training in job search strategies, interview techniques and so on, play an important part in these courses. For details:

★ **ASK** your local Jobcentre.

Open Tech Programme

The Open Tech Programme has created material which allows people to learn at their own pace and at a time and place that suits them, whether at home or at work. It is designed to widen adult career and job opportunities at technician and supervisory management levels of skill. A new open learning programme is due to be launched in April 1987 to promote the wider use of open learning in training. Details will be available from MSC VET area offices from that date. For more information see *17 Flexible learning* and *33 Training at work*.

★ **LOOK AT** the *Open Tech directory*. Jobcentres, MSC VET area offices and public libraries usually have a copy.

Training for Enterprise

This scheme provides training for the new or existing business owner or manager and for those considering setting up a business.

For those starting up a business or planning to become self-employed, there is the Business Enterprise Programme (BEP), which teaches the basic business management skills and leads to the development of a business plan. This is a part-time course. The New Enterprise Programme (NEP) and Firmstart are ideal for major business ventures, providing detailed and intensive training. There are also special courses – the Graduate Enterprise Programme and the Business Enterprise Programme (Graduates) – for recent graduates, of any discipline, who have decided to run their own businesses.

The owners and managers of established businesses can benefit from the seminars of the Private Enterprise Programme (PEP) which offers training in basic business management. There are also the Management Extension (MEP) and Graduate Gateway (GGP) programmes which operate by seconding experienced managers and recent graduates to small firms to work on growth projects.

Eligibility rules for the various enterprise training programmes vary slightly. Details may be obtained from MSC VET area offices.

Useful leaflets, which may also be obtained from area offices, are:

Management extension programme – free management to help your business grow
Management extension programme – an exciting opportunity for unemployed managers
Aiming to be a high achiever? (*graduate gateway programme*)
Private enterprise programme.

Small business training

Start-up training

There are a number of courses available:

- New Enterprise Programme (NEP) and Firmstart held at well-known business schools. They are designed for people who wish to launch businesses which have significant growth and employment potential. The NEP is a 16-week full-time programme (four weeks in residence and 12 weeks market research), and Firmstart is a part-time programme lasting about 24 weeks (most of the teaching takes place at weekends). Firmstart's part-time format makes it ideal for those who have recently started their businesses and are therefore under great pressures of time and energy.
- Business Enterprise Programme (BEP), a part-time course for those who want to set up, or have recently started, a small firm or a one-person business. BEP lasts seven days, and is split into one and two-day blocks. The whole programme should be completed within a month.
- Graduate Enterprise Programme (GEP) for recent graduates who want to start businesses which are likely to grow quickly. This is a 16-week programme involving a residential period at a training establishment and some individual market research.

Help to existing businesses:

- Private Enterprise Programme (PEP), a series of training seminars in key subjects such as marketing and financial control. Each seminar lasts for a day, although the training may be arranged over two evenings, or an afternoon and evening. Established firms pay £35 for a seminar but firms in the first year of trading are exempt from this charge.
- Management Extension Programme (MEP) and Graduate Gateway Programme (GGP). These provide small business owners with an extra management resource in the form of an experienced manager or recent graduate. After training in small business management, the managers and

graduates develop and implement – at little or no cost to the 'host firms' – a growth project. Secondments last about three months.

Access to Information Technology
So much of modern business is bound up with information technology that anyone entering this field needs to understand the language if they're going to survive. Reading books will only get you so far.

This new scheme is designed for the beginner and will provide a sure grounding in the basics. Training is available in the evenings or at weekends.

Employed, self-employed and unemployed people are eligible.

Management training
Provision for management training concentrates on the unemployed rather than on those prepared to give up their job, and priority is given to short practical courses rather than longer more academic courses. Programmes for those of a professional, executive or managerial level who are unemployed or facing redundancy (like the Bridge Programme mentioned in *5 Out of work*) concerned mainly with counselling and self-marketing are also available. A visit to the Jobcentre or the VET area office is the best starting point.

Community Programme
This offers temporary work, either full-time or part-time, for people who have been out of work for some time. Projects are sponsored by local bodies, eg councils or voluntary organisations. They involve work that is of benefit to the local community like tree planting or loft insulation but could equally be conversion of a disused building for use as a training workshop or gardening work for the physically handicapped.

Many schemes now offer training opportunities to participants.

WOMAN, 38, ON PRACTICAL COMPUTING JTS COURSE
I was always afraid of computers – my husband and daughter are the family experts! But after a few days I started to get confident – computing really isn't so different from other things – I can learn! I did a work experience project for a local high tech company, setting up a financial model for them on a spreadsheet. After only four weeks! And I now have the offer of a job....

EQUAL OPPORTUNITIES

All MSC programmes are equal opportunities programmes. They are open equally to all who are eligible, regardless of race, sex, religion or disability.

Wider Opportunities for Women
Full- or part-time courses for women wishing to return to work after a period of domestic responsibility. The courses provide training to update skills and rebuild confidence, and offer advice on the labour market and the jobfinding process.

Ethnic minorities

MSC policy is to integrate all trainees into mainstream provision where possible. But it does recognise that ethnic minorities may need special provision to help them compete on equal terms in the labour market. This includes work-related language training for those for whom English is a second language, and 'positive action' courses in job-specific skills for particular racial groups, where that group is significantly under-represented in the particular work in question.

VET REGIONAL AND AREA OFFICES

London Region

Regional Office, 236 Grays Inn Road, London WC1X 8HL. Tel: (01) 278 0363.

North East Area Office, 3rd Floor, Cityside House, Alder Street, London E1 1EW. Tel: (01) 377 1866.

South and West Area Office, Lyric House, 149 Hammersmith Road, London W14 0OL. Tel: (01) 602 7227.

London South East Area Office, Skyline House, 200 Union Street, London SE1 0LX. Tel: (01) 928 0800.

East Midlands and Eastern Region

Regional Office, 2nd Floor, 2 Clinton Street East, Nottingham NG1 3DQ. Tel: (0602) 410360.

Derby Area Office, 4th Floor, St Peters House, Gower Street, Derby DE1 1SB. Tel: (0332) 360550.

Ipswich Area Office, 2nd Floor, Crown House, Crown Street, Ipswich IP1 3HS. Tel: (0473) 218951.

Leicester Area Office, 1st Floor, Rutland Centre, Halford Street, Leicester LE1 1TQ. Tel: (0533) 538616.

Lincoln Area Office, Wigford House, Brayford Wharf, Lincoln LN5 7AY. Tel: (0522) 32266.

Luton Area Office, Ground and 1st Floor, Wesley House, 19 Chapel Street, Luton LU1 2SU. Tel: (0582) 412828.

Nottingham Area Office, 4th Floor, Lambert House, Talbot Street, Nottingham NG1 7FF. Tel: (0602) 413313.

Northern Region

Regional Office, Broadacre House, Market Street, Newcastle upon Tyne NE1 6HH. Tel: (0632) 326181.

Cleveland Area Office, 10th Floor, Corporation House, 73 Albert Street, Middlesbrough TS1 2RU. Tel: (0642) 241144.

Co Durham Area Office, Valley Street North, Darlington, Co Durham DL1 1JT. Tel: (0325) 51166.

South Tyne Area Office, 2nd Floor, Derwent House, New Town Centre, Washington, Tyne and Wear NE38 7ST. Tel: (091) 416 6161.

Newcastle Area Office, Broadacre House, Market Street, Newcastle upon Tyne NE1 6HH. Tel: (0632) 326181.

North West Region

Regional Office, Washington House, Capital Centre, New Bailey Street, Manchester M3 5ER. Tel: (061) 833 0251.

Cheshire Area Office, 1st Floor, Spencer House, Dewhurst Road, Birchwood Centre, Warrington WA3 7PP. Tel: (0925) 826515.

Cumbria Area Office, Thirlmere Block, Mobet Estate, Workington CA14 3YP. Tel: (0900) 66991.

Manchester Central Area Office, 4th and 5th Floor, Bolton House, Chorlton Street, Manchester M1 3HY. Tel: (061) 236 7222.

Manchester East Area Office, 1st Floor, 1 St Peters Square, Stockport SK1 1NN. Tel: (061) 477 8830.

Manchester North Area Office, 3rd Floor, Provincial House, Nelson Square, Bolton BL1 1PN. Tel: (0204) 397350.

Lancashire Area Office, 3rd Floor, Duchy House, Lancaster Road, Preston PR1 1HE. Tel: (0772) 59393.

Merseyside Inner Area Office, 4th Floor, Sefton House, Exchange Street East, Liverpool L2 3RS. Tel: (051) 236 0026.

Merseyside Outer Area Office, 7th Floor, Sefton House, Exchange Street East, Liverpool L2 3RS. Tel: (051) 236 0026.

South East Region

Regional Office, Telford House, Hamilton Close, Basingstoke, Hampshire RG21 1UZ. Tel: (0256) 29266.

Kent Area Office, Victory House, 6th Floor, Meeting House Lane, Chatham ME4 4PS. Tel: (0634) 44411.

Chelmsford Area Office, 2nd Floor, Globe House, New Street, Chelmsford, Essex CM1 1UG. Tel: (0245) 358548.

Fareham Area Office, 25 Thackery Mall, Fareham Shopping Centre, Hampshire PO16 0PQ. Tel: (0329) 285921 and 230880.

High Wycombe Area Office, 31 Octagon Parade, High Wycombe, Bucks HP11 2LD. Tel: (0494) 33473.

Horsham Area Office, Exchange House, Worthing Road, Horsham, West Sussex RH12 2SQ. Tel: (0403) 50244.

Reading Area Office, 26–30 Kings Road, Reading RG1 3AA. Tel: (0734) 586262.

South West Region

Regional Office, The Pithay, Bristol BS1 2NQ. Tel: (0272) 273710.

Avon Area Office, Minster House, 27 Baldwin Street, Bristol BS99 7HR. Tel: (0272) 277116.

Devon and Cornwall Area Office, 6th Floor, Inter City House, Plymouth Station, Plymouth, Devon PL4 6AA. Tel: (0752) 671671.

Gloucester Area Office, Conway House, 33–35 Worcester Street, Gloucester GL1 3AJ. Tel: (0452) 24488.

Somerset/Dorset Area Office, Crescent House, The Mount, Taunton, Somerset TA1 3TT. Tel: (0823) 59121.

West Midlands Region

Regional Office, The Registry, 21st Floor, Alpha Tower, Suffolk Street, Queensway, Birmingham B1 1UR. Tel: (021) 643 6338.

Birmingham Area Office, Metropolitan House, Hagley Road, Birmingham B16 8TG. Tel: (021) 454 3355.

Coventry Area Office, 5th Floor, Bankfield House, 163 New Union Street, Coventry CV1 2QQ. Tel: (0203) 24100.

Dudley/Sandwell Area Office, Falcon House, The Minories, Dudley, West Midlands DY2 8PG. Tel: (0384) 455391.

Staffordshire Area Office, Moorlands House, 24 Trinity Street, Hanley, Stoke on Trent ST1 5LN. Tel: (0782) 260505.

Telford Area Office, Hazeldine House, Town Centre, Telford, Shropshire TF3 4JJ. Tel: (0952) 507474.

Wolverhampton Area Office, 2nd Floor, 30 Market Street, Wolverhampton WV1 3AT. Tel: (0902) 71111.

Yorkshire and Humberside Region

Regional Office, Jubilee House, 33–41 Park Place, Leeds LS1 2RL. Tel: (0532) 446299.

Bradford Area Office, Jubilee House, 33–41 Park Place, Leeds LS1 2RL. Tel: (0532) 446299.

Hull Area Office, 4th Floor, Essex House, Manor Street, Hull HU1 1YA. Tel: (0482) 226491.

Leeds Area Office, 3rd Floor, Fairfax House, Merrion Street, Leeds LS2 8JU. Tel: (0532) 446181.

Sheffield/Rotherham Area Office, 8th Floor, Sheaf House, Pennine Centre, Hawley Street, Sheffield S1 3GA. Tel: (0742) 701911.

Wakefield, Barnsley and Doncaster Area Office, York House, 31–36 York Place, Leeds LS1 2EB. Tel: (0532) 450502.

Wales

Office for Wales, 4th Floor, Companies House, Crown Way, Maindy, Cardiff CF4 3UT. Tel: (0222) 388588.

Cardiff Area Office, 5th Floor, Phase 1 Building, Tyglas Llanishen, Cardiff CF3 4PJ. Tel: (0222) 755744.

Gwent Area Office, Government Building, Cardiff Road, Newport NPT 1YE. Tel: (0633) 56161.

Swansea Area Office, 4th Floor, Orchard House, Orchard Street, Swansea SA1 5DJ. Tel: (0792) 460355.

Wrexham Area Office, Wynnstey Block, Hightown Barracks, Kingsmill Road, Wrexham LL13 8BH. Tel: (0978) 365550.

Scotland

Office for Scotland, 9 St Andrews Square, Edinburgh EH2 2QX. Tel: (031) 225 8500.

Ayrshire, Dumfries and Galloway Area Office, 25 Bank Street, Kilmarnock KA1 1ER. Tel: (0563) 44044.

Central and Fife Area Office, 5 Kirk Loan, Edinburgh EH2 7HD. Tel: (031) 334 9821.

Glasgow City Area Office, 4th Floor, George House, 36 North Hanover Street, Glasgow G1 2AD. Tel: (041) 552 3411.

Grampian and Tayside Area Office, Argyll House, Marketgait, Dundee DD1 1UD. Tel: (0382) 29971.

Highlands and Island Area Office, 3rd Floor, Metropolitan House, 31–33 High Street, Inverness IV1 1TX. Tel: (0463) 220555.

Lanarkshire Area Office, Scomagg House, Crosshill Street, Motherwell ML1 1RU. Tel: (0698) 51411.

Lothian and Borders Area Office, 2–3 Queen Street, Edinburgh EH2 1JS. Tel: (031) 225 1377.

Dunbarton, Argyll and Renfrewshire Area Office, West Block, 5 Elmbank Gardens, Charing Cross, Glasgow G2 4PN. Tel: (041) 226 5544.

SKILLS TRAINING AGENCIES (STAs)

Skillcentres

Northern

Regional Office
3rd Floor, Maclaren House, Talbot Road, Stretford, Manchester M32 0FP. Tel: (061) 872 4111 or 4114.

Bradford
Common Road, Low Moor, Bradford, West Yorkshire BD12 0SF. Tel: (0274) 600911.

Cheshire
Castle Rise, Runcorn, Cheshire WA7 5XR. Tel: (092 85) 65921/4.

Cumbria
Glasson Industrial Estate, Maryport, Cumbria CA15 8NY. Tel: (0900) 812771/2.

East Lancashire
Eagle Street, Accrington, Lancashire BB5 1NS. Tel: (0254) 395521.

Hull
Chamberlain Road, Hull HU8 8HL. Tel: (0482) 20738.

Leeds
Parkside Lane, Leeds LS11 5SZ. Tel: (0532) 704661.

Liverpool
105 Boundary Street, Kirkdale, Liverpool L5 9YT. Tel: (051) 207 6031.

Manchester
Guinness Road, Trafford Park, Manchester M17 1SD. Tel: (061) 872 6042.

Preston
180 Longridge Road, Preston, Lancashire PR2 5AP. Tel: (0772) 652021.

Rochdale
Chichester Street, Rochdale OL16 2AG. Tel: (0706) 341514.

St Helens
Bedford Street, Park Industrial Estate, St Helens, Merseyside WA9 1PN. Tel: (0744) 34134.

Sheffield
Richmond Park Road, Sheffield S13 8HT. Tel: (0742) 446471.

Wakefield
Doncaster Road, Wakefield. Tel: (0924) 375823.

Wigan
Swan Lane, Hindley Green, Wigan WN2 5ID. Tel: (0942) 56123.

South East

Regional Office
Skyline House, 200 Union Street, London SE1 0LY. Tel: (01) 928 0770.

Barking
25 Thames Road, Barking, Essex IG11 0HR. Tel: (01) 591 2662.

Basildon
Bentalls, Cranes Farm Road, Basildon, Essex SS143BT. Tel: (0268) 3225.

Chelmsford
Farrow Road, Rodney Way, Widford Industrial Estate, Chelmsford CM1 3TF. Tel: (0245) 26533.

Deptford
2 Deptford Church Street, London SE8 4SJ. Tel: (01) 691 5721.

Enfield
Bilton Way, Enfield, Middlesex EN3 7NZ. Tel: (01) 805 1365.

Ipswich
White House Road, Ipswich, Suffolk IP1 5NX. Tel: (0473) 47464.

Lambeth
Unit 13–14, 11 Lyham Road, London SW2 5DZ. Tel: (01) 274 4106.

Letchworth
Pixmore Avenue, Letchworth, Herts SG6 1JP. Tel: (046 26) 3084.
Residence, Pixmore Avenue, Letchworth, Herts SG6 1JP. Tel: (046 26) 3084.
Letchworth Instructor Training College, Pixmore Avenue, Letchworth, Herts SG6 1JP. Tel: (046 26) 72872.

Medway
Courteney Road, Gillingham, Kent ME8 0RY. Tel: (0634) 360404. Annexe (to close).
Sittingbourne Industrial Park, Crown Quay Lane, Sittingbourne, Kent ME10 3JL. Tel: (0795) 71231.

Milton Keynes
Chesney Wold, Bleak Hall, Milton Keynes, Bucks MK6 1LX. Tel: (0908) 670001.

Norwich
Swanton Road, Mile Cross Road, Norwich NR2 4LR. Tel: (0603) 49181.

Perivale
Walmgate Road, Perivale, Greenford, Middlesex UB6 7NE. Tel: (01) 998 1451.

Peterborough
Saville Road, Westwood, Peterborough PE3 6TQ. Tel: (0733) 267242.

Twickenham
Industrial Estate, Rugby Road, Twickenham, Middlesex TW1 1DT. Tel: (01) 892 6285.
Waddon Annexe, Worsley Bridge Road, Sydenham, London SE26 5BE. Tel: (01) 658 3527.

South West

Regional Office
Bristol Skillcentre, Gill Avenue, Fishponds, Bristol BS16 2QL. Tel: (0272) 657446.

Bristol
Gill Avenue, Fishponds, Bristol BS16 2QL. Tel: (0272) 657446.

Gloucester
117 Bristol Road, Gloucester GL1 5SP. Tel: (0452) 27721.

Plymouth
Newnham Industrial Estate, Strode Road, Plympton St Mary, Plymouth, Devon PL7 4B5. Tel: (0752) 335921.

Portsmouth
Scott Road, Hilsea, Portsmouth, Hampshire PO3 5LF. Tel: (0705) 668831.

Reading
Manor Farm Road, Reading, Berkshire RG2 0JH. Tel: (0734) 864524.

Redruth
Wilson Way, Pool Industrial Estate, Redruth, Cornwall TS15 3SD. Tel: (0209) 213231.

Slough
Walpole Road, off Bath Road, Cippenham, Slough, Berkshire SL1 6BN. Tel: (062 86) 5222.

Slough Residence
Bath Road, Cippenham, Slough, Berkshire SL1 6BN. Tel: (062 86) 5222.

Somerset Training Centre
58 Salmon Parade, Bridgwater, Somerset TA6 5JT. Tel: (0278) 428494.

Southampton
West Bay Road, Southampton, Hampshire SO9 3SH. Tel: (0703) 228281.
Auckland Road, Millbrook, Southampton, Hampshire SO0 4YN. Tel: (0703) 228281.

Swindon
Faraday Road, Dorcan, Swindon SN3 5HB. Tel: (0793) 641671.

West Sussex
Churchill Industrial Estate, Chartwell Road, Lancing, West Sussex BN15 8YB. Tel: (0903) 764331.

Wales and the Midlands

Regional Office
Conference Centre, Middlemore Road, Handsworth, Birmingham B21 0BU. Tel: (021) 554 5222.

Birmingham
Middlemore Road, Handsworth, Birmingham B21 0BT. Tel: (021) 554 5222.

Cardiff
Western Avenue, Cardiff CF4 3XY. Tel: (0222) 621343.

Chesterfield
Dunstan Trading Estate, Foxwood Road, Sheepbridge, Chesterfield. Tel: (024 56) 450511.

Coventry
Binns Close, Torrington Avenue, Coventry CV4 9TB. Tel: (0203) 474544.

Leicester
Humberstone Lane, Leicester LE4 7JW. Tel: (0533) 769101.

Newport
Corporation Road, Newport, Gwent NPT 0YT. Tel: (0633) 271160.

Northampton
4 Clayfields Close, Moulton Park, Northampton NN3 1QF. Tel: (0604) 46643.

North Staffs
Clough Street, Hanley, Stoke on Trent, Staffs. Tel: (0782) 261521.

Nottingham
Lilac Grove, Beeston, Nottingham NG9 1QY. Tel: (0602) 221112.

Port Talbot
Cramic Way, Port Talbot, West Glamorgan SA13 1RY. Tel: (0639) 884691/6.

Wolverhampton
Craddock Street, Whitmore Reans, Wolverhampton WV6 0OJ. Tel: (0902) 27173.

Wrexham
Wrexham, Bersham Road, Clwyd LL13 7UH. Tel: (0978) 355555.

Scotland and the North East

Regional Office
5 Kirk Loan, Corstophine Road, Edinburgh EH12 7HD. Tel: (031) 334 9821.

Bellshill
Bellshill Industrial Estate, Bellshill, Lanarkshire ML4 3JE. Tel: (0698) 748667.

Billingham
Industrial Estate, Leeholme Road, Billingham on Tees TS23 3TE. Tel: (0642) 560811.

Dundee
4 Staffa Place, Dundee DD2 3SX. Tel: (0382) 816633.

Dunfermline
Townhill, Dunfermline, Fife KY12 0TB. Tel: (0383) 721148.

Durham
Littleburn Trading Estate, Langley Moore, Co Durham DH7 8HG. Tel: (0385) 780601.

Edinburgh
West Granton Road, Edinburgh EH5 1JB. Tel: (031) 551 1461.

Annexe
West Harbour Road, West Harbour Industrial Estate, Edinburgh EH5 1PT. Tel: (031) 552 3216.

Glasgow (Hillington)
Hillington Industrial Estate, Queen Elizabeth Avenue, Glasgow G52 4TL. Tel: (041) 810 3111.

Irvine
Ayr Road, Irvine, Ayrshire KA12 8ES. Tel: (0294) 78688.

Tyneside
Green Lane, Felling, Gateshead NE10 0LA. Tel: (091) 469 4314.

25 Radio and TV

WHAT BROADCASTING OFFERS

Since radio and TV were first invented people have wanted to use them for education. They seem to offer the perfect opportunity to give everyone access to knowledge that used to be confined to small groups of experts.

Broadcasts have rarely worked well as a method of teaching all on their own, but they have proved invaluable in getting things started or when combined with supporting materials or services. For example, in Open University courses, on average 10% of student study time is spent on broadcast material and you could probably manage without it altogether. *On the move*, the programme to teach people to read, was used for that purpose by very few people, but was used by an enormous number as a way of getting in touch with someone who would help face to face and locally. On the other hand *Make it count*, a Yorkshire Television basic maths series, led most people to buy the accompanying book and study it at home.

More and more educational broadcasts are linked to other things, perhaps a course you can do at your local college (like the language series *A vous la France!*), residential courses (discussed in *27 Leisure classes*), or a correspondence course; they may combine printed materials and local support of some sort (like Channel 4's *Write on* series and workbook to encourage people to develop their writing skills, OU programmes about young children – *The first years of life*) or publications and phone-ins (like Central's networked *Workout* series on unemployment). All the broadcasting organisations have someone responsible for educational programming and efforts are also made to work with the local education service. But there is a sense in which all broadcasting is educative. It's all a question of how you use what you see and hear. Programmes like *Panorama* or *World in action* set out to inform us and can be very useful to people on courses; *Tomorrow's world* is one thing to a casual viewer, another to an Open University technology student.

The Open College

In July 1986 Lord Young announced the setting up of a college of the air – The Open College – designed to bring together broadcasters, educationalists and sponsors to provide vocational education and training. The College will provide courses below degree level which help people improve their vocational competence. Courses will be available through a combination of broadcasting on radio and TV with local back-up provided by colleges and other learning establishments! The first courses are expected to start in September 1987. To find out more

★ **ASK** College of the Air, c/o Manpower Services Commission, St Mary's House, Moorfoot, Sheffield S1 4PQ.

Local radio

Local radio stations are very responsive to local ideas and needs. For instance, BBC Radio Leicester has been broadcasting programmes to help people in the local Asian community improve their written and spoken English. Many local radio stations have advice lines and programmes dealing with the needs of different groups in the community, such as BBC Radio Newcastle, Radio Cumbria, and Radio Merseyside and Capital Radio's *Helpline* which provides on-air information and is backed up by an off-air phone-in advice and referral service. BBC Radio York runs two evening courses on air, one for school governors, and one dealing with retirement issues. Radio Nottingham's daily programme, *TXRX*, is run in close collaboration with community groups and provides advice on a range of topics, such as employment, health etc. Women's health is dealt with and is supported by a booklet *Well woman* available from the Education Producer at Radio Nottingham. In Dundee, Radio Tay is running a very popular series of courses four nights a week in collaboration from the local colleges. New technology courses are proving especially popular.

If you think a subject of local interest could be covered and isn't, why not approach your local radio station? Approaches from groups or organisations always have a good chance. For more about how to use local radio:

★ **LOOK AT** *Using the media*, Dennis McShane, Pluto Press, 1980.

★ **WRITE TO** The Media Project, The Volunteer Centre, 29 Lower King's Road, Berkhamstead, Herts HP4 2AB.

FINDING OUT WHAT'S HAPPENING

BBC TV and radio

The BBC issues a supplement in the *Radio times* called *Learning at home*, in early September, January and March which lists programmes on BBC TV and national radio.

They also produce a *Continuing education* newsletter four times a year outlining programme plans up to 18 months ahead, which they send to all colleges and public libraries. If your library doesn't have one, tell them that they should!

★ **WRITE TO** BBC Education, London W5 2PA.

BBC local stations mostly have a full-time producer responsible for education who can give information and advice about programmes. The BBC also publishes information centrally about local radio.

★ **WRITE TO** Local Radio Education Adviser, Cliff Kitney, Room 202, Bank Buildings, 14/15 Langham Place, London W1A 1AA. Tel: (01) 927 4935.

★ **ASK** the Station Manager of your BBC local radio station (see below for addresses) for details of programmes planned locally or:

★ **LOOK AT** local editions of *Radio times*.

Independent TV and radio

Independent broadcasting (ITV and ILR), unlike the centralised BBC, is a regionally organised broadcasting system.

Independent TV

Adult education is planned at annual workshops. These three or four day meetings decide the policy for the programme year, a year ahead. The IBA has now set up the Programme Support and Development Group, whose job is to provide programme information, support materials and back-up to programmes and act as a broker between producers and support agencies. All ITV companies now have Community and Continuing Education Officers. They work together in supporting network adult education on ITV and Channel 4, and they are also involved in supporting local education programming.

Adult education programmes tend to be broadcast at certain times. They are usually on Sunday mornings and in mid-day week slots. The more popular series are becoming more accessible, eg after the 10 pm news programmes, or occasionally, at 7 pm – peak viewing time. A booklet, *TV Take up*, gives advance information (see below).

Independent Local Radio

The number of ILR stations in operation is now expanding at a steady rate towards an expected total of about 70 stations. The requirement to provide at least one hour of planned and structured education is expected of all of them. Most exceed this amount. Topics such as health education, parent education, consumerism and advice to the unemployed have been covered. There are also some interesting projects involving outside organisations and bodies such as the Open University, the Manpower Services Commission and extra-mural departments.

★ **WRITE TO** the Education Officer of your local ITV company or to the Education Officer (Adult and Continuing Education), IBA, 70 Brompton Road, London SW3 1EY. The list of ITV companies (below) includes the names of the Community and Continuing Education Officers.

★ **SEND FOR** *TV Take up*, which previews adult education on ITV and Channel 4, from The Programme Support and Development Group, Education Department, IBA (address above).

For details of other programming (those not designated 'educational' but nonetheless of particular interest and value to home learners):

★ **WRITE TO** your local ITV and ILR station. Give details of the subjects you are studying.

★ **LOOK AT** *TV Times*.

CHANNEL 4

Channel 4 is a wholly owned subsidiary of the IBA with its own board. Channel 4 has a particular responsibility to cater for interests which have not previously had much coverage on television – including taking seriously the needs of a multi-cultural society, of young people, and of people over 60. Fifteen per cent of Channel 4's time is devoted to educational programming, but much of the rest of the output aims to be educative also.

A strong emphasis is placed on viewers learning at home, and, to that end, back-up material has been prepared for a great variety of series and single programmes. Distribution of this material is arranged through the various broadcasting support agencies in England, Scotland and Northern Ireland (listed in *20 Basics*) and through other national organisations such as the National Extension College, the Libraries' Association and the National Book League. For details of the licensing scheme for copying certain programmes off-air:

★ **WRITE TO** Channel 4 Licensing Scheme, Guild Sound and Vision, 6 Royce Road, Peterborough, PE1 5YB.

The Channel 4 Educational Liaison Officer also attempts to meet with a wide variety of informal and formal educators throughout the country to discuss the exploitation of programmes in the community. The *SEE 4* newspaper, with full details of programmes, is published regularly. For the annual catalogue of publications:

★ **WRITE TO** Channel 4 Catalogue, PO Box 4000, London WC 6XJ, or Glasgow G12 9JQ, or Belfast BT2 7FE. Enclose an SAE.

★ **WRITE TO** the Educational Liaison Officer, Channel 4 Television, 60 Charlotte Street, London W1P 2AX. Tel: (01) 927 8921.

The Welsh channel – S4C

A separate fourth channel, S4C, provides a Welsh language service for Wales. All programmes in Welsh are now shown on S4C. Programmes are produced by the BBC in Wales, the local independent contractor HTV and independent companies. S4C screens over 23 hours of Welsh language programmes a week. At other times it screens Channel 4's network programmes in English.

★ **ASK** The Head of Public Relations, S4C, Sophia Close, Cardiff CF1 9XY. Tel: (0222) 43421.

PUBLICATIONS

The BBC, ITV companies and ILR stations produce books, leaflets and records arising out of their own programmes. Books and materials accompanying programmes are usually described in the programme, including information about where to buy them. Sometimes they are published by commercial publishers, sometimes by the broadcasters themselves. Both the BBC and ITV have their own publishing sides.

★ **WRITE TO** BBC Publications, PO Box 234, London SE1 3TH.

★ **WRITE TO** Programme Support and Development Group, IBA, 70 Brompton Road, London SW3 1EY.

Annual handbooks

Both the BBC and the IBA publish a handbook every year which is an invaluable source of information about how they work.

★ **LOOK AT** *BBC handbook 1986.*

★ **LOOK AT** *Television and radio 1986: IBA guide to independent broadcasting.*

You should be able to find them in the library or buy them through any bookshop. If in difficulty, contact BBC Publications and Independent Television Publications Ltd respectively.

ADDRESSES

Independent radio and television

IBA Education Department, 70 Brompton Road, London SW3 1EY. Tel: (01) 584 7011.

ITV companies

Anglia Television, Head Office, Anglia House, Norwich NR1 3JG. Tel: (0603) 615151. CCEO Ms Sylvia Shendon.

Central Independent Television, Central House, Broad Street, Birmingham B1 2JP. Tel: (021) 643 9898. CCEO Mr Rex Bird.

Border Television, Television Centre, Carlisle CA1 3NT. Tel: (0228) 25101. Education Officer Mr Clem Shaw.

Channel Television, The Television Centre, St Helier, Jersey. Tel: (0534) 73999.

Grampian Television, Queen's Cross, Aberdeen AB9 2XJ. Tel: (0224) 646464. CCEO Ms Marian Hepworth.

Granada Television, Granada Television Centre, Manchester M60 9EA. Tel: (061) 832 7211. Community liaison for adult education and religious programmes Canon Frank Wright.

HTV Wales, The Television Centre, Cardiff CF1 9XL. Tel: (0222) 21021. CEO Ms Bethan Eames.

HTV West, Television Centre, Bath Road, Bristol BS4 3HG. Tel: (0272) 778366. Education Officer Mr Gerry Dawson.

London Weekend Television, South Bank Television Centre, Kent House, Upper Ground, London SE1 9LT. Tel: (01) 261 3434. CCEO Ms Liz Woodison.

Scottish Television, Cowcaddens, Glasgow G2 3PR. Tel: (041) 332 9999. Education Liaison Officer (AE) Ms Liz Stephen.

Television South West, Derry's Cross, Plymouth PL1 2SP. Tel: (0752) 663322. Head of Education Mr Tom Goodison.

Thames Television, Education Department, International House, 149 Tottenham Court Road, London W1P 9LL. Tel: (01) 388 5199. CCEO Ms Penny French.

TVS (Television South), Television Centre, Northam, Southampton SO9 5HZ. Tel: (0703) 34211. CCEO Mr Hugh Geach.

Tyne Tees Television, The Television Centre, City Road, Newcastle-upon-Tyne NE1 2AL. Tel: (0632) 610181. CCEO Ms Sheila Browne.

Ulster Television, Havelock House, Ormeau Road, Belfast BT7 1EB. Tel: (0232) 28122. Education Officer Mr George Fleeton.

Yorkshire Television, The Television Centre, Leeds LS3 1JS. Tel: (0532) 38283. CCEO Ms Mary Hunter.

Independent Local Radio stations

ILR Aberdeen, North Sound Radio, 45 Kings Gate, Aberdeen AB2 6BL. Tel: (0224) 632234.

ILR Ayr, West Sound, Radio House, 54 Holmston Road, Ayr KA7 3BE. Tel: (0292) 283662.

ILR Belfast, Downtown Radio, PO Box 96, Newtonards, Northern Ireland BT23 4ES. Tel: (0247) 815555.

ILR Birmingham, BRMB Radio, Radio House, PO Box 555, Aston Road North, Birmingham B6 4BX. Tel: (021) 359 4481.

ILR Bournemouth, 2CR (Two Counties Radio), 5/7 Southcote Road, Bournemouth BH1 3LR. Tel: (0202) 294881.

ILR Bradford/Huddersfield & Halifax, Pennine Radio, PO Box 235, Pennine House, Forster Square, Bradford BD1 5NP. Tel: (0274) 731521.

ILR Brighton, Southern Sound, Radio House, Franklin Road, Portslade BN4 2SS. Tel: (0273) 422288.

ILR Bury St Edmunds, Saxon Radio, Long Brackland, Bury St Edmunds, Suffolk IP33 1JY. Tel: (0284) 701511.

ILR Cardiff, Red Dragon Radio, Radio House, West Canal Wharf, Cardiff CF1 5XJ. Tel: (0222) 384041.

ILR Coventry, Mercia Sound, Hertford Place, Coventry CV1 3TT. Tel: (0203) 28451.

ILR Dundee/Perth, Radio Tay, PO Box 123, Dundee DD1 9UF. Tel: (0382) 29551.

ILR Edinburgh, Radio Forth, Forth House, Forth Street, Edinburgh EH1 3LF. Tel: (031) 556 9255.

ILR Exeter/Torbay, Devon Air Radio, 35/37 St David's Hill, Exeter EX4 4DA. Tel: (0392) 30703.

ILR Glasgow, Radio Clyde, Clydebank Business Park, Clydebank, Glasgow G81 2RX. Tel: (041) 941 1111.

ILR Gloucester and Cheltenham, Severn Sound, PO Box 388, Gloucester GL1 1TX. Tel: (0452) 423791.

ILR Great Yarmouth & Norwich, Radio Broadland, 47–49 St George's Plain, Colegate, Norwich NR3 1DD. Tel: (0603) 630621.

ILR Guildford, County Sound, The Friary, Guildford GU1 4YX. Tel: (0483) 505566.

ILR Hereford/Worcester, Radio Wyvern, 5/6 Barbourne Terrace, Worcester WR1 3JN. Tel: (0905) 612212.

ILR Humberside, Viking Radio, Commercial Road, Hull HU1 2SA. Tel: (0482) 25141.

ILR Inverness, Moray Firth Radio, PO Box 271, Inverness IV3 6SF. Tel: (0463) 224433.

ILR Ipswich, Radio Orwell, Electric House, Lloyds Avenue, Ipswich IP1 3HZ. Tel: (0473) 216971.

ILR Leeds, Radio Aire, PO Box 362, Leeds LS3 1LR. Tel: (0532) 452299.

ILR Leiceter, Leicester Sound, Granville House, Granville Road, Leicester L51 7RW. Tel: (0533) 551616.

ILR Liverpool, Radio City, PO Box 194, 8/10 Stanley Street, Liverpool L69 1LD. Tel: (051) 227 5100.

ILR London, General and Entertainment Service, Capital Radio, Euston Tower, London NW1 3DR. Tel: (01) 388 1288.

ILR London, News and Information Service, London Broadcasting Company (LBC), Communications House, Gough Square, London EC4P 4LP. Tel: (01) 353 1010.

ILR Luton/Bedford, Chiltern Radio, Chiltern Road, Dunstable, Bedfordshire LU6 1HQ. Tel: (0582) 666001. 55 Goldington Road, Bedford MK40 3LS. Tel: (0234) 49266.

ILR Maidstone & Medway/East Kent, Invicta Radio (incorporating Northdown Radio and Network East Kent), 37 Earl Street, Maidstone ME14 1PF. Tel: (0622) 679061. 15 Station Road East, Canterbury, Kent CT1 2RB. Tel: (0927) 67661.

ILR Manchester, Piccadilly Radio, 127/131 The Piazza, Piccadilly Plaza, Manchester M1 4AW. Tel: (061) 236 9913.

ILR Northampton, Hereward Radio, PO Box 1557, Abington Street, Northampton NN1 2HW. Tel: (0604) 29811.

ILR Nottingham, Radio Trent, 29/31 Castle Gate, Nottingham NG1 7AP. Tel: (0602) 581731.

ILR Peterborough, Hereward Radio, PO Box 225, Bridge Street, Peterborough PE1 1JX. Tel: (0733) 46225.

ILR Plymouth, Plymouth Sound, Earls Acre, Alma Road, Plymouth PL3 4HX. Tel: (0752) 27272.

ILR Portsmouth/Southampton Ocean Sound, Whittle Avenue, Fareham, Hants PO15 5PA. Tel: (0489) 589911.

ILR Preston and Blackpool, Red Rose Radio, PO Box 301, St Paul's Square, Preston PR1 1YE. Tel: (0772) 556301.

ILR Reading, Radio 210, (Thames Valley Broadcasting), PO Box 210, Reading, Berkshire RG3 5RZ. Tel: (0734) 413131.

ILR Reigate & Crawley, Radio Mercury, Broadfield House, Brighton Road, Crawley RH11 9BJ. Tel: (0293) 519161.

ILR Sheffield and Rotherham, Radio Hallam, PO Box 194, Hartshead, Sheffield S1 1GP. Tel: (0742) 71188.

ILR Southend/Chelmsford, Essex Radio, Radio House, Clifftown Road, Southend-on-Sea, Essex SS1 1SX. Tel: (0702) 333711.

ILR Stoke-on-Trent, Signal Radio, Studio 257, 67/73 Stoke Road, Stoke-on-Trent ST4 2SR. Tel: (0782) 417111.

ILR Swansea, Swansea Sound, Victoria Road, Glowerton, Swansea SA4 3AB. Tel: (0792) 893751.

ILR Swindon/West Wiltshire/Bristol, Great Western Radio (GWR), Lime Kiln Studios, Wootton Bassett, Swindon, Wiltshire SN4 7EX. Tel: (0793) 853222.

ILR Teesside, Radio Tees, 74 Dovecot Street, Stockton on Tees, Cleveland TS18 1HB. Tel: (0642) 615111.

ILR Tyne/Wear, Metro Radio, Newcastle-upon-Tyne NE99 1BB. Tel: (091) 488 3131.

ILR Wolverhampton/Black Country, Beacon Radio, PO Box 303, 267 Tettenhall Road, Wolverhampton WV6 0DQ. Tel: (0902) 757211.

ILR Wrexham and Deeside, Marcher Sound/Sain-Y-Gororau, The Studios, Gwersyllt, Wrexham, Clwyd LL11 4AF. Tel: (0978) 752202.

BBC radio and television

BBC Educational Broadcasting Services and Education Department Controller, Educational Broadcasting, Villiers House, The Broadway, Ealing, London W5 2PA.

BBC local radio

Programme Services Editor: Greg Ainger, BBC Local Radio, Room 230, The Langham, Portland Place, London W1A 1AA. Tel: (01) 580 4468 ext 4272 or 3834 for general enquiries about education on BBC Local Radio.

Radio Bedford, PO Box 476, Hastings Street, Luton, Beds LU1 5BA. Tel: (0582) 45911.

Radio Brighton, Marlborough Place, Brighton, Sussex BN1 1TU. Tel: (0273) 680231.

Radio Bristol, 3 Tyndalls Park Road, Bristol BS99 7QT. Tel: (0272) 741111.

Radio Cambridgeshire, Broadcasting House, 104 Hills Road, Cambridge CB2 1LD. Tel: (0223) 315970.

Radio Cleveland, 91/93 Linthorpe Road, Middlesbrough, Cleveland TS1 5DG. Tel: (0642) 225211.

Radio Cornwall, Phoenix Wharf, Truro, Cornwall TR1 1UA. Tel: (0872) 75421.

Radio Cumbria, Hilltop Heights, London Road, Carlisle CA1 2NA. Tel: (0228) 31661.

Radio Derby, 56 St Helens Street, Derby DE1 3HY. Tel: (0332) 361111.

Radio Devon, St David's Hill, Exeter, Devon EX4 4DB. Tel: (0392) 21561.

BBC Essex, 198 New London Road, Chelmsford, Essex CM2 9AB. Tel: (0245) 262393.

Radio Foyle, PO Box 927, 8 Northland Road, Londonderry BT48 7HL. Tel: (0504) 266522.

Radio Guernsey, Commerce House, Les Banques, St Peter Port, Guernsey. Tel: (0481) 28977.

Radio Humberside, 63 Jameson Street, Hull HU1 3NU. Tel: (0482) 23232.

Radio Jersey, Broadcasting House, Rouge Bouillon, St Helier, Jersey. Tel: (0534) 70000.

Radio Kent, 30 High Street, Chatham, Kent ME4 4EZ. Tel: (0634) 46284.

Radio Lancashire, King Street, Blackburn, Lancashire BB2 2EA. Tel: (0254) 62411.

Radio Leeds, Broadcasting House, Woodhouse Lane, Leeds LS2 9PN. Tel: (0532) 442131.

Radio Leicester, Epic House, Charles Street, Leicester LE1 3SH. Tel: (0533) 27113.
Radio Lincolnshire, Radion Buildings, 10a Newport, Lincoln LN1 3EU. Tel: (0522) 40011.
Radio London, 35a Marylebone High Street, London W1A 4LG. Tel: (01) 486 7611.
Radio Manchester, New Broadcasting House, Oxford Road, Manchester M60 1SJ. Tel: (061) 228 3434.
Radio Merseyside, 55 Paradise Street, Liverpool L1 3BP. Tel: (051) 708 5500.
Radio Newcastle, Crestina House, Archbold Terrace, Newcastle-upon-Tyne NE2 1DZ. Tel: (0632) 814243.
Radio Norfolk, Norfolk Tower, Surrey Street, Norwich NR1 3PA. Tel: (0603) 617411.
Radio Northampton, Compton House, Abington Street, Northampton NN1 2BE. Tel: (0604) 20621.
Radio Nottingham, York House, Mansfield Road, Nottingham NG1 3JB. Tel: (0602) 415161.
Radio Oxford, 242/254 Banbury Road, Oxford OX2 7DW. Tel: (0865) 53411.
Radio Sheffield, Ashdell Grove, 60 Westbourne Road, Sheffield S10 2QU. Tel: (0742) 686185.
Radio Shropshire, 2–4 Boscobel Drive, Heath Farm, Shrewsbury, Shropshire SY1 3TT. Tel: (0743) 248484.
Radio Solent, South Western House, Canute Road, Southampton SO9 4PJ. Tel: (0703) 686185.
Radio Stoke, Conway House, Cheapside, Hanley, Stoke-on-Trent ST1 1JJ. Tel: (0782) 24827.
Radio Ulster, Broadcasting House, Ormeau Avenue, Belfast BT2 8HQ. Tel: (0232) 244400.
Radio West Midlands, Pebble Mill Road, Birmingham B5 7SA. Tel: (021) 472 5141.
Radio York, 20 Bootham Row, York YO3 7BR. Tel: (0904) 641351.

26 Learning by post

Correspondence courses
What are they like?
What do they offer?
Accreditation
Choosing
Recent developments
Accredited colleges

CORRESPONDENCE COLLEGES

Learning by correspondence course has long been a popular and succesful way of studying. This is largely because it is very flexible; you can do it when and how you want, make it fit in with your life. It has also been a very succesful method of learning for people who can't get to a college for some reason – they may have a disability, may live miles away from a college and so on.

There are also disadvantages. One is that it is a lonely method of studying; you don't have the benefit of tutors or other students on hand to talk to, compare notes with, discuss progress with. A second problem is that it is a field in which it is easy for unscrupulous people to cheat you – a potential problem when you are buying *anything* by post.

Having said that, this is part of the education system that has always been completely open; the correspondence colleges have never imposed entry qualifications on students and they've always tried to attract people from all classes by advertising in popular magazines as well as quality journals. And the field has developed in ways to deal with both of these problems – most of the important colleges in this country are 'accredited', and techniques such as 'Flexistudy' developed by the National Extension College, and the increasing use of new technology, are beginning to make the situation of the correspondence student a bit less lonely.

WHAT IS IT LIKE?

In the words of one expert on correspondence colleges, 'it's excellent, but to do it you need real character'. In other words, it's hard work, and requires self-discipline. It's not an easy way out, though some colleges seem to suggest that in their advertising, or in their names. To get fast results, you need to work hard and well; the college can only help you make the best use of your efforts.

MAN, 36
I just wanted two A-levels quickly. So I enrolled on a correspondence course. It was a package to get me through the exams I wanted. I had some previous knowledge, so I was able to do them in three months and I got good grades. When I did the exam, I more or less repeated the model answers I'd had. It worked.

MAN, 29
When I qualified to become an accountant, about 80% of us took the same correspondence course. It was so boring I could hardly bear to look at it. I finally enrolled at a four-week course of intensive lectures. But the course was still useful – all the information was there.

Practically all the correspondence colleges offer the same basic structure:

- An individual timetable depending on when you want to sit the exam.
- Complete sets of notes and information sent at regular intervals (the course units). Sometimes you may be advised to buy books as well.
- Assignments – things you do (essays etc) and send to your tutor for marking.
- Problem forms – a way of telling your tutor you're stuck, but in writing. You get a written reply.
- Self-assessment tests – list of questions so you know how much you've learnt.
- Specimen answers – answers to assignments written as a guide to how to approach the question.

So, if you do as you're told and can keep up with the work, you'll pass the exam. There's no pretence of 'educating' you – it's about passing exams. It can be lonely, and the support of your 'personal tutor' may well not be enough. You have to be determined.

WHAT DO CORRESPONDENCE COLLEGES OFFER?

Mostly a way of getting qualifications. There are a few big colleges which offer a wide range of courses – professional subjects (eg building, banking, insurance, accountancy), GCSE courses, OU preparatory courses, London University external degrees. The others tend to be more specialist, like the Northern School of Physical Therapies, The College of Estate Management, NALGO Correspondence Institute. But several of them offer GCSEs as well, so it's worth getting quite a few prospectuses. The National Extension College is rather different and has led the way in many new developments in distance learning.

Most of the following information applies mainly to the big colleges which advertise in national newspapers such as *Exchange and mart* etc. They offer:

- A prospectus – a mine of information about professional qualifications. Worth getting just for that, if you can resist the temptation to enrol at once (which they all try to get you to do).
- Prizes – some colleges give prizes to their students if they do particularly well.
- Career advice – most have a postal advice system; one or two offer face-to-face interviews as well.
- Support meetings – some of the professional courses can be done with college courses.
- Personal tutors – all offer a personal tutor. Wolsey Hall lets you talk by tape; NEC gives you your tutor's phone number if he or she gives permission.

- Guarantees – many offer you one, such as: 'if you fail your exam, we'll re-tutor you free'. One offers you your money back if you fail. But only if you've completed the whole course properly.

Costs
Vary a lot. It's like trying to compare car hire prices – there are so many special deals. Average seems to be £60 to £80 for A-level per subject, and £200 to £350 for a banking course. But do get the prospectuses and compare them!

ACCREDITATION

The Council for the Accreditation of Correspondence Colleges (CACC) operates with the approval of the DES. It is an independent body which inspects colleges and grants approval if the Council's criteria are being met. Most of the approved colleges show their accreditation certificate in their prospectus.

If you want information about where to find a particular course at an accredited college, or you want to check on whether a college you've found is accredited (and if not, whether your course is available at one that is):

★ **ASK** CACC, 27 Marylebone Road, London NW1 5JS. Tel: (01) 935 5391.

Non accredited colleges
There are many colleges that are not accredited. They offer courses in anything you can think of: photography, languages, drawing, piano playing, Swedish massage, PSV driving, religion and so on. Some are respectable but there is no easy way of knowing.

CHOOSING

Most of the correspondence colleges are private companies. Some of them use quite high-pressure sales techniques – sending follow-up letters as well as the prospectus you ask for, offering all kinds of encouragement (including discounts) to enrol. How can you tell if you're getting what you pay for? It's very hard to judge in advance how good the correspondence colleges really are. Accreditation in itself is not necessarily enough – how do you choose between two accredited colleges?

In Europe there are stricter rules governing what correspondence colleges can do. These rules ban high-pressure sales techniques, promoting courses before they've been written and various other abuses. It looks as if they won't be introduced in Britain for the moment. But you can still ask the colleges you approach the following questions, which reflect the EEC rules and which are used by CACC when it inspects a college:

- has the course material been written only for the course advertised?
- when was the last time the notes were thoroughly revised?
- is the course already written?
- do they give refunds? If so, for what?
- can they send you a specimen of the course material?

The Association of British Correspondence Colleges (ABCC)
This Association is a trade association representing nineteen of the colleges. It produces a free broadsheet and will offer advice to potential students. Its members also have an agreed code of ethics designed to maintain standards.

★ **WRITE TO** The Secretary, Association of British Correspondence Colleges, 6 Francis Grove, London SW19 4DT.

Complaints
If you're not happy with what you get, you should complain to CACC, which is the main body concerned with standards. They will take it up with the college concerned. If you have a complaint about a college that is a member of the ABCC you should also get in touch with them.

The only other channel of complaint is your local consumer protection department. They can only help with misleading adverts.

RECENT DEVELOPMENTS

Colleges change and update their courses to meet new needs and demands. In addition, new ways of using correspondence courses are developing.

Media links
More and more radio and TV programmes have printed support materials, sometimes produced by correspondence schools, and are mentioned on the programmes. It can work both ways of course – the broadcast can also be an effective bit of back up to your correspondence course. See *25 Radio and TV*.

Supported correspondence courses
Because of the problems of student isolation, and consequent high dropout rates from correspondence courses, a lot of work has gone into devising ways of providing students with more contact and support from tutors and other students. The best developed example of this is the National Extension College's Flexistudy. This involves buying your correspondence course through a local college; you get not just the course but a tutorial system with someone you can meet easily. This system is described in more detail in *17 Flexible learning*.

New technology
This type of learning, often called distance learning, is one area where modern technology can make a big impact. For example:

- many correspondence colleges now compile their courses on word processors so that they can update them more easily, cheaply and hence more often
- audio tapes have been used for some type as part of correspondence courses but video tapes are now beginning to be used as well – very appropriate where courses are dealing with practical skills
- computers are beginning to be used; for example, the National Extension College's 'Mail' system provides a method of marking student assignments that allows for very rapid marking and return of results.

Open Learning

These developments are all part of a wider movement towards what is often called Open Learning. The Open University is one example; the Manpower Services Commission runs the Open Tech Project and there are very many other developments in this field (for more information see *17 Flexible learning*).

ACCREDITED COLLEGES

The Agricultural Correspondence College, Warborough, nr Oxford OX9 8DQ. Tel: (086732) 8219. Farming.

The Association of Dispensing Opticians, 22 Nottingham Place, London W1M 4AT. Tel: (01) 935 7411/2. Preliminary and final dispensing examination courses. ADO fellowship and honours diplomas (leading to registration by General Optical Council).

British Careers Training College, Howard House, Esplanade, PO Box 253, Jersey. Tel: (0534) 79034. Particularly for overseas students.

British National Radio and Electronics School, PO Box 7, Teignmouth, Devon TQ14 0HS. Tel: (062 67) 6114. Courses and training equipment in radio, electronics and computer technology.

Burleigh College of Concise Studies, 162a College Road, Harrow, Middx. Tel: (01) 863 2020. Salesmanship.

Business Training Ltd, Sevendale House, 7 Dale Street, Manchester M1 1JB. Tel: (061) 228 6735/6. English for business for those whose first language is not English.

The Canine Studies Institute (RTC Associates), London Road, Lily Hill, Bracknell, Berks. RG12 6QN. Tel: (0344) 420898. Dog breeding.

The Chartered Insurance Institute, Tuition Service, 31 Hillcrest Road, South Woodford, London E18 2JP. Tel: (01) 989 8464. Insurance diploma and certificate courses.

Chart Foulks Lynch plc, Correspondence Courses, 53 Great Sutton Street, London EC1V 0DQ. Tel: (01) 251 4981. accountancy, banking, tax, law.

Civil Service Correspondence School, Ware, Herts. Tel: (0920) 5926. Civil service examinations. GCE.

The College of Law, Braboeuf Manor, St Catherines, Guildford, Surrey. GU3 1HA. Tel: (0483) 576711. Final examination of The Law Society (previous attendance at oral class necessary).

College of Management Training Ltd, 30 Ferndale Road, Burgess Hill, West Sussex RH15 0HG. Tel: (04446) 43560. Accountancy.

Co-operative Union Ltd, Postal Tuition Section, Stanford Hall, Loughborough, Leics. LE12 5QR. Tel: (050 982) 2333. Courses relating to the co-operative movement.

Ellis School of Surveying and Building, Albany House, Worcester WR1 3DZ. Tel: (0905) 23706. Professional and trade examinations of the building and construction industry.

The Institute of Grocery Distribution, Grange Lane, Letchmore Heath, Watford, Herts. WD2 8DQ. Tel: (09276) 7141/6. Distributive trades certificates and diplomas.

ILEX Tutorial Services, Kempston Manor, Kempston, Bedford MK42 7AB. Tel: (0234) 857711. Law and legal practice.

International Correspondence Schools, 312 High Street, Sutton, Surrey SM1 1PR. Tel: (01) 643 9568. Technical, professional, commercial, general education.

London Montessori Centre, Correspondence Division, 18 Balderton Street, London W1Y 1TG. Tel: (01) 493 0165. Courses leading to a teaching diploma in nursery and primary education.

London School of Accountancy, 23–24 Old Bailey, London EC4M 7PG. Tel: (01) 499 8250. Accountancy courses.

London School of Journalism, 19 Hertford Street, Park Lane, London W1Y 8BB. Tel: (01) 499 8250. Journalism, short story writing, English.

May's Correspondence College, Cleveland Road, London E18 2AF. Tel: (01) 989 9726. Institute of Bankers, Parts I and II.

Mercer's College, Ware, Herts. Tel: (0920) 5926. General education. Full-time and part-time courses for children of school age.

Metropolitan College, Oxford OX2 6PR. Tel: (0865) 52200. Accountancy, business, banking, hotel and catering, insurance, marketing, BTEC.

Metropolitan School of Machine Knitting, Correspondence division, 139/141 Windham Road, Bournemouth BH1 4RQ. Tel: (0202) 304581 (24 hour answering service). Tuition courses for single and double bed knitting machines.

The Methodist Study Centre, Room 70, 1 Central Buildings, Westminster, London SW1H 9NH. Tel: (01) 222 8010. Biblical and theological courses at basic, intermediary and advanced levels to equip lay and ordained Christians for work in the Church and community.

NALGO Correspondence Institute, Nalgo House, 1 Mabledon Place, London WC1H 9AJ. Tel: (01) 388 2366. Professional and vocational qualifications: GCE subjects.

National Extension College, 18 Brooklands Avenue, Cambridge CB2 2HN. Tel: (0223) 63465. Elementary courses: GCSEs and A-levels, preparatory course for Open University, degree and diploma, professional, general interest courses.

National Marine Correspondence School, 28 Hamilton Street, Birkenhead, Cheshire L41 1AL. Tel: (051) 647 6777. Courses for yachtsmen (including Department of Trade and Industry certificates).

The National School of Salesmanship Concessionaries Ltd, Sevendale House, 7 Dale Street, Manchester M1 1JB. Tel: (061) 228 6733/4. Professional diploma courses.

The National School of Salesmanship Ltd. (Address as above).

New York Institute of Photography, 16–20 High Road, Wood Green, London N22 6BX. Tel: (01) 888 1242. Photographic studies.

The Northern Institute of Massage/Northern College of Physical Therapies, 100 Waterloo Road, Blackpool, Lancs. FY4 1AW. Tel: (0253) 403548. Theoretical studies in massage plus practical work in approved centres.

Pitmans Correspondence College, Worcester Road, Wimbledon, London SW19 7QQ. Tel: (01) 947 6993. Professional and commercial courses, secretarial, and secretarial teachers' courses, general education.

The Rapid Results College, Tuition – Greater Charlton, Westminster Industrial Estate, Woolwich Road SE18 5TV. Tel: (01) 317 9636.

The School of Accountancy and Business Studies, Intertext House, 8 Elliot Place, Clydeway Centre, Glasgow G3 8EF. Tel: (041) 221 2926. Professional examination courses.

The School of Herbal Medicine Phytotherapy, Correspondence Division, 148 Forest Road, Tunbridge Wells, Kent TN2 5EY. Tel: (0892) 30400. Courses in herbal medicine.

Successful Writers School, 303–305 Burdett Road, London E14 7EL. Tel: (01) 515 9168. Comprehensive and specialist courses in all areas of creative writing.

Transport Tutorial Association, PO Box 4UZ, London W1A 4UZ. Tel: (01) 631 3833. Institute of Transport examination courses.

Trans-World Tutorial College, 9 The Esplanade, PO Box 42, Jersey. Tel: (0534) 76270. Introductory courses especially designed in preparation for careers in commerce and industry principally in developing countries.

The Wheelhouse School of Navigation, Rudley Mill, nr Hambledon, Hants PO7 6QZ. Tel: (070132) 467. Courses for yachtsmen with special reference to RYA/DTB certificates.

Wolsey Hall, Oxford OX2 6PR. Tel: (0865) 52200. General education, GCSEs and A-levels, degrees, diploma and professional courses. Preparatory courses for the Open University.

The Writing School, 16–20 High Road, Wood Green, London N22 6BX. Tel: (01) 888 1242. Courses in all forms of writing.

Other types of correspondence courses

Other types of correspondence course are described in *17 Flexible learning* and *23 The Open University*.

27 Leisure classes: part-time, weekends, holidays

Recreation plus
LEA courses
Extra-mural classes
Voluntary adult education
Residential courses
Sport
The arts

There are thousands of classes, groups and courses which meet in colleges, evening institutes, schools, adult education centres, community centres and other places. They are provided by LEAs, university and polytechnic extra-mural departments, the WEA, voluntary bodies, commercial organisations and others.

RECREATION PLUS

As well as pure recreation, enjoyment, or education for its own sake, this type of education has a number of practical uses.

- It's a way of coming back to study after a break, or coming in for the first time on a part-time basis.
- It's a way of learning important skills (eg car maintenance, French, weaving) and possibly earning money.
- It's a way of exploring things you might like to study more seriously, before committing yourself.

LEA COURSES

Every LEA has part-time adult education classes, sometimes called community education, especially in Scotland. The way these are organised in different areas is described in *16 Further education, adult education*. How they are organised in your area is described in the *Gazetteer*.

For a prospectus of courses locally, try your local library, the LEA or the WEA (see *28 The WEA*) and watch in the local press during September. Pay attention to enrolment arrangements.

Often you can't book a place but have to go and queue on a particular night and it's first come, first served. Costs are changing a lot. Some are going up steeply. If you live near the border with another LEA, it may well be worth comparing prices but you may have to pay *more* if you do go over the county boundary. You may be exempt or able to pay less if you're on social security, family income supplement, retired or unemployed. Ask at the college or centre where you enrol. Occasionally, you can pay each week, but it's rare.

Organisers (called adult tutors, adult education tutors, tutor-organisers, community education workers and various other things) try to set up classes which are:

- Successful (enough people come to make it pay).
- Useful to the community (like basics or support groups for parents).
- Approved of by the LEA (or the centre's own management committee, if there is one).

But they also respond to requests from people in the community, especially groups of people. So, if you want a class and think that your friends want a similar class (or that you can get together enough people) it's quite proper for you to contact the local organiser. Many areas have self-financing groups. That means you pay enough in fees to cover all the costs. Sometimes clubs and associations can get help with organising their own classes and get special rates.

WOMAN, 38, HOUSEWIFE
We looked everywhere for a keep fit class during the day. We found one but it's over eight miles and you need a car. So we asked the adult education tutor at the local upper school. He said we could have a class in our village hall but we would need to guarantee fifteen to enrol. If we wanted to start in the summer term and not wait till September, we would have to be self-financing. This would mean the students' fees would have to cover the cost of the tutor and the rent of the hall, making £80. So we would need 20 people all paying £4. He didn't think we would get that many people but he does have several self-financing groups.

EXTRA-MURAL CLASSES

A number of universities, polytechnics and other higher education establishments have extra-mural departments, or departments of adult education offering courses to the general public. The newer ones may be called departments or centres of continuing education. Courses may be held at the university or college itself, or elsewhere – sometimes over quite a wide area; some universities have a separate college or base for their extra-mural work.

What Do They Offer?

Evening classes, part-time day classes, short courses, summer schools, public lectures. They are often at a high academic level, and taught by HE lecturers. It is an attempt to take higher education to the people, so they're open to absolutely everyone – no previous academic knowledge is expected.

They are usually concerned with the arts and sciences in general and with local interests, so there are many courses on local history, local geography and industry. They do not restrict themselves to this sort of work however; increasingly they are offering courses relevant to the local needs. So, for example they might run courses for women, (like New Opportunities for Women), for unemployed people, or to help people update their skills and familiarise themselves with new technology.

At its most developed, as in London University, some courses may lead to a local qualification which satisfies the entry requirements of the university concerned.

Some Examples

Cambridge University Board of Extra Mural Studies
Has its base at Madingley Hall, a residential centre on the edge of Cambridge, but also runs classes mostly on an evening basis throughout East Anglia. Their 200 one-day and residential courses a year cover a very broad range of liberal education classes – Ancient History, Local History, Music, Local Geography, Archeology, Geology, and very much more. They are open to anyone over 18.

Newcastle-upon-Tyne Centre for Continuing Education
Offers traditional classes, for example philosophy, archaeology and science and a selection of new-style courses, like microprocessors in the home, New Opportunities for Women.

Trent Polytechnic Centre for Extension Studies
Runs short courses (6, 10, 11, 12 meetings) on subjects such as sociology, women and the law, disarmament or deterence, conversational French, German, Russian, Spanish, children and their problems – and more. They also have a programme of one-off events open to the public at no charge – their Open Programme held in different buildings of the Polytechnic, in Nottingham. Access can also be arranged to a wide range of lecture programmes in mainstream degree and higher diploma courses.

University of St Andrews
Offers a large programme of residential courses for families and individuals. There are cultural holidays, recreational courses and a wide range of special interest courses. All include accommodation. Details from University of St Andrews, 3 St Mary's Place, St Andrews, Fife KY16 9UY.

Similar courses are run by Lancaster and Loughborough Universities.

Brunel University, Continuing Education Department
Runs vocational and technology related updating courses, short courses, as well as accredited programmes on a part-time or distance learning basis.

More information
If there are extra-mural classes in your area, they will probably be advertised at the public library but if you want to know everything they do, write to the department concerned or phone for a prospectus. They may publish one every year in August/September or every term. Some also have short course information, mainly for the summer.

The following list of extra-mural departments shows only where they are based. Their classes are held in several counties, so wherever you are, do contact the nearest ones even if they are located in a different county.

Higher education centres with opportunities for continuing education
Main addresses of colleges and universities listed can be found in the *Gazetteer*. An address is only given in this list if the activities are run from a different centre.

England

Avon

Bath College of Higher Education – see Wiltshire.
University of Bath.
University of Bristol, Department of Extra-Mural Studies, Wills Memorial Building, Queens Road, Bristol BS8 1HR. Tel: (0272) 303629.

Berkshire

University of Reading, Department of Extra-Mural Studies, London Road, Reading, RG1 5AQ. Tel: (0734) 875234 ext 230.

Cambridgeshire

Cambridge University, Board of Extra-Mural Studies, Madingley Hall, Madingley, Cambridge CB3 8AQ. Tel: (0954) 210636.

Cheshire

North Cheshire College, Faculty of Adult and Community Studies, Museum Street Centre, Warrington, Cheshire WA1 1HU. Tel: (0925) 32712.

Devon

Dartington College of Arts, The Devon Centre, residential courses, music studies.
University of Exeter, Department of Adult and Continuing Education, St Lukes, Heavitree Road, Exeter EX1 2LU. Tel: (0392) 264956.

Durham

Durham University, Department of Adult and Continuing Education, 32 Old Elvet, Durham DH1 3JH. Tel: (0385) 64466.

Gloucestershire

College of St Paul and St Mary, Adult and Continuing Education Department.

Hampshire

University of Southampton, Department of Adult Education.

Humberside

University of Hull, Department of Adult and Continuing Education, 47/49 Salmon Grove, Hull HU6 7SZ. Tel: (0482) 465415.

Kent

The University of Kent, School of Continuing Education, Tel: (0227) 66822 ext 3380.

Lancashire

Edge Hill College, Principal Lecturer in Adult Studies.
Lancashire Polytechnic, Continuing Education Service.
Lancaster University, Extra-Mural Studies. Residential summer schools.
St Martin's College, Department of Adult Education.

Leicestershire

University of Leicester, Department of Adult Education.
Loughborough University of Technology, Centre for Extension Studies. Tel: (0509) 263171 ext 2153 or 2150. Residential summer schools catering for all the family.
Vaughan College. Free-standing part of the University of Leicester Department of Adult Education.

LONDON – GREATER

Hillingdon

Brunel University, Continuing Education Department.

Waltham Forest

North East London Polytechnic. Each faculty has a short course unit.

London – Inner

City University, Short Course Unit.
Goldsmith's College, School of Adult and Social Studies.
Imperial College, Continuing Education Office.
Polytechnic of Central London. Short Course Unit.
South Bank Polytechnic, Extra Faculty Unit.
School of Oriental and African Studies (London), Extra-Mural Department.
Thames Polytechnic (and Avery Hill College), Continuing Education Unit.
University of London, Department of Extra-Mural Studies, 26 Russell Square, London WC1B 5DQ. Tel: (01) 636 8000 ext 3850.

MANCHESTER – METROPOLITAN DISTRICTS

Manchester

The University of Manchester, Department of Extra-Mural Studies.
University of Manchester Institute of Science and Technology. Short Course Unit. Tel: (061) 236 3311 ext 2713.

Salford

The University of Salford, Short Course Unit.

MERSEYSIDE – METROPOLITAN DISTRICTS

Liverpool

The University of Liverpool, Department of Extension Studies.

Northamptonshire

Nene College, School of Humanities and Adult Education, at Park campus and at Avenue campus. Tel: (0604) 714101
The University Centre, Free-standing centre of University of Leicester Department of Adult Education. Tel: (0604) 30084.

Nottinghamshire

The University of Nottingham, Adult Education Centre, 14/22 Shakespeare Street, Nottingham NG1 4FJ. Tel: (0602) 473022.
Trent Polytechnic, Centre for Extension Studies.

Oxfordshire

The University of Oxford, Department for External Studies, Rewley House, 1–7 Wellington Square, Oxford OX1 2JA. Tel: (0865) 52901.

Staffordshire

The University of Keele, Department of Adult Education. Tel: (0782) 625116.

Surrey

The University of Surrey, Department of Educational Studies.

Sussex – East

Brighton Polytechnic, Short Courses Centre, 49 Darley Road, Eastbourne, East Sussex BN20 7SP. Tel: (0323) 33130.
The University of Sussex, Centre for Continuing Education.

Sussex – West

West Sussex Institute of Higher Education, Faculty of Further Studies.

TYNE AND WEAR – METROPOLITAN DISTRICTS

Newcastle-upon-Tyne

Newcastle-upon-Tyne Polytechnic, Recurrent Education Service.
The University of Newcastle, Centre for Continuing Education, Windsor Terrace, Newcastle-upon-Tyne NE1 7RU. Tel: (091) 232 8511 ext 2792.

Sunderland
Sunderland Polytechnic, Continuing Education Unit.

WEST MIDLANDS – METROPOLITAN DISTRICTS
Birmingham
The University of Birmingham, Department of Extra-Mural Studies.

Coventry
Warwick University, Department of Continuing Education.

Wiltshire
Bath College of Higher Education (incorporating Bath Academy of Art), Extra-Mural Department, (part of Bath College of Higher Education), Corsham Court, Corsham, Wilts SN13 0DB. Tel: (0742) 712571.

YORKSHIRE SOUTH
Sheffield
The University of Sheffield, Department of Continuing Education, Broomspring House, 85 Wilkinson Street, Sheffield S10 2GJ. Tel: (0742) 768555 ext 4920.

YORKSHIRE – WEST
Bradford
Bradford and Ilkley Community College, Adult Education Department.

Leeds
The University of Leeds, Department of Adult and Continuing Education.

WALES

Dyfed
The University College of Wales, Department of Extra-Mural Studies, Aberystwyth.

Gwynedd
University College of North Wales, Department of Extra-Mural Studies. Tel: (0248) 351151.

South Glamorgan
Cardiff University College, Department of Extra-Mural Studies, 38/39 Park Place, Cardiff CF1 3BB. Tel: (0222) 874832.

West Glamorgan
University of Swansea, Department of Extra-Mural Studies, Berwick House, 6 Uplands Terrace, Swansea SA2 0GU. Tel: (0792) 472168.

Scotland

Central
The University of Stirling, Department of Continuing Education. Tel: (0786) 73171 ext 2025.

Fife
University of St Andrews, Department of Adult Education and Extra-Mural Education, 3 St Mary's Place, St Andrews KY16 9UY. Tel: (0334) 73429. Summer courses for all the family.

Grampian
University of Aberdeen, Department of Adult Education and Extra-Mural Studies, Taylor Building, Aberdeen AB9 2UB. Tel: (0224) 480241 ext 6506.

Lothian

Heriot-Watt University, Public Relations Office.

University of Edinburgh, Department of Extra-Mural Studies, 11 Buccleuch Place, Edinburgh EH8 9LW. Tel: (031) 667 1011 ext 6246.

Strathclyde

University of Glasgow, Department of Adult Continuing Education, 57/59 Oakfield Avenue, Glasgow G12 8LW. Tel: (041) 339 8855 ext 4394.

University of Strathclyde, Department of Continuing Education.

Tayside

University of Dundee, Department of Extra-Mural Education.

NORTHERN IRELAND

Belfast

Queen's University of Belfast, Department of Extra-Mural Studies.

Coleraine

The University of Ulster, Coleraine Campus.

Londonderry

The University of Ulster, Magee Campus.

Newtonabbey

The University of Ulster, Jordanstown Campus.

VOLUNTARY ADULT EDUCATION

Some adult education centres are run by voluntary organisations like the Quakers. They are often linked to the LEA, but they may be more flexible and open to ideas from the public and more imaginative about the way they collect fees.

To find out more

These centres will advertise their courses in the same way as other adult education providers – libraries, the local press and so on – and you may not even be aware that they are not part of LEA provision.

Many are members of an organisation called the Educational Centres Association. It exists to improve educational resources and facilities for adults, and includes students and tutors equally. Member organisations try to involve students in planning programmes and running their centres. For a list of members (although it includes som LEA centres as well):

★ **SEND FOR** *Education Centres Association directory,* 50p from Secretary, Educational Ccntres Association, Chequer Centre, Chequer Street, (Bunhill Row), London EC1V 8PL. Tel: (01) 251 4158.

In Scotland, many are members of the Scottish Institute of Adult and Continuing Education.

★ **ASK** Scottish Institute of Adult and Continuing Education, 30 Rutland Square, Edinburgh EH1 2BW. Tel: (031) 229 0331.

RESIDENTIAL COURSES

A lot of places offer weekend, half-week or longer residential courses in everything – maths, sailing, climbing, walking, art, crafts, computing and so on. Some are run by LEAs at their own residential centres, some by universities, some by bodies like the Countryside Commission. There are also hotels offering study weekends. Many of these are courses for the whole family and make ideal short holidays if you like studying to relax.

Costs
Vary enormously, from £45 a week upwards. Depends very much on the sort of accommodation and level of catering.

How to find out more
Many of these courses are advertised in the press or in local libraries. If you want to plan ahead, the National Institute of Adult Continuing Education publishes a six-monthly list of residential courses. This is a descriptive list of courses, by date, with an index by subject, and it covers England, Wales and Scotland.

★ **SEND FOR** *Residential short courses*, £1 inc p&p from National Institute of Adult Continuing Education, 19b de Montfort Street, Leicester LE1 7GE. Tel: (0533) 551451. Published every January and August.

The BBC publishes lists of residential courses based on their broadcasts.

★ **SEND FOR** *Residential courses based on BBC series*, from BBC Education, London W5. Enclose a large SAE.

Overseas
There are many courses and other learning opportunities abroad – language courses at foreign universities, discovery and adventure holidays and much else. Many of these are advertised in the press.

Central Bureau for Educational Visits and Exchanges
Publishes an annual guide that lists thousands of world-wide sports, special interest and study holidays. Opportunities include arts and crafts, environment and language studies and voyages of discovery, trekking and safaris from cycling tours of China to mule safaris in the Swiss Alps.

★ **SEND FOR** *Adventure and discovery*, price £2.50, from Central Bureau for Educational Visits and Exchanges, Seymour House, Seymour Mews, London W1H 9PE. Tel: (01) 486 5101; 3 Bruntsfield Crescent, Edinburgh EH10 4HD. Tel: (031) 447 8024; 16 Malone Road, Belfast BT9 5BN. Tel: (0232) 664418/9.

SPORT

Much part-time and recreational education involves sport, and indeed sport and keep fit classes are always some of the most heavily used classes in adult education.

However, this is one type of provision where there is even more going on outside adult education classes. There is so much happening that we could not even begin to list what exists but some of the principle ways in which you can learn, or recieve tuition in a sport include:

- Sports clubs – there are clubs for every type of sport you can think of; many have links with local adult education centres but many more do not. Libraries often keep lists of local organisations, including sports clubs.
- District councils – in county areas these are responsible for a smaller, more local area than the LEA, but the metropolitan boroughs have the functions of an LEA as well as a district council. They are important as they provide recreational services like leisure centres, sports centres and swimming pools. These often include tuition as well as facilities.
- Local schools often have swimming pools these days. They will often organise swimming tuition out of school hours for their own pupils but may also offer the facility to the local population as well.

THE ARTS

This is another area of great demand and again there is much going on outside the formal provision for education and training. As well as a huge variety of classes and courses in residential colleges, extra-mural departments, adult education classes and of course in the art colleges, you will find art centres running their own classes. These might vary from great and venerable institutions to local self-help art centres, community photographic facilities, writing workshops and so on.

To find out what is available in your area:

★ **ASK** the Regional Arts Association. Their address will be available from the local library.

★ **LOOK AT** *The directory of arts centres*, free from the Arts Council of Great Britain, 105 Piccadilly, London W1V 0AU. Tel: (01) 629 9495. Lists arts centres in England, Wales and Scotland. Enclose a large SAE and unattached stamps to the value of 40p.

28 The WEA

What is the WEA?
How it works
What it does
What it costs
How to find out more

WHAT IS THE WEA?

The Workers Educational Association is a voluntary body offering part-time classes to adults country-wide. It is an organisation that you can join and so be involved in planning the local programmes. Its classes and courses are run everywhere – in schools, adult education centres, local halls and so on. It uses everyone's premises whilst remaining separate and independent, and so it tries to reach people where they live and work.

HOW IT WORKS

- Despite its name, it is not restricted to any one kind of worker – it is open to all. It was established (in 1903) to overcome the disadvantages of workers who didn't have access to established channels of education.
- It has 900 local branches each with their own officers (secretary, treasurer, chairman), who plan the local programme. You can join the WEA and be a member of the local branch – if you join a WEA class promoted by a branch you become a member automatically.
- The branches make up twenty districts, each with a district secretary (list below); in each district, there are tutor/organisers and development officers who help branches organise their programme, work with affiliated societies and recruit suitable part-time tutors. There are also industrial tutors who are concerned with trade union and industrial studies.
- Classes are all part-time, but may be in the day or evening. They sometimes have creche facilities attached to daytime classes. They may also take the form of trips to places of interest.
- The standard of education is usually high, many of their tutors are university teachers.
- They run activities in co-operation with LEAs and they have a particularly close relationship with some university extra-mural departments.
- It is unusual for WEA classes to lead to formal qualifications.

WHAT IT DOES

Varies from area to area because branches have their own ideas about local needs, and the professional staff who help them have their own interests and expertise.

Broadly their work falls into four types of education:

- For people in deprived areas, or who suffer from social or educational disadvantage (eg the elderly, the handicapped, the mentally ill, the unemployed). In a number of areas the WEA is involved in the setting up of unemployment centres.
- Trade union education (usually in conjunction with the TUC education service).
- Social and political education (eg courses for school managers, potential councillors, workers in voluntary organisations).
- Liberal education (the traditional WEA class, in subjects like philosophy, art, literature), and also preparation for higher education. As it is a democratic organisation, the interests and talents of the organiser and branch members can flourish and as a result there are many new developments.

The WEA News

This now has a circulation of nearly 30,000 and is sent to members and others interested in adult education. It is a good way to find out about new developments. For more information:

★ **ASK** Jack Taylor at the WEA national address below.

WEA Women's Studies Newsletter

A new series of this newsletter was restarted in 1984. It is published twice a year and each issue focuses on one area of women's experience. It also includes news of courses and new resources. It is available from the national office at 85p per issue, £1.60 per year.

WHAT IT COSTS

If it's a trade union course, you probably won't pay anything. Courses for unemployed people and other disadvantaged groups are usually free – but it is up to the local branch. For other courses there is a fee usually around £1.00 an hour, but again the fees may be reduced for people on benefit.

HOW TO FIND OUT MORE

The best person to contact for information about membership, classes in your area, and to ask if you want something new put on, is your branch secretary. The local library should be able to tell you his or her name; if you have difficulty, contact the district secretary.

District offices and secretaries

England

Berks, Bucks and Oxon: 6 Brewer Street, Oxford OX1 1QN. Tel: (0865) 246270. Linden West.
Eastern: Botolph House, 17 Botolph Lane, Cambridge CB2 3RE. Tel: (0223) 350978. Reg Carnell.
East Midland: 16 Shakespeare Street, Nottingham NG1 4GF. Tel: (0602) 475162. Russell Gent.
London: 32 Tavistock Square, London WC1 9EZ. Tel: (01) 387 8966. E Wallis.

Northern: 51 Grainger Street, Newcastle-upon-Tyne NE1 5JE. Tel: (091) 232 3957. M Standen.
North Western: 4th Floor, Crawford House, Precinct Centre, Oxford Road, Manchester M13 9GH. Tel: (061) 273 7652. I Harford.
Southern: 56 High Street, Southampton SO9 5UG. Tel: (0703) 229810/229819. Douglas Payne.
South Eastern: 4 Castle Hill, Rochester, Kent ME1 1QQ. Tel: (0634) 42140. Vernon Hull.
South Western: Martin's Gate Annexe, Bretonside, Plymouth PL4 0AT. Tel: (0752) 664989. Charles Butler.
Western: 17 Princess Victoria Street, Bristol BS8 4BX. Tel: (0272) 732630. Douglas A Gohl.
West Lancs and Cheshire: 7/8 Bluecoat Chambers, School Lane, Liverpool L1 3BX. Tel: (051) 709 8023. F D Connor.
West Mercia (incl N Staffs): 9/11 Digbeth, Birmingham B5 6BH. Tel: (021) 643 0717. R E Copley.
Yorkshire North: 7 Woodhouse Square, Leeds LS3 1AD. Tel: (0532) 453304/455944. C J Croft.
Yorkshire South: Chantry Buildings, Corporation Street, Rotherham S60 5GE. Tel: (0709) 372121. J R Fisher.

Wales

North Wales: 33 College Road, Bangor, Gwynned LL57 2AP. Tel: (0248) 353254. Rufus Adams.
South Wales: Tawney House, 11 Station Terrace, Cowbridge Road West, Cardiff CF5 4AA. Tel: (0222) 552277. Barry Moore.

Scotland

Scotland North: 163 King Street, Aberdeen AB2 3AE. Tel: (0224) 642725. Adrian Jones.
Scotland South East: Riddle's Court, 322 Lawnmarket, Edinburgh EH1 2PG. Tel: (031) 226 3456. Dr Mick McGrath.
Scotland West: 212 Bath Street, Glasgow G2 4HW. Tel: (041) 332 0176. Mrs Jean Barr.

Northern Ireland

Northern Ireland: 1 Fitzwilliam Street, Belfast BT9 6AW. Tel: (0232) 229718. Paul Nolan.

National address

Temple House, 9 Upper Berkeley Street, London W1 8BY. Tel: (01) 402 5608/9. General Secretary: R Lochrie.

29 Local councils

Leisure services
Community and economic development
Employment opportunities in local government

Local councils form the network through which local government works. They are responsible for a wide range of services, including seeing that your rubbish is collected and the local bus service operates reasonably reliably. Some local councils have responsibility for the education service in the area, through the local education authority (eg the metropolitan boroughs and the county councils). There are also smaller subdivisions of the councils which act as local authorities, called district councils, and there are hundreds of these in the country.

Although district councils have no responsibility for education, they are increasingly involved in various types of education and training provision through their other responsibilities and concerns. This chapter is an outline of some of the ways they might do this.

LEISURE SERVICES

This department (which may be called something else – parks, amenities, recreation and so on) will be responsible for the provision of sporting facilities such as swimming pools, tennnis courts, bowling greens, and in some areas for purpose-built sports or leisure centres. It will also have responsibility for library services, perhaps with associated arts activities.

Wherever such facilities exist, it is quite likely that various types of coaching may be available too. For example, swimming pool staff often organise swimming lessons for adults as well as children. The same is quite likely with any facility that employs professional staff. In some leisure centres, the range might be much wider than sports and might include such things as arts and crafts, drama and so on. The library service is also quite likely to run a number of activities and may host a variety of exhibitions, music and poetry events.

COMMUNITY AND ECONOMIC DEVELOPMENT

Community and economic development is concerned with improving the local environment and economy. This may include social as well as physical development of the area, and in recent years it increasingly includes developments aimed at stimulating employment. Partly because of high unemployment, partly because of concern for declining economic activity in their area (and in turn worsened employment opportunities for local residents), many district and borough councils are very involved in local economic development.

What is done in the name of community and economic development varies widely but in most versions it is likely to include some activities which are broadly educational; they are also likely to have a strong self-help flavour. Some district councils have a community development policy and may even have a community development officer. Such a person could be located in a number of different departments such as housing, planning or amenities.

Others have set up specific economic development units to research needs in the area and set up initiatives related to the local economy and employment, such as investment in land and buildings, promotion of the area for business and as a place to live, help for small businesses, for unemployed people, training workshops etc. For example, Humberside County Council established a small Economic Development Unit in the early 1980s, which has since become a separate organisation with its own staff and a substantial budget. Some of the most common ways in which help is made available include:

- the provision of facilities for people wanting to set up their own small business, such as premises, loans, maybe training courses
- setting up training facilities such as training workshops.

Training Workshops

Local councils frequently assist in the funding of women's training workshops (such as those listed in *6 Women*). They may participate in consortia running workshops or they may just run their own. Examples exist in various parts of the country and the local council should publicise the facility.

Local training workshops

LONDON – INNER

Camden

Camden Training Centre, 57 Pratt Street, London NW1 0DP. Tel: (01) 482 2103. The Centre provides courses for members of the local community, particularly unemployed adults, on a range of subjects such as building maintenance, printing, microelectronics, carpentry, small businesses and self-employment and others. Some courses are offered for women only, some are mixed. All full-time trainees receive a training allowance as well as travel costs, and childcare is available free of charge. Language support is offered on all courses where needed.

Greenwich

Charlton Training Centre, Westminster Industrial Estate, Ferranti Close, off Westfield Street, Woolwich, London SE18 5TU. Tel: (01) 317 9636. This was previously an MSC Skillcentre which has been re-opened by a group of local interests, including the borough council, called the Charlton Training Consortium. The consortium has approved courses in pneumatics/hydraulics, vehicle repair and maintenance, vehicle body repair and spraying, engineering, catering, reprographics, sheet metal work/arc welding, record press/entertainments servicing, industrial electronics, joinery/carpentry/building, co-operatives and business development. Some of their courses are for women only, they have a creche, and a sheltered industrial group which will employ people with severe disabilities to provide all the administrative services necessary to run the Centre. They also have a basic education centre.

30 Health education

What is health education?
Self-help and voluntary organisations
Correspondence courses
Radio and TV
District health authorities
Health Education Council
Parenting

WHAT IS HEALTH EDUCATION?

It can cover a wide range, not just staying healthy or dealing with illness but also sex education, mental health, parenting, family, diet and any other social aspects of life that affect general well-being. It may be provided by the medical and health services, by the educational system, by social work bodies, by voluntary bodies or on a self-help basis.

SELF-HELP AND VOLUNTARY ORGANISATIONS

There are hundreds of voluntary organisations tackling all sorts of health issues – anything from campaigns about hazards like radiation and pollution, to promoting information, advice and help about a particular area of health.

Some have developed from the women's movement.

★ **ASK** Women's Health Information Centre, 52 Featherstone Street, London EC1. Tel: (01) 251 6580. They can advise you on setting up a women's health group. The centre also produces a list of self-help groups and women's health courses, and produces broadsheets on various aspects of women's health.

It's also worth asking at local women's centres or community centres to see if there are self-help groups or branches of voluntary organisations in your area which are involved with the aspects of health education that interest you. Other useful people are your doctor or health centres, Citizens' Advice Bureau, other advice centres, and your local library.

This is a selection of voluntary organisations involved in health issues. Like many such groups, in addition to providing advice and information on an individual level, the projects will try to put you in touch with speakers for meetings or groups, and with workshops and local events if they are available.

New Approaches to Cancer (NAC) is a focus for over 200 contact points across the country, which advise on self-help, nutrition, exercise, mental approaches and complementary therapies.

★ **WRITE TO** New Approaches to Cancer, c/o The Seekers Trust, Addington Park, Maidstone, Kent ME19 5BL. Tel: (0732) 848336 (with SAE if possible).

The Terrence Higgins Trust is a registered charity set up to provide information, advice and help about AIDS (Acquired Immune Deficiency Syndrome) and related health problems and issues.

★ **WRITE TO** The Terrence Higgins Trust, BM AIDS, London WC1N 3XX. Enclose a large SAE. Their Helpline number is (01) 833 2971. This phone is staffed 7 to 10 pm weekdays and 3 to 10 pm weekends – otherwise leave messages (answerphone).

The Sickle Cell Society was set up by a group of parents and medical practitioners in 1979. Sickle Cell Disease is a very painful condition affecting people (often children) of Afro-Caribbean, Asian and East Mediterranean Origin. The Society provides help, advice and information – with branches in Birmingham, Cardiff, Liverpool, Manchester and London. Check in the telephone book for your nearest branch, or write (with an SAE) for an information pack, branch addresses and contact names.

★ **WRITE TO** The Sickle Cell Society, Green Lodge, Barretts Green Road, London NW10 7AP. Tel: (01) 961 8346/7795.

The National Extension College has two books available which might be useful for people involved in self-help groups: *Community start up*, about starting a community group and keeping it going, and *Self-help learning groups*, a practical guide for people who are organising such a group.

★ **SEND FOR** *Community start up* by Caroline Pinder, published by the National Extension College jointly with the National Federation of Community Organisations, £4.95 from the Publications Dept, National Extension College, 18 Brooklands Avenue, Cambridge CB2 2HN. *Self-help learning groups* by Maggie Falshaw, £2.95 from the same address.

CORRESPONDENCE COURSES

The National Extension College

NEC has produced an excellent course in conjunction with the College of Health, called *Taking stock, a whole life review*. They have also produced a course which is a help-yourself guide to good health in old age called *Fit for life*. For more information:

★ **WRITE TO** the National Extension College at the above address.

The Open University

The OU has a short course called Health Choices concerned with helping people make their own informed decisions about lifestyle and personal health.

★ **LOOK AT** *23 The Open University*.

RADIO AND TV

There are always a number of programmes on radio and TV, on all channels, dealing with a wide range of health issues. An excellent guide to all these programmes is produced twice a year by the IBA. It is also available on disk for microcomputers – write for further information.

★ **LOOK AT** *Broadcasts for parent education and child studies*, from Christopher Jones, IBA Education, 70 Brompton Road, London SW3 1EY.

For a general overview of educational programmes to come:

★ **LOOK AT** *TV Take up*, a six-monthly guide to educational programmes generally, including a section on health and family, from the address above.

ALTERNATIVES

Complementary, or alternative, health care is to do with approaches that differ from the traditional practices of Western medicine, and includes disciplines such as osteopathy, homeopathy, holistic medicine and alternative therapy. There is a very wide range of individuals, projects and organisations working in these areas, and it's a good idea to look for recommendations and be cautious before committing your health or money. The Institute for Complementary Medicine is a useful starting point for local contacts. They will provide a free referral to one of 67 information points around the country, and they also publish a year book with details of training organisations and identification of the meaning of the letters which appear after practitioners' names.

★ **WRITE TO** The Institute of Complementary Medicine, 21 Portland Place, London W1N 3AF. Enclose an SAE.

★ **LOOK AT** *Alternative medicine*, by Dr Andrew Stanway, £3.95 in the Penguin Health Series. A useful introduction to alternative and complementary medicine.

For a good introduction to alternative health issues and approaches:

★ **LOOK AT** *The alternative health guide*, by Brian Inglis and Ruth West, published by Michael Joseph. £12.50 – expensive but very useful.

DISTRICT HEALTH AUTHORITIES

England and Wales are divided into Regional Health Authorities, which in turn are sub-divided into District Health Authorities; in Scotland the equivalent are Health Boards, and in Northern Ireland the equivalent are Health and Social Service Boards. Most of the Districts and Boards have a health education service operating from the 'health education unit'. The District Health Education Officer is responsible to the District Medical Officer for promoting, organising and developing health education in the area, and for stimulating interest in and awareness of health education. The health education service can provide information, advice, resources and training for anyone wanting to promote health education for individuals or groups, such as the nurse or doctor for their patient, the teacher for pupils, or the speaker for an organisation. So if you want to know what's on offer, perhaps find a speaker for your group or just get help with your own talk:

★ **ASK** your District Health Education Officer. Your local District Health Authority is listed in the telephone book, or you can

★ **LOOK AT** *The hospitals and health services yearbook*.

HEALTH EDUCATION COUNCIL

The Health Education Council (England, Wales, Scotland and Northern Ireland) has resource centres for information, leaflets, resource lists (which give details of books, reports, audio-visual materials and other information) – good for someone thinking of putting on a course. It also mounts major campaigns (for example anti-smoking) and provides training for people working in health education.

★ **ASK** The Health Education Council, 78 New Oxford Street, London WC1A 1AH. Tel: (01) 631 0930.

The Scottish Health Education Group has a programme aimed at helping people make the best possible choices in relation to health and well being. Their activities include campaigns concerning alcohol, mental health and the elderly.

★ **WRITE TO** The Scottish Health Education Group, Health Education Centre, Woodburn House, Canaan Lane, Edinburgh EH10 4SG. Tel: (031) 447 8044.

PARENTING

There is no one national organisation co-ordinating all the initiatives but there is a lot going on.

At the antenatal stage you have a choice between using courses run in hospitals and clinics by people like health visitors, and groups and courses run by independent groups like the National Childbirth Trust.

At the pre-school stage there are playgroups and mother and toddler groups. The Pre-School Playgroups Association should be able to help with local contacts – addresses in *3 Studying with children*. Many adult education services run courses or informal groups for parents and there is an Open University short course, The Pre-School Child.

There is less happening as you move into older age groups though some schools run informal parent groups and there are several relevant Open University courses.

The guide to broadcasts (see above) has lists of programmes and contacts.

31 Training for voluntary work

The growth of voluntary work
Some examples
How to find out more

THE GROWTH OF VOLUNTARY WORK

One curious fact about Britain today is that although people are expected to have more qualifications for jobs, and more and more official agencies are created to help them, there is still an enormous and growing demand for unqualified people to be voluntary helpers in all sorts of work. Some of it is quite skilled and responsible work and the people organising it may have very detailed and thorough training programmes for their volunteers.

Some professions, like social work, look more favourably on newcomers who have experience before they enter the profession, and voluntary work may be a way of getting such experience. Moreover, since many organisations do train their volunteers, voluntary work is also a good way of getting some training. Some of this training is of a very high standard and if you are doing it in the course of volunteering, it will usually cost you nothing.

There are several valuable outcomes for you from doing such voluntary work and training (not to mention the useful work you may do for others). It may:

- lead on to paid work in the same field
- lead to continued voluntary work – if you are getting satisfaction from it that is a valuable outcome
- help you to decide that this sort of work is *not* for you, a very useful conclusion if you were just about to spend a lot of time and energy getting into that field
- provide you with skills (such as counselling) which you can use in the other parts of your life and work.

MAN, 35, NOW A SENIOR COMMUNITY WORKER
I left British Leyland at 21. From the age of 15 I'd been doing voluntary work in the evenings and weekends, which was infinitely more fulfilling than BL. The job provided the finances. I wasn't stretched at work. So at 21 I went to work in a children's home.

SOME EXAMPLES

There are so many that we can't list them all, but some interesting schemes which include training are:

- Marriage guidance counselling. The training is long, detailed and thorough. It gives the workers a skill – counselling – which is more and more in demand.

- Adult literacy tutoring (or adult numeracy, helping mentally handicapped people in classes etc) – all part of adult basic education. Many volunteers are involved. They all receive various training courses, and because there is a shortage of trained and experienced people, voluntary tutors often go on to become paid tutors. If you want to help in this field, enquire through the contact points listed in *20 Basics*.
- Youth work (also called youth and community work) is organised by education authorities (in Scotland community education departments) and voluntary groups such as churches, Guides and Scouts. Most groups are always on the look out for helpers. Many local authorities run training schemes and these can lead to paid part-time posts. Contact your LEA youth officer or local clubs. For full-time youth work, see *42 Things to study: youth and community work*.
- Voluntary Service Overseas. Rather a different commitment. This normally involves a two-year period of service in a developing country. You need to have a skill, profession or trade which is needed overseas, and you get paid a local wage.
- Helping in playgroups – work that many parents are involved in because their children use playgroups. They often get training for this work from LEAs or voluntary bodies like the PPA (see *3 Studying with children*). As children grow up, parents drift away from playgroups and may build on this experience to do other work.
- Citizens' Advice Bureaux and other advice work such as Samaritans, Scouting and many others.

Community action

If you want help to get things done in your own neighbourhood, it's available. If you haven't got a group near you to provide a lunch club for old people, start an adventure playground on waste land, campaign for better facilities locally or whatever, you should be able to find support. Contact your local community council or council for voluntary service (see below). They won't do it for you but should help you get started. Once established, they often run training sessions to help your group work more effectively, often in conjunction with bodies like the WEA.

HOW TO FIND OUT MORE

The National Council for Voluntary Organisations (NCVO) is a national umbrella organisation for many voluntary bodies and provides excellent information services. They also provide a useful guide to how they work.

★ **SEND FOR** *Guide to NCVO services – an aid for users*, from the NCVO, Bedford Square Press, 26 Bedford Square, London WC1B 3HU. Tel: (01) 636 4066.

They also publish a guide to over 1,300 voluntary organisations which is one useful place to start.

Details of courses, conferences and other events are carried by *Voluntary action* supplement, published in the weekly magazine, *New society*, available from most newsagents.

Wales, Scotland and Northern Ireland

★ **ASK** Wales Council for Voluntary Action, Llys Ifor, Crescent Road, Caerphilly, Mid-Glamorgan CF8 1XL. Tel: (0222) 869224.

★ **ASK** Scottish Council of Social Service for Community and Voluntary Organisations, 18/19 Claremont Crescent, Edinburgh EH7 4JW. Tel: (031) 556 3882.

★ **ASK** Northern Ireland Council for Voluntary Action, 2 Annadale Avenue, Belfast BT7 3JR. Tel: (0232) 640011.

Other information

If you want to find out which organisations locally involve volunteers you could:

★ **ASK** The council for voluntary service or volunteer bureau (in towns) or the rural community council (in rural areas). They are umbrella organisations and should know what's happening locally. To find out the address of your local one, look in the phone book or:

★ **LOOK AT** *Social services yearbook* (see *Booklist*).

Another useful body is The Volunteer Centre (UK) which provides information and advice on all aspects of volunteering. The activities of the centre's Training Unit include both consultancy and residential courses. The training programme is produced twice a year and is free on request. They are also able to offer help and advice to groups interested in

- examining their policy and practice
- developing their own training materials for use with volunteers
- producing their own advertising and publicity materials
- producing their own audio-visual materials such as slide-tape and video.

★ **SEND FOR** *Volunteer bureaux directory*, £2 inc p&p and amendment service from VBX Unit, The Volunteer Centre, 29 Lower King's Road, Berkhamsted, Herts HP4 2AB. Tel: (044 27) 73311.

Free booklet

There is a useful booklet published every six months called *VORTEX* (*Voluntary organisations register of training exercises*) which lists many useful short courses for people already working in these fields.

★ **ASK** The Organiser, VORTEX, 26 Bedford Square, London WC1B 3HU.

32 Trade union education

The Trades Union Congress (TUC) *General Federation of Trade Unions*
Individual unions

There is a legal right for trade union representatives, including union safety representatives, to have time off work for education and training connected with their union duties, and still be paid by their employer. The legal rights are embodied in the Employment Protection Consolidation Act and the Health and Safety Commission's Regulations.

Nine and a half million people in Britain belong to trade unions affiliated to the TUC and the TUC runs a variety of special education and training programmes for its members.

THE TRADES UNION CONGRESS (TUC)

Each year it offers facilities to between 30,000 and 40,000 members who want to learn more about trade unions, or to train for their work as full-time officers, shop stewards, safety representatives etc. It's done at FE and HE colleges, polytechnics, some university extra-mural departments, by the WEA, at TUC National Education Centres, or by correspondence.

Courses for trade union representatives

The TUC doesn't actually run courses; they are provided by public educational bodies. It approves them and supplies core materials – a basic set of key studies it wants all its approved courses to cover. The rest is up to the tutors. Courses are usually done by day release and take between two and ten days. The TUC pays the course fees and the employer continues to pay wages.

Who are they for?

Day-release courses are normally for trade union representatives, shop stewards and safety representatives. You have to be nominated by your union, who will forward your application to the TUC regional education officer for you.

★ **ASK** your full-time officer or union branch secretary.

He or she should have leaflets – the TUC distributes half a million a year. If for any reason they haven't got this information, you could contact the TUC regional education officer, who also arranges evening classes and day schools.

New initiatives

A new development is the growth of the TUC Unemployed Workers' Centres (see *5 Out of work*). These are not set up as educational facilities but many provide a focus for informal education, and may host classes.

TUC regional education officers

Northern: 31 Moseley Street, Newcastle-upon-Tyne NE1 1YF. Tel: (0632) 321725. T Cook.

East Midland and East Anglia: 61 Derby Road, Nottingham NG1 5BA. Tel: (0602) 472483. D F Marshall.

Yorkshire and Humberside: 1 Navigation Yard, Chatry Bridge, Wakefield WF1 5PQ. Tel: (0924) 375836. M Ball.

North Western: Baird House, 41 Merton Road, Bootle, Merseyside. Tel: (051) 933 4403. A J Johnstone.

West Midland: 1150 Stratford Road, Hall Green, Birmingham B28 8AF. Tel: (021) 777 7121. P Hughes.

South Western: Guildhall Chambers, 1 Henbury Road, Westbury-on-Trym, Bristol BS9 3HH. Tel: (0272) 501989. D Gover.

South Eastern: Education Department, Trades Union Congress, Congress House, Great Russell Street, London WC1B 3LS. Tel: (01) 636 4030. S Grinter.

Wales: 1 Cathedral Road, Cardiff CF1 9SD. Tel: (0222) 27449. J F Hannaway.

Scotland: 16 Woodlands Terrace, Glasgow G3 6ED. Tel: (041) 332 2045. L Cairns.

Northern Ireland: Northern Ireland Committee, 1/9 Castle Arcade, Belfast BT1 5DG. Tel: (0232) 241452. Training education officer, F Bunting.

Courses by post

The TUC education service runs its own correspondence courses for members of affiliated unions. For more information:

★ **WRITE TO** Congress House, Great Russell Street, London WC1B 3LS. Tel: (01) 636 4030 or contact your union branch.

INDIVIDUAL UNIONS

All unions are concerned with training their officials (whether full- or part-time). Many have their own education service. Some have residential colleges of their own. However, these will only be for members of the union concerned; you will hear about your own union's educational programme through your union paper or journal. If you want to know the education officer for most of the major unions:

★ **LOOK AT** *The education yearbook* (see *Booklist*).

In addition, larger unions may have scholarships or offer financial help to members returning to study – especially those attending adult residential colleges. These awards are usually additional to other grants.

GENERAL FEDERATION OF TRADE UNIONS

Their educational trust organises day, weekend and week-long courses and offers places on WEA and Scottish TUC courses. They also offer some grants for full-time and Open University students, and scholarships to Ruskin College. For a copy of their programme:

★ **WRITE TO** General Federation of Trade Unions Educational Trust, Central House, Upper Woburn Place, London WC1H OHY Tel: (01) 387 2578.

33 Training at work

MSC schemes
Industrial training organisations (ITOs)
Short courses
Industrial language training

MSC SCHEMES

Recent surveys have shown that companies (and countries) which invest in training are more successful than those that do not. In the UK there seems to be considerable resistance because employers are unwilling to make the investment in time and money, especially in small to medium companies. To deal with this, and to help make the point that the investment is worthwhile, MSC offers a number of schemes to help companies work out the training they need and organise it in a non-disruptive way; it also pays a contribution to the costs. Schemes are continually being developed, so talk to your MSC area office. Currently the main areas covered are:

Analysing needs

Consultancy grants to help find out how training would help you, and how best to do it. Usually an outside specialist needs to be called in to look at the whole organisation; MSC can also help you find a suitable consultant.

★ **LOOK AT** *Professional assistance in analysing training needs*, leaflet ATL60, at your Jobcentre.

Training costs

Grants to employers wanting to do training in approved areas (mainly things you do not have to do by law, eg safety training, but which would help you, eg management development, marketing).

★ **LOOK AT** *Local training grants to employers*, leaflet ATL46.

Training for change

If you are

- in a developing industry
- experiencing skill shortages
- introducing new technology

and your employees need new skills, you may be eligible for support. You need to work through your designated Industrial Training Organisation. If you do not know what that is

★ **ASK** Room E621, MSC, Moorfoot, Sheffield S1 4PQ. Tel: (0742) 704025.

★ **LOOK AT** *Pricing skills training schemes*, leaflet ATL34, at your Jobcentre.

Open learning

Through Open Tech (see *17 Flexible learning*) MSC has stimulated the development of hundreds of training packages which let you install your own training system in-house. Staff can follow the course at convenient times (even at home), and get extra support by telephone, or by arrangement. Regional centres have been set up which can help with equipment, advice or materials; for a list of these see *17 Flexible learning*. For a list of materials

★ **LOOK AT** *Open Tech directory*. See *Booklist*.

INDUSTRIAL TRAINING ORGANISATIONS (ITOs)

The Industrial Training Organisations (ITOs) are responsible for ensuring that adequate training is taking place in industry. Most of the statutory Industrial Training Boards (ITBs) have now been wound up but a few Boards have been retained; industries without statutory boards have alternative arrangements organised by the firms themselves, often through their trade associations. Some MSC grants must be processed through your ITO.

Industrial Training Organisations

Agriculture and horticulture

The Agricultural Training Board provides or secures training for all grades of employers, the self-employed and workers in the industry, from new entrants to experienced workers who wish to progress or retrain.

The Board may also train people not employed in the industry at repayment rates, which may be obtained from Board offices.

Agricultural Training Board, Bourne House, 32/34 Beckenham Road, Beckenham, Kent BR3 4PB. Tel: (01) 650 4890.

Clothing

The Clothing and Allied Products Industry Training Board provides a wide range of in-company and off-the-job training.

None of the training is for people outside the industry though the Board does give grants to companies for sandwich course students, and can provide a broad range of careers advice.

Clothing and Allied Products Industry Training Board, Tower House, Merrion Way, Leeds LS2 8NY. Tel: (0532) 441331.

Construction

The Construction Industry Training Board provides training for people not employed in the industry as well as employees, though only firms that are registered with the Board can receive grants for training. As part of its provision it runs the Bircham Newton Training Centre in Norfolk, the largest construction training centre in the world.

Construction Industry Training Board, Bircham Newton Training Centre, Bircham Newton, Nr Kings Lynn, Norfolk PE31 6RH. Tel: (0553) 776677.

Information Services, CITB, St Clements Lane, London WC2A. Tel: (01) 242 0933.

Electricity industry

Policy is made and monitored by the Electricity Supply Industry Training Committee, but the training is carried out by individual electricity boards. In addition to training for young recruits the boards provide a range of job-specific training for adults, some appropriate parts of which may be available to non-employees. This is by arrangement with the local area electricity board or CEGB local office, to which enquiries should be directed.

Electricity Supply Industry Training Committee, The Electricity Council, Education and Training Branch, 30 Millbank, London SW1P 4RD. Tel: (01) 834 2333.

Engineering

Engineering Industry Training Board, 54 Clarendon Road, Watford WD1 1LB. Tel: (0923) 38441.

For careers information contact the Engineering Careers Information Service, 54 Clarendon Road, Watford WD1 1LB. Tel: (0923) 38441.

Hotels and catering

The Hotel and Catering Training Board provides a wide range of training including a small business service for people thinking of starting up their own business in the industry, adult retraining, and careers information.

Hotel and Catering Training Board, Ramsey House, Central Square, Wembley, Middlesex HA9 7AP. Tel: (01) 902 8865.

Local government

The responsibility for training rests with the 456 local authorities. The function of the Local Government Training Board is to influence local authorities in England and Wales and others concerned to ensure that the quantity and quality of training provided is adequate to meet the needs.

Local Government Training Board, Arndale House, The Arndale Centre, Luton LU1 2TS. Tel: (0582) 451166.

Merchant navy

The Merchant Navy Training Board is a voluntary body providing training to suit the needs of seafarers and companies operating in the merchant navy.

Merchant Navy Training Board, 30/32 St Mary Axe, London EC3A 8ET. Tel: (01) 283 2922.

The offshore petroleum industry

The Offshore Petroleum Industry Training Board operates the Offshore Training Centre which provides courses covering many aspects of the exploration and drilling for, and production of, offshore oil, together with fire training for personnel employed in the offshore industry. Details of courses are available from the OPITB Information Officer.

Although all courses are open to those not employed in the offshore industry, courses are designed primarily to meet companies' requirements for their employees. The exception to this is the four-week Basic Rig Crew Course, which is designed for new entrants into the drilling industry. Full details of this course are available from the Offshore Training Centre Administrator.

Offshore Petroleum Industry Training Board, Forties Road, Montrose, Angus DD10 9ET. Tel: (0674) 72230.

Road transport

The Road Transport Industry Training Board now covers road haulage, motor vehicle retail and repair, vehicle body building and repair, furniture removals, motor factors and passenger car hire.

There are two training centres at High Ercall in Shropshire and at Livingston in Scotland. There is also Skills Assessment Service which is available to anyone whether employed in the industry or not.

Road Transport Industry Training Board, Capitol House, Empire Way, Wembley, Middlesex HA9 0NG. Tel: (01) 902 8880.

Catalogue of self-instruction and training packs, audio-visual aids and training courses from Board Publications, MOTEC, High Ercall, Telford, Shropshire TF6 6RB. Tel: (0952) 770441.

Plastics industry

The Plastics Industry Training Board opened the Plastics Processing Industry Training Centre in Telford, Shropshire in April 1985. It now runs a range of courses in most of the major processes including injection moulding, extrusion, blow moulding, blown film and vaccum forming along with a number of technical courses such as electronics, hydraulic, pneumatics, robotics and quality control. The Board also operates the polymer Open Tech providing distance learning material on all aspects of plastics processing ranging from introductory to technical levels.

Courses Administration, The Plastics Processing Industry Training Board, Halesfield 7, Telford, Shropshire TF7 4QL. Tel: (0952) 584466.

Water industry

The Water Industry Training Association provides a range of over 200 different courses covering all aspects of the water business.

Water Industry Training Association, Tadley Court, Tadley Common Road, Tadley, Nr Basingstoke, Hampshire RG26 6TB. Tel: (07356) 3011/6.

Northern Ireland

In Northern Ireland, this work is organised separately by the Northern Ireland Training Authority covering training boards for construction, distribution, engineering, food and drink, hotels and catering, office and business, road transport, textiles. For more information:

★ **ASK** Northern Ireland Training Authority and Industrial Training Boards, Swinson House, Glenmount Road, Church Road, Newtownabbey, Co Antrim BT36 7LH. Tel: (0231) 65171.

The Construction and Road Industry Training Boards are based at the Northern Ireland Training Centre.

★ **ASK** Northern Ireland Training Centre, 17 Dundrod Road, Nutts Corner, Crumlin BT29 3SP. Tel: (023 125) 466 (construction) or 653 (road transport).

SHORT COURSES

Updating skills to keep pace with technical change and development is an essential part of all work these days. There has always been a large 'short course' industry with courses being provided by professional bodies, colleges and other educational establishments, firms themselves, voluntary bodies and commercial training firms. This is a growth area with some emphasis being put on the provision of courses in new technology; but short course provision continues for in-service training and the updating of all skills. Some examples you will find throughout the book include:

- short courses for teachers (see *Teaching* in *42 Things to study*)
- short courses being run by extra-mural and continuing education departments of higher education establishments (listed in *27 Leisure classes*, though many of them are by no means recreational in intent!)
- short courses for people working in the social services field (listed in *VORTEX* and described in *31 Training for voluntary work*).

Updating skills – PICKUP

To encourage the updating of skills, the government started the PICKUP programme (it stands for professional, industrial and commercial updating). Eleven regional development agents have been appointed to encourage the work and a newsletter, *PICKUP in progress*, is published to provide up-to-date information.

★ **ASK** PICKUP Programme, Department of Education and Science, Elizabeth House, York Road, London SE1 7PH. Tel: (01) 928 9222 ext 3564.

One important part of the PICKUP programme is the *PICKUP short course directory*. It holds over 6,000 records of short vocational courses for adults nationwide and in a variety of subject areas; for example from computer applications to welding and from aboriculture to dentistry. Courses can be full- or part-time, or distance learning and are at all levels of entry, from craft to postgraduate. The directory is available on microfiche, Prestel and floppy disk.

★ **ASK** Guildford Educational Services, 164 High Street, Guildford, Surrey GU1 3HW. Tel: (0483) 579454.

INDUSTRIAL LANGUAGE TRAINING

Industrial Language Training represents a unique opportunity for workers, managers and trade unionists to tackle questions of communications and equal opportunities in the workplace.

Many companies have had to respond to their multi-racial workforce at a time when British industry is undergoing radical change in terms of economic conditions, new technology and use of human resources.

The aim of ILT is to improve the skills related to communications which will contribute to increased job access, increased job effectiveness and equal opportunities in the workplace for people of all ethnic and racial origins.

How ILT works

The ILT service now employs over 150 full-time trainers in 29 local ILT units. The service is funded by the MSC.

ILT units, which are established and managed by individual local authorities, are located in areas of high ethnic minority settlement and are co-ordinated by the National Centre for Industrial Language (NCILT).

Industrial Language Training units

National office

National Centre for Industrial Language Training, Havelock Campus, Havelock Road, Southall, Middlesex UB5 4NZ. Tel: (01) 571 2241.

Local Units

Any addresses not listed will be the main address of the college concerned, and can be found in the *Gazetteer*.

Bedfordshire

Industrial Language Training Unit, The Westbourne Centre, Westbourne Road, Bedford MK40 4PQ. Tel: (0234) 53481. Ask for: Wendy Gray.

Berkshire

Industrial Language Centre, Slough College of Higher Education, Wellington Street, Slough SL1 1YG. Tel: (0753) 25004 and 71821. Ask for: Shamim Khan.

Cambridgshire

Cambridgeshrie College of Arts and Technology, Collier Road, Cambridge. Tel: (0223) 63271. Ask for: Tony Morgan ext 2074 or his secretary ext 2054.

Derbyshire

Industrial Language Training Unit, Munday Street, Heanor, Derbyshire DE7 7DZ. Tel: (0773) 717441. Ask for: Bob Woolley.

Hertfordshire

Industrial Language Training Unit, Department of Adult Education, North Herts College, Cambridge Road, Hitchin SG4 0JD. Tel: (0462) 33914. Ask for: Prem Tiwary or Helen Reason.
And at Callowland Adult Education Centre, Leavesden Road, Watford WD2 5EP. Tel: (0923) 20270.

Lancashire

Lancashire Industrial Language Training Unit, 54/56 Blackburn Road, Accrington, Lancashire BB5 1LE. Tel: (0254) 393316. Ask for: Roger Munns.

Leicestershire

Industrial Language Unit, Charles Keene College of Further Education, Painter Street, Leicester LE1 3WA. Ask for: Paul Charlesworth.

LONDON – GREATER

Barking

Industrial Language Training Unit, Westbury Centre, Ripple Road, Barking IG11 7PT. Tel: (01) 594 3304. Ask for: Paul Lamb.

Bexley

Erith College of Technology, Tower Road, Belvedere, Kent DA17 6JA. Tel: (03224) 42331. Ask for: Ken Dixon.

Brent Industrial Language Training Unit, Ashley Gardens, Preston Road, Wembley, Middlesex HA9 8NP. Tel: (01) 908 1708/2905. Ask for: Libby Knowles.

Ealing and Hounslow

Pathway Industrial Unit, Havelock Centre, Havelock Road, Southall, Middlesex UB2 4NZ. Tel: (01) 571 2241. Ask for: Philip Baker.

Enfield

Industrial Language Training Unit, 31 Derby Road, Ponders End, Enfield EN3 4AJ. Ask for: Andy Beattie.

Newham

Industrial Language Training Unit, Newham Town Hall, East Ham, London E6 2RP. Tel: (01) 470 8176. Ask for: Elisa Christmas.

LONDON – INNER

North of the River

North London Industrial Language Training Unit, Jack Ashley Buildings, 3 Prah Road, London N4 2RA. Tel: (01) 354 0303. Ask for: Manijeh Kia-Najand.

South of the River

Industrial Language Training Unit, Southwark Institute, Hunter Close, (off Tabard Street), London SE1 4UU. Tel: (01) 403 0463 and 407 8986. Ask for: Yasmin Alibhai.

MANCHESTER – METROPOLITAN DISTRICTS

Bolton

Industrial Language Training Unit, Room 20, 3rd Floor, Bolton Metropolitan College, Clarence Street Centre, Bolton BL1 2ET. Tel: (0204) 34455. Ask for: Ann Gough.

Manchester

Industrial Language Training Unit, Manchester Business School, Booth Street West, Manchester M15 6PB. Tel: (061) 273 8228. Ask for: secretary of language department.

Oldham

Language Training Unit, Greenacres Centre, Galland Street, Greenacres, Oldham OL4 3EU. Tel: (061) 624 3668. Ask for: David Morgan.

Rochdale

Industrial Language Training Unit, Room 8, College Annexe, Baillie Street, Rochdale OL6 1JJ. Tel: (0706) 359700. Ask for: John Smith.

Tameside

Industrial Language Training Unit, Warrington House, Church Street, Ashton-under-Lyme, Tameside OL6 7PR. Tel: (061) 330 6911. Ask for: Peter Trumper.

Northamptonshire

Industrial Language Training Unit, The Lodge, Rickyard Road, The Arbours, Northampton NN3 3QZ. Tel: (0604) 410236. Ask for: Claire Bulloch.

TYNE AND WEAR – METROPOLITAN DISTRICTS

Newcastle

Industrial Language Training Unit, College of Arts and Technology, Ryehill House, Maple Terrace, Newcastle-upon-Tyne NE4 7EE. Tel: (091) 272 3464. Ask for: Desmond Watkiss.

WEST MIDLANDS

Birmingham

Industrial Language Training Unit, Handsworth Technical College, The Council House, Soho Road, Birmingham B21 9DP. Tel: (021) 551 6031 ext 222. Ask for: Clarice Brierley.

Coventry

Coventry and Warwickshire Industrial Language Service, Stoke School Site, Briton Road, Coventry CV2 4LF. Tel: (0203) 455947. Ask for: Ros Patchett.

Dudley

Language and Literacy Centre, Dudley College of Technology, The Broadway, Dudley, West Midlands DY1 4AS. Tel: (0384) 238367. Ask for: Bhajan Devsi.

Sandwell

Sandwell Industrial Language Service, Warley College of Technology, Crocketts Lane, Smethwick, Warley, West Midlands B66 3BU. Tel: (021) 558 6077. Ask for: Theo Brooks.

Walsall

Industrial Language Unit, Butts Centre, Butts Road, Walsall, West Midlands WS4 2AY. Tel: (0922) 34953. Ask for: Ram Chandola.

Wolverhampton

Industrial Language Training Unit, Room 26, Bilston Community College, Wellington Road, Bilston, West Midlands WV14 6EW. Tel: (0902) 402861. Ask for: Sujinder Sangha.

Warwickshire

North Warwickshire College of Technology and Art. Service planned. Ask for: Rosemary Collier.

YORKSHIRE – SOUTH

Sheffield

Industrial Language Training, St Barnabus Centre, Alderson Road, Sheffield S2 4UD. Tel: (0742) 552366 and 587187. Ask for: Bhupinder Panesar.

YORKSHIRE – WEST

Bradford

West Yorkshire Language Link, Auburn House, Upper Piccadilly, Bradford BD1 3NU. Tel: (0274) 305625. Ask for: John Clegg.

Calderdale

Industrial Language Training Unit, Bermerside Hall, Skircoat Green, Halifax HX3 0RZ. Tel: (0422) 62552 and 53144. Ask for: Jenny Ferris.

Kirklees

West Yorkshire Language Link, Marsh Adult Education Centre, St James Road, Marsh, Huddersfield HD1 4QA. Tel: (0484) 538418. Ask for: John Clark.

Leeds

West Yorkshire Language Link, 2 Woodhouse Square, Leeds LS3 1AD. Tel: (0532) 449603 . Ask for: Margaret Horton.

34 The private sector

What is the private sector?
Independent colleges of FE
English language schools
Business amd secretarial colleges
Independent higher education
Can you trust them?
Further information

WHAT IS THE PRIVATE SECTOR?

Most of the education described in this book is public education run by local or central government or bodies like the MSC and universities. One exception is the correspondence colleges – but there are also a number of independent colleges offering education and training which are open to adults. They cover a wide range of subjects such as advertising, modelling, photography, GCEs, business studies and computing. Some advertise on the London Underground (computers, shorthand/typing), others in small ads in the papers. Some are reputable, sincere and serious, others are more dubious. And until you get there, it's very hard to tell what you will get. Some of them have formed into associations which guarantee standards both of teaching and amenity.

Recognition

In 1982 the Department of Education and Science ceased to offer 'recognition as efficient' to colleges in the private sector. This used to be some indication of standards. In place of DES recognition, the British Council has developed an inspection and recognition scheme for colleges and other providers and is one of the organisations that established a British Accreditation Council.

The British Accreditation Council for Independent Further and Higher Education was set up in 1984 to inspect and accredit private institutions of further and higher education. It is made up of representatives of public educational bodies and operates a system of inspection and accreditation.

★ **ASK** The British Accreditation Council for Independent Further and Higher Education, 114 Chase Side, Southgate, London N14 5PN. Tel: (01) 886 6599.

Advantages and disadvantages

The main advantages of the private sector are that you may be able to join at any time of the year and there is often more individual attention.

The disadvantage is the cost compared with the public sector, but even that is worth checking as fees go up in LEA colleges, especially for overseas students.

INDEPENDENT COLLEGES OF FURTHER EDUCATION

These offer full-time courses leading to GCSEs and A-levels as well as other courses and exams. Most colleges work in terms but it is often possible to start at other times. Some specialise in courses for 17–21 year olds; some have no limit.

Some colleges are members of The Conference of Independent Further Education which is a voluntary association aimed at maintaining standards at the DES level. Members are inspected regularly by an independent panel of assessors and codes of practice and conduct are in force.

★ **SEND FOR** *List of members and guide to courses* from the Conference for Independent Further Education, PO Box 7, Moreton-in-Marsh, Gloucestershire GL36 9LP. Tel: (0386) 700683.

ENGLISH LANGUAGE SCHOOLS

There are dozens of schools (or colleges) teaching English to foreigners. Many of them mushroom in the summer to cater for youngsters from abroad.

ARELS-FELCO

Some of the larger ones have formed into the Association for Recognised English Language Teaching Establishments in Britain (ARELS-FELCO). It publishes a guide, *Learn English in Britain with ARELS-FELCO,* and guarantees minimum standards. It also acts as an examining board for courses in individual schools. The Association only includes colleges 'recognised as efficient' by the British Council. The schools run all-year-round and summer courses to suit adults and juniors. For a list of recognised English language schools:

★ **ASK** ARELS-FELCO, 125 High Holborn, London WC1V 6QD. Tel: (01) 242 3136.

★ **LOOK AT** *Education yearbook* (see *Booklist*).

BUSINESS AND SECRETARIAL COLLEGES

There's an enormous range of secretarial colleges, business schools, receptionist schools, computer schools. Their courses are often advertised in a way that suggests you could learn a lot in a very short time. If you can do a similar course at a local college you may save a lot of money by doing so and can be confident of the value of the qualifications you earn. You may find a JTS-sponsored course. These run at both LEA and private colleges. In either case, you pay no fees, and you get paid a training allowance (see *24 Training for a new job*).

INDEPENDENT HIGHER EDUCATION

The main institution in the private sector for degree study is the University of Buckingham. This opened in 1976 as an independent university outside the state system. Unlike most universities, you apply directly and courses are shorter because there are fewer holidays. The four ten-week terms start in January. Students on its two-year courses can receive mandatory LEA awards.

There are also places in the private sector which prepare students for London University external degrees. Few are residential, but fees for residential courses of this kind are over £3,500 a year. Many are listed in *DITTO* (see below).

CAN YOU TRUST THEM?

There are a number of things you can look out for:

- Do their advertisements make sense? For example, do they suggest you can get rich overnight?
- Do their fees seem fair compared with other similar places? They'll usually be more than in the public system. If they don't tell you what their fees are in writing before you go and visit, be careful.
- Do they offer qualifications recognised by other people – especially employers? If they offer their own qualifications, be suspicious. The main qualifications are explained in *41 Qualifications*.
- As many places are used by foreign students, the British Council keeps a record of complaints about them. If there are too many, they won't recommend the place to enquirers. You can ask them which places they recommend. They can't give details about each college.
- Ask your local education guidance service for adults (see *1 Advice and help*).

Complaints

If the advertisements seem misleading when compared with what you get, you can complain to the local consumer advisory service. They can take dishonest traders to court. For the address of your local office:

★ **LOOK AT** *Social services yearbook* (see *Booklist*).

The Advertising Standards Authority can investigate misleading advertisements. Send a letter indicating the nature of complaint – if possible enclose a copy of the advertisement. Phone enquiries are welcome.

★ **WRITE TO** The Advertising Standards Authority, Brook House, 2/16 Torrington Place, London WC1E 7HN. Tel: (01) 580 5555.

FURTHER INFORMATION

A directory of private colleges covering everything from accountancy and antiques to modelling and theatre arts is available and worth checking if you want to use a course in the private sector.

★ **LOOK AT** *Directory of independent training and tutorial organisations* (*DITTO*) - a guide to private colleges and training organisations. Compiled by Elizabeth Summerson and Maureen Davies, published by Careers Consultants Ltd, 12/14 Hill Rise, Richmond, Surrey TW10 6UA. Tel: (01) 940 5668. Some subject areas in DITTO have been made available as separate mini-guides. Titles are: *Getting into keep-fit, beauty, hairdressing and modelling; Getting into cookery and housekeeping; Getting into secretarial courses*; *Getting into alternative medicine*; and *Getting into creative arts and crafts*.

35 Training for self-employment

The growth of self-employment
Courses
Where to go for advice

THE GROWTH OF SELF-EMPLOYMENT

As more people lose their jobs with changes in the economy, many are becoming aware of alternatives to wage earning. One alternative is working for yourself, being self-employed, running your own business. It has always been the choice for many, but today it is the focus of much interest as a realistic way of working. After all, big business doesn't do everything. How much does it cost to service a washing machine? How many attractive handmade implements can you get from big stores? And there are traditional areas where the small business has always been dominant – electricians, plumbers, window cleaners, building sub-contractors, shopkeepers have always made up a large self-employed sector in the economy.

More people are moving towards self-employment, offering services or goods or anything that's hard to get. It's a way of working that's relevant for modern industry too – many people working with computers, for example, work as freelance consultants or started off by forming their own company.

Things to think about

What you offer has to be something that people want to buy, or you'll get very little trade. So as well as having the skills to make what you make or do what you do, you have to know how to survey the market, how to publicise your goods or services and how to get them to the customer. And a business also presents extra work of its own – tax, national insurance, VAT, accounts, records and the rest – which can't be ignored.

Perhaps the worst problem is taking the plunge – do you do it gradually or suddenly? What about the lean times when no one seems to want you, and the good times when everyone does, and you have no time to get round them all, so they may give you up. It's a big step to take – but you can get help.

With the growth of self-employment there has been a growth of advice services and training courses, to help people with all the problems involved.

COURSES

There are so many courses that only an outline of what's on offer can be given here. The advice services listed below (who may also run courses themselves) should know of extra things in your locality. People providing courses will also publicise them through libraries, the local press, advice centres and so on.

The courses described are mostly about the mechanics of running a business – if you need extra training in the technical skills you will use then look at other chapters, especially *16 Further education, adult education* and *24 Training for a new job.*

MSC courses

Described in more detail in *24 Training for a new job.* They include the New Enterprise Programme (16 weeks for people who wish to launch businesses with growth potential that will employ people), Small Business Courses (eight weeks for people wanting to set up more modest businesses), and Self Employment Courses (one or two weeks for skilled people wanting to set up a one-person business). There is also a Management Extension Programme to help with the expansion of existing small businesses. Information is available from Jobcentres. These courses (some of which may be run part time, at weekends) are also advertised in the national and local press.

Correspondence courses

The Open University

The OU's Open Business School offers a course Start Up Your Own Business.

★ **WRITE TO** Start Up Your Own Business, The Open University's Open Business School, Walton Hall, Milton Keynes MK7 6AA.

National Extension College

Offers the *Small business course*. They also publish two books, *Be your own boss starter kit* and *Growth kit*. NEC and Pan Books jointly offer services of *Breakthrough* courses on a selection of key business skills.

★ **WRITE TO** National Extension College, 18 Brooklands Avenue, Cambridge CB2 2HN. Tel: (0223) 316644.

Adult education courses

Many adult education centres, further education colleges and extra-mural departments in higher education establishments run short courses on starting a small business. Contact the people listed in *27 Leisure classes* but also keep your eyes open – they should be advertised locally.

Other courses

Project Fullemploy

Runs self-employment courses in Clerkenwell (London), West Bromwich, Bradford, Manchester, Deptford (London) and Bristol. They have a lot of experience of running courses for people from ethnic minorities though their courses are open to all.

★ **ASK** Project Fullemploy, Head Office, 102 Park Village East, London NW1 3SP. Tel: (01) 387 1222.

WHERE TO GO FOR ADVICE

The Small Firms Service

Operated by the Department of Trade and Industry, it is an information and counselling service designed to help owners and managers of small businesses with their plans and problems. It also acts as an advisory service to those thinking of starting their own business.

The information service is free. For counselling, when plans and problems can be discussed in confidence with an experienced businessperson, the first three sessions are free and a modest charge is made for any further sessions.

The Small Firms Service also produces a range of booklets intended to help those running a small business or those wishing to.

There is a list of Small Firms Centres below; you can also contact your nearest one by dialling 100 and asking for Freefone 2444 or Freefone Enterprise.

Local Small Firms Centres

South Eastern Region:
Ebury Bridge House, 2–18 Ebury Bridge Road, London SW1W 8QD. Tel: (01) 730 8451.
Carlisle House, Carlisle Road, Cambridge CB4 3DN. Tel: (0223) 63312.
Abbey Hall, Abbey Square, Reading RG1 3BE. Tel: (0734) 591733.

South West Region: 5th Floor, The Pithay, Bristol BS1 2NB. Tel: (0272) 294546.

East Midlands Region: Severns House, 20 Middle Pavement, Nottingham NG1 7DW. Tel: (0602) 581205.

West Midlands Region: 6th Floor, Ladywood House, Stephenson Street, Birmingham B2 4DT. Tel: (021) 643 3344.

Yorkshire and Humberside Region: 1 Park Row, City Square, Leeds LS1 5NR. Tel: (0532) 445151.

Northern Region: Centro House, 3 Cloth Market, Newcastle-upon-Tyne NE1 3EE. Tel: (0632) 325353.

North West Region: 3rd Floor, 320–325 Royal Exchange Building, St Ann's Square, Manchester M2 7AH. Tel: (061) 832 5282.

Sub-office for Liverpool: Graeme House, Derby Square, Liverpool L3 9HJ. Tel: (051) 236 5756.

Wales: 16 St David's House, Wood Street, Cardiff CF1 1ER. Tel: (0222) 396116/7/8/9.

Scotland: 21 Bothwell Street, Glasgow G2 6NR. Tel: (041) 248 6014.

Council for Small Industries in Rural Areas (CoSIRA)

Offers help to people thinking of starting up in business or already operating in an English rural area (and towns having a population of under 10,000 people). Technical advice on a wide range of skills is available from experts in such subjects as welding, production engineering, woodworking machinery, GR plastics and some of the traditional rural industries such as thatching, saddlery, forgework and pottery technology. Business management advice is available and also assistance with local problems with country-based organisers. Short and long-term training courses may be undertaken in some of the subjects mentioned, either in the Salisbury workshops or on the client's premises provided that the student is already in employment or attached to a Masterman. Some loan assistance is available from limited funds but this must not exceed 30% of your total project cost. CoSIRA will help you present your case to obtain the rest from private sources.

★ **SEND FOR** leaflets giving general and more specific information, from CoSIRA, Information Section, 141 Castle Street, Salisbury, Wiltshire SP1 3TP. Tel: (0722) 336255 or look in your telephone directory for the number of the nearest CoSIRA office.

In Northern Ireland, the Local Enterprise Development Unit runs short courses for people wishing to set up small businesses.

★ **ASK** Local Enterprise Development Unit, LEDU House, Upper Galwally, Newtownbreda, Belfast BT8 4AR. Tel: (0232) 691031.

Local enterprise agencies

There are over 250 enterprise agencies which have been set up around Britain, to offer advice to people interested in creating and developing new and existing small businesses. They provide free advice on finance, premises, marketing and other subjects important to the development of small businesses. For a list of local enterprise agencies:

★ **ASK** Business in the Community, 227a City Road, London EC1V 1LX. Tel: (01) 253 3716, or Scottish Business in the Community, Eagle Star House, 25 St Andrews Square, Edinburgh EH2 1AF. Tel: (031) 556 9761/2.

The co-operative business option

One way of reducing the solitude is to form a co-op. That means you work with others, not as an employer but as equals. There are local Co-operative Development Agencies in many areas to help and advise on setting up co-operatives.

★ **ASK** Co-operative Development Agency (CDA), Broadmead House, 21 Panton Street, London SW1Y 4DR. Tel: (01) 839 2988.

Your local council

Local councils have a variety of ways of helping small firms and should have a lot of local knowledge.

★ **ASK** The Chief Executive's Department of your local council. If you don't know where that is, ask in the library.

36 Teach yourself systems

What's on offer?	*Tapes and records*
Books	*Computers*

WHAT'S ON OFFER?

By 'teach yourself systems' we do not mean correspondence courses or self-help schemes like those described in *26 Learning by post* and *17 Flexible learning*, nor even radio and TV programmes. We mean the enormous range of books, records, tapes and computer programs which provide you with opportunities to study hundreds of subjects and languages.

BOOKS

'Teach yourself' and 'Made simple' books are well known, but there are many similar, cheaper, shorter learning guides as well as DIY books, car manuals, computer handbooks and many others. It's extremely hard to learn from books, unless you have previous knowledge of the subject; this applies particularly if you are trying to master a practical skill. Anyone who tries to mend their car on the basis of a manual will know this – manuals are most useful as sources of reference for people who already know what they're doing. The same goes for other subjects. It's not the fault of the books – it's just that books are not the best way to start learning anything.

If you do use books you must be satisfied with slow and difficult progress. They do not miraculously fill gaps in your knowledge; at best they help you find out how big the gaps are. Not recommended if you are a nervous beginner!

On the other hand, books do offer the chance to 'dip in' to a subject – offer a taster to find out whether you might want to pursue a subject further. Use them just like any other introductory book. And don't feel stupid if you find they're not all simple. A lot of them aren't. The subject range covered is wide; one well known series includes books on ballroom dancing, biology and billiards.

Beginners books for GCSEs and A-levels are usually very good, because that's all they are – they're designed to help you pass exams and, used correctly, they probably work.

Finding the right book

There *are* other books available as well as those advertised in magazines or as part of a series on TV. Browse around bookshops – it's free. And use your libraries. The staff should help you find the books you want; if they don't have them they can usually borrow them or they may be able to tell you where there are specialist libraries on your subject. Many libraries, bookshops and organisations publish regular booklists – and books themselves usually suggest other things to read.

TAPES AND RECORDS

These usually teach languages. They won't teach you much – just enough to get you started. And they're expensive – sometimes more than an evening class would be. Try them first at the library and only buy if you really think it works for you. Don't believe extravagant advertising claims.

WOMAN, 29
My mum learns bird songs from records. She listens and then goes out and says 'ah that's a great crested tit'. So it does work. She's spent pounds on them, she's got about ten records and they cost a bomb.

COMPUTERS

Computing is a subject in itself (see *42 Things to study* and *24 Training for a new job*). Two aspects of home computing which make the microcomputer an extra teach-yourself tool are educational programs to learn particular things and using microcomputers at home to learn programming.

Educational programs

Only a small proportion of software for home computers is for educational purposes. Much of it is mediocre; learning could be achieved as easily through more traditional methods. But look around. You will find that programs are directed at the school age range from three years old to A-level standard. Subjects range from basic reading and spelling to A-level maths and physics.

Software designed to teach people with disabilities is among the more enlightened and has been used successfully with, for example, people who are blind, autistic or who have mental handicaps.

You will find more information in the many computer magazines available – browse through them in the newsagents and find which suits your needs best.

Prices for programs for home computers such as the BBC and Spectrum range from £5 to £60. They are covered by copyright so you are not allowed to copy them unless they state they are copyright free. If you have a BBC microcomputer you can buy an adapter so you can not only obtain Teletext pages but also so that telesoftware can be transmitted directly to your computer. Most of the telesoftware is educational.

Learning programming

You can teach yourself programming using magazines and books, as well as your computer. Even if you go to a class to learn programming (and many evening classes called 'an introduction to computing' are in fact an introduction to programming) you will get a lot more from it if you can work by yourself at home as well. But the problems mentioned above about learning from books are as relevant here too. Many publishers have cashed in on the booming home computer market. Books to teach programming as well as user manuals are very varied in standard. Ask around before spending your money.

37 Alternatives

Ecology
Education
Growth and therapy
Single sex groups
Work
Politics and pressure groups
How to find out more

A lot of learning goes on outside the mainstream education system. Since you often have to pay, it could be seen as a part of the private sector. But it can often be radical; many people involved are not doing it for the money. Also, there may be no quality standards, so you do have to take a chance.

Things change very quickly in this sort of learning; groups or publications wind up and new ones are started all the time. Also the sorts of things you can study change over time. This chapter can't list everything, so instead some ideas are offered as signposts so you can start your own search. You may also be able to gather ideas from groups or projects mentioned in *1 Advice and help*, *6 Women*, *9 Ethnic minorities*, *27 Leisure classes* and *30 Health education*.

ECOLOGY

This is about understanding how people live in relation to the environment and could include learning about conservation (of energy, animal life, natural resources), self-sufficiency, or how best to live in harmony with nature. There are lots of organisations and publications – many run short courses or hold meetings where you can learn skills or acquire knowledge. A few are listed here.

Friends of the Earth. Have local groups which may be involved in different activities, varying from area to area – for example, bike repair workshops, domestic insulation projects, recycling, and campaigning against nuclear power. Offer training to volunteers too.

★ **WRITE TO** Friends of the Earth, 27 Swinton Street, London WC1.

National Centre for Alternative Technology. Just visiting the centre is one way to learn about non-harmful, non-wasteful technology and energy use, but they also run short residential courses including solar, wind and water power, organic growing and blacksmithing. For a list:

★ **WRITE TO** National Centre for Alternative Technology, Llwyngwern Quarry, Machynlleth, Powys. Tel: (0654) 2400. Enclose an SAE.

Soil Association. Mainly interested in organic farming and gardening. You have to join but it's worth it. They also run courses.

★ **WRITE TO** Soil Association, 86–88 Colston Street, Bristol BS1 5BB. Tel: (0272) 290661.

Henry Doubleday Research Association. Has 10,000 members and carries out research demonstration into ecologically sustainable methods of growing. There is a ten-acre area of demonstration organic gardens open all year round.

★ **WRITE TO** Henry Doubleday Research Association, Centre for Organic Gardening, Ryton-on-Dunsmore, Coventry CV8 3LG. Tel: (0203) 305517.

★ **LOOK AT** *Home farm*, the official magazine of the Small Farmers Association - comes out six times a year (subscription £8 a year). Covers all sorts of topics to do with organic farming and gardening, humane livestock keeping, small farming practice and rural life, with lists of courses.

★ **WRITE TO** Home Farm, Broad Lays Publishing Company, Widdington, Saffron Walden, Essex CB11 3SP. Tel: (0799) 40922.

The Tree Council. Organises annual national tree week in December and promotes tree planting and the care of trees for environmental purposes.

★ **WRITE TO** The Tree Council, 35 Belgrave Square, London SW1X 8WN. Tel: (01) 235 8854.

★ **LOOK AT** *Resurgence*, a magazine published every two months (£1.70 a copy, or £10 subscription). Articles from a 'small is beautiful' perspective – includes energy, arts and education. Lists courses, events, green/environmental activities.

★ **WRITE TO** Resurgence, Worthydale Manor Farm, Camelford, Cornwall PL32 9TT. Tel: (0840) 212711.

Working Weekends on Organic Farms (*WWOOF*). For people interested in agriculture and animal husbandry in a practical way. Can help you get experience and training in skills related to smallholding and self-sufficiency.

★ **WRITE TO** Working Weekends, 19 Bradford Road, Lewes, East Sussex.

EDUCATION

The last twenty years have seen a rapid expansion of activities in holistic education; for example, assertiveness training, co-counselling, life-planning, stress management and a host of others. All deal with the whole person – spiritual, physical, emotional, social and intellectual. Many courses help people to develop self-confidence as well as new skills and insights.

Human Potential Research Project (*HPRP*). The longest established centre for this kind of education in Europe.

★ **WRITE TO** Diana Lomax, HPRP, Department of Educational Studies, University of Surrey, Guildford GU2 5XH. Tel: (0483) 571281 ext 9191.

GROWTH AND THERAPY

This is about self discovery – understanding how your mind and body work and how you relate to other people. It's a field that's full of different approaches, theories and jargon. At first you'll probably not know the difference between transactional analysis, primal therapy, encounter groups, gestalt, or bio-energetics.

★ **LOOK AT** *Human potential resources* - a quarterly magazine from Human Potential Resources, 35 Station Road, Hendon, London NW4 4PN. The magazine has articles, listings of workshops and courses, and a calendar of events. It is intended for people who are looking for new directions in their personal development and growth. Sample copy free, yearly subscription £3.50.

★ **LOOK AT** *Self and society – the European journal of humanistic psychology* - bimonthly. Yearly subscription £8.50 from Self and Society, 62 Southwark Bridge Road, London SE1 0AS.

SINGLE SEX GROUPS

There are several organisations to contact if you want to find out about discussion groups, local events, meetings and workshops of particular interest to single sex groups. In some parts of the country there are telephone information and counselling services with easily recognised names. They are run by volunteers and are usually part time, so it may take a while to get through when you phone. Many services provide training for their volunteers.

There are a few university or polytechnic extra-mural departments and adult education institutes which run non-exam courses on literature, history or politics. Often these are run as one-offs to assess popularity. Their courses change from year to year – phone to check what's on offer. Short courses and workshops (as well as advice) are available from several organisations for people interested in knowing more about AIDS (Acquired Immune Deficiency Syndrome) and related health problems. See *30 Health education* for more information.

WORK

With new technology and changes in Britain's industries, values and lifestyles, the structure of work is changing. It no longer simply means being employed for a salary or wage, it can refer to unpaid activities, including voluntary work. There is an increase in job sharing and in different kinds of organisations, eg co-operatives. Some groups work to provide a service to the community as well as make a profit. A number of national and local organisations exist to advise and support people seeking alternative work. Only a few are mentioned here.

Co-operative Development Agency. Publishes the *National directory of new co-operatives,* £5.50 from Broadmead House, 21 Panton Street, London S1Y 4DR. There are around 100 local CDAs throughout the country which offer advice and help to people wishing to set up a co-op.

Industrial Common Ownership Movement. The National Federation of Workers Co-operatives, 7–8 Corn Exchange, Leeds LS1 7BP. Tel: (0532) 461737.

★ **WRITE TO** Foundation for Alternatives, The Rookery, Adderbury, Nr Banbury, Oxfordshire. The Foundation aims to promote pilot projects in alternative forms of social and political organisations, especially in employment. It produces directories and profiles of schemes throughout the country.

POLITICS AND PRESSURE GROUPS

If you have some idea of where you stand, these groups provide a great opportunity to learn about different topics. Organisations hold meetings, discussions, day schools or workshops on issues as diverse as agriculture, transport, economics, the media, defence and peace and the prison system. They'll probably be less helpful for learning if you're not sure where you stand or if you don't agree with the group's ideas. These events can be a great chance to learn and share ideas with influential people from politics and education.

To find out more, ask anyone you know who is involved in political activity, ask for the name of a local contact in larger libraries, or buy the publications of whichever organisation attracts you. If you're interested in trade union activities, there are some useful addresses in *32 Trade union education*. Some adult education institutes, and university and polytechnic extra-mural departments run courses about politics – see *16 Further education, adult education* for ideas on where to start looking. There is an enormous range of pressure groups.

★ **WRITE TO** Workplace Nurseries Campaign, Southbank House, Black Prince Road, London SE1 7SJ. The information officers are Penny Craig and Sean Williamson. Tel: (01) 582 7199.

★ **WRITE TO** Council for the Protection of Rural England, 4 Hobart Place, London SW1W 0HY. Tel: (01) 235 9481. There is a branch in each county – check at your local library.

★ **LOOK AT** *Directory of social change*, available at most libraries, published by Directory of Social Change, Radius Works, Back Lane, London NW3 1NL. Tel: (01) 435 8171.

★ **WRITE TO** British Society for Social Responsibility in Science, 9 Poland Street, London W1. Tel: (01) 607 9615.

HOW TO FIND OUT MORE

In larger towns and cities, radical bookshops, wholefood stores, women's centres, student unions and community centres are often the best places to find contacts. Some publish alternative guides which are mines of information. Useful magazines include *Time out* or *City limits* - even if you live outside London they can be useful starting points.

★ **LOOK AT** *Alternative London*, Otherwise Press, £3.50.

38 Do it yourself

Disadvantages
Advantages
How organised must you be?
Help you can get
Self-help groups
The Mutual Aid Centre

If you can't find a course, or don't want to use one, you can create your own.

You may not want to go to college; perhaps you can't fit it in or don't have enough money; there may not be one near or you may just not like formal places. It's quite possible to study and learn effectively without going anywhere.

Teachers can't pour knowledge or skills into you; you have to do the work. All they can do is try to make it as straightforward as possible, save you some time and tell you how well you're doing. But you do all the learning yourself. It's quite commonplace for people to teach themselves to play an instrument, to cook, or to learn to drive from a friend. This can be applied to other things – passing O-level history, learning to speak French or to type.

DISADVANTAGES

If you don't go to college you don't have:

- all the resources at hand (though you can often get them)
- anyone to tell you if what you're doing is good; so you may be uncertain, and feel that you're not really doing it because you're not at college
- someone to ask if you're not sure about something
- other people to talk to, compare notes with and share difficulties with. You may feel isolated – many people decide to go to college to avoid this.

ADVANTAGES

If you decide you want to do it on your own, these obstacles can be overcome. To start with, that sense of 'not really doing it' is false. You probably are, though you may not gain formal recognition for what you do. The chances are you will follow up the things that interest you rather than methodically work through a syllabus. You have time to stop and start when you're too busy or feeling lazy; you're free. What you are doing is learning. What you are not doing is gaining formal recognition and status for having been through an institution.

WOMAN, 30s
I started to learn about cows by keeping one. I was highly motivated, so I got a lot from books. I found that the knowledge I gleaned was from any and every source that was available. I tuned in whenever anyone said anything useful. It's more interesting to read about cows if you have one.

HOW ORGANISED MUST YOU BE?

It depends what you're doing.

If you're learning a skill

- You'll need to practise fairly regularly, so you'll need access to the thing you're learning to use, whether it's a guitar, a road roller, a typewriter or a computer. Without that, you've got problems.
- You'll need proper instructions, preferably written down. You can get them from a book or perhaps a friend. Half the battle is understanding the instructions.
- You'll need to know how to judge progress towards what you're aiming at; that could be done by watching someone else doing it or by demonstrating what you've learned to someone who can do it better than you do. If there's no one it's a bit harder.

If you're getting a qualification

If you want a qualification to show you've learnt the skill you'll almost always have to go to a college, skillcentre or somewhere else. If you want an academic qualification you can take some exams as an external candidate. You can get a syllabus from the exam board (see *41 Qualifications*).

Your main problems will be organising your work so that you cover enough topics, knowing what's expected when you do written work, and judging if you're at the appropriate standard. If you want help you're probably best off doing a correspondence course (see *26 Learning by post*).

If you're just finding out more

This is one area that's ideal for 'do it yourself'. You don't have to be organised, but you can if you like. You don't have to follow a structured course; you can start at the end and work back to the beginning or in the middle and work both ways! You can do it on your own, or organise a group of friends to meet with – many groups, like local history societies or women's study groups start that way. Some people advertise in the local paper to find others wanting to pursue the same topic.

HELP YOU CAN GET

Help may be a matter of facilities, or knowledge or just someone to talk to. You may find them all in one place, or in several.

Use your library

Your local library offers a tremendous range of resources and information. Even if the one you use is a small branch or mobile library, it is part of a larger county library service. They can get books or information you ask for and even if the county library doesn't have what you want, there is a system for libraries to borrow from each other. So do ask. Some of the services you can expect include finding out where to go for expert help on different things, locally or nationally, what local organisations exist, where the local colleges and adult education centres are, what places to visit.

As a general principle, librarians are information specialists, not guardians of books. If there's anything you need to know about anything, it's worth asking them. Although this is one of the most important services they offer, it is very much underused because so many people think libraries only lend books.

Many organisations have libraries open to the public (eg the IBA). Many of them are delighted if people ask for their help, though it will vary a lot, depending on why the library exists and how stretched they are. Your local librarian should be able to help you find specialist libraries and tell you whether they're open to you.

Museums, galleries, institutes

Places dealing in specialist information can be approached if your subject is something to do with them. You can meet some very interesting people! They may have an education officer (who is more concerned with school parties). You may get a better response if you go to a subject specialist – for instance they will often identify specimens (of coins, plants, rocks etc) for you.

★ **LOOK AT** *Museums and galleries in Great Britain and Northern Ireland*, ABC Historic Publications, annual. Lists every museum by location and subject.

For a critical guide:

★ **LOOK AT** *The good museums guide*, Kenneth Hudson, Papermac which looks at the best 400 (of 1,600). Lists by subject, outstanding special interest collections.

Local colleges or universities

Even if you're not on a course, your local college may be able to help. It's worth a try, even though sometimes you do not get far. But they could, for example:

- let you talk to one of their subject specialists; that will be easier if you find the right person and go direct to them rather than going through the bureaucracy
- introduce you to people studying your subject
- let you use the facilities of their library and other resources
- let you sit in on a few lectures or meetings
- advise you on what and what not to read.

In the end, they'll probably try to enrol you on one of their courses anyway, or they may suggest that one of the newer schemes they might be running is just for you!

Some universities do allow (and a few even encourage) people to sit in on courses, as occasional students. Those that we know of are listed in the *Gazetteer* and in the list of higher education institutions in *22 Getting a degree*. Sometimes you'll have to pay – but not always. If you approach lecturers direct they will often be happy for you to attend lectures informally, but that's more difficult where students are taught in small groups on a tutorial basis.

Some places are becoming more open, allowing people more freedom to study from home or to plan their own courses. Correspondence courses have always been home-based but that's been extended by the Open University and Flexistudy and other similar approaches to studying (listed in *17 Flexible learning*).

North East London Polytechnic has shown it is possible for people to design their own degree course through their courses by independent study. It may suit you better to use one of these half-and-half methods than to do it totally by yourself.

Education guidance services for adults
Should be able to advise you on local sources of help – they are listed in *1 Advice and help*.

Citizens' Advice Bureaux
Should be able to tell you whether there's a local education guidance service.

Broadcasts
Radio and TV programmes are a starting point for DIY learning; for more on how to use broadcasting look at *25 Radio and TV*.

Getting a course organised for yourself
Most people running courses (local colleges, local adult education services, WEAs and so on) are concerned with getting together enough people to make the courses viable. If you approach them and say 'here is a group of people wanting to learn', they'll often be pleased to organise a class and teacher. Clubs and societies you belong to (the Women's Institute, Round Table, Trades Council, National Housewives Register etc) can often provide you with such a group ready made, and many colleges run courses for, or in conjunction with local organisations. They may be equally ready to respond in the same way to an ad hoc group of people who have come together because of a common interest.

WOMAN, 30s
Jo had been doing make-up lessons from home. She had been charging enough to cover costs. She said, 'why not let me come and do it at the school?' – the FE room needed to be used more. We had to form a club. The organising secretary said it needed to be better than a few women coming along. We formed a committee. This made it sound official – right for the powers that be. The leaflet giving all the courses included the make-up club. We had an enrolment evening with the other classes. Jo made it into a course of ten lessons – we had a slendertone machine, one week hair care, one week make-up. The only snag in it was no children allowed – no creche. There's no room for one. It was a bit difficult without a creche; it put the numbers down. But it was a success, the people who came were pleased and wanted her to carry on with it.

An extra advantage of getting someone in the business to help you organise your class is that they should be able to give you guidance as to whether your instructor or teacher needs any special qualifications, training or experience. This could be important with activities involving possible danger – such as the many types of keep-fit and aerobics classes that are very popular and are frequently organised on a self-help or private enterprise basis.

The WEA

A long established self-help education service – one you can join. It has 900 local branches and by joining you can be involved in decisions about courses they put on locally. There is more information about how the WEA works in *28 The WEA*.

NASO

A national self-help voluntary adult education movement that has existed for nearly 200 years. NASO 'friendship through study' groups meet throughout the country, organising and running their own programme. Individual groups get together for regional activities which range from residential weekends to studying a particular subject in some depth, to social outings to visit a place of interest. The national office publishes discussion leaflets and a study handbook each year to help local schools with their discussion programme and publishes a bi-monthly magazine *One and all* to link the groups together in a national movement.

The national office also organises study tours abroad, a See Britain Summer School annually and activity weekends to complement studies in the handbook.

Groups vary in size from 5 to 25 people and each group finds its own meeting place which can be a community centre, church hall or a member's home. There is a small national membership fee but the study handbook, which is sold at a reduced rate to members, is available to the general public (1986 edition £3.50).

★ **ASK** National Adult School Organisation, Norfolk House, Smallbrook,Queensway, Birmingham B5 4LJ. Tel: (021) 643 9297.

SELF-HELP GROUPS

A long established method of study in some countries though not well established here apart from some of the organisations mentioned above.

The Attleborough experiment

Attleborough is a small town in Norfolk. For the last few years there has been an adult education experiment to set up a self-help learning network. Students decide what they want to learn and are helped to find people and resources in the local community that can help. A programme has been made by BBC TV (contact BBC Enterprises) and a booklet has been published describing the experiment.

★ **SEND FOR** *The Attleborough experiment*, £3 inc p&p from the National Extension College, 18 Brooklands Avenue, Cambridge CB2 2HN. Tel: (0223) 316644.

THE MUTUAL AID CENTRE

An organisation to encourage self-help. They have a number of projects, some of them educational, and all including some education.

Studying on your way to work

One of their first projects was an experiment to see if it's possible to organise regular study sessions for people travelling to work by train – while travelling. They found that many people were enthusiastic to do it and British Rail were helpful in organising it. There are now a number of 'brain trains' and they've produced a booklet telling you how to set up your own if you are interested.

★ **LOOK AT** *Go to work on a brain train*, Mutual Aid Press, Paper No 1, £1 from The Mutual Aid Centre (see below).

The Motorists' Co-operative

The longest running project is in Milton Keynes and is a way of beating garage bills but also of overcoming that fear of mechanical things many of us have. The £6 a year membership entitles you to a special members' discount on spare parts and accessories sold in the shop and special rates for DIY. There is always a qualified mechanic to advise you if you don't know what to do, plus MOT testing.

★ **ASK** MKOK, Waterside, Peartree Bridge, Milton Keynes MK6 3BX. Tel: (0908) 606848 . Contact Bill Dredge.

Publications

Mutual aid in a selfish society, a plea for strengthening the co-operative movement, £1.20.

Hello, can I help you? The growth of telephone answering services, which includes a directory of telephone-giving advice services, £1.30. For these, and more information:

★ **ASK** The Mutual Aid Centre, 18 Victoria Park Square, London E2 9PF. Tel: (01) 980 6263.

MONEY

39 Money: what for, where from

WHAT WILL YOU NEED MONEY FOR?

All study costs something. Sometimes you will have to pay the costs yourself, sometimes you can get help. This chapter tells you about some of the organisations which help financially when you are studying. Not everything is covered – it's too complicated. And if you have any problems you'll need precise legal information, which you can get from the booklets and sources of advice listed below.

You can use these notes to identify the things you need money for; then look at your grant (allowance, bursary, award – whatever it's called it still means money which somebody is giving you so you can study) and see whether it covers all of them. If not, you may have to spend your own money or get more from somewhere else.

For most courses

Course fees, exam fees, travel, equipment (from pens and paper to protective clothing).

For full-time courses

Money to support you and your family (including two homes if you have to live away) and residence fees; union dues; meals. You may also want to continue paying national insurance contributions.

Most grants cover fees, books and equipment. Sometimes travel and meals, and for full-time courses 'maintenance' (money to stay alive). This is based on a minimum standard of living. You're never rich on a grant (though it's possible to be better off, or no worse off, than you were).

Fee waivers

Sometimes colleges or adult education centres waive fees. LEAs often do for unemployed people, people on supplementary benefit or others who can't find the money for fees. What happens in your area may be a question for individual colleges and centres, or your LEA may have a policy for all of its adult and further education. The policy of LEAs with regard to fee waivers for adult education classes is explained in the *Gazetteer*. For individual colleges, ask the college concerned. Some other organisations may also have fee reduction policies. This is indicated (where we know about it) in the relevant chapter, but do always ask.

MSC COURSES

All trainees on full-time Job Training Scheme courses are paid an allowance which is updated every year. There is a basic allowance and extra allowances for dependants, travel, and midday meals where they are not provided free of charge. Part-time courses may not cost you anything but you won't get an allowance.

For a more detailed explanation of allowances see *24 Training for a new job*.

Sponsorship

The MSC may also pay its normal allowance plus course fees to people it sponsors to go on approved courses run by other people. To get sponsorship the course must meet certain requirements.

YTS

People on YTS are paid at least £27.30 a week in the first year and £35 in the second year, and any travel costs over £3 a week. Some employers make up the YTS allowance to a higher level. There are no deductions for National Insurance or superannuation while you are given a training allowance.

LEA GRANTS

LEAs in England and Wales give grants for many courses. There are two kinds:

Mandatory grants - they have to give them to you if you satisfy the conditions; the government decides who should be eligible and how much the grants will be – all the LEA does is check your eligibility and make the payments. The equivalent grants in Scotland are paid centrally by the Scottish Education Department.

Discretionary grants - they don't have to pay them but can. They are explained in *40 LEA grants*. In Scotland, LEAs only pay discretionary grants.

BURSARIES FOR ADULT COLLEGES

You can get one of these if you're going to one of the eight adult residential colleges (described in *21 Adult residential colleges*). They're much the same as ordinary LEA grants except they are paid direct by the central government education departments. You must apply through the college concerned, by filling in an application form by 5 July of the year you're starting. The college will do the rest. Similarly, if you live in Scotland you must complete a form and return it to the Scottish Education Department (address below).

★ **SEND FOR** *Adult education bursaries* from The Awards Officer, Adult Education Bursaries, c/o Ruskin College, Oxford OX1 2HE.

★ **ASK** Scottish Education Department, Awards Branch, Haymarket House, Clifton Terrace, Edinburgh EH12 5DT, or the Department of Education for Northern Ireland, Rathgael House, Balloo Road, Bangor BT19 2PR.

AWARDS FOR AUXILIARY MEDICAL WORK

These are mandatory grants but paid by the DHSS (the Scottish Education Department in Scotland, Department of Health and Social Services in Northern Ireland). Only for dental therapists, hygienists, occupational therapists, physiotherapists, orthoptists, radiographers. In Northern Ireland, the DHSS also gives grants for social work courses.

★ **ASK** DHSS, Student Grants (PSM) NI2, Norcross, Blackpool FY5 3TA; SED Awards Branch, Haymarket House, Clifton Terrace, Edinburgh, EH12 5DR; or Department of Health and Social Services, Dundonald House, Upper Newtownards Road, Belfast BT4 3S4.

SPONSORSHIP BY EMPLOYERS

Many employers (including the armed forces) offer money to students on BTEC, SCOTVEC higher courses and first degree courses in a number of subjects. To get one you may have to agree to work for the employer afterwards for a set time (two years or more). They range from £200 to £2,590 per year and you may receive up to £1,380 a year sponsorship without losing your grant. If you have a National Engineering Scholarship, the maximum allowed without loss of grant is £1,730. For a list of sponsorships available:

★ **SEND FOR** *Sponsorships 1987*, £1.55 inc p&p from MSC, COIC, Department CW, ISCO5, The Paddock, Frizinghall, Bradford BD9 4HD.

★ **SEND FOR** *Industrial sponsorship and the universities central admissions scheme*, free from UCCA, PO Box 28, Cheltenham, Gloucester GL50 1HY. This leaflet covers university sandwich courses.

POSTGRADUATE AWARDS

You get money to do higher degrees either from the education departments or the research councils, depending on the subject of study and where you live.

What are they?

Bursaries are tied to institutions. Studentships are not. You have to have a good degree and good academic references. They are all competitive and hard to get. Both grants are calculated rather like mandatory grants, though studentships are worth a bit more.

DES awards

For humanities, information science and librarianship:

★ **SEND FOR** *Postgraduate awards booklets, 1, 2 and 3* from DES, Publishing Despatch Centre, Honeypot Lane, Stanmore, Middlesex HA7 1AZ.

Research councils

Agricultural and Food Research Council

★ **SEND FOR** *Regulations governing postgraduate awards, Regulations governing postgraduate awards for food research and training, Schools fellowships,* from AFRC, Studentships' Section, 160 Great Portland Street, London W1N 6DT. Tel: (01) 580 6655.

Economic and Social Research Council

★ **SEND FOR** *ESRC studentship handbook* and *ESRC bursary handbook* from ESRC, Research and Training Administrative Division, 160 Great Portland Street, London W1N 6BA. Tel: (01) 637 1499.

Medical Research Council

★ **SEND FOR** *Research studentships* and *Advanced course studentships* from MRC Training Awards, 20 Park Crescent, London W1N 4AL. Tel: (01) 636 5422.

Natural Environment Research Council

★ **SEND FOR** *NERC Training awards* from NERC University Support Section, Polaris House, North Star Avenue, Swindon SN2 1EU. Tel: (0793) 40101.

Science and Engineering Research Council

★ **SEND FOR** *SERC studentships and fellowships* from SERC, Secretary's Department, RTSS, Polaris House, North Star Avenue, Swindon SN2 1ET. Tel: (0793) 26222. SERC is trying to encourage graduate engineers and scientists to continue with their studies.

Scotland
Students living in Scotland apply to the Scottish Education Department.

★ **WRITE TO** SED, Students' Awards Branch, Haymarket House, Clifton Terrace, Edinburgh EH12 5DT. Tel: (031) 337 2477.

Northern Ireland
Students living in Northern Ireland apply to the Department of Education for Northern Ireland.

★ **WRITE TO** DENI, Rathgael House, Balloo Road, Bangor, Co Down BT19 2PR. Tel: (0247) 66311.

SUPPLEMENTARY BENEFIT

The 21 hours rule
To claim supplementary benefit you have to be available for work (unless you are a single parent or someone who is not required to sign on, eg because of age or disability). If you are on a full-time course that's not possible, but it may be possible while doing a part-time course. Under the 21 hours rule you may study for up 21 hours a week (classroom and supervised study) without losing benefit,

as long as you are available for work, and that means being willing to leave the course to take a job immediately if a vacancy occurs.

The rules are complicated and vary according to how old you are and what sort of course you're doing. To check how the rules affect you:

★ **ASK** your local DHSS office.

★ **LOOK AT** *Opening doors,* published by the Further Education Unit. Most libraries should have a copy.

Social security benefits

There are certain things you may be able to claim once you're a full-time student. They include rent rebates, free prescriptions, free dental treatment, glasses, milk for your children – there is a full list in the CPAG booklet mentioned below. You will be eligible for these too if you receive supplementary benefit, though you will still have to apply for them.

★ **LOOK AT** *CPAG national welfare benefits handbook*, from Child Poverty Action Group, 1 Macklin Street, London WC2 5NH.

Dependants' allowances

Parents on grants who are not eligible for the dependants' allowance may be able to claim from the DHSS Student Unit.

★ **SEND FOR** form HS1 from the DHSS Student Unit, North Fylde Central Office, Norcross, Blackpool FY5 3TA.

EDUCATIONAL CHARITIES

There are some charities which give grants to students. Any grant is usually small (around £75) and aimed at people under 21. But it is possible to get one, though you may feel that you spend more than that in writing letters and applications. The demand for such help has also increased in recent years making them harder to get.

Directories

There are directories which list the addresses of charities. They are large, expensive books which you should find in libraries.

★ **LOOK AT** *Charities digest*, Family Welfare Association.

★ **LOOK AT** *Directory of grant-making trusts*, Charities Aid Foundation.

★ **LOOK AT** *The grants register*, Macmillan.

★ **LOOK AT** *The education yearbook* (see *Booklist*). It has a section on educational charities.

Educational Grants Advisory Service

Can give limited help with finding money for study from suitable charities but it is overwhelmed with enquiries. It prioritises and gives precedence to the long-term unemployed and single parents. Sources of help for adults from this source are very limited – there is often an upper age limit of 25. It is more likely that you will manage to get help if you meet financial hardship during a course; it is not common to find full funding for a course this way.

★ **WRITE TO** The Student Adviser, Educational Grants Advisory Service, Family Welfare Association, 501/505 Kingsland Road, London E8 4AU. Please do not phone.

MORE INFORMATION

The Department of Education and Science
Issues *Grants to students – a brief guide, Guides to grants – designated courses.* These are available from DES, Room 4/50, Elizabeth House, York Road, London SE1 7PH.

Guides to grants – postgraduate awards 1, 2 and 3, Guides to grants – postgraduate awards for librarianship and information science. These are available from DES, Publications Despatch Centre, Honeypot Lane, Stanmore, Middlesex HA7 1AZ.

Scottish Education Department
Issues *Guide to student allowances* available from SED, Awards Branch, Haymarket House, Clifton Terrace, Edinburgh EH12 5DT.

National Union of Students
The NUS grants adviser can help with specific cases, or put you in touch with someone local who can.

★ **WRITE TO** Grants Department, NUS, 461 Holloway Road, London N7 6LJ. Enclose an SAE.

Department of Education for Northern Ireland
Issues *Guide to students grants* available from DENI, Rathgael House, Balloo Road, Bangor, Co Down BT19 2PR.

40 Money: LEA grants

Mandatory grants
How much is a mandatory grant?
Discretionary grants

There are grants available for many courses. There are two kinds:

- Mandatory grants – they have to give them to you.
- Discretionary grants – they don't have to give them to you, but can. These are the main sources of finance for educational courses.

Apply to your LEA in the first instance; they're responsible for deciding whether you're eligible, how much for, and for paying it. If you live in Scotland apply to the Scottish Education Department and if you live in Northern Ireland apply to the local Education and Library Board.

MANDATORY GRANTS

These must be paid to anyone who does a 'designated' course, as long as you satisfy the conditions. All are higher education and almost all are full-time or sandwich courses; except for a few part-time teacher training courses. The DES decides grant levels and provides the regulations. Both are revised annually.

Designated courses

These are full-time or sandwich courses leading to:

- a first degree from a university or the CNAA
- a Diploma of Higher Education
- BTEC Higher National Diploma Awards
- an initial teaching qualification including the one-year Postgraduate Certificate in Education or Art Teachers' Certificate or Diploma
- a university certificate or diploma course lasting at least three years
- certain other courses specifically designated as being 'comparable' to first degree courses. These include a three-year course for the Graduate Diploma in Drama at the Welsh College of Music and Drama, and a three-year sandwich course for the Associateship of the Association of Certified Accountants at the Polytechnic of the South Bank and many others.

For a list of designated 'comparable' courses:

★ **SEND FOR** *Guides to grants: designated courses*, from DES, Room 4/50, Elizabeth House, York Road, London SE1 7PH.

Part-time teacher training courses
The only part-time courses that attract mandatory grants are initial teacher training courses. If you are interested:

★ **WRITE TO** DES, Room 4/21, Elizabeth House, York Road, London SE1 7PH.

Eligibility – some catches

Even if you are on a designated course, there are conditions you must meet if the grant is to be mandatory. If you don't meet them, you can still try for a discretionary grant. The main conditions are:

- You've been ordinarily resident in the British Isles for three years up to the beginning of the academic year in which your course begins.
- Your residence here hasn't, during those three years, been wholly or mainly for the purposes of full-time education.
- You must apply to your LEA in writing before the end of your first term.
- You haven't, in the LEA's opinion, shown yourself, by your conduct, to be unfit to get a grant. If you are declared unfit and want to fight it, consult the NUS Grants Adviser.
- You haven't already done various types of further education. The regulations say you're OK if you have not previously attended a course of advanced further education of more than two years. A period of one term's attendance or less is usually disregarded. If you have already attended an advanced course, consult your LEA, even if this course was taken abroad.

So, you're OK if your previous study was:

- a course at one of the long-term adult residential colleges for which you are entitled to a DES bursary
- a course of study leading to a range of 'specified' qualifications that are recognised for entry into HE.

Specified qualifications

'Specified' qualifications include:

- a foundation course credit of the Open University
- GCE A-level or SCE Higher in two subjects
- certificates of completion of a full-time art, drama or music foundation course lasting two years or more
- ONC/OND, BTEC certificate or diploma
- attestation of fitness of the Scottish Universities Entrance Board
- European or Internationale Baccalaureate.

For the precise legal definition:

★ **LOOK AT** *Awards regulations*, Statutory Instrument no 1397, amended 1986. Available from HMSO.

HOW MUCH IS A MANDATORY GRANT?

Basic rates

Rates quoted are for 1986/87.

- living at home with your parents: £1,510 pa
- living/lodging in London: £2,246 pa

- living/lodging outside London: £1,901
- if your board and lodging at college is provided free: £831 pa.

Extras for everyone
If you have to attend the course for more than 30 weeks and 3 days (25 weeks and 3 days for Oxbridge college) for the additional weeks:

- living at home with your parents: £27.85 per week
- lodging/living in London: £51.05 per week
- lodging/living outside London: £39.75 per week.

If your course is 45 weeks or more, you'll receive a grant for all 52 weeks.

Extras especially for adults

- two homes: if you have dependants in your first home and have to live away, up to £455 per year
- mature students: up to £740 if you are aged 26 or over and have earned at least £12,000 from employment during the three years before the start of your course
- dependants: one spouse or other adult (mum, dad, but not common law wife or husband) – £1255
- dependent children: under 11, £250 pa; 11–15, £515 pa; 16–17, £680 pa; 18+ £965 pa
- single parents: one child (living with you), £1,255 pa; other children, as above
- if the LEA says you're not eligible for dependant's allowances, you can apply for a special hardship allowance from the DHSS
- during the holidays: up to £45.20 per week if you'd suffer hardship otherwise, at the LEA's discretion (ie you have to prove it to them)
- disablement: at the LEA's discretion, up to £565 pa.

Your income
If you have an income of over £460 they'll start reducing your grant. But you can have any scholarships worth up to £1,380 without your grant being affected. Some other types of income are also disregarded.

Parents
If you're under 25, the LEA will take your parents' income into account unless:

- you've been self-supporting for any three years before the academic year in which your course begins (including time off for looking after your children, and periods of registered unemployment)
- you have been married for at least three years before the start of your course
- your parents earn less than £8,700 per year after allowances.

Spouse's contribution to grant
If you are over 25 (or satisfy the authority that they don't need to take your parent's income into account), they will expect your spouse to contribute if he or she is earning enough.

The LEA doesn't count your spouse's income in full – it gives him or her various allowances. If, after that, his or her income is less than £6,800, you get the full grant. If, for example, it's £8,000 after allowances they take off £181 from your grant.

Spouse's allowances – how they work them out
The LEA doesn't just take your spouse's income as it is. They deduct various things from it; what's left is called the residual income, and that's what they use to judge the spouse's contribution. The deductions are:

- other dependants (parents etc but not spouse), £1130
- mortgage interest for which you get tax relief
- contributions to pension schemes for which you get tax relief
- the gross amounts of any other superannuation and 50% of the gross amounts of life assurance premiums which qualify for relief under the Income Tax Acts
- sometimes the cost of domestic help (up to £895)
- usually an allowance if your spouse is also on a grant; if you have other dependent children the contribution is reduced by £90 for each one.

Special cases
There are some special arrangements for

- sandwich courses
- some part-time teacher training courses
- divorced or separated students
- members of religious orders.

Appeals
If you want to appeal because you've been refused a grant or don't think you've been given the right amount, appeal to the LEA. If you're really dissatisfied, write to the DES. This is not an appeal in a legal sense, but the DES may take up your case with the LEA if they feel all the facts have not been taken into account. But the DES cannot force the LEA to change its mind.

DISCRETIONARY GRANTS

Grants for further education and part-time courses are almost always discretionary. There's not much to say about them; apply to your LEA and see what they say. Broadly:

- LEAs running access courses often provide grants for them (these are described in *18 Adult routes*)
- full-time A-level courses or courses at a similar level, eg BTEC National Diploma sometimes attract grants
- full-time GCSE courses – very rarely
- part-time courses – GCSE, A-level or anything else – almost never
- Open University courses – see *23 The Open University*.

It is not just a question of money you could receive. Getting a grant usually means your fees are paid as well – not getting a grant means they're not, and fees are high.

How much?

If you are taking a designated course but can't get a mandatory grant (for example, you can't meet the residence qualification), and the LEA do give you a discretionary grant, they must pay you the same as a mandatory grant.

If you are not taking a designated course and the LEA decides to give you a discretionary grant they can give you what they like.

Appeals

If you're not eligible for a mandatory grant and are turned down for a discretionary grant (as is often the case since only limited funds are available) you can ask the LEA why they've turned you down (although they don't have to tell you). You can then appeal to the education office. It may be worthwhile talking to local councillors, especially if they're on the education committee. It may even be worthwhile writing to your MP. There's still a chance that you won't be successful, but you will have a better chance of success through asking than through staying quiet.

The Department of Education and Science issue a booklet each year which explains the grant system in more detail.

★ **SEND FOR** *Grants to students: a brief guide*, from Department of Education and Science, Room 4/50, Elizabeth House, York Road, London SE1 7PH.

★ **SEND FOR** *Guide to students allowances*, from Scottish Education Department Awards Branch, Haymarket House, Clifton Terrace, Edinburgh EH12 5DT.

★ **SEND FOR** *Guide to student grants*, from Department of Education for Northern Ireland, Rathgael House, Balloo Road, Bangor, Co Down BT19 2PR.

SUBJECTS AND PLACES

41 Qualifications

About qualifications
What are they?
Who needs them?
The main qualifications
What is the same as what else?

ABOUT QUALIFICATIONS

Although getting a qualification is by no means the only purpose of education, it is still the heart of the education and training system. There are over 1,200 listed in the main reference book on the subject, *British qualifications* – everything from PhD (Doctor of Philosophy) to FInstBCS (Fellow of the Institute of Burial and Cremation Administrators); from HND (Higher National Diploma) to RP (Registered Plumber). And there are any number of more unusual ones which may or may not be reputable, depending on your point of view.

Most qualifications give you letters after your name, but there are some important exceptions, eg General Certificate of Education (GCE), City and Guilds, Royal Society of Arts (RSA) and MSC Skillcentre certificates. So this chapter looks at qualifications in general – what they are, who needs them, who awards them, what they are worth and how you get them.

WHAT ARE THEY?

A qualification is a way of proving to the world that you have learned enough about something to satisfy certain other people who already know about it. There are two main types, which correspond roughly to the difference between education and training. They are:

General qualifications (*education*) - accepted by a very wide range of people. They can be used to get you into many jobs, higher education or training courses. The main ones are the Certificate of Secondary Education (CSE), the General Certificate of Education (GCE) (both of which will become GCSE in June 1987), Scottish Certificate of Education (SCE) and degrees (BA, BSc, BEd and so on).

Specific qualifications (*training*) - recognised by a very wide range of people. Can be used to prove your competence at one type of job or activity. Examples are the City and Guilds Craft Certificate in Plumbing, Fellow of Institute of British Bakers (FIBB), Associate of the Institute of Chartered Accountants (ACA), State Registered Nurse (SRN). Most do involve a certain amount of general education, mainly in English and maths, in addition to skills relevant to the job.

Recognised qualifications

Anyone can award qualifications but they have to be 'recognised' in some way for the qualification to be worth anything. Books can tell you a lot about specific qualifications for specific jobs – the bodies which award the main nationally recognised ones are dealt with below.

A recognised qualification may imply a number of things. For example:

- It may be accepted by the Department of Education and Science (DES) and by pretty well anyone, as with GCE.
- It may be accepted by particular people for particular things, eg a BA of one university being accepted by another university for entry to its postgraduate courses; an HND being accepted by the Open University to give exemption from some parts of its degree courses; a professional body accepting a qualification for entry into membership.

So you should check the value of any qualification you're going to take for the purpose you want to use it for.

WHO NEEDS THEM?

Essential

There are some things you can't be unless you have the right qualifications – for example a doctor, nurse, barrister, solicitor, priest, school teacher, architect, engineer. To find out what qualifications you must have to practise particular professions, you will have to ask the body that governs that profession. To find out who that is:

★ **LOOK AT** *British qualifications* (see *Booklist*).

Desirable

To enter most professions and trades, it's helpful to have either a general qualification or the right specific one – for example technicians, laboratory workers, secretaries, caterers, office workers, careers officers, computer programmers and operators, civil servants. But things are a bit fluid; some employers seem to despise 'bits of paper' and prefer people with practical experience; most universities, polytechnics and colleges of higher education admit mature students without the 'usual qualifications' if they're satisfied that the applicant is 'suitable'.

MAN, 40s, ON SKILLCENTRE FITTING COURSE
I worked for years, know the trade inside out. I wanted to stop being self-employed and get a job with the Gas Board. Because I didn't have the qualifications they wouldn't take me, so I'm at the Skillcentre to prove I've been trained.

Useful

In smaller firms, or for your own business, experience is often enough, as with bricklaying, plumbing, agricultural work, carpentry, motor mechanics, car body repairing, fitting, dressmaking. But increasingly you have to have a qualification to be considered semi-skilled or skilled, especially in large firms.

To sum up, for some purposes a qualification is a must. For others, it is a help, though you may be able to manage without if you can show that you have the necessary knowledge and skill. For everything else, it is totally unnecessary.

Do you need one?
There's no easy answer. But if you don't know already you can ask at the Jobcentre. You can also ask firms working in your chosen field (ask for the personnel or training officer) or you can look at one of the reference books that deal with jobs and careers.

★ **LOOK AT** *Equal opportunities: a careers guide for women and men, Careers encyclopaedia* and *Annual careers guide: opportunities in the professions, industry, commerce and the public service* (see *Booklist*).

THE MAIN QUALIFICATIONS

General Certificate of Secondary Education (GCSE)
This is now replacing the O-level system in England, Wales and Northern Ireland, but not so far in Scotland. People taking GCSE will no longer have to choose between O-levels, CSE and joint 16-plus exams – it's a single system with a single scale of grades. The first GCSE examinations will be taken in summer 1988. There will still be A-levels.

In Scotland, O- and H-grades will remain the same.

If you're aiming to use your GCSEs to apply for jobs, some companies may want A, B or C grades at GCSE (previously O-levels) or O-grades in maths and English. Others think that formal educational qualifications are not necessarily an indication of your abilities and talents, and may use other ways to find out what you can do.

- The new examination will involve a minimum of 20% practical coursework, eg aurals in languages (including English), fieldwork in geography, lab work in the sciences. This coursework will be assessed by the teacher or course tutor throughout the course (continuous assessment).
- The grades will be based on what students know, understand and can do (criterion referenced).
- Grades awarded will be A, B, C (equivalent to the current GCE and to CSE grade 1) and then D, E, F, G (equivalent to CSE grades 2–5).

There are special provisions for mature students in GCSE. The syllabus, called GCSE (mature), will be designed for one-year courses and will take into account the different patterns of study and different needs of mature students. Mature students are people over 17, ie over statutory school age.

There is a list of examination boards under *Examining groups for the GCSE* below. At present, the examination groups are still in the early stages of preparing syllabuses for mature students, and they are following rather different lines.

★ **WRITE TO** the examinations board nearest to you in your examining group area for up-to-date details.

In the interim period until summer 1988 when GCSEs take over O-levels, GCEs will run alongside. But there are now no more students taking new GCEs – the last students to begin these were in 1986.

- Qualifications in maths and English are becoming more and more necessary to enter any sort of white collar work expecially if you have no other qualification or experience. There was once a job advertised for a furniture remover that asked for four O-levels!
- A-levels or Highers are needed to enter civil service executive grades and many professions, and are the usual way for school leavers to get into universities, polytechnics and colleges of higher education for degree studies, but not necessarily so for adults (see *22 Getting a degree*).

Exams are taken in June. There are single subject exams in almost everything: English, maths, biology, French, Gujerati, photography and so on.

Scotland

The Scottish H-grade is not directly equivalent to GCE A-level being based on a shorter, less specialised course of study.

Possession of an appropriate number of H-grade passes qualifies the holder for admission to all Scottish universities and colleges, to universities and colleges elsewhere in the United Kingdom and for exemption from the preliminary examinations of most professional bodies. Examinations are taken in late April/May.

Examining groups for the GCSE

GCSE is administered by six examining groups. Each group has a number of examinations boards:

London and East Anglian Group (*LEAG*)

East Anglian Examinations Board, The Lindens, Lexden Road, Colchester CO3 3RL. Tel: (0206) 549595.

London Regional Examinations Board, Lyon House, 104 Wandsworth High Street, London SW18 4LF. Tel: (01) 870 2144.

University of London School Examinations Board, Stewart House, 32 Russell Square, London WC1B 5DP. Tel: (01) 636 8000.

Midlands Examining Group (*MEG*)

East Midlands Regional Examinations Board, Robins Wood House, Robins Wood Road, Aspley, Nottingham NG8 3NR. Tel: (0602) 296021.

Oxford and Cambridge Schools Examinations Board, 10 Trumpington Street, Cambridge CB2 1QB. Tel: (0223) 64326.

Oxford and Cambridge Schools Examinations Board, Elsfield Way, Oxford OX2 8EP. Tel: (0865) 54421.

Southern Universities Joint Board, Cotham Road, Cotham, Bristol BS6 6DD. Tel: (0272) 736042.

The West Midlands Examinations Board, Norfolk House, Smallbrook, Queensway, Birmingham B5 4NJ. Tel: (021) 643 2081.

University of Cambridge Local Examinations Syndicate, Syndicate Buildings, 1 Hills Road, Cambridge CB1 2EU. Tel: (0223) 61111.

Northern Examining Association (NEA)

Associated Lancashire Schools Examining Board, 12 Harter Street, Manchester M1 6HL. Tel: (061) 228 0084.

Joint Matriculation Board, Manchester M15 6EU. Tel: (061) 273 2565.

Northern Regional Examinations Board, Wheatfield Road, Westerhope, Newcastle-upon-Tyne NE5 5JZ. Tel: (091) 286 2711.

North West Regional Examinations Board, Orbit House, Albert Street, Eccles, Manchester M30 0WL. Tel: (061) 788 9521.

Yorkshire and Humberside Regional Examinations Board, 31–33 Springfield Avenue, Harrogate, North Yorkshire HG1 2HW. Tel: (0423) 66991.

Yorkshire and Humberside Regional Examinations Board, Scarsdale House, 136 Derbyshire Lane, Sheffield S8 8SE. Tel: (0742) 557436.

Northern Ireland Schools Examinations Council (NISEC)

Northern Ireland Schools Examinations Council, Beechill House, 42 Beechill Road, Belfast BT8 4RS. Tel: (0232) 704666.

Southern Examining Group (SEG)

Associated Examining Board, Stag Hill House, Guildford, Surrey GU2 5XJ. Tel: (0483) 506506.

South East Regional Examinations Board, 2–10 Mount Ephraim Road, Tunbridge Wells, Kent TN1 1EU. Tel: (0892) 35311/2/3/4.

Southern Regional Examination Board, Avondale House, 33 Carlton Crescent, Southampton SO9 4YL. Tel: (0703) 32312.

The South Western Examinations Board, 23–29 Marsh Street, Bristol BS1 4BP. Tel: (0272) 273434.

University of Oxford Delegacy of Local Examinations, Ewert Place, Banbury Road, Summertown, Oxford OX2 7BZ. Tel: (0865) 54291.

Welsh Joint Education Committee (WJEC)

Welsh Joint Education Committee, 245 Western Avenue, Cardiff CF5 2YX. Tel: (0222) 561231.

Ways of preparing for GCSE

You can study for them by attending a day or evening, full- or part-time course at an FE college, adult education centre or evening institute, by using a correspondence course, going to a private college or totally on your own, by private study.

If you do it by correspondence or by yourself, you enter as an external or private candidate. You will sit the exam at a local centre (probably an FE college), with other people – internal and external candidates. You will have to make your own arrangements with the examination board and the centre. Some centres don't take external candidates, or may only do so in summer, or for some boards, or for some subjects. It's a thorny question, so check up early.

Useful information to get - Contact the nearest examinations board in your examination group area for details of rules, syllabus and timetable.

Past examination papers - With O-levels, the pattern was often the same for several years, so you could work out some things you might be asked. GCSE syllabuses are new, so old O-level papers won't be relevant any more – though interesting to look at.

Examiner's reports - Most useful as they say how questions were answered and what the examiner was looking for. Some boards sell them on their own, some include them in other reports, but some only distribute them to institutions, so you have to ask a lecturer to show them to you. However, until the first GCSE exam results are known, only reports on O-levels/O-grades are available.

★ **LOOK AT** *All about GCSE: a clear and concise summary* by Maureen Mobley, Chris Emerson et al, Heinemann 1986.

Qualifications below GCSE
A number of new exams have been developed (eg by City and Guilds, RSA, the Associated Examining Board) to test skills in English and maths below O-level. The Certificate of Extended Education (CEE) is useful for mature students:

★ **ASK** Oxford and Cambridge Schools Examination Board for the regulations and syllabus.

Degrees (BA, BSc, MA)
A degree – any degree – is the qualification that opens doors more than any other. Having a degree (being a graduate) allows you to apply for a large range of higher level jobs which are increasingly closed to non-graduates (eg in the civil service). But you may need further training after graduating as being a graduate is never in itself a licence to practise any profession. Degrees which seem to prepare you only for a specific job (like a BEd, law degree, engineering degree and so on) can be just as useful in getting a wide range of jobs as a BA.

Degrees are awarded by universities or the Council for National Academic Awards (CNAA), explained more fully in *22 Getting a degree*. They come at different levels with many different names.

First degrees
BA (Bachelor of Arts), BSc (Bachelor of Science), LLB (Bachelor of Laws), BEd (Bachelor of Education) and many more. It usually takes three or four years of full-time study to get one.

Honours degrees
Are usually more specialist and more academically demanding than pass or general degrees and are usually graded 1st, 2nd or 3rd class. Don't confuse with honorary degrees (see below).

DipHE
The Diploma in Higher Education (DipHE) is a qualification in its own right but is also equivalent in standard to the first two years of a degree. After further study, it can lead on to a degree.

Higher degrees
MA (Master of Arts), MSc (Master of Science) etc. Mainly taken after following a course for a year. MPhil (Master of Philosophy) is usually taken by doing research for two years. BPhil (Bachelor of Philosophy) can be taken in different ways.

Some MAs mean other things: Oxford and Cambridge BAs can become MAs after a few years without further study, and some universities (like those in Scotland) call some of their first degrees MA.

Doctors' degrees
Like PhD (Doctor of Philosophy) they are awarded after doing several years' research – at least three years full-time, more part-time. Can be in any subject, not just philosophy or medicine.

There are other degrees which universities award for even more advanced work.

Honorary degrees
Are awarded to distinguished people who don't have to do anything but be distinguished!

Ways of preparing for degrees
Higher education is the term used to describe all degree level studies and is discussed in greater detail in *22 Getting a degree* and *23 The Open University*.

City and Guilds of London Institute
Offers qualifications mainly for industry. Covers a wide range – over 200 technical subjects, including engineering, construction, information technology, travel and tourism, hotels and catering and hairdressing. Usually studied on day release or block release at a college of FE after you have got a job.

Schemes cover three industrial functions: operative, craft, technician. The level depends on what you want to do. It is possible to progress to high career levels no matter which levels you start at.

More and more adults are doing City and Guilds to improve their qualifications. In recent years about one third of candidates have been over 21. City and Guilds has now developed exams and qualifications in communication skills and numeracy, which could be useful to adults wanting to improve their basic education. There are schemes in home economics, photography, amateur gardening and creative studies which are also suitable for adults.

★ **SEND FOR** *List of publications and candidate's guide,* free from Sales Section, City and Guilds of London Institute, 76 Portland Place, London W1N 4AA. Tel: (01) 580 3050.

Business and Technician Education Council (BTEC)
Covers England, Wales and Northern Ireland. For Scotland, see SCOTVEC (below). Awards qualifications for a wide range of fields including agriculture, business and finance, computing and information systems, construction, design, distribution, hotel, catering and leisure services, engineering, public administration and science. There are also pre-vocational and continuing education courses.

Awards are at four levels; the precise entry requirements vary from subject to subject, and they may be variously studied full or part time, by day or block release, or by sandwich course:

First Diploma or Certificate - intended for students of 16 and over with few or no academic qualifications. The Certificate course is one year part-time; the Diploma course is one year full-time or two years part-time.

National Diploma or Certificate - intended for students of 16 and over with four or more O-levels, grade one CSEs, or a BTEC First award or equivalent qualifications eg CPVE. The Certificate course is two years part-time; the Diploma course is two years full-time or three years part-time or sandwich.

Higher National Diploma or Certificate - intended for students of 18 and over with an A-level and some O-levels or BTEC National award. The Certificate course is two years part-time; the Diploma course is two years full-time or three years part-time or sandwich.

Continuing Education Certificate/Diploma and Units – designed for adults and students normally at least 21 years old. Continuing Education Units are short courses leading to a BTEC Certificate of Achievement. They can be put together to gain a BTEC Continuing Education Certificate or Diploma. Entry qualifications vary according to the individual course and students may be admitted on the basis of suitable experience and proven ability instead of formal qualifications.

BTEC courses are usually done at FE colleges or polytechnics. Some may be done by distance learning – such opportunities are described in *17 Flexible learning*. ntry requirements, length of course and mode of study vary from subject to subject. For a more detailed explanation:

★ **SEND FOR** *Information sheet no 1* and *The BTEC selection for adults*, free from the Publications Despatch Unit, BTEC, Central House, London WC1H 0HH. Tel: (01) 388 3288. For further information ask for the Information Service.

Scottish Vocational Education Council (SCOTVEC)

SCOTVEC offers a range of nationally recognised occupational qualifications in: technology, science, agriculture, food and hospitality services, information technology, public administration, business administration, clerical and secretarial studies, art/design and printing and textiles. Advanced courses are open to people who have completed an appropriate National Certificate programme (or its equivalent), or in some cases to students who possess an appropriate group of SCE H- and O-grades or GCE A- and O-levels. Some students may qualify, at the discretion of a college principal, for admission on grounds of maturity and experience.

Successful candidates are awarded Higher National Certificates or Higher National Diplomas, depending on the level of course. You can improve your qualifications by further study. The courses are offered at colleges of further education and Central Institutions in Scotland but there is some provision for distance learning (see *17 Flexible learning*). For further information:

★ **WRITE TO** SCOTVEC, 38 Queen Street, Glasgow G1 3DY. Tel: (041) 248 7900.

Merger of SCOTBEC and SCOTEC
In March 1985, the Scottish Vocational Education Council was formed with responsibility for business and technician education. It took over the functions originally performed by the Scottish Business Education Council (SCOTBEC) and the Scottish Technical Education Council (SCOTEC).

The National Certificate
In 1984 vocational education in Scotland changed with the implementation of the government's Action Plan for the education of 16 to 18 year olds. The effect was to replace all existing FE courses below degree level by a new modular structure. Programmes of study (both full- and part-time) take into account the personal and social development of students and the needs of a wide range of users including industry and commerce, professional and technician bodies, trade associations and statutory bodies. Programmes of study leading to the National Certificate are made up of modules, most of which last 40 hours, although there is provision for half, double, treble and, exceptionally, quadruple modules (160 hours). The National Certificate replaced SCOTEC and SCOTBEC courses at non-advanced level and some City and Guilds craft courses.

★ **ASK** your local college.

★ **SEND FOR** *Guide to courses for 1986–87* from SCOTVEC, 38 Queen Street, Glasgow G1 3DY. Tel: (041) 248 7900.

RSA (Royal Society of Arts)
The RSA offers a wide range of examinations and assessment schemes in office, secretarial and business studies, computers and information technology, languages and general training for work.

Single subject examinations are offered at Stage 1 Elementary, Stage 2 Intermediate and Stage 3 Advanced, over five series in an academic year – Autumn, New Year, Easter, Whitsun and Summer. Candidates can enter for as many examinations as they wish.

Also available is a range of new communicative examinations in languages from Level 1 to 4. Languages offered are French, German, Italian and Spanish.

There are also higher level qualifications such as the post A-level Diploma for Personal Assistants and the graduate level Diploma for Bilingual Secretaries. The Profile Schemes in communication, numeracy, process skills and general skills – which is a composite version of the three separate profiles – offer a system of accreditation alongside subject disciplines and a variety of courses, eg GCSE.

The Certificate of Continuing Education is available to students in the adult education sector with modest academic achievements, who wish to increase their confidence in order to return to work or proceed to further education.

Schemes are also available for young people and adults whose native language is not English.

★ **SEND FOR** *RSA guide,* 75p, and *Single subject syllabus*, £1.20, from RSA Examinations Board (Publications), Murray Road, Orpington, Kent BR5 3RB. Tel: (0689) 32421.

London Chamber of Commerce and Industry Examinations Board
A major examining body for business studies, secretarial and foreign language examinations established by the business community for the business community and with an in-built criterion of 'employability'. It is internationally recognised by employers and professional bodies. These examinations may be taken at schools and colleges of FE and HE in this country and overseas.

Single subject examinations at three stages – first, second and third level – are held four times a year (series 1–4). Group awards are also available for certain related groups of subjects taken at one sitting.

The Group Certificate in Commercial Studies (first level) and The Group Certificate in Business Studies (second level) are business-orientated general education examinations. They are of value to people wanting work in an office or who are fairly new to the business environment.

The third level Group Diploma in managerial principles gives in-depth knowledge of specific areas of business work.

Group secretarial qualifications – Secretarial Studies Certificate, Private Secretary's Certificate and the highest qualification of its kind, the Private and Executive Secretary's Diploma. Group office technology examinations – First Certificate in Office Technology and Second Certificate in Office Technology.

Secretarial language examinations in French, German and Spanish; Secretarial Language Certificate; Advanced Secretarial Language Certificate; Secretarial Language Diploma.

Oral foreign language examinations (foreign language for industry and commerce) can be taken in any language throughout the year at four levels – preliminary, threshold, intermediate and advanced.

New examinations include office/information technology.

Booklets of the regulations and syllabuses are available. Price on application. State whether you are interested in business, secretarial or language examinations.

★ **WRITE TO** Director, London Chamber of Commerce and Industry Examinations Board, Marlowe House, Station Road, Sidcup, Kent DA15 7BJ. Tel: (01) 302 0261/4 or (01) 309 0440 (for group secretarial and group office technology examinations only).

WHAT IS THE SAME AS WHAT ELSE?

The equivalence of different qualifications is tortuous; each institution that demands one qualification will decide for itself whether another one is worth the same to them. A national system to compare different qualifications does not yet exist although one is being developed for vocational qualifications.

ECCTIS
The Educational Counselling and Credit Transfer Information Service has been established to provide such a service. It has developed a national computerised information bank on courses in further and higher education. More information about its current work is given in *1 Advice and help* and *22 Getting a degree.*

Teaching qualifications

The DES at Mowden Hall is responsible for determining whether overseas teaching qualifications are acceptable for qualified teacher status in England and Wales. The General Teaching Council in Scotland will assess teaching qualifications obtained outside Scotland (including English and Welsh ones) to see if they are acceptable for teaching in Scotland.

★ **ASK** DES, Mowden Hall, Staindrop Road, Darlington, Durham DL3 9BG. Tel: (0325) 460155.

★ **ASK** General Teaching Council for Scotland, 5 Royal Terrace, Edinburgh EH7 5AF. Tel: (031) 556 0072.

Scotland

★ **SEND FOR** *Guide to equivalences* from SCOTVEC, 38 Queen Street, Glasgow G1 3DY. Tel: (041) 248 7900. Published by SCOTVEC and City and Guilds.

Overseas qualifications

The British Council has an equivalence service for anyone who has an overseas grant, and who wishes to know how it is regarded in the UK.

★ **ASK** The National Academic Recognition Information Centre for the United Kingdom (NARIC), British Council, 10 Spring Gardens, London SW1A 2BN.

The National Union of Students also offers an advisory service to member student unions.

★ **ASK** The National Union of Students, 461 Holloway Road, London N7 6LJ. Tel: (01) 272 8900.

Alternatives to A-levels

There are a number of special courses for adults designed as alternatives to A-levels for getting in to higher education – see *18 Adult routes*.

However, all sorts of qualifications can be used to support applications for entry to higher education and a number of technical qualifications are widely accepted as equal to A-level, such as BTEC and SCOTVEC qualifications. One regional advisory council has produced a booklet listing such alternatives in its area:

★ **SEND FOR** *Alternatives to A-level: guide to BTEC National Diploma and Certificate courses 1985/1987*, 60p, from Regional Advisory Council for Further Education, London and South Eastern Region, Tavistock House South, Tavistock Square, London WC1H 9LR. Tel: (01) 388 0027.

42 Things to study

This is an alphabetical list of areas of study of interest to adults. It is not intended to be a comprehensive careers index but outlines a variety of subjects you can study at various levels and in different ways. It is possible to study many general and vocational subjects at local colleges. Other more specialised subjects may only be available at a few colleges in the country. This list includes:

- subjects offered only in specialist colleges
- subjects for which there is a central application procedure
- subjects where there are special information and advice facilities available
- special information or more detailed course directories are available
- subjects in which adults are frequently interested.

ACCOUNTANCY

Can be studied at clerical, technician and professional levels in FE and HE colleges, polytechnics and private colleges. A one-year full-time foundation course gives exemption from the first part of the qualifying examinations of the main accountancy professional bodies and is available at over 30 colleges.

Each branch of accountancy has its own professional body which will advise on courses and training.

★ **ASK** Institute of Chartered Accountants in England and Wales, Chartered Accountants' Hall, Moorgate Place, London EC2P 2BJ. Tel: (01) 628 7060.

★ **ASK** Institute of Chartered Accountants of Ireland, 11 Donegall Square South, Belfast BT1 5JE.

★ **ASK** Chartered Institute of Certified Accountants (NI), c/o B R McGuire and Co, Suite 1, The Shopping Centre, Carryduff BT8 8DW.

★ **ASK** Chartered Association of Certified Accountants, 29 Lincoln's Inn Fields, London WC2A 3EE. Tel: (01) 242 6855.

★ **ASK** Institute of Cost and Management Accountants, 63 Portland Place, London W1N 4AB. Tel: (01) 637 2311.

★ **ASK** Association of Certified Accountants, Scottish Branch, Charlotte House, Queen Street, Glasgow G1 3DN. Tel: (041) 204 1578.

★ **ASK** Chartered Institute of Public Finance and Accountancy, 3 Robert Street, London WC2N 6BH. Tel: (01) 828 7661. (You must be employed in a financial capacity in an approved public service organisation.)

★ **ASK** Association of Accounting Technicians, 21 Jockey's Fields, London WC1R 4BN. Tel: (01) 405 4961. (Offers open-entry one-year part-time certificate.)

AGRICULTURE AND HORTICULTURE

Some FE colleges have departments of agriculture or horticulture. There are also over 60 colleges specialising in agriculture, horticulture, forestry and agricultural engineering with courses at all levels. For a summary of the courses, qualifications and colleges in England, Wales and Scotland:

★ **SEND FOR** *Agriculture, horticulture and forestry courses – full-time and sandwich – in the UK* (50p including p&p) from the National Consultative Committee for Agricultural Education, 2 Looms Lane, Bury St Edmunds, Suffolk IP33 1HE. Tel: (0284) 64977.

★ **SEND FOR** *Courses and training for careers in horticulture* (£1.00 plus 18p p&p) from the Institute of Horticulture, c/o Royal Horticulture Society, PO Box 313, 80 Vincent Square, London SW1P 2PE. Tel: (01) 834 4333.

★ **SEND FOR** *Courses in agriculture in the United Kingdom* (£3.00 including p&p) from the Agricultural Education Association, c/o Mr P Biglin, Askham Bryan College of Agriculture and Horticulture, Askham Bryan, York YO2 3PR. Tel: (0904) 702121.

★ **LOOK AT** the Agricultural Training Board in *33 Training at work*.

★ **ASK** Careers Education and Training Advice Centre, National Agricultural Centre, Stoneleigh, Kenilworth, Warwickshire CV8 2LZ. Tel: (0203) 555100.

★ **ASK** The Landscape Institute, 12 Carlton House Terrace, London SW1Y 5AH.

★ **ASK** about the City and Guilds certificates in amateur gardening from Section 11, City and Guilds of London Institute, 46 Britannia Street, London WC1X 9RG. Tel: (01) 278 2468.

For a summary of courses in Northern Ireland:

★ **SEND FOR** *Agricultural courses in Northern Ireland* from the Department of Agriculture, Dundonald House, Upper Newtownards Road, Belfast BT4 3SF.

ARCHITECTURE

Can be studied at technician and professional levels in FE and HE colleges respectively. Professional architects must be registered with the Architects Registration Council of the UK (ARCUK).

★ **SEND FOR** *Schools of architecture recognised by the Royal Institute of British Architects* (£1.45 including p&p) from RIBA, Publications Department, Finsbury Mission, Moreland Street, London EC1V 8VB. Tel: (01) 251 0791. Also *A career in architecture,* £2.00 inclusive.

★ **SEND FOR** *A career as an architectural technician,* free from British Institute of Architectural Technicians, 397 City Road, London EC1V 1NE. Tel: (01) 278 2206.

★ **ASK** Royal Institute of British Architects (RIBA), 66 Portland Place, London W1N 4AD. Tel: (01) 580 5533 for further information. Bookshop or personal callers only. All correspondence to Moreland Street (address above).

ARMED SERVICES

Offers wide ranging education and training opportunities, with special training for different branches given by the services themselves, often leading to recognised qualifications. Minimum entry requirement is the passing of aptitude tests and a medical, but some levels of entry demand academic qualifications.

★ **ASK** at any Army Careers Information Office, Royal Air Force Careers Information Office, or Royal Navy and Royal Marines Careers Information Office listed in your telephone directory.

ART, CRAFT AND DESIGN

Taught in many FE colleges. There are also over 60 specialist colleges called colleges of art, colleges of art and design. Don't confuse them with colleges of arts and technology, another name for a general college, though it may well have an art department. For information on full-time industrial design courses:

★ **LOOK AT** *Design courses in Britain*, (£3.75 plus 25p p&p) from Design Council, 28 Haymarket, London SW1Y 4SU. Tel: (01) 839 8000.

There is a central application procedure for courses leading to a CNAA first degree in art and design:

★ **SEND FOR** *CNAA first degree courses in art and design, Registration Scheme*, from Art and Design Admissions Registry, Penn House, 9 Broad Street, Hereford HR4 9AP. Tel: (0432) 266653. Application forms are issued on receipt of application fee of £5.00 for UK students and £15.00 for overseas students.

★ **ASK** Business and Technician Education Council, Central House, Upper Woburn Place, London WC1H 0HH. Tel: (01) 388 3288 for details of design courses.

These subjects may of course be studied without preparing for an exam and there are numerous art and craft courses in FE colleges and adult education centres as well as at the specialist art colleges. There are also a number of art centres around the country which run classes and have other facilities as well.

★ **LOOK AT** *Directory of arts centres,* free from the Information Section, Arts Council of Great Britain, 105 Piccadilly, London W1V 0AU. Tel: (01) 629 9495. This gives details of arts centres in England, Scotland and Wales, most of which run workshops in arts, crafts and theatre.

★ **ASK** The British Institute of Interior Design, IC Devonshire Avenue, Beeston, Nottingham NG9 1BS. Tel: (0602) 221255

★ **ASK** City and Guilds of London Institute, 46 Britannia Street, London WC1X 9RG. Ask for Section 23 for information on fashion, embroidery, soft furnishing and upholstery, flower arrangement, toymaking, basketry, textiles and ceramics; Section 25 for photography.

AVIATION

Learning to fly is a very expensive business – you can't do it on your own, even if you have a plane, and you must be medically fit. British Airways and the Armed Services sponsor training.

There are a few LEA colleges offering courses; one governed by the DES and Department of Trade; and several private ones. Every pilot must hold a professional pilot's licence given by the Civil Aviation Authority.

★ **ASK** Civil Aviation Authority, Flight Crew Licensing, Aviation House, 129 Kingsway, London WC2B 6NN. Tel: (01) 405 6922 for information and medical advice.

★ **SEND FOR** *Where to fly* (75p including p&p) from the Aircraft Owners and Pilots Association, 50A Cambridge Street, London SW1V 4QQ. Tel: (01) 834 5631. It gives information on the private pilot's licence as well as a list of private clubs which offer training

★ **SEND FOR** *CAP 53, The private pilot's licence* (£1.75 plus 45p p&p) from Printing and Publishing Services, Greville House, 37 Gratton Road, Cheltenham, Gloucestershire GL50 2BN. It gives details of the syllabus and requirements for a pilot's licence.

BEAUTY WORK

Taught at FE colleges and many private colleges. Usually people of over 17 years are preferred. Check that the course offered is a nationally recognised one – not all are acceptable to employers and professional bodies. Beauty consultants are generally trained by large cosmetic houses or department stores for demonstration and sales work.

★ **ASK** British Association of Beauty Therapy and Cosmetology, Suite 5, Wolseley House, Oriel Road, Cheltenham, Gloucestershire GL50 1TH. Tel: (0242) 570284 for a list of recognised colleges and careers information.

BROADCASTING AND FILM

There are some traineeships with the BBC and IBA – studio manager, production, camera work, and secretarial. Most people are experienced in a particular field prior to entry. There are a few courses at FE, HE, or at private colleges. Bristol University has a postgraduate certificate course in radio/film/television. Some polytechnics have photographic degrees with substantial film and photographic content. Some of the women's training workshops listed in *6 Women* provide courses in film and video.

★ **ASK** Appointments Department or Engineering Recruitment Officer, BBC, Broadcasting House, London W1A 1AA. Tel: (01) 580 4468.

★ **ASK** Independent Broadcasting Authority, 70 Brompton Road, London SW3 1EY. Tel: (01) 584 7011 for addresses of individual independent companies.

★ **ASK** National Film and Television School, Beaconsfield Film Studies, Station Road, Beaconsfield, Bucks. Tel: (04946) 71234 about their postgraduate diploma in film making and their short courses (some for women only) for those who already work in the industry to update and improve skills.

★ **SEND FOR** *Film and TV training, a guide to colleges* (£2.50 including 30p p&p) from British Film Institute, 81 Dean Street, London W1V 6AA. Tel: (01) 437 4355.

BUILDING AND CONSTRUCTION

Taught in more than 250 universities, polytechnics and colleges in the UK. Qualifications range from BTEC to postgraduate. Institute exams also available.

★ **LOOK AT** the Construction Industry Training Board in *33 Training at work.*

★ **SEND FOR** *List of building courses* (£4.40 including p&p) from the Chartered Institute of Building, Englemere, King's Ride, Ascot, Berkshire SL5 8BJ. Tel: (0990) 23355.

BUSINESS STUDIES

Widely available as a subject at most FE and HE colleges, at many private colleges. Further details of the main business studies courses can be obtained from BTEC and SCOTVEC.

★ **SEND FOR** *Business studies,* free from DES, Room 2/11, Elizabeth House, York Road, London SE1 7PH. Tel: (01) 934 9566.

★ **LOOK AT** *The BGA guide to business schools* (£6.00 including p&p) from Business Graduates Association, Canberra House, 315 Regent Street, London W1R 8DE. Tel: (01) 637 7611.

★ **ASK** The Institute of Marketing, Moor Hall, Cookham, Maidenhead, Berkshire SL6 9QH. Tel: (0628) 24922.

CAREERS WORK

Courses are available at a number of colleges and one specialist college: Kent College for the Careers Service, College Road, Hextable, Swanley, Kent BR8 7RN. Tel: (0322) 64407/8.

★ **SEND FOR** *Training for the careers service,* and *A career as a careers officer,* free from Local Government Training Board, 4th Floor, Arndale House, The Arndale Centre, Luton LU1 2TS. Tel: (0582) 451166.

CIVIL SERVICE

The variety of employment opportunities in the Civil Service means a wide range of qualifications are useful. Training is mainly internal, either within your own department or at the Civil Service's own college. The Civil Service will also help with outside qualifications. Anyone under 18 is entitled to day release for any course they want to take. People over 18 can apply for day release which may be given for qualifications appropriate to their work. An adult FE scheme operates through which the Civil Service gives financial help (about 80%) for courses studied in your own time. These can range from a GCSE to an Open University degree.

★ **ASK** Civil Service Commission, Alencon Link, Basingstoke, Hampshire. Tel: (0256) 29222.

INFORMATION TECHNOLOGY

Both the BBC and IBA have programmes on computing. Details in *Radio times* and *TV times*. Also look at *25 Radio and TV* for information on how to find out about such programmes in advance. Details of local courses in Scotland and Northern Ireland are available from Network (Scotland) and the Referral Service (Northern Ireland). Addresses for these services are listed in *20 Basics*. Courses are also available in specific skills, eg programming. Courses are held at FE and HE colleges, private companies or colleges. Check with the National Computing Centre to see which private colleges follow their training recommendations. Ask for the Threshold department. Some computer manufacturers run their own courses. City and Guilds are offering a course, Computer Literacy 953, as well as courses in programming and information processing. For details:

★ **WRITE TO** City and Guilds of London Institute (for the address see *41 Qualifications*).

★ **ASK** National Computing Centre Ltd, Oxford Road, Manchester M1 7ED. Tel: (061) 228 6333.

★ **ASK** British Computer Society, Information Department, 13 Mansfield Street, London W1M 0BP. Tel: (01) 637 0471 for details of professional qualifications and the Society's examination.

★ **LOOK AT** *Computers users yearbook*, £52.95, published by Computing Publications Ltd. Your local library should have a copy.

★ **SEND FOR** *Computerfax, a guide to BBC and Open University resources in computing 1986–87* (25p) from Broadcasting Support Services, PO Box 7, London W3 6XJ. Enclose a large SAE.

★ **SEND FOR** *Microelectronics, electronics, computing and information technology courses in Scotland*, free from Microelectronics Educational Development Centre, Paisley College, High Street, Paisley PA1 2BE. Tel: (041) 887 2158.

★ **ASK** University of Cambridge Local Examinations Syndicate, Publications Section, 1 Hills Road, Cambridge CB1 2EU. Tel: (0223) 61111. Modules available on information technology course; computer literacy, word processing, spreadsheets, databased, videotex and information systems, programming, computer control technology, microelectronics.

DANCE AND DRAMA

There are a wide variety of courses in dance, drama and the performing arts in LEA colleges and specialist schools of dance or of drama as well as many small private schools teaching dance. Further information on recreational courses can be obtained from LEAs. For specialist dance training:

★ **ASK** The Council for Dance Education and Training, 5 Tavistock Place, London WC1H 9SS. Tel: (01) 388 5770 for a list of accredited dance schools and courses on full-time professional acting and stage management.

★ **ASK** The National Council for Drama Training, 5 Tavistock Place, London WC1H 9SS. Tel: (01) 387 3650 for information on accredited full-time professional acting and stage management courses.

★ **SEND FOR** free prospectus from the Conference of Drama Schools, Central School of Speech and Drama, Embassy Theatre, Eton Avenue, London NW3 3HY. Tel: (01) 722 8183.

★ **SEND FOR** free list of some drama schools in England and Wales from DES, Room 2/11 Elizabeth House, York Road, London SE1 7PH. Tel: (01) 934 9566.

DISTRIBUTION

General and specialised courses at all levels. Areas covered include retail distribution, wholesale distribution, warehousing, mail order and individual trades like bookselling and grocery. One specialist college:

The College for the Distributive Trades, 30 Leicester Square, London WC2H 7LE. Tel: (01) 839 1547.

DRIVING

Getting a licence to drive a car

Learning to drive a car is usually done through a private motoring school. The Department of Transport keeps a register of approved driving instructors (known as DOT approved).

★ **ASK** Department of Transport, 2 Marsham Street, London SW1P 3EB. Tel: (01) 212 3434. They do not publish their register of approved driving instructors but will tell you if a particular instructor is on it.

Advanced motoring

The Institute of Advanced Motorists Test is available for experienced drivers. Courses are run by private motoring schools, local authorities and 180 local members' groups.

★ **ASK** your local authority Road Safety Officer for details of courses in your area.

★ **ASK** Institute of Advanced Motorists, 359/365 Empire House, Chiswick High Road, London W4 4HS. Tel: (01) 994 4403 for general information and details of associate member schemes through which holders of the Advanced Driving Test give you driving practice.

Heavy goods vehicle (HGV) driving

HGV driving can be learnt with a private driving school, through a Road Transport Industry Training Board scheme or with a private employer (who may train you for a fee, even if you are not employed by them).

★ **LOOK AT** the Road Transport Industry Training Board in *33 Training at work*.

★ **LOOK AT** *A guide to the heavy goods vehicle driving test and licences* by David P Saye.

Taxi driving

Taxi drivers must be licenced by the local licencing authority – usually your council (though, in London, the Public Carriage Office issues licences). You must be at least 21 to drive a taxi, and pass a stringent medical test. You must pass a police exam or, in London, a Public Carriage Office exam to get a licence. The exam consists of a driving test in the taxi and an oral and practical test of your knowledge of the area. Acquiring 'the knowledge' (of the location) can be a formidable task in a large city and will require months of research in your own time. The London branch of the Taxi Drivers' Association runs a course of training for 'the knowledge' where hours of attendance are flexible.

★ **ASK** the Public Carriage Office, 15 Penton Street, London N1 9PU. Tel: (01) 278 1744 or your local police for details of their tests.

★ **ASK** the Taxi Drivers' Association, 9/11 Woodfield Road, London W9 2BA. Tel: (01) 286 1046 for details of their course of training. Local branches of the Taxi Drivers' Association may also be able to help if you live outside London.

Driving instruction

The Driving Instructors' Association and the Associated Examining Board jointly award the Diploma in Driving Instruction. The Diploma has five Modules in its structure which are each examined in a two-hour examination. You can study for the first module and then take a break for a while, as long as you complete the course within five years of passing the first one.

Chauffeur driving

Private courses run by larger motoring schools. Rolls Royce also runs courses, about nine a year in Crewe. You must have a clean driving licence on the day you start your course. They are mainly for Rolls Royce or Bentley drivers but they do accept drivers of other makes.

★ **ASK** Rolls Royce Motors Ltd, Pyms Lane, Crewe, Cheshire CW1 3PL. Tel: (0270) 255155 ext 3496.

Motor bikes

Inexpensive training courses are run mainly by local authorities and by Star Rider – their scheme is known as the 'Star Riders' scheme. These courses are open to people of all ages. They usually cover riding skills, maintenance and the law as it affects two wheeled vehicles. The aim is to prepare a rider for Part 1 and Part 2 of the motorcycle test. Part 1 is conducted by the local authorities, or by Star Rider for people who have taken their courses. People who have not taken a course are tested for Part 1 at a Department of Transport Test Centre. Part 2 is always taken at a DOT Test Centre.

★ **ASK** your local authority road safety department about their training courses.

★ **ASK** Star Rider, Federation House, 2309/11 Coventry Road, Sheldon, Birmingham B26 3PB. Tel: (021) 742 4296 for the address of your local Star Rider training centre.

ENGINEERING

Widely available as a subject at FE and HE colleges and at private colleges. A degree is now necessary for registration as a chartered engineer.

★ **ASK** Engineering Careers Information Service, 54 Clarendon Road, Watford, Herts WD1 1LB. Tel: (0923) 38441 for their leaflet on education and training and for a set of their career leaflets.

★ **ASK** Women's Engineering Society, 25 Foubert's Place, London W1V 2AL. Tel: (01) 437 5212 for advice on women training for engineering careers. Enclose an SAE for careers information sheet.

ENGLISH

Can be studied at all levels. Make sure you know what your aims are – are you studying English for pleasure, because you want a better job, or to teach English? Studying English can be part of improving your basic education, (see *Basic education* below). If you want to teach English, see the sections *Teaching* and *Teaching English as a foreign language* (below).

Learning English as a foreign language

Courses range from short, part or full-time holiday courses to those lasting three months or more. The level varies from basic English to university degree entrance standard. Make sure you have the right course for your needs. Courses are run by private language schools and by local education authority colleges.

★ **ASK** British Association of State Colleges in English Language Teaching (BASCELT), The Secretary, c/o South Thames College, 50–52 Putney Hill, London SW15 6QX, for course details for foreign students in the state sector.

★ **ASK** Association for Recognised English Language Teaching Establishments in Britain (ARELS/FELCO), 125 High Holborn, London WC1V 6QD. Tel: (01) 242 3136.

Basic education

LEAs run courses in basic English and maths and English as a second language. They are usually part-time and could be held in colleges of FE, community centres, local adult institutes or in your own home. See courses listed in *20 Basics* and *33 Training at work*.

FASHION, TEXTILES AND LEATHERWORK

Taught at all levels from practical craft courses to degree standard. Courses are held in all types of places, including FE colleges, art colleges and colleges of HE. Courses are biased toward design or production. Some specialist colleges:

London College of Fashion, 20 John Prince's Street, London W1M 9HE. Tel: (01) 629 9401. Courses include fashion design, tailoring, embroidery and clothing technology.
Cordwainers College, 182 Mare Street, London E8 3RE. Tel: (01) 985 0273. Full-time courses in footwear design and manufacture. Also full-time courses in leathergoods production/design and rural saddlery.
The Royal School of Needlework, 25 Princes Gate, London SW7 1QE. Tel: (01) 589 0077. Day and evening part- and full-time courses in design and embroidery.

★ **LOOK AT** the Clothing and Allied Products Industry Training Board in *33 Training at work*.

NB Central application procedure for courses leading to a CNAA first degree in art and design including fashion design – see *Art and design* (above).

FOOD

Courses from hostess cookery to hotel and hospital catering. Taught in adult education classes, many FE and HE colleges and a few specialist LEA colleges:

Birmingham College of Food and Domestic Arts, Summer Row, Birmingham B3 1JB. Tel: (021) 235 2774.
Hotel and Catering College, Ballywillan Road, Portrush, County Antrim, N. Ireland BT56 8JL. Tel: (0265) 823768.
Glasgow College of Food Technology, 230 Cathedral Street, Glasgow G1 2TG. Tel: (041) 552 3751.

★ **LOOK AT** Hotel and Catering Industry Training Board in *33 Training at work*.

HAIRDRESSING

Training for hairdressing can be through a hairdressing apprenticeship or a full-time course at an FE college or private college.

★ **ASK** The Hairdressing Council, 12 David House, 45 High Street, South Norwood, London SE25 6HJ. Tel: (01) 771 6205. Its leaflet *A career in hairdressing* is available at 50p including postage. It does not circulate material on careers as it exists for already qualified hairdressers.

★ **ASK** National Hairdressers Federation, 11 Goldington Road, Bedford MK40 3JY. Tel: (0234) 60332 for general information.

HEALTH EDUCATION

★ **LOOK AT** *30 Health education*.

INSURANCE

Can form part of a business studies course, but also available as a subject on its own. Training is done by employers and by external courses at the CII's College of Insurance at Sevenoaks.

★ **ASK** Careers Information Officer, Chartered Insurance Institute, 20 Aldermanbury, London EC2V 7HY. Tel: (01) 606 3835 for details of examinations and courses. The CII offers advisory interviews for those seriously interested in insurance as a career.

★ **ASK** Secretary, British Insurance Brokers Association, BIBA House, 14 Bevis Marks, London EC3M 5DJ. Tel: (01) 623 9043 for careers information.

JOURNALISM

The number of people training for journalism each year is small. You can take a full-time course in newspaper, periodical or radio journalism or in fashion writing before going into employment. Training is controlled by the National Council for the Training of Journalists and is most often with a local newspaper. Training in periodicals is controlled by the Periodicals Training Committee.

★ **ASK** The Newspaper Society, Whitefriars House, 6 Carmelite Street, London EC4Y OBL. Tel: (01) 583 3311 for information on training in journalism.

★ **ASK** The London College of Fashion, 20 John Prince's Street, London W1M 0BJ. Tel: (01) 629 9401 for details of its fashion writing course.

★ **ASK** The London College of Printing, Elephant and Castle, London SE1 6SB. Tel: (01) 735 8484 for details of its courses.

★ **ASK** Periodical Training Committee, Imperial House, Kingsway, London WC2B 6UN. Tel: (01) 836 8798 for information on a career in periodical journalism.

LANGUAGES

Can be studied on their own at all levels or as part of a broader course, eg business studies, secretarial, European studies. Available at all types of colleges, including private language colleges, and by correspondence course. Flexible study arrangements are frequently available – for example evening classes might include access to a language laboratory in your own time.

★ **SEND FOR** *Part-time and intensive language study: a guide for adult learners,* Information Guide No 8, 1982 (£1.20 plus 45p p&p) for information on types of language courses in Britain. Produced by the Centre for Information on Language Teaching and Research (CILT) and available from CILT Mailorder, 20 Carlton House Terrace, London SW1Y 5AP. Tel: (01) 839 2626.

★ **SEND FOR** *A guide to language courses in polytechnics and similar institutions,* published by Standing Conference of Heads of Modern Languages, Lancashire Polytechnic, Preston PR1 2TQ. Information on full-time courses *not* at universities.

★ **ASK** The Institute of Linguists, 24A Highbury Grove, London N5 2EA. Tel: (01) 359 7445.

LAW

The training of solicitors and barristers in England and Wales is very different to the Scottish system, so check further if you are interested in Scottish law. Training starts after A-levels or a degree, although clerical staff can begin at a lower level. Courses of professional training are available at HE colleges throughout the country.

★ **ASK** The Law Society, 113 Chancery Lane, London WC2A 1PL. Tel: (01) 242 1222 for details of solicitors' training in England and Wales.

★ **ASK** Law Society of Scotland, Law Society's Hall, PO Box 75, Drumsheugh Gardens, Edinburgh EH3 7YR. Tel: (031) 226 7411 for details of solicitors' training in Scotland. For advocated training, Clerk of Faculty, Faculty of Advocates, Parliament House, Edinburgh EH1 1RF.

★ **ASK** The Law Society of Northern Ireland, 90 Victoria Street, Belfast BT1 3GN. Tel: (0232) 231614.

★ **ASK** The Under Treasurer, Inn of Court of Northern Ireland, Royal Courts of Justice, Belfast BT1 3JF.

★ **ASK** The Council of Legal Education, 4 Gray's Inn Place, London WC1R 5DX. Tel: (01) 405 4635 for details of barristers' training for the Bar of England and Wales.

★ **ASK** the Institute of Legal Executives, Kempston Manor, Kempston, Bedford MK42 7AB. Tel: (0234) 857711 for details of legal executive training and exams.

LIBRARIANSHIP AND INFORMATION SCIENCE

Professional librarians and information scientists usually take a specialised undergraduate or postgraduate course at a university or polytechnic. The Library Association is the largest body for such professionals. It maintains a register of Chartered Members open to graduates who meet its requirements. The Institute of Information Scientists has exams for the Certificate in Information Science, designed for graduates working as information scientists who are not able to take a specialised postgraduate course. Support staff can study for City and Guilds qualifications or BTEC National awards with library options.

★ **SEND FOR** *How to become a chartered librarian,* free from The Library Association, 7 Ridgmount Street, London WC1E 7AE. Tel: (01) 636 7543. This is the largest professional body for library and information workers.

★ **ASK** The Institute of Information Scientists, 44 Museum Street, London WC1A 1LY. Tel: (01) 831 8003 for details of training in information science.

MANAGEMENT STUDIES

See also *Business studies*. Many courses are available in management studies at FE and HE colleges and private colleges. Specialist courses include distribution, food, hotel, recreation and business studies. See sections under these headings. The Diploma in Management Studies is a good way of doing a management qualification part time; it takes three years and is available in about 30 polytechnics. Masters degrees in management by distance learning are available through Henley, The Management College (listed under Oxfordshire in the *Gazetteer*).

★ **ASK** Management Consultancies Association, 11 West Harkin Street, London SW1X 8JL.

★ **ASK** City and Guilds of London Institute, 76 Portland Place, London W1N 4AA especially for the Guest House and Small Establishment Management Course (No 491).

MATHEMATICS

Can be studied from first steps with adult numeracy schemes to degree and post-degree levels. Widely available at FE and HE colleges and many private colleges. Basic numeracy provision is described in *20 Basics*. Polymaths and trimaths are introductory courses for people who might want to go on to take a degree level course – they are described in *18 Adult routes*.

★ **SEND FOR** *Using your maths* from the Department of Education and Science, Elizabeth House, York Road, London SE1 7PH. Tel: (01) 934 9566.

MEDICINE

Students need at least 3 Cs in A-levels to study for a degree in medicine. More frequently three Bs are the minimum requirement, and occasionally three As. This is the first step to becoming a doctor. After a degree, medical students must still study and get practical experience, before they can register as doctors with the General Medical Council.

★ **ASK** British Medical Association, BMA House, Tavistock Square, London WC1H 9JP. Tel: (01) 387 4499 for information on medical training and entry requirements. Large SAE required.

MINING AND QUARRYING

Courses are limited in number and mainly found at FE and HE colleges in large mining or quarrying areas. There is one specialist college which runs courses at BTEC Higher and degree level only: Camborne School of Mines, Trevenson, Poole, Redruth, Cornwall TR15 3SE. Tel: (0209) 714866.

Distance learning is available at Doncaster Institute of Higher Education and is explained in *17 Flexible learning*.

MOTOR MECHANICS

Can be studied through an apprenticeship, YTS or a full-time course at college.

★ **LOOK AT** the Road Transport Industry Training Board in *33 Training at work*.

★ **SEND FOR** *Careers information*, free from Institute of The Motor Industry, Fanshaws, Brickendon, Hertford, Herts SG13 8PQ.

★ **SEND FOR** *The retail motor industry* from Motor Agents Association, 201 Great Portland Street, London W1N 6AB.

There are courses at a number of the women's training workshops listed in *6 Women*. For an interesting self-help project, look at the Motorists' Co-op in Milton Keynes described in *38 Do it yourself*.

MUSIC

Courses in general musicianship and for those wanting to be professional musicians are taught in many specialist colleges and in universities, polytechnics and colleges of HE. Lower level courses are available in colleges of FE. Training for teachers of music follows the same pattern as teacher training in general.

★ **ASK** Department of Education and Science, Elizabeth House, York Road, London SE1 7PH. Tel: (01) 934 9000 and the Scottish Education Department, New St Andrews House, Edinburgh EH1 3SY. Tel: (031) 556 8400 for information on courses including teacher training.

★ **ASK** UK Council for Music Education and Training, 13 Back Lane, South Luffenham, Oakham, Leicestershire LE15 8NQ. Tel: (0727) 58296 for advice on education and training.

★ **ASK** your local education authority music adviser for advice – they are geared to helping young people but may be able to help informally.

★ **ASK** your local Army Careers Information Office for details on entry to the Army and Women's Royal Army Corps – both have bands.

★ **LOOK AT** *The British music yearbook*, available at larger libraries, for information on courses, colleges, grants and organisations.

NAVIGATION

Adult entry to the Merchant Navy is severely restricted. For those already employed there are schemes of training, including correspondence and block release courses leading to Certificates of Competency awarded by the Department of Transport. Degree courses in nautical marine, and maritime studies include periods of sea service. FE and HE colleges, mainly in the port towns often offer courses in fishing and yachting.

★ **ASK** the local Merchant Navy Establishment Office situated in any major seaport near your home.

★ **LOOK AT** *The directory of shipowners, shipbuilders and marine engineers* available at large local libraries for addresses of all UK based shipping companies and of overseas companies with UK agents.

★ **WRITE TO** College of the Sea, 202 Lambeth Road, London SE1 7JW. Tel: (01) 261 9539 for information on correspondence courses.

★ **LOOK AT** the Merchant Navy Training Board in *33 Training at work*.

NURSERY NURSING

Two-year full-time courses leading to the examinations of the National Nursery Examinations Board (NNEB) are available at colleges of FE throughout the country. There are also private colleges which offer NNEB and their own certificates. Scottish NNEB offers a course leading to the Scottish Nursery Nursing Certificate.

★ **ASK** NNEB, Argyle House, 29/31 Euston Road, London NW1 2SD. Tel: (01) 837 5458 for a list of colleges and a general information sheet. Enclose an SAE.

★ **ASK** SNNEB, 38 Queen's Street, Glasgow G1 3DY. Tel: (041) 204 2271.

★ **ASK** Association of Nursery Training Colleges, 26 Wilbraham Road, Fallowfield, Manchester M14 6JX. Tel: (061) 224 4560.

NURSING

Nurse training programmes are usually based in Schools of Nursing but more academic courses are based in colleges of HE. There are some differences between training schemes in Scotland and those in England and Wales. Check with the Regional Health Authority (Health Board in Scotland).

★ **LOOK AT** *Directory of schools of nursing*, published by HMSO.

There are several specialist courses in nursing, such as midwifery and health visiting, which can be taken after general nursing training. Like doctors, nurses must cover an 'approved' training programme only.

★ **ASK** ENB, Careers Advisory Centre, 2b Margaret Street, London W1N 7LB. Tel: (01) 631 0979 for lists of approved training centres and general careers information.

★ **SEND FOR** the DHSS leaflet *Nursing* (ref NLI) from DHSS Leaflets Unit, PO Box 21, Stanmore, Middlesex HA7 HAY.

OCCUPATIONAL THERAPY

There are 15 occupational therapy training schools. Upper age limit for training is 40. Application for England, Wales and Scotland through clearing house. For details of all courses, including Northern Ireland:

★ **SEND FOR** *A career in occupational therapy* from the College of Occupational Therapists, 20 Rede Place, London W2 4TU. Tel: (01) 229 9738/9.

OPTHALMIC OPTICS

Opthalmic opticians take a degree course at one of five universities or the Glasgow College of Technology, followed by a year's practice under supervision, before they can register as fully qualified with the General Optical Council. Dispensing opticians train through full-time, part-time or correspondence courses at one of three colleges and register after three years as fully qualified.

★ **ASK** British College of Opthalmic Opticians, 10 Knaresborough Place, London SW5 0TG. Tel: (01) 373 7765 for details of training.

★ **ASK** Association of British Dispensing Opticians, 22 Nottingham Place, London W1M 4AT. Tel: (01) 935 7411 for details of training.

OSTEOPATHY

The recognised qualification is Diploma in Osteopathy. Courses leading to this are available at:

British School of Osteopathy, 1/4 Suffolk Street, London SW1Y 4HG. Tel: (01) 930 9254/8.
European School of Osteopathy, 104 Tonbridge Road, Maidstone, Kent ME16 8SL. Tel: (0622) 671558.

★ **SEND FOR** free leaflets from the General Council and Register of Osteopaths, 21 Suffolk Street, London SW1Y 4HG and from the British Naturopathic and Osteopathic Association at the same address as the British College of Naturopathy and Osteopathy.

PHOTOGRAPHY

Courses at craft, technician and professional level are available at FE and HE colleges. These may be in general photography or specialised areas like medical and press photography.

★ **ASK** British Institute of Professional Photography, Amwell End, Ware SG12 9HN. Tel: (0920) 4011 for details of colleges offering training. Enclose an SAE.

★ **SEND FOR** *Directory of photographic courses* (£7.25) from Henry Greenwood and Co Ltd, 28 Great James Street, London WC1N 3HL. Tel: (01) 404 4202.

★ **ASK** City and Guilds of London Institute, Section 25, 46 Britannia Street, London WC1X 9RG.

PHYSIOTHERAPY

Most applications to the 35 schools are through the Central Admissions Department of the Chartered Society of Physiotherapy. There is no rigid upper age limit but applicants are not usually accepted over 35. For details of courses:

★ **SEND FOR** *The skilful touch: a career as a chartered physiotherapist* from the Chartered Society of Physiotherapy, 14 Bedford Row, London WC1R 4ED. Tel: (01) 242 1941/46.

PRINTING

Taught in many LEA colleges. One specialist college:
London College of Printing, Elephant and Castle, London SE1 6SB. Tel: (01) 735 8484. The college offers a wide range of courses.

★ **ASK** Institute of Printing, 8 Lonsdale Gardens, Tunbridge Wells, Kent TN1 1NU. Tel: (0892) 38118/9 for details of membership of the Institute.

PROFESSIONAL AND PUBLIC ADMINISTRATION

Can be studied on its own, or as part of a business studies course, at FE and HE colleges and correspondence colleges.

★ **ASK** Local Government Training Board, 8 The Arndale Centre, Luton LU1 2TS. Tel: (0582) 21111 for information on careers in local government. Also information on BTEC certificate in public administration.

★ **ASK** Institute of Chartered Secretaries and Administrators, 16 Park Crescent, London W1N 4AH. Tel: (01) 580 4741.

★ **SEND FOR** *Administration, the flexible professional career*, published by the Institute of Chartered Secretaries and Administrators (address above) specifically designed to give information to the 24–35 age group.

RADIOGRAPHY

Training through courses mainly held in hospitals leading to state registration. Two main branches – diagnostic (examining parts of the body) and therapeutic (treatment of disease). Most radiographers work in the diagnostic branch.

★ **ASK** College of Radiographers, 14 Upper Wimpole Street, London W1M 8BN. Tel: (01) 935 5726 for its free leaflets and details of courses and exams.

RECREATION

Courses cover everything from sports and arts administration to country park management. Can be studied at certain FE and HE colleges, full and part time. See the section *Sport* (below).

★ **ASK** Institute of Leisure and Amenity Management, Ilam House, Lower Basildon, Reading RG8 9NE. Tel: (0491) 873558 for details of training.

★ **ASK** Arts Council of Great Britain, Training Officer, 150 Piccadilly, London W1V 0AU. Tel: (01) 629 9495 for information on arts administration training. It will also send you monthly job lists if you send SAEs.

★ **SEND FOR** *Directory of training opportunities in countryside conservation and recreation,* free from Countryside Commission, Publications Despatch Department, 19–23 Albert Road, Manchester M19 2EQ.

★ **ASK** Section 26, City and Guilds of London Institute, 76 Portland Place, London W1N 4AA.

RELIGION

Can be studied at universities, polytechnics and colleges of HE and at specialist colleges. There is also growing provision of courses and conferences, part-time and local, with an emphasis on personal development and experiential learning where entry qualifications rely on factors other than high academic achievement. Some provide accreditation for work. Contact your religious leader for advice or contact the education staff direct through one of the contact points listed below .

Church of England

The Church of England has an adult education officer or link in each diocese.

★ **ASK** Rev Robin Bennett, Church of England General Synod Board of Education, Church House, Dean's Yard, London SW1P 3NZ. Tel: (01) 222 9011.

United Reformed Church

★ **ASK** Rev Terry Oakley for information on part-time adult education and training and the Rev Michael Dunford for adults wanting to train for the ministry, both at 86 Tavistock Place, London WC1 49RT. Tel: (01) 837 7661.

Roman Catholic Church

★ **ASK** the Vocational Director of your diocese for information on entering the priesthood, a monastery or convent or contact Father Patrick Purnell SJ, National Catechetical Association, 23 Kensington Square, London W8. Tel: (01) 937 7523 for information on part-time education.

Methodist Church

★ **ASK** Candidates Secretary, No 1 Central Buildings, Westminster, London SW1. Tel: (01) 222 8010.

Baptist Church

★ **ASK** Rev WCR Hancock, Secretary for Ministry, Baptist Union of Great Britain and Ireland, Baptist Church House, 4 Southampton Row, London WC1B 4AB. Tel: (01) 405 9803. Offers Christian Training Programme via local tutors or correspondence material.

Church of Scotland

★ **ASK** Rev R Blakey, Board of Education, 121 George Street, Edinburgh EH2 4YN. Tel: (031) 225 5722.

Scottish Episcopal Church

★ **ASK** Rev J Clarke, Communications Officer, General Synod Office, 21 Grosvenor Crescent, Edinburgh EH12 5EE. Tel: (031) 225 6357/8 for information on training for the non-stipendiary ministry.

★ **ASK** Miss C Matthews, 24 Barossa Place, Perth. Tel: (0738) 23578 for information on training as a Lay Missioner.

Church of Ireland

★ **ASK** Rev P Semple, Theological College, Braemor Park, Rathgar, Dublin 14. Tel: Dublin 97–55–06.

Church in Wales

★ **ASK** Rev Canon D Williams, Provincial Director, Education and Communications Centre, Woodland Place, Penarth, South Glamorgan CF6 2EX. Tel: (0222) 705278.

Board of Deputies of British Jews

★ **ASK** Mr Stuart Polak, Education Officer, Woburn House, Upper Woburn Place, London WC1H 0EP. Tel: (01) 387 3952.

SCIENCE

Many courses are available from preparatory to post-degree. Available at FE and HE colleges and private colleges. A number of access courses are science based; these, and polyphysics, are described in *18 Adult routes*.

★ **SEND FOR** *Science and technology,* free from DES, Room 2/11, Elizabeth House, York Road, London SE1 7PH. Tel: (01) 934 9566.

SECRETARIAL STUDIES

Can be studied at all levels from basic courses requiring no qualifications to post degree level courses at colleges of FE and HE and many private colleges throughout the country. Different secretarial specialisations include agriculture, medical, legal, languages – with corresponding examinations. Further details on the main secretarial courses can be obtained from BTEC, SCOTVEC and RSA (addresses in *41 Qualifications*). See also the section *Business studies* (above).

SELF-EMPLOYMENT

If you are interested in being self-employed or running your own business, there are lots of training courses you can do. See *35 Training for self-employment*.

SPEECH THERAPY

Qualification is through a degree course at a university, polytechnic, college of HE, or at the specialist college:

Centre for Clinical Communication Studies, City University, Northampton Square, London EC1V 0HB. Tel: (01) 253 4399 ext 4612. Also offers a two year postgraduate course.

All courses will consider applications from mature students.

★ **SEND FOR** *Speech therapy as a career*, free from the College of Speech Therapists, Harold Poster House, 6 Lechmere Road, London NW2 5BU. Tel: (01) 459 8521.

SOCIAL WORK

Taught in many colleges; mature entry is very common. If over 25, you may not need any formal qualifications.

★ **ASK** The Information Service, Central Council for Education and Training in Social Work or

★ **SEND FOR** *Leaflet 2 – Professional training for social work*, and *Leaflet 2:1* (a list of recognised social work qualifying courses). Free from Central Council for Education and Training in Social Work.
England: Derbyshire House, St Chad's Street, London WC1H 8AD. Tel: (01) 278 2455.
Wales: West Wing, 10A St David's House, Wood Street, Cardiff CF1 1ES. Tel: (0222) 26257.
Scotland: Ivanhoe House, 9 South St David Street, Edinburgh EH2 2BW. Tel: (031) 556 2953.
Northern Ireland: 14 Malone Road, Belfast BT9 5BN. Tel: (0232) 665390.

SPORT

Sports facilities (including coaching) are available everywhere through adult education centres, local council recreation centres, private provision and local and national clubs. Courses in sports management and related studies are offered by selected colleges of FE and HE. Recreation management courses cover sports centres and sports clubs. See also the section *Recreation* (above).

★ **ASK** Sports Council, 16 Upper Woburn Place, London WC1H 0QP. Tel: (01) 388 1277 for details of recreation management training and coaching courses.

SURVEYING, LAND AND PROPERTY SERVICES

There are several branches; the main ones are building surveying, general practice, land agency and agriculture, land surveying, minerals, planning and development, and quantity surveying. There are two levels of entry: professional and technician.

There are two ways to qualify at the professional level: either by a full-time, sandwich or part-time course leading to a recognised degree or diploma, or by taking the professional qualifying exams by part-time or distance learning. Candidates also have to pass a Test of Professional Competence – a period of practical experience followed by a practical test.

At technician level, qualification is through BTEC courses.

★ **WRITE TO** The Society of Surveying Technicians, Drayton House, 30 Gordon Street, London WC1H 0AX. Tel: (01) 388 8008.

★ **ASK** Royal Institution of Chartered Surveyors, Education and Membership Department, 12 Great George Street, Parliament Square, London SW1P 3AD. Tel: (01) 222 7000 for details of courses and routes to qualification – they publish a range of free leaflets on different branches of surveying.

★ **ASK** Incorporated Society of Valuers and Auctioneers, Education Office, 3 Cadogan Gate, London SW1X 0AS. Tel: (01) 235 2282 for a list of colleges running their qualifying exams and for general information.

★ **ASK** Director of Courses, College of Estate Management, Whiteknights, Reading RG6 2AW. Tel: (0734) 861101 for details of their courses which include correspondence courses for most professional qualifying exams in estate management, surveying and estate agency.

TEACHING

Initial teacher training

Mostly studied at HE colleges, though specialist certificates are available at some FE colleges. Maths and English at O-level or equivalent are now compulsory for all students wishing to train as teachers. Mature entrants are welcome. Several specially designed and shortened courses are available for those qualified and experienced in areas related to businees studies and craft design and technology. A tax free bursary of £1,250, on top of mandatory award entitlement, is available to trainee teachers on one- or two-year courses in mathematics, physics and craft design and technology. Most teacher training courses are at degree or postgraduate level. There are also many in-service courses for qualified teachers.

Ask for the following, which are free from the DES at the address below:

A career in teaching
Teaching mathematics and science
Teaching business studies in secondary schools
Design your future: teaching craft design and technology
Bursary scheme for trainee teachers
My teacher: teaching in primary schools
Grants for students: a brief guide
Addresses of colleges offering specially designed short courses for CDT and business studies.
Short courses and long courses – which lists courses for qualified teachers.

★ **ASK** Department of Education and Science, Room 2/11, Elizabeth House, York Road, London SE1 7PH. Tel: (01) 934 9000.

★ **ASK** Scottish Education Department, 43 Jeffrey Street, Edinburgh EH1 1DN. Tel: (031) 556 9233 for information on teacher training in Scotland.

★ **ASK** Department of Education for Northern Ireland, Rathgael House, Balloo Road, Bangor, Co Down BT19 2PR. Tel: (0247) 466311.

Teaching English as a foreign language (TEFL)
Courses, full- or part-time, vary in length from one month to one year. Some are for qualified teachers wanting to train for something new, others for people new to teaching. TEFL qualifications include postgraduate teaching certificates, higher degrees/diplomas in linguistics, RSA certificates, Trinity College diplomas and many others. Some institutions award their own qualification – not all are widely accepted. Check with your local education authority or any private employer you may hope to work for before setting out on a course. Courses are run by colleges of FE and HE, universities, polytechnics and private schools. Local education authority grants may be available. One specialist residential local education authority college running courses in TEFL:

Eaton Hall International, Retford, Nottinghamshire DN22 0PR. Tel: (0777) 706441.

★ **ASK** British Association of State Colleges in English Language Teaching (BASCELT), The Secretary, c/o South Thames College, 50–52 Putney Hill, London SW15 6QX, for details of colleges in the state sector running TEFL courses.

★ **ASK** English Teaching Information Centre, The British Council, 10 Spring Gardens, London SW1A 2BN. Tel: (01) 930 8466 for TEFL/TESL *Academic courses in the UK 1986–1987*.

★ **ASK** ARELS/FELCO, 125 High Holborn, London WC1V 6QD. Tel: (01) 242 3136 for a list of recognised private schools which run TEFL courses.

TRADITIONAL CRAFTS

Traditional crafts include blacksmithing, farriery, wrought ironwork, thatching, saddlery, furniture making and restoration, pottery and clay technology. Courses are available at colleges of FE, specialist centres and, depending on the nature of the craft, at different levels. See entry under *Fashion, textiles and leatherwork* for Cordwainers College which runs saddlery courses.

★ **ASK** Council for Small Industries in Rural Areas (CoSIRA), Castle Street, Salisbury, Wiltshire SP1 3TP. Tel: (0722) 336255. It will advise on training and setting up your own business and give information on its own courses and college courses.

★ **WRITE TO** Society of Dyers and Colourists, PO Box 244, 82 Grattan Road, Bradford, Yorkshire BD1 2JB. Tel: (0274) 725188.

WELSH

Can only be studied at a few colleges in the country; also part-time courses at adult education centres in Wales. S4C broadcasts in Welsh and includes several education programmes – see *25 Radio and TV*. Two colleges which run specialist courses are:

The University College of Wales, Aberystwyth, Dyfed. Tel: (0970) 3177. Offers external arts degrees taught in Welsh, including Welsh and Welsh history. Students working at home receive tapes in Welsh as part of the teaching materials.

The Polytechnic of Wales, Pontypridd, Mid Glamorgan, CF37 1DL. Tel: (0443) 405133. It has a Welsh Language Unit running courses in Welsh.

★ **ASK** Welsh Office Education Department, Ty-Nant, 180 High Street, Swansea SA1 1NI.

WOMEN'S STUDIES

A relatively new subject due to the development of the women's liberation movement. It can involve looking at the role of women in society, past and present and women's contributions to literature, art, music and so on. It can be studied for its own sake in adult education in classes or at women's centres. We know of five universities which offer a postgraduate qualification in women's studies (Kent, York, Sheffield, Sussex and Bradford). There are others where women's studies forms part of a postgraduate course. The Polytechnic of Central London also runs a diploma in women's studies course. See *6 Women*.

★ **ASK** Feminist Library and Information Centre, Hungerford House, Victoria Embankment, London WC2N 6PA. Tel: (01) 930 0715 for *Women's studies courses in the UK* (£1.25 plus 25p p&p).

YOUTH AND COMMUNITY WORK

In England, Wales, Scotland and Northern Ireland 18 colleges offer two year full-time courses (some incorporating a social work qualification). In addition there are one-year full-time courses for graduates and experienced workers. Part-time courses are available in London and Northern Ireland. Teaching qualifications are accepted as qualifying for youth and community work. A number of BEd courses offer it as an option.

★ **SEND FOR** *Training for professional youth and community work* from the National Youth Bureau, 17/23 Albion Street, Leicester LE1 6GD. Tel: (0533) 554775.

Gazetteer: places to study

HOW THE GAZETTEER IS ORGANISED

The *Gazetteer* is a list of course providers over the whole country. It is organised by LEAs (though they do not run all the facilities listed) since the LEA has the responsibility for further and adult education in each area; the name of the LEA is probably familiar to most people living there.

The Gazetteer is divided up into:

- England
- Wales
- Scotland
- Northern Ireland
- Channel Islands and the Isle of Man.

Within these sub-divisions, the LEAs are listed alphabetically, except for Northern Ireland where colleges are listed alphabetically by town.

The former metropolitan counties in England (ie London, Manchester, Merseyside, Tyne and Wear, West Midlands, South Yorkshire and West Yorkshire) are listed in their respective alphabetical positions; the metropolitan districts and Greater London boroughs are listed alphabetically within them. Inner London has not been divided into boroughs as it is covered by a single LEA.

The order used in this list is also used in all the lists of providers found throughout the book.

WHAT IS LISTED?

Each entry starts with a description of how that LEA organises its adult and further education provision, including costs, fee concessions for particular groups of people, the provision of basic education, and any contact point for further information.

The list that follows is headed with the location of any educational guidance services for adults in the area – these should be the first point of contact if you have difficulties using the system, or don't know what you want.

This is followed by a list of:

- all further education colleges maintained by the LEA, including colleges of agriculture, art, building etc
- any free-standing adult education centres maintained by the LEA (ie adult education colleges, institutes or centres which run as independent units but not adult education centres which are part of a school or other establishment)
- all institutions providing higher education in the area (ie universities, polytechnics and colleges and institutes of higher education, Scottish Central Institutions – and a few other places)

- any establishments offering types of course which we think are of particular interest to adults such as distance learning, access, NOW and preparatory courses, industrial language training units.

The name and address of each institution listed is followed by a series of abbreviations in italics, indicating any such activities of special interest to adults available at the college or centre. Further information about these activities is given in the respective chapter, including more detailed lists which provide alternative addresses (where the activity concerned is run at a sub-centre). There will also be a bit more detail about the provision including a person to contact (where relevant, and where we have been able to find out).

Activities listed

ARC: long term adult residential college, see *21 Adult residential colleges*
DL: distance learning or flexible study, see *17 Flexible learning*
Drop-in Centre: drop-in basic education centre, see *20 Basics*
EGS: educational guidance service for adults, see *1 Advice and help*
EM: extra-mural or continuing education department or short course unit in higher education institution, see *27 Leisure classes*
HE: higher education, see *22 Getting a degree*
HE Prep: higher education preparatory or access course, see *18 Adult routes*
ILTU: industrial language training unit, see *33 Training at work*
MS: mature student entry scheme (to higher education), see *22 Getting a degree*
NOW: New Opportunities for Women, see *19 Starting again*
Occ: occasional students (in higher education), see *22 Getting a degree*
Open College: open college scheme, see *18 Adult routes*
Polymaths: see *18 Adult routes*
Polyphysics: see *18 Adult routes*
PTHE: part-time degree courses, see *22 Getting a degree*
SRC: short term adult residential college, see *27 Leisure classes*
Trimaths: pre-polymaths course, see *18 Adult routes*
TW: training workshop, see *6 Women* and *29 Local councils*

This information should only be used as a starting point. Though colleges may plan to run courses, they do cancel them if insufficient students enrol. Equally, if there is strong demand, they may put on additional courses. So always start by asking the college concerned for more information about the courses you are interested in.

England

Avon

Adult education provision in Avon is made through 14 areas. Courses cost 57p per hour for vocational and 91p per hour for non-vocational courses. Fee concessions are decided at authority level and reductions of 25% are available to old aged pensioners and 75% to registered unemployed people. Basic education is available free.

Education Guidance Service for Adults

Avon Network (Education Guidance Centre for Adults), Quay Street, Bristol B71 2JL. Tel: (0272) 299822.
City of Bath Technical College, Avon Street, Bath BA1 1UP. Tel: (0225) 312191 ext 209.

Bath College of Higher Education, (incorporating Bath Academy of Art), Newton Park, Newton St Loe, Bath BA2 9BN. Tel: (022 17) 3701. *HE, EM* (see Bath Academy of Art, Wiltshire).
Bath University, Claverton Down, Bath BA2 7AY. Tel: (0225) 826826. *HE, MS, PTHE.*
Bristol Polytechnic, Coldharbour Lane, Frenchay, Bristol BS16 1QY. Tel: (0272) 656261. *HE, PTHE, NOW.*
Bristol University, Senate House, Tyndall Avenue, Bristol BS8 1TH. Tel: (0272) 303030. *HE, EM, Occ.*
Bristol Women's Workshop, 144 Wells Road, Totterdown, Bristol BS4 2AC. Tel: (0272) 711672. *Women's TW.*
Brunel Technical College, Ashley Down, Bristol BS7 9BU. Tel: (0272) 41241. *DL.*
City of Bath Technical College, Avon Street, Bath BA1 1UP. Tel: (0225) 312191. *DL, HE Prep, EGS.*
Filton Technical College, Filton Avenue, Filton, Bristol BS12 7AT. Tel: (0272) 694217. *DL, HE Prep.*
Norton-Radstock College, South Hill Park, Radstock, Bath BA3 3RW. Tel: (0761) 33161. *EGS.*
Nursery Nurses' College, 1 Worcester Terrace, Clifton, Bristol BS8 3JW. Tel: (0272) 738129 and 731542.
Soundwell Technical College, St Stephen's Road, Soundwell, Bristol BS16 4RL. Tel: (0272) 675101.
South Bristol Technical College, Marksbury Road, Bedminster, Bristol BS3 5JL. Tel: (0272) 661105. *DL, EGS, HE Prep, NOW.*
Trinity College, Stoke Hill, Stoke Bishop, Bristol BS9 1JP. Tel: (0272) 682803. *HE, Occ.*
Weston-Super-Mare College of Further Education, Knightstone Road, Weston-Super-Mare BS23 2AL. Tel: (0934) 21301. *DL.*

Bedfordshire

General adult education classes are provided through 14 community colleges based on upper/secondary schools and with various out-centres. Four colleges (Barnfield, Bedford, Dunstable and Luton) also run adult classes and there is a residential college for short adult courses at Woburn and a craft centre at Bedford. The countywide Special Adult Learning Programmes (SALP) run basic education classes (free) and courses for special groups in the community. Bedfordshire has a standard fee policy; non-vocational courses cost 82p per hour, or 41p for students under 18 years and not in full-time education; while vocational courses cost 35p per hour. OAPs, full-time students and unemployed or disabled people pay no fees. Students living outside Bedfordshire do not pay higher fees.

Education Guidance Services for Adults

Adult Education Centre (Bedford College of Higher Education), 10 Rothsay Gardens, Bedford. Tel: (0234) 47914.
Charles Street Adult Education Centre, Drop-in Advice and Counselling Service, Charles Street, Luton LU2 0EB. Tel: (0582) 38348.

Barnfield College, New Bedford Road, Luton LU3 2AX. Tel: (0582) 507531. *DL.*
Bedford College of Higher Education, Cauldwell Street, Bedford MK42 9AH. Tel: (0234) 45151. *HE, PTHE, DL, EGS.*
Bedfordshire Industrial Language Training Unit, The Westbourne Centre, Westbourne Road, Bedford MK40 4PQ. Tel: (0234) 53481. *ILTU.*
Challney Community College, Stoneygate Road, Luton LU4 9TJ. Tel: (0582) 599921. *DL, EGS.*
Charles Street Adult Education Centre, Charles Street, Luton LU2 0EB. Tel: (0582) 38348. *EGS.*
Cranfield Institute of Technology, Cranfield, Bedford MK43 0AL. Tel: (0234) 750111, and at Silsoe College, Silsoe MK45 4DT. Tel: (0525) 60428.*HE, Occ, DL,* and at Royal Military College of Science, Shrivenham, Swindon, Wiltshire SN6 8LA. Tel: (0793) 782551.
Dunstable College, Kingsway, Dunstable LU5 4HG. Tel: (0582) 696451. *DL.*
Elstow Craft Centre, Elstow, Bedford MK42 9XP. Tel: (0234) 50594. *NOW.*
Lea Manor Community College, Northwell Drive, Luton LU3 3TL. Tel: (0582) 595124. *DL.*
Luton College of Higher Education, Park Square, Luton LU1 3JU. Tel: (0582) 34111. *HE, PTHE, DL.*

Maryland Residential College, Leighton Road, Woburn, Milton Keynes MK17 9JD. Tel: (052 525) 688. *SRC.*
Redborne Community College, Flitwick Road, Ampthill MK45 2NU. Tel: (0525) 404462.
Special Adult Learning Programmes, Westbourne Centre, Westbourne Road, Bedford MK40 1JD. Tel: (0234) 64454, and at Charles Street Adult Education Centre, Luton (above). *DL.*

Berkshire

Adult education (including basic education) is organised through departments of adult education at Bracknell, Langley, Newbury and Windsor further education colleges except in the former Reading borough area, where there is a separate adult college. Courses run in schools or village halls will usually be administered by the nearest college. Fees are set at LEA level and concessions are available for retired, unemployed and many disabled people as well as others; if in doubt, ask. Basic literacy and numeracy teaching is free. The county runs a short-term residential college for adults at Wokingham.

*Education Guidance Service for Adults*Reading Adult College, 18 Cross Street, Reading RG1 1SW. Tel: (0734) 581754.

Berkshire College of Agriculture, Hall Place, Burchetts Green, Maidenhead, Berks. Tel: (062 882) 4444.
Berkshire College of Art and Design, Raymond Road, Maidenhead SL6 6DS. Tel: (0628) 24302.
Bracknell College, Church Road, Bracknell RG12 1DJ. Tel: (0344) 420411. *DL, NOW.*
Bulmershe College of Higher Education, Bulmershe Court, Woodlands Avenue, Earley, Reading RG6 1HY. Tel: (0734) 663387. *HE, Occ, PTHE.*
College of Estate Management, Whiteknights, Reading RG6 2AW. Tel: (0734) 861101. *DL.*
Easthamstead Park Educational Centre, Wokingham, Berks. RG11 3DF. Tel: (0734) 780686. *SRC.*
Langley College of Further Education, Station Road, Langley, Slough SL3 8BY. Tel: (0753) 49222.
Newbury College of Further Education, Oxford Road, Newbury RG13 1PQ. Tel: (0635) 42824.
Reading Adult College, Wilson Centre, Wilson Road, Reading RG3 2RW. Tel: (0734) 55575. *EGS DL. Basic Education,* Tel: (0734) 589900.
Reading College of Technology, Kings Road, Reading RG1 4HJ. Tel: (0734) 583501. *DL.*
Reading University, Whiteknights, Reading RG6 2AH. Tel: (0734) 875123. *HE, EGS, EM.*
Slough College of Higher Education, Wellington Street, Slough SL1 1YG. Tel: (0753) 34585. *HE, DL, ILTU.*
Windsor and Maidenhead College, Claremont Road, Windsor SL4 3AZ. Tel: (075 35) 862111 and Boyn Hill Avenue, Maidenhead. Tel: (0628) 25221.

Buckinghamshire

Adult education in the county is organised through nearly 30 centres operating mainly in school premises. A good deal of the programme is held during evenings but there is a growing provision of day-time, weekend and holiday courses – some of which is on a residential basis. There is a standard rate of fees in the county and there are concessions for OAPs, the unemployed, under 18s and those receiving supplementary benefits. There is also an arrangement to enrol for courses organised within the school curriculum.

For more information ask: G S Cook, Education Department, County Hall, Aylesbury, Bucks HP20 1UZ. Tel: (0296) 395000 ext 8913.

Education Guidance Service for Adults
Youth and Community Department, County Hall, Aylesbury HP20 1UZ. Tel: (0296) 395000 ext 674.

Amersham College of Further Education Art and Design, Stanley Hill, Amersham HP7 9HN. Tel: (02403) 21121. *DL.*
Aylesbury College of Further Education and Agriculture, Oxford Road, Aylesbury HP21 8PD. Tel: (0296) 34111. *DL.*
Buckinghamshire College of Higher Education, Queen Alexandra Road, High Wycombe HP11 2JZ. Tel: (0494) 22141/9. *DL, HE.*
Milton Keynes College, Chaffron Way, Leadenhall West, Milton Keynes MK6 5LP. Tel: (0908) 668998. *DL.*

Milton Keynes Women and Work, 1 The Bakehouse, 6 Church Street, Wolverton, Milton Keynes, Bucks MK2 5JN. Tel: (0908) 310372. *Women's TW*.
National Film and Television School, Beaconsfield Studios, Station Road, Beaconsfield, Bucks. Tel: (049 46) 71234.
University of Buckingham, Hunter Street, Buckingham MK18 1EG. Tel: (0280) 814080. *HE, MS*.

Cambridgeshire

Part-time adult education is provided by the countywide Community Education Service. This is organised mainly in schools (community colleges and village colleges) most of which have some child care facilities, but also in the county's five further education colleges and in one separate adult college (Peterborough). Apart from classes in the further education colleges, all fees are decided by individual centres, as are concessions. These are generally available to retired, unemployed and disabled people as well as to the under 18s. Basic education (literacy, numeracy and English as a second language) courses cost substantially less than other subjects (about 30p per hour compared to 70p).

Education Guidance Services for Adults
Education Desk, c/o Cambridge Jobcentre, Guildhall Chambers, Cambridge. Tel: (0223) 64941.
Peterborough Education Guidance Service for Adults (PEGS), Community Education, Touthill Close, City Road, Peterborough PE1 1UJ. Tel: (0733) 310101 ext 247.
Isle College, Wisbech PE13 2JE. Tel: (0945) 582566.

Bottisham Village College, Lode Road, Bottisham, Cambridgeshire CB5 9DL. Tel: (0223) 811372. *DL*.
Cambridge College of Further Education, Newmarket Road, Cambridge CB5 8EG. Tel: (0223) 357545. *DL*.
Cambridgeshire College of Arts and Technology, Collier Road, Cambridge CB1 2AJ. Tel: (0223) 63271. *DL, ILTU, MS, HE, PTHE*.
Cambridgeshire Farm College, Milton, Cambridge CB4 4DB. Tel: (0223) 860701. *MS*.
Cambridge Intercollegiate Applications Office, Kellet Lodge, Tennis Court Road, Cambridge CB2 1QJ. Tel: (0223) 333308. *HE, EM*.
Cambridge Training and Development Ltd, Unit 43, Clifton Industrial Estate, Cherry Hinton Road, Cambridge CB1 4FB. Tel: (0223) 214346.
Cambridge University Board of Extra-Mural Studies, Madingley Hall, Madingley, Cambridge CB3 8AQ. Tel: (0954) 210636. *EM* (Cambridge University), *SRC*.
Cambridge Women's Resource Centre, 7c Station Road, Cambridge CB1 2JB. Tel: (0223) 321148. *Women's TW*.
Huntingdonshire College, California Road, Huntingdon PE18 7BL. Tel: (0480) 52346.
Isle College, Ramnoth Road, Wisbech PE13 2JE. Tel: (0945) 582561/6. *EGS, DL*.
Peterborough College of Adult Education, Brook Street, Peterborough PE1 1TU. Tel: (0733) 61361.
Peterborough Regional College, Park Crescent, Peterborough PE1 4DZ. Tel: (0733) 67366. *DL*.

Cheshire

Adult education in the county is organised as part of the further education service. Courses are run in Cheshire's six colleges of further education but most are held in over 40 school-based adult education centres, or community centres. Fees, which are fixed at county level, are from 54p to 64p per hour for vocational subjects and 90p an hour for non-vocational subjects. There is no charge for basic education, which is run by adult literacy tutors in the colleges. Fee remissions are also decided at county level and are available to old age pensioners, the unemployed and under 18s as well as others on application on grounds of hardship.

Burton Manor, Burton, South Wirral, Cheshire L64 5SJ. Tel: (051) 336 5172. *SRC*.
Cheshire College of Agriculture, Reaseheath, Nantwich, Cheshire. Tel: (0270) 625131.
Chester College, Cheyney Road, Chester CH1 4BJ. Tel: (0244) 375444. *HE, MS*.
Crewe and Alsager College of Higher Education, Crewe Road, Crewe CW1 1DU. Tel: (0270) 500661. *HE, PTHE*.
Halton College of Further Education, Kingsway, Widnes WA8 7QQ. Tel: (051) 423 1391.

Macclesfield College of Further Education, Park Lane, Macclesfield SK11 8LF. Tel: (0625) 27744. *DL.*

Mid-Cheshire College of Further Education, Hartford Campus, Northwich CW9 8AQ. Tel: (0606) 75281. *DL. HE Prep, NOW.*

North Cheshire College, Padgate Campus, Fearnhead, Warrington WA2 0DB. Tel: (0925) 814343. *DL, EGS, EM, HE, HE Prep, NOW, Occ, MS, Open College scheme.*

South Cheshire College, Dane Bank Avenue, Crewe CW2 2AB. Tel: (0270) 69133. *DL, Open Tech.*

South Trafford College of FE, Manchester Road, West Timperley, Altrincham, Cheshire WA14 5PQ. Tel: (061) 973 7064. *DL.*

West Cheshire College of Further Education, Eaton Road, Handbridge, Chester CH4 7ER. Tel: (0244) 677677. *DL, EGS.*

Cleveland

Most recreational and leisure courses are organised by further education centres but meet in schools and community centres. There are two free-standing centres. The six colleges of further education do offer some recreational courses and several courses for adults which provide a second chance. Fees are established by the education committee and are around 80p per class meeting. Tuition is free to people in receipt of unemployment benefit and to those in financial hardship, receiving supplementary benefit. No charge is made for courses in basic education and those specifically designed for handicapped students. People in receipt of the state National Insurance Retirement Pension and under 18s, pay half fees. Basic education is organised by the following six centres:

Acklam Further Education Centre, The Hustler Adult Wing, Hall Drive, Acklam, Middlesbrough. Tel: (0642) 818480.

Bertram Ramsey Further Education Centre, Prissick Base, Marton Road, Middlesbrough. Tel: (0642) 315063.

Billingham Further Education Centre, Sixth Form College, Marsh House Avenue, Billingham. Tel: (0642) 563285.

Langbaurgh Further Education Centre, Ormesby Road, Middlesbrough. Tel: (0642) 313088.

Redcar Further Education Centre, Aske Road, Redcar. Tel: (0642) 477173. *DL.*

William Newton Further Education Centre, William Newton Centre, Junction Road, Norton, Stockton. Tel: (0642) 554001. *SRC, EGS* (planned).

Help can also be obtained by applying at any branch library. Information can be obtained from the education office. Tel: (0642) 248155 ext 3055 and 3067. (Open University offices in Middlesbrough.) Information on all courses can be obtained from the *Further education in Cleveland* pack, available in all libraries. This includes a booklet *Education for leisure* which has an index of courses offered throughout the county. The universit*ies* of Durham and Leeds have extra-mural centres at Stockton and Middlesbrough.

Brotton Further Education Centre, Linden Road, Brotton, Saltburn, Cleveland TS12 7RJ. Tel: (0642) 76305. *DL.*

Cleveland College of Art and Design, Green Lane, Middlesbrough TS5 7RJ. Tel: (0642) 821991 and Church Square, Hartlepool TS24 7EX. Tel: (0429) 263211.

Cleveland Technical College, Corporation Road, Redcar TS10 1EZ. Tel: (0642) 473132. *DL.*

Guisborough Agricultural Centre, Avenue Place, Redcar Road, Guisborough, Cleveland TS14 6AX. Tel: (0287) 33870. *DL* (planned).

Hartlepool College of Further Education, Stockton Street, Hartlepool TS25 7NT. Tel: (0429) 275453. *DL, EGS.*

Kirby College of Further Education, Roman Road, Linthorpe, Middlesbrough TS5 5PJ. Tel: (0642) 813706.

Longlands College of Further Education, Douglas Street, Middlesbrough TS4 2JW. Tel: (0642) 248351. *DL, EGS, ILTU* (planned).

Middlesbrough Women's Training Centre, 4th Floor, Sun Alliance House, Albert Road, Middlesbrough. Tel: (0642) 244223. *Women's TW.*

Redcar Further Education Centre, Ashe Road, Redcar TS10 2BP. Tel: (0642) 477173. *DL.*

Stockton-Billingham Technical College, The Causeway, Billingham TS23 2DB. Tel: (0642) 552101. *DL.*

Stockton Further Education Centre, William Newton Further Education Centre, Junction Road, Norton, Stockton-on-Tees, Cleveland TS20 1PR. Tel: (0642) 554001.

Teesside Polytechnic, Borough Road, Middlesbrough TS1 3BA. Tel: (0642) 218121. *Polymaths, HE, PTHE, Occ.*

Cornwall

Cornwall's adult education service runs courses in the community wherever facilities are available – there are no separate institutes. Classes are organised through 12 centres and cost a minimum of 80p per hour. The under 19s (for exam courses), people on supplementary benefit, the unemployed, those on invalidity benefit or OAPs pay 50p per hour. There is no charge for basic education.

For more information ask: Sheila Richards. Tel: (0736) 64746.

Education Guidance Service for Adults

NETWORK, Department of Continuing and Adult Education, Hayne Corfe Centre, Sunningdale, Truro TR1 3ND. Enquiries to John Hurst (0872) 74503.

Callington/Launceston Centre, Torr House, Stoke Climsland, Callington, Cornwall. Tel: (0579) 70563. *DL.*

Camborne School of Mines, Trevenson Pool, Redruth TR15 3SE. Tel: (0209) 714866. *HE.*

Cornwall Education Centre, Church Road, Pool, Redruth TR15 3PU. Tel: (0209) 716631. *PTHE.*

Cornwall College of Further and Higher Education, Redruth TR15 3RD. Tel: (0209) 712911. *DL, HE.*

Falmouth School of Art, Woodlane, Falmouth TR11 4RA. Tel: (0326) 313269/312948. *HE.*

Restormel Adult Continuing Education Centre, Mid-Cornwall College of Further Education, Sedgemoor, Bodmin Road, St Austell PL25 5AB. Tel: (0726) 67911. *DL, EGS.*

Carrick Adult Continuing Education, 61 Lenon Street, Truro. Tel: (0872) 79867. *DL.*

Cumbria

Adult education in Cumbria is organised with further education and the Youth and Community service. Most classes take place in schools or community centres but some are held in the further education colleges. Fees are currently 92p per hour and concessions are available, countywide, to retired or unemployed people and also the under 18s. There is no charge for basic education.

For more information ask: Mr A Drysdale (ext 2514) or Mrs L Kerry (ext 2050), 5 Portland Square, Carlisle CA1 1PU. Tel: (0228) 23456.

Barrow-in-Furness College of Further Education, Howard Street, Barrow-in-Furness LA14 1LU. Tel: (0229) 25017.

Carlisle Technical College, Victoria Place, Carlisle CA1 1HS. Tel: (0228) 24464. *DL, Open College scheme.*

Charlotte Mason College of Education, Rydal Road, Ambleside LA22 9BB. Tel: (096 63) 3066. *HE.*

Cumbria College of Agriculture and Forestry, Newton Rigg, Penrith, Cumbria CA11 OAH. Tel: (0768) 63791.

Cumbria College of Art and Design, Brampton Road, Carlisle CA3 9AY. Tel: (0228) 25333.

Kendal College of Further Education, Milnthorpe Road, Kendal LA9 5AY. Tel: (0539) 24313.

West Cumbria College, Park Lane, Workington CA14 2RW. Tel: (0900) 64331. *NOW, HE Prep, PTHE, DL.*

Derbyshire

Responsibility for providing adult education in Derbyshire is divided between 19 'Adult Principals' working over geographical areas and by three further education colleges. The majority of classes are organised through adult education centres (often using schools) but some are held in the colleges. The county determines fees for vocational classes and the local centres for non-vocational courses. There are concessions for retired and unemployed people, people on supplementary benefit and disability pensions. Basic education is, in general, organised separately and is free to students.

For more information apply to the nearest appropriate centre. Community education policies are under development, and will result in changes of this organisation during 1987.

Ashbourne Adult Education Centre, Cokayne Avenue, Ashbourne, Derbyshire. Tel: (0335) 43206. *DL.*
Chesterfield College of Technology and Arts, Infirmary Road, Chesterfield S41 7LL. Tel: (0246) 31212. *DL, HE Prep, NOW.*
Derby College of Further Education, Wilmorton, Derby DE2 8UG. Tel: (0332) 73012. *DL, EGS.HE Prep, NOW.*
Derbyshire College of Agriculture and Horticulture, Broomfield, Morley, Derbyshire DE7 6DN. Tel: (0332) 831345. *ARC, MS.*
Derbyshire College of Higher Education, Kedleston Road, Derby DE3 1GB. Tel: (0332) 47181. *DL, HE, HE Prep, MS, Occ, PTHE.*
High Peak College of Further Education, Harpur Hill, Buxton SK19 9JZ. Tel: (0298) 71100. *DL, HE Prep, MS.*
North East Derbyshire College of Further Education, Rectory Road, Clowne, Chesterfield S43 4BQ. Tel: (0246) 810332.
South East Derbyshire College, Field Road, Ilkeston DE7 5RS. Tel: (0602) 324212 (and also at Heanor). *DL, ILTU, NOW.*

Devon
Adult education classes in the county are organised through the community education service. Courses are run through adult education centres, 21 community colleges and five further education colleges but may also be held in other places (such as village halls). In addition, some schools are experimenting with back to school schemes. Fees are decided locally – an average cost per hour would be in the range of 60p to 80p. Basic education classes are integrated with other courses in some areas but there is also a countywide programme. There is also no standard policy for fee reductions; they are decided at local level. The county also runs a residential centre offering short courses for adults. This operates as part of Devon Centre for Continuing Education (see below).

Education Guidance Service for Adults
NETWORK, Advice Service for Adult Education, Herondyke, West Charleton, Kingsbridge TW7 2AA. Tel: (054853) 289. *DL.*

Bicton College of Agriculture, East Budleigh, Budleigh Salterton, Devon EX9 7BY. Tel: (0395) 68353.
Bideford Community College, Abbotsham Road, Bideford, North Devon. Tel: (02372) 76400. *DL.*
College of St Mark and St John, Deriford Road, Plymouth PL6 8BH. Tel: (0752) 777188. *HE.*
Devon Centre for Continuing Education, Dartington College of Arts, Totnes TQ9 6EH. Tel: (0803) 862267. *HE Prep, NOW, HE, EM.*
East Devon College of Further Education, Bolham Road, Tiverton EX16 6SH. Tel: (0884) 254247/9. *DL, EGS, NOW, HE Prep.*
Exeter College, Hele Road, Exeter EX4 4JS. Tel: (0392) 77977. *DL.*
Exeter College of Art and Design, Earl Richards Road North, Exeter EX2 6AS. Tel: (0392) 263263. *HE, Occ.*
Exeter University, Northcote House, The Queen's Drive, Exeter EX4 4QJ. Tel: (0392) 263263. *HE, EM, Occ.*
North Devon College, Sticklepath, Barnstaple EX31 2BQ. Tel: (0271) 45291. *DL.*
Plymouth College of Art and Design, Tavistock Place, Plymouth PL4 8AT. Tel: (0752) 264714. *DL.*
Plymouth College of Further Education, King's Road, Devonport, Plymouth PL1 5QG. Tel: (0752) 264709. *DL.*
Plymouth Polytechnic, Drake Circus, Plymouth PL4 8AA. Tel: (0752) 221312. *HE, PTHE, Occ, Polymaths.*
Rolle College, Exmouth EX8 2AT. Tel: (0395) 265344. *HE, Occ, HE Prep, PTHE.*
Royal Naval Engineering College, Manadon, Plymouth PL5 3AQ. Tel: (0752) 553740. *HE.*
St Clare's Adult Education Centre, Fore Street, Seaton, Devon. Tel: (0297) 21904. *DL.*
Seale-Hayne College, Newton Abbot, Devon TQ12 6NQ. Tel: (0626) 52323. *HE.*

Sidmouth College, Primley Road, Sidmouth, Devon. Tel: (039 55) 4823. *DL.*
South Devon College of Arts and Technology, Newton Road, Torquay TQ2 5BY. Tel: (0803) 213242. *DL, NOW.*

Dorset

The county's adult education service is organised mainly through nine area adult education centres but also through further education or technical colleges. Most centres are school-based but there are separate centres in Bournemouth, Dorchester, Swanage, Weymouth, Gillingham, Sturminster and Christchurch. In addition, Dorset runs a 'back to school' scheme for adults. Fees, which are fixed at county level, vary from between 42p and 83p an hour for most non-vocational subjects to nothing (basic education is free of charge) with vocational subjects working out at under 40p an hour. Fee reductions are determined at authority level but principals have some discretion. Concessions are available to retired people, holders of invalidity pensions, people under 18 in full-time education and the unemployed, and remissions for others on a low income (at present, under £5800 a year).

For more information, contact: County Adult Education Office, Education Department, Portman House, Richmond Hill, Bournemouth BH2 6ER. Tel: (0202) 22151. The County Adult Literacy and Numeracy Scheme is part of the Adult Education Service with its own structure.

Further information from: Mrs E Stow, County Co-ordinator, Commanders House, Constitution Hill Road, Poole, Dorset BH14 0QB. Tel: (0202) 682167.

Bournemouth and Poole College of Art and Design, Wallisdown Road, Poole, Dorset BH12 5HH. Tel: (0202) 533011.
Bournemouth and Poole College of Further Education, North Road, Parkestone, Poole BH14 0LS. Tel: (0202) 747600. *DL.*
Dorset College of Agriculture and Horticulture, Kingston Mauward, Dorchester, Dorset DT2 8PY. Tel: (0305) 4738.
Dorset Institute of Higher Education, Wallisdown Road, Wallisdown, Poole BH12 5BB. Tel: (0202) 524111. *HE, PTHE, MS.*
Weymouth College, Cranford Avenue and Newstead Road, Weymouth. Tel: (0305) 774911 (both sites). *DL, EGS.*

Durham

The provision of adult education classes is divided between the six colleges run by the county and a large number of adult education, youth and community 'areas' which are mainly school-based. The county also runs Beamish Hall, which provides short residential courses for adults. Apart from Beamish Hall courses, fees are fixed at county level. Non-vocational subjects work out between 65p and 86p an hour, charges for vocational subjects vary according to the course. Fee concessions are also fixed at county level and reductions are available to retired people, the unemployed and the under 18s. Fees are not charged for basic education classes.

Beamish Hall Residential College, Stanley, Durham DH9 ORG. Tel: (0207) 233147. *SRC.*
Bishop Auckland Technical College, Woodhouse Lane, Bishop Auckland DL14 6JZ. Tel: (0388) 603052.
Darlington College of Technology, Cleveland Avenue, Darlington DL3 7BB. Tel: (0325) 467651. *DL.*
Derwentside College, Park Road, Consett DH8 5EE. Tel: (0207) 502906. *Drop-In Centre, basic education.*
Durham College of Agriculture and Horticulture, Houghall, Durham DH1 3SG. Tel: (0385) 61351.
Durham University, Old Shire Hall, Durham DH1 3HP. Tel: (0385) 64466. *HE, EM, NOW, Occ.*
New College Durham, Framwellgate Moor Centre, Durham DH1 5ES. Tel: (0385) 62421. *DL, EGS, HE Prep, ILTU, HE.*
Peterlee College, Peterlee SR8 1NU. Tel: (091) 586 2225. *DL.*

Essex

The county's further education branch provides a comprehensive range of adult learning opportunities in its 11 colleges and 37 adult and joint adult and youth centres. Currently over 80000 adult students access opportunities each year on courses which range across examination and non-examination subjects, vocational and non-vocational subjects and recreation, academic and cultural activities. Fees are determined by the county education committee and courses cost £1 per hour with a 50% reduction for examination courses and old age pensioners. In addition, adults in receipt of a means tested benefit are entitled to a 75% reduction and basic education students are charged £4.45 per term. In exceptional circumstances the principal or head of centre can waive fees completely.

For more information, guidance and advice about adult learning opportunities available locally, contact your local adult centre or college. For general information about opportunities available across the county, ring the Information Service on Colchester(0206) 47737, Southend (0702) 354411, Epping (0378) 77948 or Chelmsford (0245) 267222 ext 2680.

Basildon College of Further Education, Nethermayne, Basildon SS16 5NN. Tel: (0268) 28928l.
Braintree College of Further Education, Church Lane, Bocking, Braintree CM7 5SN. Tel: (0376) 21711. *DL.*
Essex Institute of Higher Education, Victoria Road South, Chelmsford CM1 1LL. Tel: (0245) 354491. *HE, PTHE, MS.*
Chelmsford College of Further Education, Dovedale, Moulsham Street, Chelmsford CM2 0JQ. Tel: (0245) 265611.
Colchester Adult Education Centre, Greyfriars, High Street, Colchester. Tel: (0206) 42242. *EGS.*
Colchester Institute, Sheepen Road, Colchester CO3 3LL. Tel: (0206) 570271. *DL, HE, HE Prep.*
Debden House, Debden Green, Loughton, Essex IG10 2NZ. Tel: (01) 508 3008. *SRC.*
Essex University, Wivenhoe Park, Colchester CO4 3SQ. Tel: (0206) 862286. *HE, MS, Occ, DL.*
Harlow College, College Gate, The High, Harlow CM20 1LT. Tel: (0279) 441288. *DL, EGS, HE Prep.*
Loughton College of Further Education, Borders Lane, Loughton IG10 3SA. Tel: (01) 508 8311. *DL.*
Southend College of Technology, Carnarvon Road, Southend-on-Sea SS2 6LS. Tel: (0702) 353931.
Thurrock Technical College, Woodview, Grays RM16 4YR. Tel: (0375) 371621. *DL.*
Wansfell College, Theydon Bois, Epping, Essex CM16 7LF. Tel: (037 881) 3027.
Writtle Agricultural College, Writtle, Chelmsford, Essex CM1 3RR. Tel: (0245) 420705.

Gloucestershire

Most classes are organised through about 70 centres (mainly school-based) and LEA colleges. Basic education is provided free of charge but fees for non-vocational subjects work out at around 88p an hour and are fixed countywide. Eligibility for fee reductions is decided at centre level and concessions should be available to retired people, the under 18s as well as others in need, upon request. Some schools allow adults to return and study if requested but this is a limited arrangement.

For more information, contact: The Education Office Annexe, 92–96 Westgate Street, Gloucester. Tel: (0452) 425418.

Education Guidance Service for Adults.

Guidelines (Educational Guidance Service for Adults). EGSA for the county. Get in touch by phone. See *1 Advice and help*.

The College of St Paul and St Mary, The Park, Cheltenham GL50 2RH. Tel: (0242) 513836. *HE, EM, EGS, PTHE, HE Prep.*
Gloucestershire College of Agriculture, Hartpury GL19 3BE. Tel: (045 270) 283.
Gloucestershire College of Arts and Technology, Oxstalls Lane, Gloucester GL2 9HW. Tel: (0452) 26321. *DL, EGS, MS, Occ, Polymaths, PTHE, HE, Trimaths.*
Mid-Gloucestershire Technical College, Stratford Road, Stroud GL5 4AH. Tel: (045 36) 3424. *DL.*
Royal Agricultural College, Cirencester GL7 6JS. Tel: (0285) 2531. *HE.*
Royal Forest of Dean College, Cinderford GL14 2JY. Tel: (0594) 22191. *DL, EGS.*

Hampshire

Adult education in the county is organised through 13 area institutes which are also responsible for youth and community service provision. Five of these are based on FE colleges. Each institute co-ordinates the work of up to 10 local adult education centres based on schools, community centres and purpose-built or adapted premises.

In addition, all colleges of further education, Portsmouth Polytechnic, the Hampshire College of Agriculture and Calshot Activities Centre offer a wide range of learning opportunities for adults.

The department of adult education at Southampton University and the Workers' Educational Association, in co-operation with the Local Education Authority, provide an extensive programme of liberal studies and a number of special projects such as return to study and second chance for women schemes.

Hampshire has recently introduced a scheme to enable adults to join appropriate courses in sixth form colleges and secondary schools.

The county has 26 designated community schools which, as well as being local adult education centres within the institute structure, provide a focus for local community involvment, activity and recreation.

Adult basic education, including English as a second language, is provided – free of charge – through the institutes, each of which has a specialist member of staff who co-ordinates this aspect of the work. A county adviser provides central support and acts as a County Referral point. Tel: Winchester (0962) 54411 ext 477.

Fees for vocational courses are fixed at county level, currently 47p per hour with a half rate for students under 18. Non-vocational fees are determined by the Institute Management Committee and thus vary from institute to institute. On average these work out at approximately 98p per hour. All institutes charge reduced non-vocational fees for young people and senior citizens and have discretion to waive or reduce fees for both vocational and non-vocational students in cases of hardship. All adult basic education, parent education and most courses for the disadvantaged are provided free of charge.

For more information contact the Further Education Division, Education Department, The Castle, Winchester (0962) 54411 ext 536 for general adult education; ext 477 for adult basic education.

Education Guidance Service for Adults

Southampton Educational Information Centre for Adults, c/o The Argyle Centre, Argyle Road, Southampton SO2 0BQ. Tel: (0703) 332676.

Basingstoke Technical College, Worting Road, Basingstoke RG21 1TN. Tel: (0256) 54141. *HE Prep, MS, DL.*

The College of Maritime Studies, Warsash, Southampton SO3 7ZL. Tel: (048 95) 6161. *HE, DL, PTHE.*

Cricklade College, Charlton Road, Andover SP10 1EJ. Tel: (0264) 63311. *DL.*

Eastleigh College of Further Education, Chestnut Avenue, Eastleigh SO5 5HT. Tel: (0703) 614444. *DL.*

Fareham Adult Education Centre, Wickham Road, Fareham. Tel: (0329) 280709.

Farnborough College of Technology, Boundary Road, Farnborough GU14 6SB. Tel: (0252) 515511. *DL.*

Highbury College of Technology, Dovercourt Road, Cosham, Portsmouth PO6 2SA. Tel: (0705) 383131. *DL, HE, EGS.*

King Alfred's College, Sparkford Road, Winchester SO22 4NR. Tel: (0962) 62281. *HE, PTHE, Occ.*

La Sainte Union College of Higher Education, The Avenue, Southampton SO9 5HB. Tel: (0703) 228761. *HE, PTHE.*

Portsmouth College of Art, Design and Further Education, Winston Churchill Avenue, Portsmouth PO1 2DJ. Tel: (0705) 826435. *DL, EGS.*

Portsmouth Polytechnic, Museum Road, Portsmouth PO1 2QQ. Tel: (0705) 827681. *HE, PTHE.*

Southampton Institute of Higher Education, East Park Terrace, Southampton SO9 4WW. Tel: (0703) 229381. *DL, Polymaths, HE, PTHE.*

Southampton Technical College, St Mary Street, Southampton SO9 4WX. Tel: (0703) 635222. *DL, EGS, HE Prep.*

University of Southampton, Southampton SO9 5NH. Tel: (0703) 559122. *HE, EM, NOW.*

South Downs College of Further Education, College Road, Purbrook Way, Havant. Tel: (070 14) 57011. *DL.*

The Tertiary College, Bishopsfield Road, Fareham PO14 1NH. Tel: (0329) 220844. *DL, HE Prep, NOW.*

Winchester School of Art, Park Avenue, Winchester SO23 8*DL*. Tel: (0962) 61891. *HE.*

Hereford and Worcester

Adult education in the county is organised through a mixture of institutes, centres and colleges. Some are school-based, others are centres administered by further education colleges. Fees, which are set at county level, work out at £11.50 per hour per week (for a 36 hour week) for vocational subjects and 75p an hour for non-vocational subjects. Basic education is free when the student is taught by a volunteer but costs 75p an hour when taught by paid staff. Concessions, again set at county level, are available to retired people and under 18s as well as others in cases of hardship.

Malvern Hill College is administered by the independent, voluntary trust, the Wyvern Trust.

Education Guidance Service for Adults

Education Guidance for Adults. EGSA for the county. Get in touch by phone. See *1 Advice and help*.

Evesham College of Further Education, Cheltenham Road, Evesham WR11 6LP. Tel: (0386) 41091. *DL.*

Herefordshire College of Agriculture, Holme Lacey, Hereford HR2 6LL. Tel: (043 273) 316. *DL.*

Herefordshire College of Art and Design, Folly Lane, Hereford HR1 1LT. Tel: (0432) 273359. *DL.*

Herefordshire Technical College, Folly Lane, Hereford HR1 1LS. Tel: (0432) 267311. *DL.*

Kidderminster College of Further Education, Hoo Road, Kidderminster DY10 1LX. Tel: (0562) 820811. *HE, DL, PTHE.*

Malvern Hills College for Adult Education, Albert Road North, Malvern WR14 2TW. Tel: (068 45) 65351. *EGS.*

North Worcestershire College, School Drive, Stratford Road, Bromsgrove B60 1BB. Tel: (0527) 79500. *DL, HE Prep.*

Pershore College of Horticulture, Avonbank, Pershore, Worcester. WR10 3JP. Tel: (0386) 552443. *DL.*

Redditch College, Peakman Street, Redditch B98 8DW. Tel: (0527) 63607/9 and 68221/2. *DL.*

Worcester College of Higher Education, Henwick Grove, Worcester WR2 6AJ. Tel: (0905) 428080. *HE, Occ, MS, PTHE.*

Worcester Technical College, Deansway, Worcester WR1 2JF. Tel: (0905) 723383. *DL, NOW.*

Worcestershire College of Agriculture, Hundlip, Worcester WR3 8SS. Tel: (0905) 51310. *DL.*

Hertfordshire

Adult education is a fully integrated part of the work of the county's further education colleges, where about half of all classes are run. The activities of other evening centres are administered through departments in further education colleges by full-time organisers. Fees (set by the county) work out at 47p an hour for vocational subjects and 94p for non-vocational subjects. Basic education is free. Guidelines for fee reductions are provided by the county, but colleges can also decide to reduce fees on the grounds of hardship. Reductions should be available for retired people, the unemployed, supplementary benefit claimants and the under 18s. About half of the centres arrange some form of child care provision.

WOW courses may be run in the county by Cambridge Training and Development (see Cambridgeshire).

Education Guidance Service for Adults

Educational Guidance for Adults, Hatfield Polytechnic, PO Box 109, Hatfield AL10 9AB. Tel: (070 72) 79499.

Cassio College, Langley Road, Watford WD1 3RH. Tel: (0923) 40311. *DL.*

Dacorum College, Marlowes, Hemel Hempstead HP1 1HD. Tel: (0442) 63771.*NOW.*

De Havilland College, The Campus, Welwyn Garden City, AL8 6AN. Tel: (0707) 326318. *DL, NOW.*

East Herts College, Turnford, Broxbourne EN10 6AF. Tel: (0992) 466451. *DL.*

Hatfield Polytechnic, PO Box 109, College Lane, Hatfield AL10 9AB. Tel:(070 72) 79490. *Polyphysics, NOW, HE, PTHE, EGS, MS, HE Prep, Occ, DL.*

Hertfordshire College of Agriculture and Horticulture, Oaklands, St Albans AL4 OJA. Tel: (0727) 50651. *ARC, MS.*

Hertfordshire College of Art and Design, 7 Hatfield Road, St Albans AL1 3RS. Tel: (0727) 64414. *HE, PTHE.*

Hertfordshire College of Building, St Peter's Road, St Albans AL1 3RX. Tel: (0727) 54273.

Hertfordshire College of Higher Education, Wall Hall, Aldenham, Watford WD2 8AT. Tel: (09276) 2511. *HE, Occ.*

North Herts College, Cambridge Road, Hitchin SG4 0JD. Tel: (0462) 32351 and at Letchworth. *DL, ILTU.*

St Albans College, 29 Hatfield Road, St Albans AL1 3RJ. Tel: (0727) 60423. *PTHE, HE Prep, MS, DL.*

Stevenage College, Monkswood Way, Stevenage SG1 1LA. Tel: (0438) 312822. *DL.*

Ware College, Scotts Road, Ware SG12 9JF. Tel: (0920) 5441. *DL.*

Watford College, Hempstead Road, Watford WD1 3EZ. Tel: (0923) 57500. *HE, DL.*

Humberside

Although some adult education provision is made by further education colleges, most courses are organised in school-based centres or in nine institutes of further education, in more than 200 locations throughout the county. A review of adult education is being undertaken, but at present, fees are set at county level and work out at 32p per hour for vocational subjects and 75p per hour for non-vocational courses. Basic literacy and numeracy teaching is free. Concessionary fees of £6 per term are available to retired or unemployed people, the under 18s, and disabled people without a full-time job and also to those on family income supplement and supplementary benefit. About a quarter of the centres have special facilities for disabled people and about a fifth organise some sort of child-care provision.

For more information, contact: The Director of Education, County Hall, Beverley, North Humberside, HU17 9BA. Tel: (0482) 867131.

Education Guidance Service for Adults

EGSA, c/o Careers Information Centre, Careers Office, Union Street, Albion Street, Hull HU2 8HB. Tel: (0482) 223081 ext 240.

Beverley College of Further Education, Gallows Lane, Beverley, North Humberside HU17 7DT. Tel: (0482) 869450. *HE Prep.*

Bishop Burton College of Agriculture, Beverley, North Humberside HU17 8QG. Tel: (0401) 50481.

Cottingham Institute of Further Education, Harland Way, Cottingham, North Humberside HU16 5PX. Tel: (0482) 842329.

East Yorkshire College of Further Education, West Street, St Mary's Walk, Bridlington, North Humberside YO16 5JW. Tel: (0262) 672676. *DL, EGS, MS, NOW.*

Grimsby College of Technology, Nuns Corner, Grimsby, South Humberside DN34 5BQ. Tel: (0472) 79292. *DL, HE Prep* (planned).

Hessle Institute of Further Education, Boothferry Road, Hessle, North Humberside HU13 9AR. Tel: (0482) 648600.

Hornsea Institute of Further Education, Eastgate, Hornsea HU18 1DW. Tel: (040 12) 3942.

Howden Institute of Further Education, Derwent Road, Howden DN14 7AL. Tel: (0430) 30131.

Hull College of Further Education, Queen's Gardens, Hull HU1 3DG. Tel: (0482) 29943. *HE Prep.*

Hull University, Hull HU6 7RX. Tel: (0482) 46311. *HE, EM, PTHE, Occ, NOW, MS.*

Humberside College of Higher Education, Cottingham Road, Hull HU6 7RT. Tel: (0482) 41451. *PTHE, DL, HE.*

Market Weighton Institute of Further Education, Spring Road, Market Weighton, York YO4 3JF. Tel: (0696) 73450.

North Lindsey College of Technology, Kingsway, Scunthorpe, South Humberside DN17 1AJ. Tel: (0724) 855022. *HE Prep.*

Pocklington Institute of Further Education, Kilnwick Road, Pocklington, York, Humberside YO4 2LL. Tel: (075 92) 2409.

South Holderness Institute of Further Education, Station Road, Preston, Hull HU12 8UZ. Tel: (0482) 897534.

South Hunsley Institute of Further Education, East Dale Road, Melton, North Ferriby HU14 3HS. Tel: (0482) 633162.

Swanland Adult Education Centre, Old School, Main Street, Swanland, North Ferriby HU14 3NE. Tel: (0482) 633559.

Withernsea Institute of Further Education, Hull Road, Withernsea, North Humberside HU19 2EQ. Tel: (096 42) 2750.

Isle of Wight

Non-vocational adult education is run through a department of the Isle of Wight College of Arts and Technology with classes held in the college itself and in local schools. The cost of classes works out at 80p an hour. Individual tuition using voluntary tutors is free of charge and where classes are run in the college the usual concessions on fees are available. The county council decides categories of students eligible for reduced fees (including retired people, unemployed people, the under 18s and hearing-impaired people) and the college determines the extent of the concession. The Isle of Wight also has a 'back to school' scheme for adults to study alongside children.

For more information, tel: (0983) 526631.

Isle of Wight College of Arts and Technology, Medina Way, Newport PO30 5TA. Tel: (0983) 526631. *DL.*

Isles of Scilly

The Isles' one secondary school in St Mary's acts as an evening centre for classes and various groups. Activities have to be self-financing although the council of the Isles of Scilly may provide a room, heating and lighting. The fee for groups of not less than eight people is £1 per hour.

For more information contact the Headmaster, St Mary's Secondary School. Tel: (0720) 22929.

Kent

Following a major countywide reorganisation in 1986 Kent is now operated on a six area basis. Adult education in non-vocational subjects is organised through 17 free-standing education centres. In addition to this the adult education service make use of approximately 50 schools in the county. Some of the centres are associated with schools or colleges, others are quite separate. Ten of the centres have playgroup or creche provision during the day and eight have wheelchair access and/or lifts or toilets for disabled people. The more vocational courses are provided by colleges. Fees in the centres are decided at county level and costs are approximately 50p for vocational subjects to 97p for the standard non-vocational rate. There are a wide range of concessions available to the unemployed and the retired. Basic education courses are free to students. Schools allow adults to study alongside children. The University of Kent at Canterbury, The School of Continuing Education and the WEA also hold classes on the authorities premises. The county has two residential colleges, Kingsgate House, Broadstairs and Eversley College, Folkestone, which are available for short residential courses for adults.

Education Guidance Service for Adults

The Open University, Wyvern House, 230/232 London Road, East Grinstead, West Sussex. Tel: (0342) 27821.

Ashford Adult Education Centre, Associate House, Queens Road, Ashford, Kent. Tel: (0233) 21768.

The Arts Centre, The New Metropole, The Leas, Folkestone, Kent. Tel: (0303) 55070.

Canterbury Christ Church College, North Holmes Road, Canterbury CT1 1QU. Tel: (0227) 65548. *HE, MS, PTHE.*

Canterbury College of Art, New Dover Road, Canterbury CT1 3AN. Tel: (0227) 469371. *HE.*

Canterbury College of Technology, New Dover Road, Canterbury CT1 3AJ. Tel: (0227) 66081. *DL.*

Dartford Adult Education Centre, East Hill House, East Hill Drive, Dartford, Kent. Tel: (0322) 21897.

Dover Adult Education Centre, Westmount, Folkestone Road, Dover, Kent. Tel: (0304) 202413.

Eversley College, Coolinge Lane, Folkestone, Kent. Tel: (0303) 58188. *SRC.*

Gillingham Adult Education Centre, Green Street, Gillingham, Kent. Tel: (0634) 50235. *NOW.*

Hadlow College of Agriculture and Horticulture, Hadlow, Nr Tonbridge, Kent TN11 OAL. Tel: (0732) 850551.

Hilderstone Adult Education Centre, St Peters Road, Broadstairs, Kent CT10 2AQ. Tel: (0843) 69171 (also at Margate and Ramsgate). *NOW.*

Kingsgate College, Convent Road, Broadstairs, Kent CT10 3PX. Tel: (0843) 61903. *SRC.*

Kent College for the Careers Service, College Road, Hextable, Swanley BR8 7RN. Tel: (0322) 64407.

Maidstone College of Art, Oakwood Park, Oakwood Road, Maidstone ME16 8AG. Tel: (0622) 57286. *HE.*

Medway Adult Education Centre, Eastgate, Rochester, Kent. Tel: (0634) 45359. *NOW.*

Medway College of Design, Fort Pitt, Rochester ME1 1DE. Tel: (0634) 44815. *HE, MS, Occ.*

Merchant Navy College, Greenhithe, Kent DA9 9NY. Tel: (0322) 845050. *DL.*

Mid-Kent Adult Education Centre, 9 Sittingbourne Road, Maidstone, Kent. Tel: (0622) 55808.

Mid-Kent College of Higher and Further Education, Horsted, Maidstone Road, Chatham ME5 9UQ. Tel: (0634) 44470. *HE, DL, PTHE.*

North West Kent College of Technology, Pelham Road, Gravesend DA11 0HN. Tel: (0474) 65233.

Sevenoaks Division Adult Education Centre, Swanley School, St Mary's Road, Swanley, Kent. Tel: (0322) 65869.

Sheppey Adult Education Centre, Shepping School, Minster Road, Minster, Sheerness, Kent. Tel: (0795) 875059.

South Kent Adult Education Service, Earlscliffe AEC, Shorncliffe Road, Folkestone, Kent CT20 2NB. Tel: (0303) 56537. *NOW.*

Sittingbourne College Adult Studies Centre, College Road, Sittingbourne ME10 1LF. Tel: (0795) 25124. *DL.*

South Kent College of Technology, Shorncliffe Road, Folkestone. Tel: (0303) 56661 (also centres at Dover and Ashford). *DL.*

Thanet Technical College, Ramsgate Road, Broadstairs CT10 1PN. Tel: (0843) 65111.

Tonbridge Adult Education Centre, Avebury Avenue, Tonbridge, Kent. Tel: (0732) 35413.

Tunbridge Wells Adult Education Centre, Monson Road, Tunbridge Wells TN1 1LS. Tel: (0892) 27317.

University of Kent at Canterbury, The Registry, Canterbury CT2 7NZ. Tel: (0227) 66822. *HE, EM, PTHE, Occ, NOW, MS.*

The Victoria Centre for Adult Education, Darnley Road, Gravesend, Kent. Tel: (0474) 534051/534026. *EGS.*

West Kent College of Further Education, Brook Street, Tonbridge TN9 2PW. Tel: (0732) 358101.

Wye College, University of London, Wye, Near Ashford TN25 5AH. Tel: (0233) 812401. *HE.*

Lancashire

Adult education classes are run by eight further education or tertiary colleges, and by five separate adult education centres. Who provides what, depends on which of the county's 12 adult education districts you live in. Classes are held in schools as well as the centres and colleges. Most adult courses cost about 85p an hour but basic education is provided free. Retired people and those under 18 pay only 40p an hour while unemployed people are charged no fee.
For further information ring Adult Education Department, County Hall, Preston. Tel: (0772) 54868.

Lancashire College of Adult Education is a purpose-built college offering a programme of residential courses for adults. Alston Hall also provides such courses in a country house setting.

Education Guidance Services for Adults

Stand 18, Nelson and Colne College, Scotland Road, Nelson, B69 6YT. Tel: (0282) 603151.

Accrington and Rossendale College, Sandy Lane, Accrington BB5 2AW. Tel: (0254) 35334. *Open College, DL.*

Adult Studies Division, Room 310, Glenburn School, Yewdale, Skelmersdale WN8 6LU. Tel: (0695) 22926.

Alston Hall Adult Residential College, Longridge, Preston PR3 3BP. Tel: (077 478) 3589. *SRC.*
Blackburn College, Feilden Street, Blackburn BB2 1LH. Tel: (0254) 55144. *DL, Open College.*
Blackpool and the Fylde College of Further and Higher Education, Ashfield Road, Bispham, Blackpool FY2 0HB. Tel: (0253) 52352 *DL, Open College.* Also Fleetwood Nautical Campus, Broadwater, Fleetwood DYZ 8JZ. Tel: (039 17) 29123. *DL.*
Burnley College, Shorey Bank, Off Ormerod Road, Burnley BB11 2RX. Tel: (0282) 36111. *ILTU, HE Prep, Open College.*
Edge Hill College of Higher Education, St Helens Road, Ormskirk L39 4QP. Tel: (0695) 75171. *NOW, Occ, HE, MS, PTHE.*
Lancashire College of Adult Education, Southport Road, Chorley, Lancs PR7 1NB. Tel: (025 72) 76719.
Lancashire College of Agriculture and Horticulture, Myerscough Hall, St Michaels Road, Bilsborrow, Preston PR3 ORY. Tel: (0995) 40611.
Lancashire Industrial Language Training Unit, 54/56 Blackburn Road, Accrington. Tel: (0254) 393317. *ILTU.*
Lancashire Polytechnic, Preston PR1 2TQ. Tel: (0772) 22141. *EM, HE, MS, Occ, PTHE, Polyphysics, EGS NOW, HE Prep.*
Lancaster and Morecambe College, Morecambe Road, Lancaster LA1 2TY. Tel: (0524) 66215. *DL, Open College.*
Lancaster College of Adult Education, St Leonards House, St Leonardgate, Lancaster LA1 1NN. Tel: (0524) 60141. *HE Prep, Open College.*
Lancaster University, University House, Lancaster LA1 4YW. Tel: (0524) 65201. *HE, EM, Occ, MS, PTHE, HE Prep, EGS.*
Runshaw Tertiary College, Longdale Road, Leyland, Preston PR5 2DQ. Tel: (0772) 432511. *NOW, DL, EGS.*
Nelson and Colne College, Scotland Road, Nelson BB9 7YT. Tel: (0282) 603151. *Open College, NOW, EGS, DL, PTHE.*
St Martin's College, Bowerham, Lancaster LA1 3JD. Tel: (0524) 63446. *HE, EM, MS, EGS.*
W.R.Tuson College, St Vincent's Road, Fulwood, Preston PR2 4UR. Tel: (0772) 716511. *Open College.*

Leicestershire

Most of the county's community education is run through 36 community colleges (some are listed below) and community centres. Some classes are run in the five further education colleges, adult education centres and Leicester College of Adult Education. Fees are set by the centres individually, but the average hourly rate is 65p almost everywhere. Some reductions are decided locally but throughout the county, a fee remission scheme is operated for the financially disadvantaged. Basic education is free, and though organised separately, runs in many colleges and centres. The county has a well-established 'back to school' scheme for adults.

For further information contact Education Offices, County Hall, Glenfield, Leicester. Tel: (0533) 871388.

The Beauchamp College, Ridge Way, Oadby, Leicester LE2 5TP. Tel: (0533) 715809.
The Bosworth College, Leicester Lane, Desford, Leicester LE9 9LJ. Tel: (045 57) 2910.
Brockington College, Mill Lane, Enderby, Leicester LE9 5LG. Tel: (0533) 867944/863722. *DL.*
Brooksby Agricultural College, Brooksby, Melton Mowbray, Leicester LE14 2LJ. Tel: (066 475) 291.
Charles Keene College of Further Education, Painter Street, Leicester LE1 3WA. Tel: (0533) 56037. *HE Prep, ILTU.*
Coalville Technical College, Bridge Road, Coalville, Leicester LE6 2QR. Tel: (0530) 36136.
Co-operative College, Stanford Hall, Loughborough, Leicester LE12 5QR. Tel: (050 928) 2333. *ARC.*
Hinckley College of Further Education, London Road, Hinckley LE10 1HQ. Tel: (0455) 632388. *DL.*
Leicester College of Adult Education, Wellington Street, Leicester. Tel: (0533) 545250.
Leicester Polytechnic, PO Box 143, Leicester LE1 9BH. Tel: (0533) 551551. *HE, PTHE.*

Leicester University, University Road, Leicester LE1 7RH. Tel: (0533) 522522. *HE, EM, MS, PTHE.*

Loughborough College of Art and Design, Radmoor, Loughborough LE11 3BT. Tel: (0509) 261515. *HE.*

Loughborough Technical College, Radmoor, Loughborough LE11 3BT. Tel: (0509) 215831. *NOW, DL.*

Loughborough University of Technology, Loughborough LE11 3TU. Tel: (0509) 263171. *HE, EM, PTHE.*

Lutterworth Community College, Bitteswell Road, Lutterworth, Leicester LE17 4EW. Tel: (045 55) 4103.

Melton Mowbray College of Further Education, Asfordby Road, Melton Mowbray LE13 0HJ. Tel: (0664) 67431. *MS, NOW, DL.*

South Fields College of Further Education, Aylestone Road, Leicester LE2 7LW. Tel: (0533) 541818. *DL.*

Vaughan College, St Nicholas Circle, Leicester LE1 4LB. Tel: (0533) 571368. *EM.*

Wigston College of Further Education, Station Road, Wigston Magna, Leicester LE8 2DW. Tel: (0533) 885051. *DL.*

Lincolnshire

Eleven full-time area tutors organise most adult education in the county, six are based in schools, four in colleges and one in a separate adult centre (in Louth). Almost three-quarters of the classes are held in schools, others in village halls and colleges. Fees (which are set at county level) work out at below 50p an hour for vocational courses and 96p an hour for courses in non-vocational subjects. Initial basic education is free. People under 18, and those on MSC schemes are entitled to reduced fees as are retired people and people on supplementary or unemployment benefit. The county also runs Horncastle Residential College offering short courses for adults.

For more information, contact: The County Education Office, Newland, Lincoln. Tel: (0522) 29931.

Education Guidance Service for Adults

Educational Guidance Service, Castlegate Centre, Castlegate, Grantham NG31 9AP. Tel: (0476) 66273.

Bishop Grosseteste College, Newport, Lincoln LN1 3DY. Tel: (0522) 27347. *HE.*

Boston College of Further Education, Rowley Road, Boston PE21 6JF. Tel: (0205) 65701. *DL.*

Gainsborough College of Further Education, Morton Terrace, Gainsborough DN21 2SU. Tel: (0427) 2942. In September 1987, this college will be amalgamated with Lincoln College of Technology to produce North Lincolnshire College.

Grantham College of Further Education, Stonebridge Road, Grantham NG31 9AP. Tel: (0476) 63141. *DL, EGS, NOW.*

Horncastle Residential College, Mareham Road, Horncastle LN9 6BW. Tel: (065 82) 2449. *SRC.*

Lincoln College of Technology, Cathedral Street, Lincoln LN2 5HQ. Tel: (0522) 30641. *DL.* See Gainsborough College of Further Education.

Lincolnshire College of Art and Design, Lindum Road, Lincoln LN2 1NP. Tel: (0522) 23268.

Louth Adult Education Centre, James Street, Louth. Tel: (0507) 603784.

Stamford College, Drift Road, Stamford PE9 1XA. Tel: (0780) 64141.

LONDON – GREATER

Education Guidance Service for Adults

BBC Radio London, Education Advice Line, 35a Marylebone High Street, London W1A 4LG. Tel: (01) 486 7040. Open year round on Thursday 3.00 to 5.00 pm. Ask for: Patsy Brown.

Barking and Dagenham

Adult education in the borough is organised through Barking College of Adult Education, which has eight branches sharing school buildings for evening courses only, plus it's own purpose-adapted premises at its headquarters and a further branch where both day and evening courses are offered. Fees work out at around 45p an hour with concessions available for the retired and unemployed, low income groups, as well as under 18s. Basic education is integrated with other adult education. There is also a 'drop-in literacy' scheme run over the summer months. Child care provision is organised at the college headquarters.

For more information, contact: The Principal, Barking College of Adult Education, Fanshawe Crescent, Dagenham, Essex. Tel: (01) 595 3237/8.

Barking College of Technology, Dagenham Road, Romford RM7 0XU. Tel: (0708) 66841. *DL.*
North East London Polytechnic, Barking Precinct, Longbridge Road, Dagenham, Essex RM8 2AS. Tel: (01) 590 7722. or West Ham Precinct, Romford Road, London E15 4LZ.

Barnet

Adult education in the borough is organised as an integral part of further education. Classes are held in Barnet and Hendon colleges as well as other centres. Fees are 32p an hour for vocational courses and 85p an hour for non-vocational ones. Basic education is free. Fee concessions are usually available to retired, unemployed and disabled people, anyone on supplementary benefit and also the under 18s (for vocational classes only).

Barnet College of Further Education, Wood Street, Barnet, Herts EN5 4AZ. Tel: (01) 440 6321. *DL*
Hampstead Garden Suburb Institute, Central Square, London NW11 7BN. Tel: (01) 455 9951 and (01) 458 5669.
Hendon College of Further Education, Corner Mead, Grahame Park Way, Colindale NW9 5RA. Tel: (01) 200 8300. *DL* (business studies).
Jew's College, 44a Albert Street, Hendon, London NW4. Tel: (01) 203 6427. *HE, MS, Occ.*

Bexley

There are four exclusive use adult centres in Bexley and eight evening centres. Fees are fixed at borough level with some concessions for second and subsequent enrolments. Free or concessionary enrolment is available to the unemployed, pensioners, handicapped and single parents. Basic literacy and numeracy teaching is provided free. Some child care provision is available.

For more information, contact: LC Martin, Principal Assistant Further Education Officer, Town Hall, Crayford DA1 4EN. Tel: (01) 303 7777 ext 559.

For information about basic education, contact: Mrs R Hambrook at Crayford Manor Centre (see below). Specific provision for the unemployed, linked with a guidance unit is now available.

For more information contact the Adult Education Development Officer, Gerry Smith at Erith College (see below).

Bexley Adult Education Centre, 5 Brampton Road, Bexleyheath, Kent DA7 4EZ. Tel: (01) 303 2541. *NOW.*
Crayford Manor House Adult Education Centre, Mayplace Road East, Crayford, Kent DA1 4HB. Tel: (0322) 521463.
Erith College of Technology, Tower Road, Belvedere, Kent DA17 6JA. Tel: (032 24) 42331. *PTHE, ILTU.*
Lamorbey Park Adult Education Centre, Burnt Oak Lane, Sidcup, Kent DA15 9BY. Tel: (01) 300 3054. *EM.*
Rose Bruford College of Speech and Drama, Lamorbey Park, Sidcup DA15 9DF. Tel: (01) 300 3024. *HE.*
Sidcup Arts Centre, Grassington Road, Sidcup, Kent DA14 9BY. Tel: (01) 300 1056.

Brent

In Brent there are four main centres providing adult education, two adult and community education centres and two community schools. Fees are standard for all courses including basic education – £15 per year per course (or pro rata per term). Fees are waived for registered disabled students, those on supplementary benefit, pensioners, the long-term unemployed (over eight months), students under 18 and students still living with unemployed or retired parents.

For more information contact: The Further Education Advisory Officer, Education Offices, PO Box 1, Chesterfield House, 9 Park Lane, Wembley, Middlesex HA9 7RW. Tel: (01) 900 5421.

Brent Industrial Language Training Unit, Ashley Gardens, Preston Road, Wembley, Middlesex HA9 8NP. Tel: (01) 908 1708 and 2095. *ILTU.*

Kilburn Polytechnic, Priory Park Road NW6 1YB. Tel: (01) 328 8241.

Willesden College of Technology, Denzil Road NW10 2XD. Tel: (01) 451 3411. *DL, NOW.*

Bromley

Adult education classes are held in adult education premises, schools and rented halls. Course fees are approximately 85p per hour for a basic course and 43p per hour for old aged pensioners and reduced fees may be granted at the discretion of the principal. There is no fee for basic education.

For more information, ring: (01) 464 3333 ext 4516.

Bromley Adult Education Service, Aylesbury Road, Bromley, Kent.. Tel: (01) 460 8812 or (01) 464 5745.

Bromley College of Technology, Rookery Lane, Bromley Common, Kent BR2 8HE. Tel: (01) 462 6331. *DL.*

Orpington College of Further Education, The Walnuts, High Street, Orpington, Kent BR6 0T2. Tel: (0689) 39336. *DL.*

Ravensbourne College of Design and Communication, Walden Road, Chislehurst BR7 5SN. Tel: (01) 468 7071. *HE.*

Croydon

There are two day/evening and seven evening centres, all entirely separate to Croydon College, and under the aegis of an organiser at the Education Department, Taberner House, Park Lane, Croydon CR9 1TP. Tel: (01) 760 5461. Special provision is also made for adult basic literacy and numeracy and for English as a second language. Fee levels vary, with various concessions available, but many are in the region of 60p per hour.

Coombe Cliff Adult Education Centre, Coombe Cliff, Coombe Road, Croydon, Surrey CR0 5SP. Tel: (01) 686 9191. *DL, PTHE, HE Prep, EM.*

Croydon College, College Road, Fairfield, Croydon, Surrey CR9 1DX. Tel: (01) 686 5700. *EGS, HE, PTHE, DL.*

South Norwood Adult Education Centre, 194 Selhurst Road, London SE25. Tel: (01) 656 0905. *DL, EM.*

Spurgeon's College, South Norwood Hill SE25 6DJ. Tel: (01) 653 0850. *HE, MS* only, *PTHE.*

Ealing

Most adult education classes in the borough are held in local schools and are set up by one of two area organisers. Fees vary with the length of class between £15 and £30 a year, with concessions for vocational courses. Fee reductions are available to retired people, under 18s and disabled people. There is no charge to the unemployed or their dependents. Basic education fees are £2 a year – no charge to the unemployed or their dependents.

Acton Technical College, Mill Hill Road, Acton W3 8UX. Tel: (01) 993 2344. *DL, HE Prep.*

Ealing College of Higher Education, St Mary's Road, Ealing W5 5RF. Tel: (01) 579 4111. *HE, MS, Occ, PTHE.*

Norwood Hall Institute of Horticultural Education, Norwood Green, Southall, Middlesex UB2 4LA. Tel: (01) 574 2261.

Pathway Further Education Centre, Havelock Road, Southall, Middlesex UB2 4NZ. Tel: (01) 571 2241. *ILTU, NOW.*

Southall College of Technology, Beaconsfield Road, Southall, Middlesex UB1 1DP. Tel: (01) 574 3448. *NOW.*

Enfield

Adult education is integrated within the borough's further education system and classes are held in colleges, schools and other establishments. Courses are organised by Enfield College of Further Education through six area offices. A two thirds reduction is made for students receiving state retirement pension, the registered unemployed and disabled. For students under 18, the fees are halved. Adult literacy and numeracy are organised by the college and based at Ponders End Library, College Court, High Street EN3 4EY. Tel: (01) 805 5855.

The borough also runs Theobalds Park College which organises short residential courses for adults.

Capel Manor Horticultural and Environmental Centre, Bullsmoor Lane, Waltham Cross, Herts. EN7 5HR. Tel: (0992) 763849. *DL, MS.*

Enfield College, 73 Hertford Road, Enfield. Tel: (01) 443 3434. *ILTU, DL, EGS, HE Prep* (planned), *NOW.*

Middlesex Polytechnic, 114 Chase Side, Southgate N14 5PN. Tel: (01) 886 6599. *MS, HE, Occ, PTHE.*

Oak Hill College, Chase Side, Southgate N14 4PS. Tel: (01) 449 0467. *HE, Occ, MS.*

Southgate Technical College, High Street, Southgate N14 6BS. Tel: (01) 886 6521. *NOW, Occ, PTHE.*

Theobalds Park College, Bulls Cross Ride, Waltham Cross, Herts EN7 5HW. Tel: (0992) 37255. *SRC.*

Haringey

The two colleges of further education provide a number of courses for adults in a wide range of disciplines. The course lengths vary from eight weeks to a year. Special arrangements are made for women and members of ethnic minority groups. The adult education service concentrates on recreation and leisure classes, with some examination courses. It also encompasses the borough's adult literacy service and provides part-time ESL courses. ESL courses with a vocational bias are offered at Haringey College. Opportunities for adults are listed in college prospectuses, and are summarised in the publication *Learning for living*, distributed, free of charge, throughout Haringey in September of each year.

For information about English as a second language, tel: (01) 348 3028.

For information about adult literacy, tel: (01) 348 6600.

Education Guidance Service for Adults

Haringey Adult Education Service, White Hart Lane Centre, Wood Green N22 5SJ. Tel: (01) 888 0952.

Haringey College, Park Road, Bounds Green, London N11 2QF. Tel: (01) 888 7123.

Haringey Women's Training and Education Centre, Lordship Lane, London N17. Tel: (01) 801 6233. *Women's TW.*

Tottenham College of Technology, High Road, Tottenham N15 4RU. Tel: (01) 802 3111. *HE Prep.*

Harrow

All adult education in the borough is provided through Harrow College of Further Education largely through its department of adult studies. Classes are held in the college itself (which runs a playgroup) and also in other premises throughout the borough. In September 1987 the authority is reorganising all post-16 education and from that date courses currently run by Harrow College of Further Education will be transferred to Directorates of Adult and Continuing Education in three new colleges. Vocational courses cost 32p per hour for non-advanced courses and 50p for advanced courses. Non-vocational courses are 73p per hour. A nominal fee of £1.50 per term is charged to part-time students of literacy, numeracy, English for speakers of other languages and to disabled students and their helpers. An additional £1 registration fee is charged for each course. Pensioners and those in receipt of certain state welfare benefits pay 25% of standard fees.

Elm Park College (from 1 September 1987), Elm Park, Stanmore, Middlesex HA7 4BQ. Tel: (01) 954 0961. *DL* (planned), *HE Prep.*

Greenhill College (from 1 September 1987), Lowlands Road, Harrow, Middlesex HA1 3AQ. Tel: (01) 422 2388. *DL* (planned), *HE Prep, NOW* (planned).

Harrow College of Further Education, Uxbridge Road, Hatch End, Pinner, Middlesex HA5 4EA. Tel: (01) 428 0121. *HE Prep.*

Harrow College of Higher Education, Northwick Park, Watford Road, Harrow, Middlesex HA1 3TP. Tel: (01) 864 5422. *HE, PTHE.*

Weald College (from 1 September 1987), Brookshill, Harrow, Middlesex HA3 6RP. Tel: (01) 954 0671. *DL* (planned), *HE Prep, NOW* (planned).

Havering

The Havering College of Adult Education provides a programme of day and evening courses at various centres throughout the borough. It works closely with the Havering Technical College to blur the vocational/non-vocational divide. Adults are encouraged to study alongside sixth form pupils. There are also close links with the youth and community service and the social services department etc. The standard hourly fee in the academic year 1986/87 is 80p. The concessionary fee for senior citizens not in receipt of supplementary pension or other qualifying benefit is 34p. The lower concessionary fee is 26p. The fees and concessions policy is authority wide, although the principal has power to waive fees in cases of financial harship. Basic education (literacy, numeracy etc) is an integral part of the adult education programme and is available at the lower concessionary fee.

Contact Miss J Webb Tel: (040 24) 45798.

For general enquiries about the Havering College of Adult Education, tel: (040 24) 40832 or 53242. A programme of courses is freely available on request either by phone or in writing to the principal.

Havering College of Adult Education, Headquarters Office, Dury Falls Campus, Wingletye Lane, Hornchurch, Essex RM11 3TB. Tel: (040 24) 40832 and 53242.

Havering Technical College, Ardleigh Green Road, Hornchurch, Essex RM11 2LL. Tel: (040 24) 55011. *PTHE, DL.*

Hillingdon

In addition to classes at the technical college, classes in the borough are run through eleven adult education centres – five of which are full-time adult centres, the remainder being part-time school-based centres. Five centres have special facilities for disabled people and three arrange some kind of regular child care. Classes cost approximately £48 for a 28-week, one night a week course, with reductions available to retired, unemployed or disabled people and those under 18. Adult literacy teaching is charged at a special rate of £10 for the course, and English as a second language classes at £16 for the course.

All enquiries to: Adult Education Office, 86 Long Lane, Ickenham, Middlesex UB10 8SX. Tel: (0895) 676690.

Brunel University, Uxbridge UB8 3PH. Tel: (0895) 74000. *DL, HE, MS, EM.*

London Bible College, Green Lane, Northwood, Middlesex HA6 2UW. Tel: (09274) 26061. *DL, HE.*

Uxbridge Technical College, Park Road, Uxbridge UB8 1NQ. Tel: (0895) 30411. *DL, NOW.*

Hounslow

Adult education works closely with the youth community, sports halls and community schools, to provide a comprehensive service for Hounslow. Twelve centres organise classes, some of which are held in separate premises, most in schools (some of which allow adult students to work alongside children). All centres are accessible to students in wheelchairs. The cost of classes works out at under 40p an hour with reductions available to people receiving state benefits (widows or retirement pensions, unemployment or supplementary benefit etc) and to the under 18s. Basic education costs about 8p an hour.

The borough has established an Open Learning Unit to advise on most open learning systems. Details from the Assistant Education Officer (FE), Civic Centre, Lampton Road, Hounslow.

For more information contact: Spring Grove Centre, Thornbury Road, Isleworth, Middlesex *TW7* 4HG. Tel: (01) 568 3697.

Cranford Community School, High Street, Cranford, Middlesex. *TW5* 9PD. Tel: (01) 897 2001. *DL.*

Hounslow Borough College, London Road, Isleworth, Middlesex TW7 4HS. Tel: (01) 568 0244.

West London Institute of Higher Education, Gordon House, 300 St Margarets Road, Twickenham, Middlesex *TW1* 1PT. Tel: (01) 891 0121. *HE, HE Prep, PTHE, MS.*

Kingston upon Thames

The Adult Education Service in Kingston has three day and five evening centres with a central office at the Guildhall. The cost of courses ranges from 75p to 98p per hour with adult literacy and basic education charged at 22p per hour. Fee reductions are available to unemployed, retired or disabled people and the under 18's.

For more information contact: Guildhall II, Kingston upon Thames. Tel: (01) 546 2121 ext 2615/6.

Hillcroft College, South Bank, Surbiton, Surrey KT6 6DF. Tel: (01) 399 2688. *ARC.*
King Athelstan Centre, Villiers Road, Kingston upon Thames. Tel: (01) 546 3729.
King Charles Centre, Hollyfield Road, Surbiton. Tel: (01) 399 8180.
Kingston College of Further Education, Kingston Hall Road, Kingston upon Thames, Surrey KT1 2AQ. Tel: (01) 546 2151.
Kingston Polytechnic, Penrhyn Road, Kingston upon Thames, Surrey KT1 2EE. Tel: (01) 549 1366. *HE, PTHE, Occ.*
Maulden Main Centre, Cocks Crescent, Blagdon Road, New Maulden, Surrey. Tel: (01) 942 9639.

Merton

Merton Institute of Adult Education provides non-vocational courses throughout the borough while the technical college deals with vocational work. About half of the classes are organised in separate adult education premises, the remainder are run in schools, community centres and other locations (such as old people's homes). Fees work out at about 80p per hour and the unemployed, retired or registered disabled qualify for reduced fees as do the under 18s. Basic education costs £1 per course.

For more information, contact the Institute.

Merton Institute of Adult Education, Whatley Avenue, London SW20. Tel: (01) 543 9292. *NOW.*
Merton College, Morden Park, London Road, Morden, Surrey SM4 5QX. Tel: (01) 640 3001. *HE Prep.*
Wimbledon School of Art, Merton Hall Road SW19 3QA. Tel: (01) 540 0231. *HE.*

Newham

Adult education is organised by departments in Newham Community College. Classes are run in the three centres linked to the college (Little Ilford, Canning Town and Barclay Hall) as well as in local schools. Fees for classes work out at around £1 a week with reductions available to those resident in Newham who are under 18, retired, unemployed or registered disabled. Basic education is free of charge to these groups. The borough also runs Debden House in Loughton as a residential college offering short courses to adults.

Newham Community College, East Ham Centre, High Street South, East Ham, London E6 4ER. Tel: (01) 472 1480. or West Ham Centre, Welfare Road, Stratford, London E15 4HT. Tel: (01) 555 1422. *DL, HE Prep, MS, NOW.*
Industrial Language Training Unit, Room 24, London Borough of Newham, The Chief Executive's Department, East Ham Town Hall, London E6 2RP. Tel: (01) 470 8176 ext 3475/3476.
Newham Parents Centre, 745–747 Barking Road, Plaistow E13. Tel: (01) 472 2000. *Drop-in Centre* (literacy).

Redbridge

Redbridge Institute of Adult Education organises more than 300 classes throughout the borough in schools, community centres and halls. Fees for non-vocational subjects are £55.70 for one year for over 18s and £27.85 for under 18s. Fees for vocational subjects are £35.40 for one year for over 18s and £17.70 for under 18s. Basic education costs 50% of the non-vocational cost. Reduced fees are available to retired, unemployed or disabled people and for those joining second non-vocational classes.

For more information, contact the Institute.

Redbridge Institute of Adult Education, Valentines High School (Upper), Cranbrook Road, Ilford, Essex IG2 6HX. Tel: (01) 554 6727 and 4400.
Redbridge Technical College, Littleheath, Romford RM6 4XT. Tel: (01) 599 5231. *DL.*

Richmond

Richmond Adult and Community College is the main provider of adult education in the borough offering classes in centres, schools and halls. At present, fees work out in the 85p to £1 an hour range. Adult basic education is free. Fee reductions are available to retired, unemployed or disabled people as well as those under 18. The full-time centres at Clifden and Parkshot have special facilities for disabled people and child care provision.

For more information, contact the Richmond Adult and Community College (see below).

Richmond Adult and Community Centre, The Clifden Centre, Clifden Road, Twickenham, Middlesex. Tel: (01) 891 5907 *EGS.*
Richmond Adult College, Parkshot, Richmond, Surrey TW9 2FE. Tel: (01) 940 5278. *DL, NOW.*
Richmond-upon-Thames Tertiary College, Egerton Road, Twickenham TW2 7SJ. Tel: (01) 892 6656. *DL, PTHE, MS, NOW.*
St Mary's College, Strawberry Hill, Twickenham, Middlesex TW1 4SX. Tel: (01) 892 0051. *HE.*

Sutton
The centre for adult studies in the borough is Sutton College of Liberal Arts (SCOLA) which runs about half of its classes on its own premises (accessible to wheelchair users) and half in local schools. Course fees work out at around 80p an hour for most courses. O- and A-level classes at Carshalton College work out at around 30p an hour. Initial literacy tuition is free but beyond this, basic education costs about 33p an hour. Retired or unemployed people are entitled to fee reductions and others who find it hard to pay full fees may be eligible.

For more information, contact Carshalton College of FE (see below).

Carshalton College of Further Education, Nightingale Road, Carshalton, Surrey SM5 2EJ. Tel: (01) 647 0021.
Sutton College of Liberal Arts, St Nicholas' Way, Sutton, Surrey SM1 1EA. Tel: (01) 661 5067.

Waltham Forest
The borough's adult education service is organised in nine centres (four of which arrange regular child care provision). Five of the centres are school-based; the others are separate. Fees for 30-week courses are £23, shorter courses are proportionately less. Within the basic education section there are second chance opportunities from basic skills work to Fresh Start courses. These are arranged on a part-time basis ranging from a few hours to substantial, structured, part-time courses. All courses are free within this section. Open learning opportunities (which includes flexistudy) is an option. Further details on request. For enquiries relating to the borough adult education service, contact: Community and Further Education Branch, Graylaw House, 394 High Road, Leyton, London E10 6QE. Tel: (01) 527 5544; for enquiries specifically relating to the Basic Education Section, contact: Chestnuts House, 398 Hoe Street, London E17 9BR. Tel: (01) 521 4311.

North East London Polytechnic, Holbrook Road, London E15 4LZ. Tel: (01) 590 7722. *HE, EM, PTHE, MS, NOW.*
Waltham Forest College, Forest Road E17 4JB. Tel: (01) 527 2311/ 2268/9. *HE Prep.*
YMCA National College, 642a Forest Road, Walthamstow, London E17 3EF. Tel: (01) 520 5599. *DL.*

LONDON – INNER

Education in the Inner London boroughs is provided by the Inner London Education Authority (ILEA). Part-time day and evening classes are organised by adult education institutes (AEIs) which each have a headquarters and a number of branches, many of which are school-based, or centres together with detached classes. Many centres offering daytime courses will have some kind of child care provision. The cost of adult education courses in Inner London works out at about 43p an hour. Students not resident in an ILEA borough are charged one and a half times the normal fee and no concessions are available. ILEA residents who are retired, unemployed, deaf or under 18 pay £1 for any number of courses as do students doing basic education courses or people claiming supplementary benefit or family income supplement.

Information about which adult education course is running where can be found in *Floodlight*, an annual guide available in libraries or from newsagents and bookstalls price 50p.

Education Guidance Services for Adults
Camden Adult Learning Advice (CALA), 58 Phoenix Road, London NW1 1EU. Tel: (01) 388 4666.

Greenwich Education and Training Advice Centre (GRETA), 12/14 Wellington Street, Woolwich, London SE18 6PF. Tel: (01) 854 2993.
Hackney Education Advice Service, Edith Cavell School, Enfield Road, London N1 5AZ. Tel: (01) 254 4180.
Hammersmith And Fulham Education and Training Advice for Adults, 241 King Street, London W6 9LP. Tel: (01) 741 8441.
Education Advice Service for Islington Adults (EASIA), 12 Barnsbury Road, Islington NW1 0HB. Tel: (01) 278 3761/2.
Kensington and Chelsea Learning Advice for Adults, 51 Golborne Road, W10 5NR. Tel: (01) 968 8532.
Lambeth Educational Opportunities (LEO), 166a Stockwell Road, London SW9. Tel: (01) 733 3155.
Open College of South London, Manor House, 58 Clapham Common, North Side, London. Tel: (01) 228 2015. DL.
Information and Advice Network on Southwark Education and Training (INSET), 175 Rye Lane, Peckham, London SE15 4TL. Tel: (01) 635 9111.
Tower Hamlets Education Advice Ltd (THEA), The Education Shop, 75 Roman Road, London E2. Tel: (01) 981 3164.
Wandsworth Education Shop, 86 Battersea Rise, London SW11 1EJ. Tel: (01) 350 1790.
Westminster Educational Advice, Beauchamp Lodge, 2 Warwich Crescent W2 6NE. Tel: (01) 289 0339. It is hoped that the project will be moving to: 36 Church St, London NW8.

Architectural Association School of Architecture, 34/36 Bedford Square WC1B 3ES. Tel: (01) 636 0974. *HE.*
Avery Hill College, Bexley Road, Eltham SE9 2PQ. Tel: (01) 850 0081. *HE, HE Prep.*
The Bookplace, 13 Peckham High Street, London SE15. Tel: (01) 701 1757. *Drop-In Centre.*
British School of Osteopathy, 1/4 Suffolk Street SW1V 4HG. Tel: (01) 930 9254.
Brixton College, 56 Brixton Hill SW2 1QS. Tel: (01) 737 1166. *DL.*
Brixton Women's Motor Mechanic Project (see Women's Motor Mechanic Workshop Ltd)
The Byam Shaw School of Art, 70 Campden Street W8 7EN. Tel: (01) 727 4711. *HE.*
Camden Adult Education Institute, 87 Holmes Road, NW5 3AX. Tel: (01) 267 1414.
Camden Training Centre, 57 Pratt Street, London NW1. Tel: (01) 482 2103. *TW.*
The Central Institute of Adult Education, Longford Street, London NW1. Tel: (01) 388 7106.
Central School of Art and Design, Southampton Row WC1B 4AP. Tel: (01) 405 1825. *HE.*
Central School of Speech and Drama, Embassy Theatre, 64 Eton Avenue NW3 3HY. Tel: (01) 722 8183. *HE.*
Centre for Clinical Communication Studies, The City University, Northampton Square, London EC1V 0HB. Tel: (01) 253 4399 ext. 4607 and 4612. *HE, MS.*
Charlton Training Centre, Westminster Industrial Estate, Ferrant's Close, off Westfield Street, Woolwich, London SE18 5TU. Tel: (01) 317 9636. *TW.*
Chelsea School of Art, Manresa Road SW3 6LS. Tel: (01) 351 3844. *HE.*
City and East London College, Pitfield Street N1 6BX or Bunhill Row EC1. Tel: (01) 638 4171. *DL, HE Prep.*
The City and Guilds of London Art School, 124 Kennington Park Road SE11 4DJ. Tel: (01) 735 2306.
New Central for Adult Education (formerly The City Lit Centre for Adult Studies), Stukeley Street, Drury Lane WC2B 5LJ. Tel: (01) 242 9872. *EM, DL, HE Prep.*
City of London Polytechnic, 31 Jewry Street EC3N 2EY. Tel: (01) 283 1030. *HE, MS, Occ, PTHE.*
City University, Northampton Square EC1V OHB. Tel: (01) 253 4399. *EM, HE, HE Prep, Occ.*
Clapham/Battersea Adult Education Institute, 6 Edgeley Road, London SW4 6EL. Tel: (01) 622 2965.
The College for the Distributive Trades, 30 Leicester Square WC2H 7LE. Tel: (01) 839 1547.
Cordwainers Technical College, Mare Street, Hackney E8 3RE. Tel: (01) 985 0273.
Fulham Chelsea Institute, Beaufort House School, Lillie Road SW6 1UF. Tel: (01) 385 6166, or (01) 589 2044.
Garnett College, Downshire House, Roehampton Lane SW15 4HR. Tel: (01) 7896533. *HE, MS.*
Guildhall School of Music and Drama, Barbican EC2Y 8DT. Tel: (01) 628 2571. *HE.*

Hackney Adult Education Institute, Chelmer Road E9 6BZ. Tel: (01) 533 2426.

Hackney College, Kelton House, 89/115 Mare Street E8 4RG. Tel: (01) 985 8484. *HE Prep.*

Hammersmith and North Kensington Adult Education Institute, Wornington Road, W10 5QQ. Tel: (01) 969 4171.

Hammersmith and West London College, Gliddon Road, Barons Court, London W14 9BL. Tel: (01) 741 1688. *HE Prep.*

Hammersmith Neighbourhood Literacy Scheme, 31, Fulham Palace Road, London W6. Tel: (01) 741 2660. *Drop-in Centre.*

Holborn Law Tutors, 200 Greyhound Road, London W14 9RY. Tel: (01) 385 3377. *DL, HE, Occ, PTHE.*

Islington Adult Education Institute, Jack Ashley Buildings, 3 Prah Road, London N4 2RA. Tel: (01) 354 0303. *ILTU.*

Kentish Town Women's Workshop, 169 Malden Road NW5. Tel: (01) 267 0688. *Women's TW.*

Kingsway-Princeton College, Sidmouth Street, Gray's Inn Road WC1H 8JB. Tel: (01) 837 8185. *DL, HE Prep.*

Laban Centre for Movement and Dance, University of London, Goldsmith's College, New Cross SE14 6NW. Tel: (01) 692 4070. *HE.*

Lambeth Adult Education Institute, Strand Centre, Elm Park, SW2 2EH. Tel: (01) 737–1234.

Lambeth Women's Workshop Unit C22, Park Hall Trading Estate, Martell Road, West Norwood. Tel: (01) 670 0339. *Women's TW.*

Lee Community Education Centre, 1 Aislibie Road, London SE12. Tel: (01) 852 4700.

Lewisham Women's Training Centre Ltd, 78b Blackheath Hills, London SE10. *Women's TW.*

The London Academy of Music and Dramatic Art, Tower House, 226 Cromwell Road SW5 O5R. Tel: (01) 373 9883.

London Business School, Sussex Place, Regent's Park, London NW1 4SA. Tel: (01) 262 5050. *HE, PTHE.*

London College of Fashion, 20 St John Prince's Street W1M 9HE. Tel: (01) 629 9401.

London College of Furniture, 41/71 Commercial Road E1 1LA. Tel: (01) 247 1953.

London College of Music, 47 Great Marlborough Street W1V 2AS. Tel: (01) 437 6120. *HE.*

London College of Printing, Elephant and Castle SE1 6SB. Tel: (01) 735 8484. *HE.*

London Contemporary Dance School, 16 Flaxman Terrace, London WC1H 9AT. Tel: (01) 387 0152/0161. *HE, MS.*

The London Foot Hospital and School of Chiropody, Fitzroy Square W1P 6AY. Tel: (01) 636 0602.

The London Institute, Camberwell School of Art and Crafts, Peckham Road SE5 8UF. Tel: (01) 703 0987. *HE.*

London International Film School, 24 Shelton Street WC2H 9HP. Tel: (01) 240 0168. *HE.*

Mary Ward Centre, 42 Queen Square, London WC1N 3AG. Tel: (01) 831 7711.

Marylebone/Paddington Adult Education Institute, Amberley Adult Centre, Amberley Road W9. Tel: (01) 286 1900.

Montefiore Community Education Centre, Deal Street, Hanbury Street, E1 5JB. Tel: (01) 247 5028.

Morley College, 61 Westminster Bridge Road SE1 7HT. Tel: (01) 928 8501. *NOW.*

North London College, 444 Camden Road, London N7 0SP. Tel: (01) 609 9981. *NOW, HE Prep.*

Paddington College, 25 Paddington Green W2 1NB. Tel: (01) 402 6221. *HE Prep, DL.*

Polytechnic of Central London, 309 Regent Street WIR 8AL. Tel: (01) 580 2020. *HE, PTHE, EM.*

Polytechnic of North London, Holloway Road N7 8DB. Tel: (01) 607 2789. *HE, PTHE, MS, Occ.*

Information and Advice Network on Southwark Educational Training (INSET), 175 Rye Lane, Peckham, London SE15 4TL. Tel: (01) 635 9111.

Putney and Wandsworth Adult Education Institute, Manrese House, Holybourne Avenue SW15. Tel: (01) 789 8255/6.

Ravensbourne Institute, Crofton School, Ewhurst Road, Brockley SE4 1AG. Tel: (01) 690 0720.

Roehampton Institute of Higher Education, Roehampton Lane SW15 5PJ. Tel: (01) 878 5751. *HE, MS, DL, EM, Occ, PTHE.*

Royal Academy of Dramatic Art, 62/64 Gower Street WC1E 6ED. Tel: (01) 636 7076. *HE.*

Royal Academy of Music, Marylebone Road NW1 5HT. Tel: (01) 935 5461. *HE.*

Royal Academy Schools, Burlington Gardens, W1V 0DS. Tel: (01) 734 9052. *HE.*

Royal College of Art, Kensington Gore SW7 2EU. Tel: (01) 584 5020. *HE.*

Royal College of Music, Prince Consort Road, South Kensington SW7 2BS. Tel: (01) 589 3643. *HE.*

Royal College of Nursing, Institute of Advanced Nursing Education, 20 Cavendish Square W1M 0AB. Tel: (01) 409 3333.

St Martin's School of Art (the London Institute), 107 Charing Cross Road WC2H 0DU. Tel: (01) 437 0611. *HE.*

South Bank Polytechnic, Borough Road SE1 0AA. Tel: (01) 928 8989. *DL, EM, HE, PTHE, HE Prep, EGS.*

South East London College, Lewisham Way SE4 1UT. Tel: (01) 692 0353. *HE Prep.*

South Lewisham Adult Education Institute, Malory School, Launcelot Road, Downham, Bromley BR1 5EB. Tel: (01) 698 4113.

South London College, Knights Hill, West Norwood SE27 0TX. Tel: (01) 670 4488 and Tooley Street, Tower Bridge SE1. Tel: (01) 407 1831. *DL, HE Prep, MS.*

South Thames College, Wandsworth High Street SW18 2PP. Tel: (01) 870 2241. *HE Prep.*

Southwark College, The Cut SE1 8LE. Tel: (01) 928 9561. *HE Prep, Polymaths, DL.*

South Greenwich Adult Education Institute, Haimo Road, Eltham SE9 6DZ. Tel: (01) 850 3632.

Southwark Adult Education Institute, Queen's Road Centre, St Mary's Road, London SE15 2EA. Tel: (01) 639 1178. *ILTU, NOW, EGS.*

Southwark Women's Workshop, 164/180 Union Street, London SE1 0LH. Tel: (01) 261 0575. *Women's TW.*

South West London College, Tooting Broadway SW17 0TQ. Tel: (01) 672 2441/3.

Streatham and Tooting Adult Education Institute, Ernest Bevin School, Beechcroft Road SW17 7DF. Tel: (01) 767 5315.

Thamesside Adult Education Institute, 1a Burrage Grove, Woolwich SE18 7LJ. Tel: (01) 855 9044.

Thames Polytechnic incorporating Avery Hill College, Wellington Street SE18 6PF. Tel: (01) 854 2030. *HE Prep, Polymaths, EGS, HE, PTHE, NOW.*

Tower Hamlets Adult Education Institute, Smithy Street, off Jubilee Street E1 3BW. Tel: (01) 790 3358.

Trinity College of Music, 11–13 Mandeville Place W1M 6AQ. Tel: (01) 935 5773. *HE.*

Vauxhall College of Building and Further Education, Belmore Street, Wandsworth Road SW8 2JY. Tel: (01) 928 4611. *NOW, MS, HE Prep.*

Walk-In-Numeracy, 22 Exhibition Close, White City, London W12. Tel: (01) 740 6675. *Drop-in Centre.*

Westminster College, Battersea Park Road SW11 4JR. Tel: (01) 720 2121. *HE Prep.*

Women's Motor Mechanic Workshop Ltd, Bay 4R, 1/3 Brixton Road, London SW9 6DE. Tel: (01) 582 2574, *Women's TW.*

Woolwich College, Villas Road SE18 7PN. Tel: (01) 855–1216 and Morgan Park SE7 8LN. Tel: (01) 855 0322. *HE Prep.*

The Working Men's College, Crowndale Road NW1 1TR. Tel: (01) 387 2037.

COLLEGES OF UNIVERSITY OF LONDON

University of London, Senate House, Malet Street, London WC1E. 7HU. Tel: (01) 636 8000. EM through many colleges below.

Birkbeck College, Malet Street WC1E 7HX. Tel: (01) 580 6622. *HE, PTHE.*

Courtauld Institute of Art, 20 Portman Square W1H 0BE. Tel: (01) 935 9292. *HE.*

Goldsmiths' College, Lewisham Way, New Cross SE14 6NW. Tel: (01) 692 7171. *HE Prep, MS, HE, PTHE, EM, Occ.*

Heythrop College, 11/13 Cavendish Square W1M 0AN. Tel: (01) 580 6941. *HE.*

Imperial College of Science and Technology SW7 2AZ. Tel: (01) 589 5111. *HE, Occ, EM.*

Institute of Archaeology, 31/34 Gordon Square WC1H 0PY. Tel: (01) 387 6052. *HE, Occ.*

Institute of Education, 20 Bedford Way WC1H 0AL. Tel: (01) 636 1500. *HE, Occ.*

King's College, London, Kings, Queens and Chelsea (KQC.), Kensington Campus, Campden Hill Road, W8 7AH. Tel: (01) 937 5411. Strand WC2R 2LS. Tel: (01) 836 5454, 552 Kings Road, SW3 6LX. Tel: (01) 351 2488. *HE.*

London School of Economics and Political Science, Houghton Street WC2A 2AE. Tel: (01) 405 7686. *HE, PTHE.*

Queen Mary College, Mile End Road E1 4NS. Tel: (01) 890 4811. *HE.*

Royal Veterinary College, Royal College Street NW1 0TU. Tel: (01) 387 2898. *HE.*

School of Oriental and African Studies, Malet Street WC1E 7HP. Tel: (01) 637 2388. *HE, EM, Occ.*

The School of Pharmacy, 29/39 Brunswick Square WC1N 1AX. Tel: (01) 837 7651/8. *HE.*

School of Slavonic and East European Studies, Senate House, Malet Street WC1E 7HU. Tel: (01) 637 4934. *HE, Occ.*

University College, Gower Street WC1E 6BT. Tel: (01) 387 7050. *HE, Occ.*

University of London Department of Extra-Mural Studies, 26 Russell Square WC1B 5DQ. Tel: (01) 636 8000. *EM* only.

Westfield College, Kidderpore Avenue, Hampstead NW3 7ST. Tel: (01) 435 7141. *HE.*

Wye College (see Kent).

Royal Holloway and Bedford College (see Surrey).

UNIVERSITY OF LONDON MEDICAL SCHOOLS

Charing Cross and Westminster Medical School, The Reynolds Building, St Dunstan's Road W6 8RP. Tel: (01) 748 2040. *HE.*

King's College School of Medicine and Dentistry, Denmark Hill SE5 8RX. Tel: (01) 274 6222. *HE.*

London Hospital Medical College, Turner Street E1 2AD. Tel: (01) 377 7000. *HE.*

Middlesex Hospital Medical School, W1P 7PN. Tel: (01) 636 8333. *HE.*

Royal Free Hospital School of Medicine, Rowland Hill Street, London NW3 2PF. Tel: (01) 794 0500. *HE.*

St Bartholomew's Hospital Medical College, West Smithfield EC1A 7BE. Tel: (01) 606 7404. *HE.*

St George's Hospital Medical School, Cranmer Terrace SW17 0RE. Tel: (01) 672 1255. *HE.*

St Mary's Hospital Medical School, Norfolk Place, Paddington W2 1PG. Tel: (01) 723 1252. *HE.*

United Medical and Dental Schools of Guy's and St Thomas's Hospital, Albert Embankment SE1 7EH. Tel: (01) 928 9292. *HE.*

MANCHESTER – METROPOLITAN DISTRICTS

Bolton

Adult education is provided in Bolton through Bolton Metropolitan College (mainly by the Faculty of Community Education) which is responsible for all non-advanced further education, adult and community education within the borough. Classes, activities and courses are offered in a variety of centres and locations across the borough. As well as using traditional adult education centres many community buildings, including two Community Education Centres, are fully utilised. Outreach approaches are also seen as essential.

There is an authority wide fee policy. Vocational courses cost £20.70 for two hours a week over 36 weeks. Non-vocational courses cost 65p per student per course hour; £2 per standard course of two hours per week for nine weeks for old aged pensioners and widows/widowers. Those in receipt of unemployment or supplementary benefit have their fees remitted.

Basic education is also provided by the Faculty of Community Education within the Adult Basic Education Unit. The co-ordinator is Mrs Irene Brunskill, Clarence Street Centre, Bolton Metropolitan College, Bolton BL1 2ET. Tel: (0204) 25500.

ESL activities are promoted by the Speak Teach English Project. Contact: Mrs Liza Hadjar, Clarence Street Centre. BUILDS (Language Development Scheme for Ethnic Minority Unemployed) contact: Mrs Patsy Williamson, Derby Street Centre. Tel: (0204) 385129.

Details of classes and provision available (late August) are in a supplement produced annually for the *Bolton evening news.*

Bolton Institute of Higher Education, Deane Road, Bolton BL3 5AB. Tel: (0204) 28851. *HE, Occ, PTHE, Polymaths, MS.*

Bolton Metropolitan College, Manchester Road, Bolton BL2 1ER. Tel: (0204) 31411.

Clarence Street Centre, Bolton BL1 2ET. Tel: (0204) 34455. Horwich Centre, Victoria Road, Bolton BL6 6ED. Tel: (0204) 696722. *DL, HE Prep, ILTU.*

Bury

Adult education is provided through the College of Adult Education which offers courses at centres throughout the borough. Adult education is also provided by Bury Metropolitan College of Further Education which has two sites.

Fees for most courses cost around 57p per hour (adult basic education 24p an hour) and there is a 50% reduction for people on state retirement pensions and many people on supplementary or unemployment benefit. No fees for people under 18.

Some courses are accredited to the Manchester OpenCollege *F*ederation and a new development is Open Learning.

For details, tel: (061) 766 5118. Courses are advertised in *Live and learn*, a newspaper-style prospectus and Bury Education and Training Advice, based at the college, will have up to date details.

Educational Guidance Service for Adults

Bury Education and Training Advice (BETA), College of Adult Education, Whitfield Centre, Higher Lane, Whitfield, Bury BL9 0DA. Tel: (061) 766 5118.

Bury Metropolitan College, Market Street, Bury BL9 OBG. Tel: (061) 761 4327.

College of Adult Education, Arts and Crafts Centre, Broad Street, Bury BL9 0DA. Tel: (061) 764 2351.

Whitefield Centre, Higher Lane, Whitefield. Tel: (061) 766 5118. *NOW, EGS, DL.*

Manchester

Community education in Manchester takes place within two areas of community education, a college of adult education, two tertiary colleges, a further education college, and a community college for further education. They have details of all classes held in their areas. Manchester Education Committee also publish a guide to all non-vocational classes for adults in the city, available free from the Continuing Education Department. The standard fee for most courses is £7.40 per term (students are also allowed to pay as they go at 80p a meeting) but this is higher at the College of Adult Education (£10.60 per term or £1 per meeting). Reduced fees are available to women over the age of 60, men over 65, the under 18s, people in receipt of unemployment, supplementary, disablement and handicap benefit or family income supplement plus spouses of unemployed people who have not registered for benefit and YTS trainees who pay 30p per class meeting. Fees are higher for non-Manchester residents. Basic education classes are organised separately and are free. The city also runs an Open College scheme.

For more information, contact: The Continuing Education Department, Education Offices, Crown Square, Manchester.M60 3BB. Tel: (061) 234 7077.

Education Guidance Service for Adults

Manchester Education Advice Service for Adults, 9 Anson Road, Victoria Par, Manchester M14. Tel: (061) 224 8241.

The Birtles Centre, Town Centre, Wythenshawe, Manchester M22 5RF. Tel: (061) 499 1455.

College of Adult Education, Cavendish Street, All Saints, Manchester M15 6BP. Tel: (061) 273 5335.

Miles Platting Community Education Centre, Holland Street, Manchester M10 7AF. Tel: (061) 205 3594.

Moseley Road Centre, Fallowfield, Manchester M14 6WQ. Tel: (061) 224 8241.

Basic Skills Unit, South Manchester Community College, The Birtles Centre, Wythenshaw Town Centre, Manchester M22 5RF. Tel: (061) 499 1455. *DL, EGS, Open College.*

College of Adult Education, Cavendish Street, All Saints M15 6BP. Tel: (061) 273–5335. *ILTU, DL, NOW, HE Prep, MS.*

Central Manchester College, Centre of Building, Faculty of Construction, Lower Hardman Street, Manchester M3 3ER. Tel: (061) 831–7791.

Central Manchester College, Openshaw Centre, Whitworth Street, Manchester M11 6BP. Tel: (061) 223–8282.

Central Manchester College, St John's Centre, Lower Hardman Street, Manchester M3 3FP. Tel: (061) 831 7091.

De la Salle College, Hopwood Hall, Middleton M24 3XH. Tel: (061) 643 5331. *HE, MS, Occ.*

Manchester Business School, University of Manchester, Booth Street, West, Manchester M15 6PB. Tel: (061) 273 8228. *ILTU, PTHE, MS, HE.*

Manchester Polytechnic, Administrative Centre, All Saints M5 6BH. Tel: (061) 228 6171. *Polymaths, Polyphysics, HE, PTHE, Open College.*

Manchester University M13 9PL. Tel: (061) 273 3333. *HE, PTHE, EM, MS.*

Moss Side Community Education Centre, 40 Embden Walk, Moss Side Shopping Centre, Manchester M14 5NW. Tel: (061) 226 841123.

North Hulme Centre, Jackson Crescent, Hulme M15 5AL. Tel: (061) 226–2293/3362. *EGS, HE Prep, Open College.*

North Manchester College, Abraham Moss Centre, Crescent Road M8 6UH. Tel: (061) 740 1491. *DL, HE Prep, NOW, Open College.*

North Manchester College, Moston Centre, Ashley Lane, Moston M9 1WH. Tel: (061) 205–7525.

Royal Northern College of Music, 124 Oxford Road M13 9RD. Tel: (061) 273 6283. *HE.*

South Manchester Community College, Fielden Park Centre, Barlow Moor Road, West Didsbury M20 8PQ. Tel: (061) 434 4821 or Wythenshawe Park Centre, Moor Road, M23 9BQ. Tel: (061) 902 0131. *DL, MS, EGS, Open College, HE Prep.*

University of Manchester Institute of Science and Technology, PO Box 88, Sackville Street M60 1QD. Tel: (061) 236 3311. *HE, EM, MS.*

Wheler Community Education Centre, Wheler Street, Higher Openshaw M11 1DH. Tel: (061) 223 9126.

Withington Centre for Community Education, 3 Mauldeth Road, Withington M20 9NE. Tel: (061) 224 8271. *DL, NOW.*

Women's Skill Centre Group, Mancoda, 12 Moseley Street, Manchester M2 3AQ. *Women's TW.*

Oldham

The community education service is organised through 15 separate centres which also use school premises for classes. Fees, which work out at under 60p an hour, can be reduced for retired or unemployed people also the under 18s and anyone on supplementary benefit or family income supplement. Basic education is provided at no cost to the student. Ten of the centres have special facilities for disabled people while nine arrange some kind of child care provision for their students.

For more information, contact: J D Hoyland. Tel: (061) 678 4223.

Adult Basic Education Project for Ethnic Minorities, Werneth Park CEC, Frederick Street, Oldham. Tel: (061) 626 9389.

Oldham Centre for Community Education, Chaucer Street OL1 1BA. Tel: (061) 624 3957. *ILTU, NOW.*

Oldham College of Technology, Rochdale Road OL9 6AA. Tel: (061) 624 5214. *Open College.*

Oldham Industrial Language Training Unit, Greenacres Centre, Galland Street, Greenacres, Oldham. Tel: (061) 624 3668. *ILTU, DL.*

Rochdale

Classes for adults are provided through Rochdale College of Adult Education, either in the college, which has a creche, or in local schools or centres. Most fees are fixed at 51p an hour but five community schools arrange their own fees for non-structured classes. Fee reductions are available to people under 18, or retired or unemployed and, in cases of hardship, to anyone. Adult basic education is free.

For more information, contact: Mr Rothwell, The Registrar, Rochdale Colleges. Tel: (0706) 521100.

Rochdale College of Adult Education, St Mary's Gate OL12 6RY. Tel: (0706) 345346.

Rochdale College of Arts and Design, St Mary's Gate OL12 6RY. Tel: (0706) 345346. *DL, HE Prep, MS, NOW.*

Rochdale Industrial Language Training Unit, Room 8, College Annexe, Baillie Street, Rochdale, OL16 1JJ. Tel: (0706) 359700. *ILTU.*

Rochdale Technical College, St Mary's Gate OL12 6RY. Tel: (0706) 345346.

Salford

Two centres (Eccles and Swinton) organise adult education in Salford, running about a quarter of the courses on their own premises (which provide some child care) and the majority in schools, community centres or youth clubs. Fees for non-vocational courses are £20 per term year but reductions are available to retired, unemployed or disabled students as well as under 18s and any full-time students. Basic education is free.

For more information, contact: Chief Education Officer, City of Salford Education Office, Chapel Street, Salford M3 5LT. Tel: (061) 832 9751.

Eccles Adult Education Centre, Green Lane, Patricroft, Eccles M30 ORP. Tel: (061) 789 1894.
Salford College of Technology, Frederick Road, Salford M6 6PU. Tel: (061) 736 6541.
The University of Salford, Salford M5 4WT. Tel: (061) 736 5843. *HE, PTHE, MS.*
Swinton Adult Education Centre, Victoria House, Victoria Park, Swinton, Manchester M27 1DZ. Tel: (061) 794 5798.
Worsley College of Further Education, Walkden Road, Worsley, Manchester M28 4QD. Tel: (061) 702 8272.

Stockport

Classes are run through 13 adult education centres and also in schools. Basic education is free and charges for other classes work out at under 65p an hour. Reduction in fee charges are available for people under 18, those in receipt of state retirement benefit, disability benefit, supplementary benefit or registered unemployed. Others may qualify for reduced fees on grounds of financial hardship. All centres have some special facilities for disabled people.

Stockport College of Technology, Wellington Road South, Stockport, Cheshire SK1 3UQ. Tel: (061) 480 7331. *DL, MS, HE Prep, HE, PTHE.*

Tameside

Adult education is run through a department of the College of Technology which publishes an annual programme describing courses. Various centres are used, also the college, schools and libraries. Two centres in Ashton and Hyde arrange regular child care provision. Fees work out at under 50p an hour and reductions are available to retired, unemployed or disabled people – also under 18s. Adult basic education is free and there are a small number of special classes for the disabled which are also free. The department offers flexistudy courses.

For more information, contact: Barbara Burgess, Adult Education. Tel: (061) 330 6911.

Tameside Education Advice Service for Adults, Warrington House, Church St, Ashton under Lyne OL6 7PR. Tel: (061) 330 6911.

Tameside College of Technology, Beaufort Road, Ashton-under-Lyne, Tameside, Greater Manchester OL6 6NX. Tel: (061) 330 6911. *DL, MS, ILTU.*

Trafford

Adult education in the borough is organised through the two colleges of further education and their three annexes. Fees for non-vocational courses are currently 78p per hour (senior citizens pay 40p) while vocational courses charged at the Nationally agreed rates. Tuition for all courses is free to registered unemployed people and to under 18s for most courses.

For more information contact: The Post School and Buildings Section, Education Offices, Town Hall, Sale, Greater Manchester M33 1YR. Tel: (061) 872 2101.

North Trafford College of Further Education, Talbot Road, Stretford, Manchester M32 0XH. Tel: (061) 872 3731.
South Trafford College of Further Education, Manchester Road, West Timperley, Altrincham, Cheshire WA14 5PQ. Tel: (061) 973 7064.

Wigan

Community education in the borough is run through two tertiary colleges and ten other centres (most based on community high schools). The tertiary colleges have special facilities for disabled people and three other centres that have some arrangements for child care. Fees vary according to the type of course: many work out at under 30p an hour and fees above 50p an hour are unlikely. The under 18s and most people receiving state benefits or pensions are entitled to

reduced fees. Basic education is free. The borough has a 'back to school' scheme for adults and other opportunities are available through flexistudy and the Open College scheme.
For more information, contact: Mrs Bridget Fielding, CLEO (see below).

Education Guidance Service for Adults
Contact for Learning and Educational Opportunities (CLEO), Education Department, Gateway House, Standishgate, Wigan WN1 1XL. Tel: (0942) 827912.

Leigh College, Railway Road, Leigh WN7 4HX. Tel: (0942) 608811. *DL, NOW.*
Wigan College of Technology, Parsons Walk, Wigan WN1 1RR. Tel: (0942) 494911. *Polymaths, HE, PTHE, Open College, DL, Drop-in basic education.*

MERSEYSIDE – METROPOLITAN DISTRICTS

Knowsley

Adult education in Knowsley is run through the Knowsley Adult Centre in Prescot and in departments of the two colleges of further education, with classes running in schools and the colleges. Fees for classes cost over £1 per hour (except for basic education which is free), but reductions are available for the unemployed. The authority operates a 'back to school' scheme for adults.
For more information contact: Mr G Evans-Hughes or Mr J D Fleming, Adult Education and Youth Service, Education Department, Huyton Hey Road, Huyton, Merseyside.

Kirkby College of Further Education, Cherryfield Drive, Kirkby L32 8SF. Tel: (051) 443 4324. *DL, HE Prep, MS.*
Knowsley Adult Centre, Knowsley Central Tertiary College, 10 Church Street, Prescot, Merseyside L34 3LA. Tel: (051) 430 9444. *DL, NOW.*
Knowsley Central Tertiary College, Rupert Road, Huyton, Merseyside L36 9UT. Tel: (051) 480 6151. *DL, EGS.*
Women's Technology Training Ltd, Hardman Street, Liverpool. *Women's TW.*

Liverpool

Community education in the city is run through 26 centres and four colleges. Over half the classes are held in schools but colleges and separate centres are also used . The authority has a 'back to school' scheme for adults. Fees for courses are based on 50p an hour and tuition is provided free to students under 18 years of age, those in receipt of state retirement pensions and the unemployed. Basic education is provided free through courses in colleges and centres. There is also a specialised referral and resource centre (at Canning Street Adult Centre, 73 Canning Street, Liverpool 8). One centre (Prince Edwin Centre, Roscommon Street, Liverpool 8) arranges child care on a regular basis and has special facilities for disabled people.

City College, Myrtle Street, Liverpool L7 7HE. Tel: (051) 708 0423, or Colquitt Street, Liverpool L1 4DB. Tel: (051) 709 0541 (nautical and catering courses).
Charles Wooton Centre, 248 Upper Parliament Street, Liverpool 8. Tel: (051) 708 9698.
South Mersey College of Further Education, Childwall Campus, Childwall Site, Childwall Abbey Road, Liverpool L16 0JP. Tel: (051) 722 5705. *NOW, HE Prep,* also Riversdale Campus, Riversdale Road, Liverpool L19 3QR. Tel: (051) 427 1227 and 427 7901/2.
C F Mott Campus of Liverpool Polytechnic, Liverpool Road, Prescot L34 1NP. Tel: (051) 489 6201. *HE, MS.*
Liverpool Institute of Higher Education, Stand Park Road, Liverpool L16 9JD. Tel: (051) 722 2361. *HE, MS, PTHE.*
Liverpool Polytechnic, Rodney House, 70 Mount Pleasant, Liverpool L3 5UX. Tel: (051) 207 3581. *Polymaths, HE, PTHE.*
Liverpool University, PO Box 147, Liverpool L69 3BX. Tel: (051) 709 6022. *HE, EM, MS.*
Millbrook College of Commerce, Bankfield Site, Bankfield Road, Liverpool L13 0BQ. Tel: (051) 259 1124, also at Muirhead Site, Muirhead Avenue East, Liverpool L11 1ES. Tel: (051) 226 0111. *NOW.*
Newsham Drive Adult Centre, 83 Newsham Drive, Liverpool L6 7UM. Tel: (051) 263 5153.

Sandown College of Further Education, Mabel Fletcher Centre, Sandown Road, Liverpool L15 4JB. Tel: (051) 733 7211. *HE Prep*, and Old Swan Centre, Broad Green Road, Liverpool L13 5SQ. Tel: (051) 220 9311. *HE Prep, NOW*.

Windsor Street Adult English Language Centre, Windsor Street, Liverpool L8 8EE. Tel: (051) 708 0520.

Women's Technology Scheme, Merseyside Trade Union Community and Unemployment Resource Centre, 24 Hardman Street, Liverpool L1 9AX. Tel: (051) 709 4356. *Women's TW*.

St Helens

Continuing education in the metropolitan borough is organised through St Helens College with classes run on its campuses, in community schools and other venues. Several schools encourage adults to join normal courses. Creche facilities are available at most venues. A wide range of Leisure Opportunities courses are organised by the community leisure department. Fees for most vocational courses cost under 30p an hour and non-vocational courses cost 50p an hour. Basic education is provided free. No charge is made to people in receipt of unemployment benefit, state retirement pension, supplementary benefit, family income supplement, invalidity benefit, housing benefit or anyone under 18.

St Helens College, School of Art and Design, Victoria Square, St Helens, Merseyside WA10 1DY. Tel: (0744) 28343, also Newton le Willows Campus, Crow Lane East, Newton le Willows WA12 9TT. Tel: (092 52) 4656.

St Helens College, Water Street, St Helens WA10 1PZ. Tel: (0744) 33766. *DL*.

Sefton

The district's adult education service is run through two further education colleges in Bootle and Southport and by separate adult centres in Crosby, Formby and Maghull. Vocational courses cost £19.40 for one year, two hours per week. Non-vocational courses cost £1.65 for two hours per week, but may also include VAT. For vocational courses half fee rates are available to old aged pensioners, full-time students 18 and over and the registered disabled. Vocational courses are free to those aged 16 and 17 who are either at work or in full-time education, those in receipt of family income supplement, the registered unemployed, those on supplementary benefit or on MSC or ITB courses. Non-vocational courses are charged at half rate to the registered disabled, those on family income supplement, the registered unemployed, those on supplementary benefit, or on MSC or ITB. Basic education is provided free.

For more information contact: Mr D D Sherwell, Senior Education Officer (Establishments). Tel: (051) 933 6003.

Crosby Adult Centre, Cambridge Road, Seaforth, Liverpool L21 1EZ. Tel: (051) 928 0765.

The Hugh Baird College of Technology, Balliol Road, Bootle, Merseyside L20 7EW. Tel: (051) 922 6704. *MS*.

Southport College of Art and Technology, Mornington Road, Southport, Merseyside PR9 0TT. Tel: (0704) 42411.

Wirral

Adult education provision is organised through Wirral Metropolitan College, with classes run on its sites, in local schools and community centres. Two centres provide regular child care and have special facilities for disabled people. Fees depend on the type of course, but apart from basic education which is free, they range between 50 and 90p an hour. Retired or unemployed people and the under 18s are entitled to half fees but full fee remission is available at the discretion of the Centre Head. There is a range of Second Chance courses on offer and the Carlett Park site of the college runs a full range of courses by flexible study (ask for their *Learnaway* booklet).

Borough Road Site, Birkenhead L42 9QD. Tel: (051) 653 5555.

Carlett Park Site, Eastham L62 3AY. Tel: (051) 327 4331. *EGS, HE Prep, DL*.

Conway Education Centre (Teachers Centre), Conway Street, Birkenhead. Tel: (051) 647 7000 ext 599. *NOW, Drop-in* (basic education).

Wirral Metropolitan College, Withens Lane Site, Wallasey, Wirral L45 7LT. Tel: (051) 653 5555. *NOW, DL, Drop-in Centre* (basic education).

Norfolk

Norfolk adult education service is organised through 60 centres, grouped into five areas, which run classes in schools and village halls throughout the county. There is also a scheme for adults to study in some schools. Fees for exam courses are 63p per hour. Other courses are run on a self-financing basis so fees vary. Basic education and lipreading costs 42p per hour. Retired people, those on supplementary or unemployment benefit and family income supplement qualify for reduced fees as do people receiving standard housing supplement and the under 18s. Those on state retirement benefit quality for reduced fees for their second and subsequent courses.

For more information contact:
East Norfolk Area Office (Great Yarmouth). Tel: (0493) 856647. Ask for: Mrs Wendy Walton.
South Norfolk Area Office (Thetford).Tel: (0842) 5492. Ask for: Paul Amison.
West Norfolk Area Office (Kings Lynn). Tel: (0553) 772766. Ask for: Sue Cara.
North Norfolk Area Office (North Walsham). Tel: (0692) 405930. Ask for: Christine Spencer.
Central Norfolk Area Office (Norwich). Tel: (0603) 621314. Ask for: Bernard Godding.

Education Guidance Service for Adults

Educational Guidance Service for Adults in Kings Lynn and West Norfolk (EGAL), Orchard Hall, Room 0409, NORCAT, Tennyson Avenue, Kings Lynn, Norfolk PE30 2QW. Tel: (0553) 761144 ext 287.

Great Yarmouth College of Art and Design, Trafalgar Road, Great Yarmouth NR30 2LB. Tel: (0493) 843557.
Great Yarmouth College of Further Education, Southtown, Great Yarmouth NR31 0JU. Tel: (0493) 655261.
Norfolk College of Agriculture and Horticulture, Easton, Norwich NR9 5DX. Tel: (0603) 742105.
Norfolk College of Arts and Technology, Tennyson Road, Kings Lynn PE30 2QE. Tel: (0553) 761144. *DL, EGS, HE Prep, MS, NOW* (planned).
Norfolk City College of Further and Higher Education, Ipswich Road, Norwich NR2 2LJ. Tel: (0603) 660011. *DL, HE, MS, NOW.*
Norwich School of Art, St George Street, Norwich NR3 1BB. Tel: (0603) 610561. *HE.*
Univeristy of East Anglia, Norwich NR4 7TJ. Tel: (0603) 56161. *HE, PTHE.*
Wensum Lodge, 169 King Street, Norwich NR1 1QE. Tel: (0603) 666021/2.

Northamptonshire

The county's adult education service is run through about 100 village centres, 25 adult education centres and five further and higher education colleges. Most courses are run in schools and colleges; a few schools may allow adult students to join school courses on request. Fees range from 32p an hour for vocational courses at non-advanced levels to 72p an hour for general adult courses. The unemployed, those in receipt of certain social security benefits and basic education students pay no course fees; the retired and full-time students under 19 pay reduced fees. Knuston Hall runs short residential courses for adults.

For more information contact: Northamptonshire County Council, Education Department, Northampton House, Northampton NN1 2HX. Tel: (0604) 256312 or Area Adult Education Office, William Knibb Centre, Montagu Street, Kettering, Northants NN16 8AE. Tel: (0536) 84319 or Area Adult Education Office, Brackley Road, Towcester. Tel: (0327) 51222.

Education Guidance Service for Adults

Adult Preparation Training, The Military Road Centre, Military Rd, Northampton NN1 3ET. Tel: (0604) 28259, 30311 or 28041. *EGS.*

Industrial Language Training Unit, The Lodge, Rickyard Road, The Arbours, Northampton NN3 3QZ. Tel: (0604) 410236. *ILTU.*
Military Road Centre, Military Road, Northampton NN1 3ET. Tel: (0604) 30311. *ILTU.*
Knuston Hall Residential College, Irchester, Wellingborough, NN9 7EU. Tel: (0933) 312104. *SRC.*
Nene College, Park Campus, Moulton Park, Northampton NN2 7AL. Tel: (0604) 715000. *HE, MS, NOW, DL.*
Northamptonshire College of Agriculture, West Street, Moulton NN3 1RR. Tel: (0604) 491131.
Northampton College of Further Education, St Gregory's Road, Booth Lane South, Northampton NN3 3RF. Tel: (0604) 403322.

Tresham College, George Street, Corby, Northants NN17 1QA. Tel: (0536) 203252. *DL.*
University Centre, Barrack Road, Northampton NN2 6AF. Tel: (0604) 30084. *PTHE, EM* (part of Leicester University and runs extra-mural courses for local students).
Wellingborough College, Church Street, Wellingborough NN8 4PD. Tel: (0933) 224165.

Northumberland
Twenty adult associations organise the county's adult education activities which are held in school and community premises. Flexistudy and Second Chance courses whereby adults join in the regular sixth form A-level courses, also operate at some centres. Most charge fees fixed at county level but two are experimenting with alternative fee arrangments. Courses in vocational-educational subjects cost under 50p per hour while non-exam activities cost 75p per hour. Retired people and those registered unemployed qualify for considerably reduced fees. An education guidance service is being developed at Adult Education Guidance Project, 56 Front Street West, Bedlington NE22 5UB. Tel: (0670) 826810. Northumberland residents also have access to LEASA in Newcastle.

Northumberland College of Agriculture, Kirkley Hall, Ponteland, Newcastle-upon-Tyne NE20 0AQ. Tel: (0661) 24141.
Northumberland Technical College, College Road, Ashington NE63 9RG. Tel: (0670) 813248. *DL, HE Prep.*
Open Door Basic Skills/Open Learning Unit, Salisbury Street, Blyth. Tel: (0670) 353818. *NOW, DL.*
North East Open Learning Access Centre. Tel: (0670) 811516. Consultancy on learning/training needs with back-up support for learners.

Nottinghamshire
Adult education is organised by the ten colleges of further education and four community schools, with classes being held in schools, colleges, village halls and community adult centres. Fees are standard throughout the county; non-vocational courses cost 65p an hour plus an enrolment fee. The cost of vocational classes varies according to the level of the course, and its length. Remission of fees is available to old aged pensioners, the unemployed and the handicapped, full-time students under 18 and people on supplementary benefit. Others may be given remission – ask. Basic education is free. General enquiries about all adult basic education should be made to the Berridge Centre, Stanley Road, Forest Fields, Nottingham NG7 6HW. Tel: (0602) 473003.

Education Guidance Service for Adults
Open University East Midlands Regional Enquiry Service, The Octagon, 143 Derby Road, Nottingham NG7 1PH. Tel: (0602) 473072.

Arnold and Carlton College of Further Education, Digby Avenue, Mapperley, Nottingham NG3 6DR. Tel: (0602) 876503. *DL, MS.*
Basford Hall College of Further Education, Stockhill Lane, Basford, Nottingham NG6 0NB. Tel: (0602) 704541.
Broxtowe College of Further Education, High Road, Chilwell, Nottingham NG6 4AH. Tel: (0602) 228161. *HE Prep, DL.*
Clarendon College of Further Education, Pelham Avenue, Nottingham NG5 1AL. Tel: (0602) 607201. *DL, HE Prep.*
Eaton Hall International, Retford, Nottingham. Tel: (0777) 706441. *DL.*
Fairham Community College, Farnborough Road, Clifton, Nottingham NG11 9AE. Tel: (0602) 213606/844668.
Kirkby Adult Centre, Tennyson Street, Kirkby-in-Ashfield, Nottingham, NG17 7DH. Tel: (0623) 751691.
Newark Technical College, Chauntry Park, Newark-on-Trent NG24 1PB. Tel: (0636) 705921. *DL.*
North Nottinghamshire College of Further Education, Carlton Road, Worksop S81 7HP. Tel: (0909) 473561. *DL, HE Prep.*
Nottinghamshire College of Agriculture, Brackenhurst, Southwell NG25 0QF. Tel: (0636) 812252.
Nottingham Women's Training Centre, High Pavement, Nottingham NG1 1HN. Tel: (0602) 586236. *Women's TW.*

Dukeries Community College, Whinney Lane, New Ollerton, Newark, Notts NG22 9TD. Tel: (0623) 860304. *NOW*.

People's College of Further Education, Maid Marian Way, Nottingham NG1 6AB. Tel: (0602) 417721. *HE Prep, DL*.

South Nottinghamshire College of Further Education, Greythorn Drive, West Bridgford, Nottingham NG2 7GA. Tel: (0602) 812125. *NOW, MS, DL*.

Sutton Centre, High Pavement, Sutton-in-Ashfield, Notts NG17 1EE. Tel: (0623) 554554 ext 255.

Trent Polytechnic, Burton Street, Nottingham NG1 4BU. Tel: (0602) 418248. *HE, PTHE, EM, MS, Occ*.

University of Nottingham, University Park, Nottingham NG7 2RD. Tel: (0602) 506101. *HE, PTHE, EM, MS*.

West Nottinghamshire College of Further Education, Derby Road, Mansfield NG18 5BH. Tel: (0623) 27191.

Oxfordshire

The county's community education service is run through 29 centres. Five further education colleges also provide courses for adults. Fees vary from centre to centre but for all courses they are in the region of 70 to 90p per hour. Entitlement to fee concessions is also decided at local level; so is the decision of whether or not to charge for basic education. Oxford University runs Rewley House as part of its department for external studies and it holds short residential courses for adults.

Educational guidance is available throught the Links in Information Services on Education (LIAISE). The LIAISE index is available in libraries, colleges and centres throughout the country and gives details of over 4000 courses and contact names for further information and guidance. It offers an advisory service in the summer in libraries and other centres.

Abingdon College of Further Education, Northcourt Road, Abingdon OX14 1NA. Tel: (0235) 21585. *DL*.

Henley, The Management College, Greenlands, Henley-on-Thames, Oxford RG9 3AU. Tel: (0491) 571454. *DL*.

North Oxfordshire Technical College and School of Art, Broughton Road, Banbury, Oxon OX16 9QA. Tel: (0295) 52221. *DL*.

Open University, Southern Region, Regional Enquiry Service, Foxcombe Hall, Boars Hill, Oxford OX1 5HR. Tel: (0865) 730731.

Oxford College of Further Education, Oxpens Road, Oxford OX1 1SA. Tel: (0865) 245871. *DL*.

Oxford Polytechnic, Gipsy Lane, Headington, Oxford OX3 0BP. Tel: (0865) 64777. *HE, PTHE, Occ, DL*.

Oxford University, University Offices, Wellington Square, Oxford OX1 2JD. Tel: (0865) 56747. *HE, EM* (see Rewley House).

Plater College, Pullens Lane, Oxford OX3 ODT. Tel: (0865) 67626. *ARC*.

Rewley House, Wellington Square, Oxford OX1 2JA. Tel: (0865) 52901. *EM*.

Ruskin College, Oxford OX1 2HE. Tel: (0865) 58376. *ARC*.

Rycotewood College, Priest End, Thame OX9 2AF. Tel: (084 421) 2501.

South Oxfordshire Technical College, Deanfield Avenue, Henley-on-Thames, Oxon RG6 1UM. Tel: (0491) 573501. *DL*.

University College, Buckland, Oxon SN7 8QX. Tel: (036 787) 202. *HE*.

Westminster College, North Hinksey, Oxford OX2 9AT. Tel: (0865) 247644. *HE*.

West Oxfordshire Technical College, Holloway Road, Witney, Oxon OX8 7EE. Tel: (0993) 3464. *DL*.

Shropshire

Adult and community education is organised through adult education departments in three further education colleges and through one adult centre in Shrewsbury. Many classes however, are run in schools. Fees are decided at the level of individual centres but don't usually cost more than 80p an hour. Reductions of 50% may be available to retired, unemployed or disabled people, those doing basic education courses, people on family income supplement or supplementary benefit or anyone in financial hardship.

For more information contact: Mrs M Bailey, Further Education Department, The Shire Hall, Abbey Foregate, Shrewsbury, Shropshire SY2 6ND. Tel: (0743) 254343.

Bridgnorth and South Shropshire College of Further Education, Stourbridge Road, Bridgnorth WV15 6AL. Tel: (074 62) 4431. *DL.*

Harper Adams Agricultural College, Newport TF10 8NB. Tel: (0952) 820280. *HE.*

Second Chance, The Gateway Education and Arts Centre, Chester Street, Shrewsbury SY1 1NB. (0743) 55159. *DL.*

Second Chance, Adult Basic Education, Albert Road Centre, Oswestry, Shropshire. Tel: (0691) 653681. *DL.*

Shrewsbury College of Arts and Technology, London Road, Shrewsbury SY2 6PR. Tel: (0743) 51544. *DL.*

Telford College of Arts and Technology, Haybridge Road, Wellington, Telford TF1 2NP. Tel: (0952) 641122. *DL, HE Prep, NOW.*

Walford College of Agriculture, Walford, Baschurch SY4 2HL. Tel: (0939) 260461.

Somerset

Community education in the county is run in colleges, local schools and community education centres. Fees are set by individual establishments but on average courses cost around £1 an hour. Fees for basic education vary; in some areas they are free, in others a nominal charge is made. Fee reductions are determined locally but will usually be available for retired people, under 18s and the unemployed. Basic education is provided in most establishments. The county co-ordinator for adult basic education is Mrs Veronica Gardiner. Tel: (0749) 74688.

For more information contact: Miss Corinne James Tel: (0823) 73451 ext 5719.

Education Guidance Services for Adults

Education Advisory Service for Adults for Gloucestershire, Avon, Wiltshire and Somerset, The Open University, 41 Broad Street, Bristol BS1 2EP. Tel: (0272) 299641.

Yeovil College Education Guidance Service, Ilchester Road, Yeovil, Somerset BA21 3BA. Tel: (0935) 23921. *HE Prep.*

Bridgwater College, Bath Road, Bridgwater, Somerset TA6 4PZ. Tel: (0278) 55464. *DL, HE Prep.*

Burnham Further Education Centre, Technical Street, Burnham-on-Sea TA8 1PM. Tel: (0278) 783057. *NOW.*

Dillington College, Ilminster, Somerset TA19 9DT. Tel: (046 05) 2427. *SRC.*

Frome Community College, Park Road, Frome BA11 1EU. Tel: (0373) 65353. *WOW.*

Ilminster Adult Education Centre, Dittan Street, Ilminster TA19 0BW. Tel: (046 05) 3195.

Minehead Community Education Centre, Middle Street, North Hill, Minehead TA24 5JJ. Tel: (0643) 2986.

Somerset College of Agriculture and Horticulture, Cannington, Bridgwater TA5 2LS. Tel: (0278) 652226.

Somerset College of Arts and Technology, Wellington Road, Taunton TA1 5AX. Tel: (0823) 83403.

Strode College, Church Road, Street BA16 0AB. Tel: (0458) 42277.

Wellington Community Education Centre, 10 Courtland Road, Wellington TA21 8ND. Tel: (082 347) 3000. *DL, MS.*

Yeovil College, Ilchester Road, Yeovil BA21 3BA. Tel: (0935) 23921. *DL, EGS.*

Staffordshire

Adult education classes are run through the county's further education colleges and through some 50 adult centres (largely school-based). The county also has two colleges providing short residential courses for adults (Wedgwood and Pendrell Hall). Fees for non-residential courses work out at 60p per hour per course. Fee reductions are set at county level and retired, registered unemployed or disabled people are usually eligible, as are the under 18s and anyone in financial hardship.

For more information contact: FE Department, Education Offices, Tipping Street, Stafford ST16 2DH. Tel: (0785) 223121.

Burton-upon-Trent Technical College, Lichfield Street, Burton-upon-Trent DE14 3RL. Tel: (0283) 454041. *DL.*

Cannock Chase Technical College, The Green, Cannock WS11 1UE. Tel: (054 35) 5811/3.
Cauldon College of Further and Higher Education, Stoke Road, Shelton, Stoke-on-Trent ST4 2DG. Tel (0782) 202561. *HE Prep, DL.*
Keele University, Keele ST5 5BG. Tel: (0782) 621111. *MS, HE, EM, Occ.*
Leek College of Further Education and School of Art, Stockwell Street, Leek ST13 6DP. Tel: (0538) 382506. *DL, EGS.*
Lichfield College, Cherry Orchard, Lichfield WS14 9AN. Tel: (0543) 262150.
Newcastle-under-Lyme College, Liverpool Road, Newcastle-under-Lyme ST5 2DF. Tel: (0782) 611531.
North Staffordshire Polytechnic, College Road, Stoke-on-Trent ST4 2DE. Tel: (0782) 744531. *DL, HE Prep, HE, PTHE.*
Pendrell Hall, Codsall Wood, Wolverhampton WV8 1QP. Tel: (090 74) 2398. *SRC.*
Staffordshire College of Agriculture, Rodbaston, Penkridge, Stafford ST19 5PG. Tel: (0785) 2209. *DL.*
Stafford College of Further Education, Earl Street, Stafford ST16 2QR. Tel: (0785) 42361. *HE Prep, DL.*
Stoke-on-Trent Technical College, Loughton Centre, Lightwood Road, Loughton, Stoke-on-Trent. Tel: (0782) 821222. *DL, HE Prep.*
Tamworth College of Further Education, Croft Street, Upper Gungate, Tamworth B79 8AE. Tel: (0827) 62344. *DL.*
Wedgwood Memorial College, Barlaston, Stoke-on-Trent, Staffs ST12 9DG. Tel: (078 139) 2105.

Suffolk

Suffolk adult education is offered through six area community education teams, although in the areas with a further education college, provision is linked with the college adult education department. Course fees are set at county level and work out at about 80p an hour. Basic education is cheaper; classes may cost up to 40p an hour but individual help is free. Fee reductions on other courses are usually available to certain unemployed, retired or disabled people and those under 18. Some local schools may permit adult students. Education guidance services are available from each area office.

Education Guidance Service for Adults

Suffolk Educational Advisory Service for Adults, Education Department, Grimwade Street, Ipswich IP4 1LJ. Tel: (0473) 55801 ext 4414.

Belstead House Adult Residential Centre, Belstead, Ipswich IP8 3NA. Tel: (0473) 686321. *SRC.*
Chadacre Agricultural Institute and Farm Training Centre, Shimpling, Bury St Edmunds, Suffolk IP29 4DU. Tel: (0284) 830388.
Lowestoft College, St Peter's Street, Lowestoft NR32 2NB. Tel: (0502) 83521. *DL, MS, PTHE, HE Prep.*
Otley College of Agriculture and Horticulture, Otley, Ipswich IP6 9EY. Tel: (047 385) 350. *ARC, DL, MS, EM, HE Prep.*
Suffolk College of Higher and Further Education, Rope Walk, Ipswich IP4 1LT. Tel: (0473) 55885. *DL.*
West Suffolk College of Further Education, Out Risbygate, Bury St Edmunds IP33 3RL. Tel: (0284) 701301. *DL.*

Surrey

Adult education, including basic education, is organised through nine institutes of adult education, which run courses in their own premises (which means lots of daytime classes), as well as in other centres such as schools and halls. Fees for vocational classes are set at county level and cost £17 (under 18s) and £24 (over 18s) per course. Fees for non-vocational courses are set by the institutes and may cost anything between 50p to over £1 per hour as they have to be self-financing. Basic education may cost up to 65p an hour. Retired and unemployed people usually qualify for fee reductions as do the under 18s (but for vocational courses only).

For more information contact: Mr Francis Verity, Area Education Office, 14/16 North Street, Guildford GU1 4AF. Tel: (0483) 572881.

Brooklands Technical College, Heath Road, Weybridge LT13 8TT. Tel: (0932) 53300. *DL*.
East Surrey College, Gatton Point, Redhill RH1 2JX. Tel: (0737) 72611. *DL*.
Epsom School of Art and Design, Ashley Road, Epsom KT18 5BE. Tel: (037 27) 28811.
Guildford County College of Technology, Stoke Park, Guildford GU1 1EZ. Tel: (0483) 31251. *DL, HE Prep*.
Hillcroft College, South Bank, Surbiton, Surrey KT6 6DF. Tel: (01) 399 2688. *ARC for women*.
Merrist Wood Agricultural College, Worplesdon, Guildford, Surrey GU3 3PE. Tel: (0483) 232424.
Mid-Surrey Adult Education Institute, Dene Street, Dorking RH4 2DA. Tel: (0306) 883351. *DL*.
North East Surrey College of Technology, Reigate Road, Ewell KT17 3DS. Tel: (01) 394 1731. *DL, HE, PTHE*.
Royal Holloway and Bedford New College (University of London), Egham Hill, Egham TW20 0EX. Tel: (0784) 34455. *HE, Occ*.
Spelthorne Adult Education Institute, 36 Kingston Road, Staines, Middlesex TW18 4LN. Tel: (0784) 57372.
Surrey University, Guildford GU2 5XH. Tel: (0483) 571281. *HE, DL, EM*.
Waverley Adult Education Institute, Bridge Street, Godalming GU7 3DU. *NOW*.
West Surrey College of Art and Design, Falkner Road, The Hart, Farnham GU9 7DS. Tel: (0252) 722441. *HE, HE Prep, MS*.
Woking and Chertsey Adult Education Institute, Danesfield Centre, Grange Road, Woking GU21 4DA. Tel: (048 62) 21425.

Sussex – East

Community education in the county is organised through colleges of further and higher education, community colleges, some schools and separate centres (some linked to colleges). Each sets its own fees but courses are around 85p an hour. Reductions are also decided at local level but will usually be available to retired or unemployed people and those under 18. Adult literacy and numeracy are provided by part-time tutors based in colleges and adult centres. The Friends Centre in Brighton is an independent voluntary adult education centre.

For further information contact: FE Section, Education Department, County Hall, Lewes BN7 1SG. Tel: (0273) 475400 ext 657.

Education Guidance Service for Adults

The Open University, South Eastern Region, Wyvern House, 230/232 London Road, East Grinstead, West Sussex. Tel: (0342) 27821.
Brighton College of Technology, Pelham Street, Brighton BN1 4FA. Tel: (0273) 685971. *DL*.
Brighton Friends Centre, Ship Street, Brighton BN1 1AF. Tel: (0273) 27835.
Brighton Polytechnic, Moulsecoomb, Brighton BN2 4AT. Tel: (0273) 693655. *DL, HE, PTHE*.
Corsica Hall Conference Centre, Cricketfield Road, Seaford BN25 1BT. Tel: (0323) 893556. *SRC*.
Eastbourne College of Arts and Technology, St Anne's Road, Eastbourne BN21 2HS. Tel: (0323) 644711.
Further Education Centre, (Lewes Technical College sub-department), Hillcrest Road, Newhaven BN9 9EA. Tel: (9273) 513329.
Hastings College of Arts and Technology, Archery Road, St Leonards on Sea TN38 0HX. Tel: (0424) 423847. *DL*.
Lewes Technical College, Mountfield Road, Lewes BN7 2XH. Tel: (079 16) 6121.
Plumpton Agricultural College, Lewes, East Sussex BN7 3AE. Tel: (0273) 890454.
Portslade Community College, Chalkey Road, Portslade BN4 2WS. Tel: (0273) 416300. *DL, EGS*.
Pyke House, Upper Lake, Battle TN33 0AN. Tel: (042 46) 2495. *SRC*.
Sussex University, Falmer, Brighton BN1 9RH. Tel: (0273) 606755. *HE, MS, EM*.

Sussex – West

The adult education service in the county operates through 22 departments: some are school-based, others are part of, or linked to, colleges of technology at Chichester, Crawley and Worthing. Fees, which are decided locally, range between 75p and £1 an hour (basic education may be cheaper or free). Fee reductions are usually available to unemployed, retired or disabled people as well as those under 18, who are still in full-time education. One centre (Hazelwick School, Crawley) has purpose-built facilities for disabled people.

For more information contact: County Adviser for Adult Education. Tel: (0243) 777776.

Education Guidance Service for Adults
The Open University, South Eastern Region, Wyvern House, 230/232 London Road, East Grinstead, West Sussex. Tel: (0342) 27821.

Chichester College of Technology, Westgate Fields, Chichester PO19 1SB. Tel: (0243) 786321. *DL, HE Prep, NOW.*
Crawley College of Technology, College Road, Crawley RH10 1NR. Tel: (0293) 25686. *DL.*
Forest Community School, Comptons Lane, Horsham, Sussex. Tel: (0403) 61088. *DL.*
Northbrook College of Design and Technology, (inc Worthing College of Technology and West Sussex College of Design), Littlehampton Road, Goring by Sea. Tel: (0903) 31116. *DL.*
West Sussex College of Agriculture and Horticulture, Brinsbury House, North Heath, Pulborough, West Sussex RA20 1DL. Tel: (079 82) 5222.
West Sussex College of Design, Union Place, Worthing, West Sussex BN11 1LQ. Tel: (0903) 31116.
West Sussex Institute of Higher Education, The Dome, Upper Bognor Road, Bognor Regis, Sussex PO21 1HR. Tel: (0243) 865581. *HE, MS.*

TYNE AND WEAR – METROPOLITAN DISTRICTS

Gateshead

Non-vocational education in the district is organised through 41 school-based centres, seven youth and community centres, three adult education centres and Gateshead Technical College. Basic education is provided free but fees for other classes cost between 50 and 70p per hour. Retired people and under 18s pay only one third of full fees.

For further information contact: Mr Peter Stout, Community Education Officer, The Town Hall, Prince Consort Road, Gateshead NE8 4ER. Tel: (091) 477 1011.

Gateshead Technical College, Durham Road, Gateshead NF9 5BN. Tel: (091) 477 0524. *DL, HE Prep.*

Newcastle-upon-Tyne

Adult education in the city is organised through eight centres but classes are held in schools, colleges, church halls, private houses and many other sorts of accommodation throughout Newcastle. Child care provision is available in some cases. Fees for evening classes work out at 50p an hour. A wide range of concessions are offered in line with the authority's fees policy, but there is a standard £2 registration fee for all categories. There are also flexible learning opportunities. *Citywise*, a newspaper detailing adult education opportunities in Newcastle, in liaison with other providers, is published each August.

For more information contact: Peter Thurst, Further Education Office. Tel: (091) 232 8520 ext 5368.

Education Guidance Service for Adults
Linked Educational Advisory Service for Adults (LEASA), College House, Northumberland Road, Newcastle-upon-Tyne NE1 8ST. Tel: (091) 232 9735.

Heaton Education Centre, Trewhitt Road, Newcastle-upon-Tyne NE6. Tel: (091) 2655725. *DL.*
Newcastle-upon-Tyne College of Arts and Technology, Maple Terrace, Newcastle-upon-Tyne NE4 7SA. Tel: (091) 2738866. *TD Prep, DL, HE Prep, ILTU.*
Newcastle-upon-Tyne Polytechnic, (Centre for Continuing Education and Training), Wynne-Jones Centre, Ellison Place, Newcastle-upon-Tyne NE1 8ST. Tel: (091) 232 6002 ext 4066. *EM, DL, Polymaths, HE, PTHE, MS, HE Prep, ILTU, Occ, EM, EGS.*
Newcastle-upon-Tyne University, Newcastle-upon-Tyne NE1 7RU. Tel: (091) 232 8511. *PTHE, HE, NOW, EM, Occ.*
Todds Nook's Adult Education Centre, Monday Crescent, Newcastle-upon-Tyne NE4. Tel: (091) 273 3758.

North Tyneside

Adult education in the borough is organised through the college of further education, the adult education centre at Hawkeys Lane and 35 school-based centres organised into four areas (Killingworth, Wallsend, Whitley Bay and North Shields/Tynemouth). Fees for vocational courses.

cost £10 for ten weeks. The borough also runs adult associations enabling members to attend any number of courses for £20.50 (some of which run for more than 20 weeks). Fees for vocational courses are £16 per year. Basic education is free. Retired people and the under 18s are entitled to special low fees, while unemployed or disabled people pay no fees. Adults may be admitted to some sixth form courses in schools.

For more information contact: Mr H B Donkin, Assistant Director of Education, Education Offices, The Chase, North Shields, Tyne and Wear. Tel: (091) 257 6621.

Adult Education Centre, Hawkeys Lane, North Shields, Tyne and Wear. Tel: (091) 257 0115. *NOW*.

North Tyneside College of Further Education, Embleton Avenue, Wallsend, Tyne and Wear NE28 9NJ. Tel: (091) 262 4081. *DL*.

South Tyneside

Adult education classes in the borough are organised by the Senior Officer, Adult Education, Youth and Community Service. There are no separate adult education centres. Classes are held in 'shared-use schemes', with local schools, youth and community centres, social services and other establishments. Courses fall into various fee categories. Standard fee concessions apply: unemployed people (and husband/wife) pay only half fees as do retired people, disabled people (special classes are free) and the under 18s. Adult literacy and basic education is provided free. All but one centre has purpose-built or adapted facilities for disabled people and all arrange child care in some form at some time. A wide ranging programme of adult education is organised for unemployed people and their families in conjunction with the Adult Education Development Project – which is a joint venture between the LEA, Durham University and WEA. For details, tel: (0632) 568093. Look out too for a new Return to Learn Centre which is planned.

For more information contact: Mr John McKay, Teacher's Centre, Bede Burn Road, Jarrow NE32 5BA. Tel: (091) 489 8466.

Education Guidance Service for Adults

Linked Educational Advisory Service for Adults (LEASA), Centre for Continuing Education, 3 Green Terrace, Sunderland SR1 3PZ. Tel: (091) 567 6474, or West Park Community Centre, Whitehall Street, South Shields. Tel: (091) 456 8093.

Hebburn Technical College, Mill Lane, Hebburn, Tyne and Wear NE31 2ER. Tel: (091) 483 2741.

South Tyneside College, St George's Avenue, South Shields, Tyne and Wear NE34 6ET. Tel: (091) 456 0403. *DL, HE Prep*.

Sunderland

A wide variety of adult education courses are provided, mostly in the evenings. Courses include languages, crafts, technical subjects, arts, home economics, office skills, GCE O-level and Return to Study courses, and a range of recreational activities. Fees are based on the rate of 75p per course hour but reduced fees at the rate of 25p per course hour are available to under 18s, retired and unemployed people.

For details contact: Adult Education Organiser, 270 Hylton Road, Sunderland, Tyne and Wear SR4 7XJ. Tel: (0783) 40533.

Education Guidance Service for Adults

Linked Educational Advisory Service (LEASA), Centre for Continuing Education, 3 Green Terrace, Sunderland SR1 3PZ. Tel: (0783) 76474.

Monkwearmouth College of Further Education, Stansfield Street Annexe, Sunderland SR5 1EB. Tel: (0783) 71193. *HE Prep*.

Sunderland Polytechnic, Edinburgh Building, Chester Road, Sunderland SR1 3SD. Tel: (0783) 76191. *DL, EGS, Occ, HE, PTHE, EM, MS*.

Wearside College of Further Education, Sea View Road West, Grangetown, Sunderland SR2 9LH. Tel: (091) 670794. *DL, Trimaths, NOW*.

Warwickshire

The county's adult education service is organised through 31 local centres. Over half of the classes are run in schools but about one third are held in further education colleges. The rest are run in halls or separate premises. Fees for vocational courses are fixed at below 35p an hour while non-vocational courses will cost under 70p an hour. Basic education works out at 71p an hour. Unemployed people pay no fees while retired people and those under 18 in full-time education pay half fees. A few schools allow adult students.

For more information contact: Andrew Young, The Education Department, 22 Northgate Street, Warwick. *ILTU.*

East Warwickshire College of Further Education, Lower Hillmorton Road, Rugby CV21 3QS. Tel: (0788) 73133. *DL, HE Prep, MS, NOW.*

Mid-Warwickshire College of Further Education, Warwick New Road, Leamington Spa CV32 5JE. Tel: (0926) 311713. *MS, HE Prep.*

North Warwickshire College of Technology and Art, Hinckley Road, Nuneaton CV11 6BH. Tel: (0203) 349321. *DL, MS, NOW, HE Prep.*

South Warwickshire College of Further Education, The Willows, Alcester Road, Stratford-upon-Avon CV37 9QR. Tel: (0789) 66245. *DL, HE Prep, MS, EGS.*

Warwickshire College of Agriculture, Moreton Hall, Moreton Morrell, Warwickshire CV35 9BL. Tel: (0926) 651367.

WEST MIDLANDS – METROPOLITAN DISTRICTS

Birmingham

Birmingham's integrated adult education youth and community service is organised through 12 adult education areas. The Birmingham Athletic Institute provides a specialist programme of physical education and recreational activities. The adult education service provides classes and activities in over 50 schools throughout the city, and at four free standing adult education centres, in addition to a number of centres offering adult education alongside general community activities.

A termly fee of £11.50 (for a ten-week course) is charged for an unlimited number of classes within a basic education course but, otherwise, a minimum fee of £11.50 is charged for one course. A reduced fee of £5.50 is charged to retired, unemployed or disabled people, single parents, under 18s and people nominated by the social services department. There is local discretion to allow further reductions.

Basic education is provided as part of the general adult education programme throughout the city, but individual home tuition is also available. Birmingham further education colleges have joined together in a consortium to develop an Open Learning System for adult training and retraining using grant aid from the Manpower Services Commission Open Tech Unit. The Resources Unit for this collaborative project is at Garretts Green College.

A Return to Learn scheme is being developed to provide an educational programme, individually tailored to meet the needs of adults who wish to return to education. It is designed to provide a planned and integrated curriculum pattern for adults which will provide a ladder of educational opportunity from basic numeracy and literacy into further and higher education and training.

Education Guidance Service for Adults

Adult Learners Enquiry Centre (ALEC), Central Library, Chamberlain Square, Birmingham B3 3BU. Tel: (021) 233 2260.

Aston University, Gosta Green, Birmingham B4 7ET. Tel: (021) 359 3611. *HE.*

Avoncroft College, Stoke Heath, Bromsgrove, Worcester B60 4JS. Tel: (0527) 31331. *SRC.*

Birmingham Athletic Institute, 201 Balsall Heath Road, Highgate, Birmingham B12 9DL. Tel: (021) 440 1021.

Birmingham College of Food and Domestic Arts, Summer Row, Birmingham B33 1JB. Tel: (021) 235 2774.

Birmingham Women's Workships, Unit 65, 14 George Street, Balsall Heath, Birmingham B12. *Women's TW.*

Bournville College of Art and Design, Linden Road, Bournville, Birmingham B30 1JX. Tel: (021) 472 0953.

Bournville College of Further Education, Bristol Road South, Birmingham B31 2AJ. Tel: (021) 476 8211. *HE Prep, DL, EGS, NOW.*

Bournville Institute, Selly Oak Area Office, Selly Park Girls School, Pershore Road, Birmingham B29 7PL. Tel: (021) 472 2340. *NOW.*

The Brasshouse Centre, 50 Sheepcote Street (off Broad Street), Birmingham B1 2HR. Tel: (021) 643 0114.

Brooklyn Technical College, Aldridge Road, Great Barr, Birmingham B44 8NE. Tel: (021) 360 3543. *DL, NOW.*

City of Birmingham Polytechnic, Perry Barr, Birmingham B42 2SU. Tel: (021) 356 6911. *Polymaths, Occ, HE, NOW, PTHE, DL, EGS MS.*

Department of Recreation and Community Services, Sutton Coldfield Area, Moat House, Lichfield Road, Sutton Coldfield. Tel: (021) 355 3634 *NOW.*

Erdington Adult Institute, Marsh Hill Adult Education Centre, Marsh Hill, Erdington, Birmingham B23 7EY. *NOW.*

Fircroft College, Bristol Road, Selly Oak, Birmingham B29 6LH. Tel: (021) 472 0116. *ARC.*

Garretts Green College, Garretts Green Lane, Birmingham B33 0TS. Tel: (021) 743 4471. *EGS, NOW, DL.*

Hall Green Area Office, Department of Recreation and Community Services, 49 Poplar Road, Kings Heath, Birmingham B14 7AA. Tel: (021) 444 2680.

Hall Green Technical College, Cole Bank Road, Hall Green, Birmingham B28 8ES. Tel: (021) 778 2311. *DL, EGS.*

Handsworth Technical College, The Council House, Soho Road, Handsworth, Birmingham B21 9DP. Tel: (021) 551 6031. *DL, NOW, ILTU.*

Hodge Hill Adult Education Centre, Bromford Road, Birmingham B36 8HB. Tel: (021) 783 3741. *NOW.*

Kingstanding Institute, Perry Barr Area Office, Kings School, Dulwich Road, Kingstanding, Birmingham B44. Tel: (021) 382 1803.

Matthew Boulton Technical College, Sherlock Street, Birmingham B5 7DB. Tel: (021) 440 2681. *MS, NOW, HE Prep.*

Newman College, Genner's Lane, Bartley Green, Birmingham B32 3NT. Tel: (021) 476 1181. *HE, MS.*

Recreation and Community Services, Edgbaston Area Office, 110 High Street, Harborne, Birmingham B15. Tel: (021) 427 9819.

Sparkbrook Area Adult Education, Sparkbrook Area Office, Sparkhill Centre, Stratford Road (corner Newton Road), Sparkhill, Birmingham, B11 4LE. Tel: (021) 772 1893. *NOW.*

Sutton Coldfield College of Further Education, Lichfield Road, Sutton Coldfield, West Midlands B74 2NW. Tel: (021) 355 5671. *HE Prep.*

Department of Recreation and Community Services, Sutton Coldfield Area, Moat House, Lichfield Road, Sutton Coldfield, West Midlands B74 2NN. Tel: (021) 355 3634. *NOW.*

University of Birmingham, PO Box 363, Birmingham B15 2TT. Tel: (021) 472 1301. *HE, PTHE, MS, EM.*

Westhill College, Weoley Park Road, Selly Oak, Birmingham B29 6LL. Tel: (021) 472 7245. *HE, MS.*

Yardley Area Office, Stone Hall, 1083 Warwick Road, Acocks Green, Birmingham B27 6QT. Tel: (021) 706 2744.

Coventry

Adult education is based on 26 centres throughout the city and almost all classes are run in school premises or community and youth centres. Fees for most classes are set centrally and the standard fee is £13.50 for a ten-week course. Some classes are organised by community associations and may have different charges and eligibility for fee reductions, for most classes though, the unemployed, retired people and the under 18s qualify for reductions.

For more information contact: The Community Education Office. Tel: (0203) 25555 ext 2892 or 2152.

Coventry (Lanchester) Polytechnic, Priory Street, Coventry CV1 5FB. Tel: (0203) 24166. *HE, PTHE, Polymaths, NOW, MS.*

Coventry Technical College, The Butts, Coventry CV1 3GD. Tel: (0203) 57221. *DL.*

Coventry and Warwickshire Industrial Language Service, Stoke School Site, Briton Road, Coventry CV2 4LF. Tel: (0203) 455947. *ILTU* only.
Henley College Coventry, Henley Road, Bell Green, Coventry CV2 1ED. Tel: (0203) 611021. *DL, EGS, ILTU.*
Hereward College of Further Education, Bramston Crescent, Tile Hill Lane, Coventry CV4 9SW. Tel: (0203) 461231. *MS* (disabled students only).
Sidney Stringer School and Community College, Cox Street, Coventry CV1 5NL. Tel: (0203) 51756.
Stoke Park School and Community College, Dane Road, Coventry CV2 4JW. Tel: (0203) 450215. *DL, EGS, HE, MS, NOW, PTHE.*
Tile Hill College of Further Education, Tile Hill Lane, Tile Hill, Coventry CV4 9SU. Tel: (0203) 461444. *DL, HE Prep.*
Warwick University, Coventry CV4 7AL. Tel: (0203) 523523. *HE Prep, HE, PTHE, EM.*
Westham House College, Barford, Warwick CV35 8DP. Tel: (0926) 624206. *SRC.*

Dudley

Leisure time learning is organised by three colleges in the district (Dudley, Stourbridge and Halesowen) and three community colleges provided at 11 centres based in colleges and schools. Provision is also made for adults to study alongside school pupils. The minimum fee is 70p per hour for non-vocational courses, with an authority policy of 50% reduction for pensioners, unemployed people and under 18s entitled to reductions. Adult basic education is run from the Language and Literacy centre at the College of Technology.

For more information contact: Mr G Daniels, Dudley Metropolitan Borough Education Services, Westox House, 1 Trinity Road, Dudley. Tel: (0384) 55433 ext 4205.

Dudley College of Technology, The Broadway, Dudley DY1 4AS. Tel: (0384) 53585. *DL, ILTU, HE Prep, NOW.*
Halesowen College, Whittingham Road, Halesowen B63 3NA. Tel: (021) 550 1451. *DL.*
Stourbridge College of Technology and Art, Hagley Road, Stourbridge DY8 1QO. Tel: (038 43) 78531. *HE.*

Sandwell

Adult education classes in the borough are run mainly in secondary high schools, in Sandwell College of Further and Higher Education and in Wednesbury Adult Centre, there are also adult literacy classes in a variety of centres. Non-vocational classes cost £14.70 for a 20-week course of two hours per week, and recreational classes similarly but for one and a half hours per week. Vocational classes are £23 for the usual 20 weeks, two hours per week. Reductions are available to old age pensioners, unemployed people as well as under 18s.

For more information contact Mr J D Gotham, Sandwell Department of Education, Highfields, High Street, West Bromwich B70 8RG. Tel: (021) 525 7366 ext 59.

Sandwell College of Further and Higher Education, Chance Campus, Crocketts Lane, Warley, West Midlands B66 3BU. Tel: (021) 569 4590/4650/4656. *MS, HE, PTHE, DL.*

Solihull

The adult education service in Solihull operates through 17 centres using part-time staff. The majority of courses are run as evening classes in secondary schools. Day classes are held in buildings such as youth clubs or church halls. Fees for 1986/7 work out at 65p an hour for vocational, exam-based courses and 90p an hour for non-vocational leisure classes. Basic education fees are lower at 30p an hour. Fee reductions are available for retired or unemployed people and also those under 18. Solihull also runs a 'back to school' scheme for adults.

For more information contact: Mr H C Stephens, Adult Education Office, Moat Lane, Solihull. Tel: (021) 704 6680.

Solihull College of Technology, Blossomfield Road, Solihull B91 1SB. Tel: (021) 705 6376. *DL, EGS, HE Prep.*

Walsall

Part-time non-vocational classes for adults in the borough are organised through the Community and Education Service and based on 26 centres. Around three quarters of classes are run in schools or community centres, the rest in hospitals, adult centres and college premises. Over half of the centres have purpose-built or specially adapted facilities for disabled people. Course fees work out at around 45p an hour for most courses (basic education is free), but some are run by school-based community associations which determine their own fees and concessions. Normal courses offer fee reductions to widows and widowers as well as the retired, unemployed and under 18s.

For more information contact: The Youth, Community and Adult Education Organiser, The Education Department, Civic Centre, Darwell Street, Walsall WS1 1DQ. Tel: (0922) 21244 ext 2313.

Butts Community Centre, Butts Road, Walsall. Tel: (0922) 23480. *ILTU.*
Walsall College of Technology, St Pauls Street, Walsall WS1 1XN. Tel: (day) (0922) 34953 (evening) (0922) 392348. *HE Prep.*
West Midlands College of Higher Education, Gorway Road, Walsall WD1 3BD. Tel: (0922) 29141. *HE.*

Wolverhampton

The college of adult education organises courses throughout Wolverhampton, using adult education centres, colleges, schools and community centres. Courses, including basic education, cost approximately 30p an hour. Concessions are available automatically for retired or unemployed people and the under 18s – and others, at the discretion of full-time staff. The college offers special Return to Study courses as well as EGS and HE Prep.

Bilston Community College, Westfield Road, Bilston, Wolverhampton WV14 6ER. Tel: (0902) 42871. *DL, HE Prep, ILTU.*
The Polytechnic, Wolverhampton, The Molineux, Molineux Street, Wolverhampton WV1 1SB. Tel: (0902) 313000. *HE, PTHE, Occ.*
Wulfrun College of Further Education, Paget Road, Wolverhampton WV6 8DU. Tel: (0902) 26512. *DL, HE Prep, NOW.*

Wiltshire

Classes for adults in the county are organised through departments in six further education colleges. Classes are held in the colleges themselves and also in associated adult centres, schools and community centres. Some schools allow adult students. Some colleges and two centres operate regular child care provision. Fees for courses start at £13.65 for one hour per week for vocational courses for the year and 80p an hour for non-vocational ones. Basic education costs £1 per year. Retired people are usually entitled to a reduction in fees for non-vocational and vocational courses. People under 18 are allowed reduced fees for vocational courses only (free if they are unemployed) and deaf or blind people pay lower fees for special courses. Other reductions for other categories may be available at the discretion of the colleges. Distance learning packages are available from the county establishments and enquiries should be made to the nearest college.

Education Guidance Service for Adults
The Adult Guidance Unit, Old College Building, Victoria Road, Swindon SN1 1PT. Tel: (0793) 618866
West Wiltshire Adult Guidance Service. A network service. See *1 Advice and help.*

Bath College of Higher Education (incorporating Bath Academy of Art), Newton Park, Newton St Loe, Bath BA2 9BN. Tel: (022 17) 3701. *HE, EM.*
Chippenham Technical College, Cocklebury Road, Chippenham SN15 3QD. Tel: (0249) 650501. *DL.*
Swindon College, Department of Adult Studies, Ferndale Road, Swindon, Wiltshire SN2 1HL. Tel: (0793) 613313. *DL.*
Lackham College of Agriculture, Lacock, Near Chippenham, Wiltshire SN15 2NY. Tel: (0249) 656111.
Royal Military College of Science, Shrivenham, Swindon SN6 8LA. Tel: (0793) 782551. *HE.*
Salisbury College of Art, Southampton Road, Salisbury SP1 2LW. Tel: (0722) 26122.
Salisbury College of Technology, Southampton Road, Salisbury SP1 2LW. Tel: (0722) 23711. *DL.*

Trowbridge Technical College, College Road, Trowbridge BA14 0ES. Tel: (022 14) 66241. *DL, EGS.*

Urchfont Manor Residential College, Near Devizes, Wiltshire SN10 4RG. Tel: (038 084) 495. *SRC.*

Bath College of Higher Education is run by Avon LEA, while the Royal Military College (at Shrivenham) is run by the Ministry of Defence although it does admit some civilians.

Yorkshire – North

As well as full and part time courses provided by the authority's colleges of further education a wide range of both vocational and non-vocational courses are provided at various centres throughout the county.

These centres are run by a part time head of centre and are located in Bedale, Castleton, Catterick Garrison, Clifton, Easingwold, Glaisdale, Great Ayton, Huntington, Malton, New Earswick, Northallerton, Pickering, Richmond, Ryedale, Stokesley, Tadcaster, Thirsk, Upper Wensleydale, Wensleydale and Whitby.

It is the policy of the authority not to charge tuition or examination fees to those registered unemployed in receipt of benefit and providing they are not employed, their spouses. In addition, fees are subsidised for students under the age of 18 and for people in receipt of the state retirement pension, supplementary benefit or family income supplement. Several colleges are running OWLET (Other Ways to Learn – Education and Training) – a tutor-sponsored, home-based learning scheme and also Restart courses.

Askham Bryan College of Agriculture and Horticulture, Askham Bryan, York YO2 3PR. Tel: (0904) 702121.

Bedale Agricultural Centre, Benkhill Drive, Bedale, North Yorks DL8 2EA. Tel: (067 72) 2344. *MS.*

College of Ripon and York St John, York Campus, Lord Mayor's Walk, York Y03 7EX. Tel: (0904) 56771. *NOW, HE, PTHE, MS, Occ.*

Craven College, High Street, Skipton BD23 1JY. Tel: (0756) 61411. *DL.*

Easingwold Agricultural Centre, Hambleton Way, Easingwold, North Yorks YO6 3EF. Tel: (0347) 21735.

Grantley Hall College, Grantley Hall, Near Ripon, North Yorks. Tel: (076 586) 259. *SRC.*

Harrogate College of Arts and Technology, Hornbeam Park, Hookstore Road, Harrogate HG2 8QT. Tel: (0423) 879466. *DL.*

North Riding College, Filey Road, Scarborough YO11 3AZ. Tel: (0723) 362392. *EM, PTHE, HE, MS, Occ.*

Pickering Agricultural Centre, Swainsea Lane, Piickering, North Yorks YO18 8NE. Tel: (0751) 73431.

Scarborough Technical College, Lady Edith's Drive, Scarborough YO12 5RN. Tel: (0723) 372105. *MS, Occ, DL.*

York College of Arts and Technology, Tadcaster Road, Dringhouses, York YO2 1UA. Tel: (0904) 704141. *DL.*

York University, Heslington, York YO1 5DD. Tel: (0904) 430000. *PTHE, HE, Occ.*

YORKSHIRE – SOUTH – METROPOLITAN DISTRICTS

Barnsley

The community education service in Barnsley provides formal and informal education opportunities for the community including adult education and community development. Local schools and community education centres are extensively used. Fees (which are fixed at district level) work out at 32p an hour for vocational (exam-orientated) classes and 75p an hour for non-vocational leisure classes. Concessions are available for the under 18s, pensioners and the unemployed. There are special fees for basic education. The authority runs a 'back to school' scheme for adults and an adult basic education unit attached to West Barnsley Community Education Service.

For more information contact any of the providers listed.

Barnsley College of Art and Design, Fairfield House, Churchfield, Barnsley S70 2BH. Tel: (0226) 285623/299869.

Barnsley College of Technology, Church Street, Barnsley S70 2AX. Tel: (0226) 299191. *DL, EGS, HE Prep.*

East Barnsley Community Education Service, Community Education Centre, Barnsley Road, Wombwell, Barnsley S73 8HT. Tel: (0226) 753406 and 752384.

Northern College, Wentworth Castle, Stainborough, Barnsley, Yorks S75 3ET. Tel: (0226) 285426. *HE Prep, MS, NOW, ARC.*

West Barnsley Community Education Service, Eldon Centre, Eldon Street North, Barnsley. Tel: (0226) 245381.

Doncaster

Adult education in the district is organised through the Don Valley Institute and the Metropolitan Institute of Higher Education; most classes are held in schools. Fees are fixed throughout the district and work out at 32p per hour for vocational classes and 63p an hour for non-exam courses. Non-vocational fees are reduced for retired people and others receiving state benefits and the under 18s; classes are free for the unemployed.

Doncaster Metropolitan Institute of Higher Education, Waterdale, Doncaster DN1 3EX. Tel: (0302) 22122. *MS, PTHE, DL.*

Don Valley Institute of Further Education, Beechfield School, Chequer Road, Doncaster DN1 2AF. Tel: (0302) 66896.

Rotherham

The three centres below organise adult education in Rotherham. Fees are 75p per hour for non-vocational classes and 32p per hour for most vocational courses. Fees are waived or reduced for those in receipt of benefit, retired people, under 18s and YTS trainees.

For more information contact: Mr C Morecroft. Tel: (0709) 382121 ext 3197, or the Educational Guidance Service.

Education Guidance Service for Adults

Educational Guidance for Adults, The Guidance Centre, Howard Street, Rotherham S65 1DD. Tel: (0709) 374902.

Rockingham College of Further Education, West Street, Wath-on-Dearne, Rockingham, Rotherham S63 6PX. Tel: (0709) 874310. *DL.*

Rotherham College of Arts and Technology, Eastwood Lane, Rotherham S65 1EG. Tel: (0709) 362111. *NOW.*

Rother Valley College of Further Education, Doe Quarry Lane, Dinnington, Sheffield S31 7NH. Tel: (0909) 568681. *HE Prep.*

Sheffield

Sheffield's adult education service is organised through eleven divisions, one integrated with a college of further education. Classes are usually held in adult centres based in schools. Fees for courses work out at between 30 and 50p an hour in all centres and standard concessions are available to retired, unemployed and disabled people, full-time students and the under 19s – (also to their husbands/wives). There are no charges for basic education. All centres will attempt to provide creche facilities for daytime classes if possible.

For more information contact: Education Department, PO Box 67, Leopold Street, Sheffield S1 1RJ. Tel: (0742) 735686.

Education Guidance Service for Adults

Sheffield Educational Information Service for Adults (SEISA), AEUW House, Furnival Gate, Sheffield S1 3SL. Tel: (0742) 735360.

Granville College, Granville Road, Sheffield S2 2RL. Tel: (0742) 760271. *DL.*

Normandale Adult Education Division, Myers Grove Campus, Wood Lane, Sheffield S6 5HG. Tel: (0742) 340216.

Norton/Woodseats Adult Education Division, Rowlinson Campus, Dyche Lane, Sheffield. Tel: (0742) 878161. *HE Prep.*

Richmond College, Spinkhill Drive, Sheffield S13 8FD. Tel: (0742) 392621.

Sheffield Caribbean Outreach Project, Philadelphia Centre, West Don Street, Sheffield S6 3BH. Tel: (0742) 333416. All forms of *ABE, Return to Study for Afro-Caribbean students, HE Prep.*

Sheffield City Polytechnic, Pond Street, Sheffield S1 1WB. Tel: (0742) 20911. *Polymaths, HE, PTHE, NOW, Occ, DL.*
Sheffield University, Western Bank, Sheffield S10 2TN. Tel: (0742) 768555. *HE, EM, MS.*
Shirecliffe College, Shirecliffe Road, Sheffield S5 8XZ. Tel: (0742) 768301. *HE Prep.*
South Yorkshire Industrial Language Unit, Earl Marshall Campus, Earl Marshall Road, Sheffield S4 8LA. Tel: (0742) 619255. *ILTU.*
Stannington College, Myers Grove Lane, Sheffield S6 5JL. Tel: (0742) 323163. *DL.*
Stocksbridge College, Hole House Lane, Stocksbridge, Sheffield S30 5BN. Tel: (0742) 884530. *DL.*
Walkley Institute for Continuing Education, South Road, Sheffield 6. Tel: (0742) 330360. *HE Prep, NOW.*
Women's Technology Training Workshop, Tritech, Thomas Street, Sheffield S1 4LE. Tel: (0742) 756297. *Women's TW.*

YORKSHIRE – WEST – METROPOLITAN DISTRICTS

Bradford

Adult education is organised through the district's three colleges, but most classes are held in local schools or community centres. Course fees work out at about 30p an hour for vocational subjects and 50p an hour for non-vocational ones. Basic education is free. Fee reductions are available to retired, unemployed or disabled people also under 18s and others on low incomes. Bradford Adult Education Centre is part of Leeds University extra-mural department.

Education Guidance Service for Adults
Educational Advisory Service for Adults (EASA), Central Library, Princes Way, Bradford BD1 1NN. Tel: (0274) 753658.

Bradford Adult Education Centre, Mornington Villas, off Mannington Lane, Bradford BD8 7HB. Tel: (0274) 487054. *NOW, PTHE.*
Bradford and Ilkley Community College, Great Horton Road, Bradford BD7 1AY. Tel: (0274) 753026 (also at Wells Road, Ilkley). *HE, PTHE, HE Prep, EM, ARC, EGS, MS, NOW, Occ, DL.*
Keighley Technical College, Cavendish Street, Keighley BD21 3DF. Tel: (0535) 665421. *DL, NOW, MS.*
Shipley College, Exhibition Road, Shipley BD18 3JW. Tel: (0274) 595731. *HE Prep, NOW.*
University of Bradford, Bradford BD7 1DP. Tel: (0274) 733466. *HE, PTHE.*
West Yorkshire Language Link, Third Floor, Auburn House, Upper Picadilly, Bradford BD1 3NV. Tel: (0274) 305625. *ILTU* only

Calderdale

The adult education service is organised in four operational areas: Todmorden, Calder and Ryburn, Halifax and Ashlar. Courses are offered throughout the year at 80p per hour. Remedial education to assist people to read, write, calculate and speak English are provided free. Basic education classes cost half the standard charge – 40p per hour. Fee remissions are available for retired people, full-time students and those in receipt of unemployment, supplementary and invalidity benefit or family income supplement. Special schemes operate to assist the housebound elderly and the handicapped.

For more information contact: The Adult Education Service, Northgate House, Northgate, Halifax HX1 1UN. Tel: (0422) 57257 ext 2529 or your local area office.

Education Guidance Service for Adults
The Shop, 2 Crossley Street, Halifax. Tel: (0422) 42106.
Adult Education Centre, Wharf Street, Sowerby Bridge. Tel: (0422) 831973.
Adult Education Centre, Horton House, Horton Street, Halifax. Tel: (0422) 65344.
Adult Education Centre, Church Lane, Brighouse. Tel: (0484) 714019.
Adult Education Centre, Calder College, Burnley Road, Todmorden OL14 7BX. Tel: (070 681) 2743.
The Education Shop, 2 Crossley Street, Halifax. Tel: (0422) 42106. *EGS, Drop-in Centre* (basic education).
Percival Whitley College of Further Education, Francis Street, Halifax HX1 3UZ. Tel: (0422) 58221. *DL.*

West Yorkshire Language Link, ILT Calderdale, Bermerside Hall, Skircoat Green, Halifax HX3 OR2. Tel: (0422) 62552/53144. *ILTU* only

Kirklees

Educational opportunities for adults are offered by the authority's adult and continuing education service, colleges of further education, Huddersfield Polytechnic and West Yorkshire Language Link. Basic education is provided free of charge, as are all courses for the under 18s. Full or part time remission of most other fees are available for the unemployed, the retired and those in receipt of social security benefits. Fees for non-vocational classes are 72p an hour. A full educational guidance service is offered to adults by the Kirklees Careers Service. Careers officers are available to give information and advice on careers and educational and training opportunities.

For more information contact: Miss C M Lambert, Oldgate House, 2 Oldgate, Huddersfield, West Yorkshire HD1 6QW. Tel: (0484) 537399 ext 247.

Dewsbury College, Halifax Road, Dewsbury WF13 2AS. Tel: (0924) 465916. *NOW, DL, HE Prep.*
Huddersfield Institute of Continuing Education (including West Yorkshire Language Link), Marsh Adult Education Centre, St James's Road, Marsh, Huddersfield HD1 4QU. Tel: (0484) 538418. *ILTU.*
Huddersfield Polytechnic, Queensgate, Huddersfield HD1 3DH Tel: (0484) 22288. *HE, PTHE.*
Huddersfield Technical College, New North Road, Huddersfield HD1 5NN. Tel: (0484) 36521. *DL, Trimaths.*
North East Kirklees Institute of Adult Education, Batley and Dewsbury Adult Education Centre, Park Road, Batley WF17 5LP. Tel: (0924) 472623.
North West Kirklees Institute of Adult Education, Town Hall, Church Street, Cleckheaton BD19 3RH. Tel: (0274) 870125.
South Kirklees Institute of Adult Education, Huddersfield Road, Holmfirth, Huddersfield HD7 1AR. Tel: (0484) 684937. *NOW.*

Leeds

Adult education in Leeds is mainly provided through eleven area organisations and the Joseph Priestley Institute of Further Education. Most activities take place in schools and community centres. Fees are 60p per hour for non-vocational courses, 32p per hour for exam-based vocational classes, A very large programme in literacy, numeracy, ESL and other basic skills is provided either free or at a nominal charge. There are fee concessions for the retired, disabled and under 18s, and people on means-tested benefits are admitted free of charge. Special attention is paid to providing educational opportunities for the unemployed.

For more information contact: Mr S H Menzis, FE Section, 6th Floor West, Merrion House, 110 Merrion Centre, Leeds LS2 8DT. Tel: (0532) 462766.

Education Guidance Services for Adults

Drop-in Education and Advice Centre, (Basic Education), 54 The Corn Exchange, Vicar Lane, Leeds LS1 7BR. Tel: (0532) 468089.
Education Advice for Adults, Bramley Community Centre, Waterloo Lane, Bramley, Leeds 13. Tel: (0532) 556231, or Education Advice for Adults, Upper Wortley Centre, Ashley Road, Leeds 12. Tel: (0532) 798435.

Airedale and Wharfedale College of Further Education, Calverley Lane, Horsforth LS18 4RQ. Tel: (0532) 581723. *DL.*
City of Leeds College of Music, Cookridge Street, Leeds LS2 8BH. Tel: (0532) 452069 or 435526.
East Leeds Women's Workshop, 161 Harehills Lane, Leeds L38. Tel: (0532) 499031. *Women's TW.*
High Technology Training Centre, 38 Sweet Street, Leeds LS11 9AJ. Tel: (0532) 435511. *Women's TW.*
Icom Women's Linkup, 14 George Street, Leeds. Tel: (0532) 432474. *Women's TW.*
Jacob Kramer College, Vernon Street, Leeds LS2 8PH. Tel: (0532) 439931.
Joseph Priestley Institute of Further Education, 71 Queen Street, Morley, Leeds LS27 8DZ. Tel: (0532) 533749. *DL.*
Kitson College of Technology, Cookridge Street, Leeds LS2 8BL. Tel: (0532) 430381. *NOW.*
Leeds College of Building, North Street, Leeds LS2 7QT. Tel: (0532) 430765. *DL.*

Leeds Polytechnic, Calverley Street, Leeds LS1 3HE. Tel: (0532) 462903. *EM, HE Prep, HE, MS, PTHE.*

Leeds University, Leeds LS2 9JT. Tel: (0532) 431751. *HE, EM, MS, PTHE, NOW, Occ.*

Park Lane College of Further Education, Park Lane, Leeds LS3 1AA. Tel: (0532) 443011. *DL, HE Prep, NOW.*

Swarthmore Education Centre, 2/7 Woodhouse Square, Leeds 3. Tel: (0532) 432210. *DL, NOW.*

Thomas Danby College, Roundhay Road, Leeds LS7 3BG. Tel: (0532) 494912. *HE Prep* (planned).

Trinity and All Saints' College, Brownberrie Lane, Horsforth, Leeds LS18 5HD. Tel: (0532) 584341. *HE, MS.*

West Yorkshire Language Link, 2 Woodhouse Square, Leeds LS3 1AD. Tel: (0532) 449603. ILTU only.

Wakefield

Adult education in Wakefield is based in the three main centres of the district college and ten outlying centres which are, on the whole, in school premises and are where most classes are held. Disabled, retired and unemployed people are entitled to fee reductions as are the under 18s. Basic education is provided free. One centre makes regular provision for child care, another also has specially adapted facilities for disabled people.

Education Guidance Service for Adults

Bretton Hall Continuing Education Unit, Bretton Hall College of Higher Education, West Bretton, Near Wakefield WF4 4LG. Tel: (092 485) 261. *HE Prep, NOW.*

Bretton Hall College, West Bretton, Wakefield WF4 4LG. Tel: (092 485) 261. *EGS, DL, HE, MS.*

Wakefield District College, Wakefield Centre, Margaret Street, Wakefield WF1 2DH . Tel: (0924) 370501, or Whitwood, Four Lane Ends, Castleford WF10 5F. Tel: (0977) 554571, or Station Road, Hensworth, Pontefract WF9 4JP. Tel: (0243) 610585. *DL, NOW.*

Wales

Clwyd

Adult education is run in 17 main centres, as well as in many minor rural centres, schools, FE colleges and clubs. Classes cost around 75p per hour. Adult literacy tuition is free; there is a reduced charge for numeracy and other basic education classes. Reduced fees are charged to retired, unemployed or disabled people. There is also a centrally organised Homebased Learning scheme.

For more information contact: Gerson Davies. Tel: (0352) 2121 ext 533.

Education Guidance Service for Adults

Education for Adults Referral Service (EARS), Adult Education Office, Rhyl High School, Grange Road, Rhyl, Clwyd. Tel: (0745) 31609.

Llandrillo Technical College, Rhos on Sea, Colwyn Bay, Clwyd LL28 4HZ. Tel: (0492) 46666.

North East Wales Institute of Higher Education, Cartrefle Cefn Road, Wrexham, Clwyd LL13 9NL. Tel: (0978) 290390. *HE, DL.*

Victoria Youth Centre, Hill Street, Wrexham, Clwyd.

Dyfed

Adult education is run in 17 FE centres; classes take place in schools in rural areas. Courses cost 83p per hour. Basic education is free. Reduced fees are charged to senior citizens and unemployed people. There is also an open and distance learning scheme for home study and an Open Tech Unit which prepares students for vocational courses, at the County Education Office (details below) ext 4506 and 4534.

For further information contact: County Education Office, The Further Education Section, Education Section, Pibwrlwyd Carmarthen SA31 2NH. Tel: (0267) 233333.

Aberystwyth University College of Wales, University of Wales, Old College, King Street, Aberystwyth. Tel: (0970) 3177. *DL, EM, HE, PTHE.*

Carmarthenshire College of Technology and Art, Alban Road, Llanelli SA15 1NG.Tel: (0554) 759165, or Ammanford Site, Ammanford SA18 3TA; Carmanthen Site, Pibwrlwyd, Carmanthen SA31 2NH; Dyfed Site, Jobswell Road, Carmanthen SA31 3HY.
Ceredigion College of Further Education, Llanbadarn Campus, Aberystwyth SY23 2BP. Tel: (0970) 4511, or Cardigan Site, Park Place, Cardigan SA43 1AB. Tel: (0239) 612032.
College of Librarianship Wales, Llanbadarn Fawr, Aberystwyth, SY23 3AS. Tel: (0970) 3181. *HE, DL.*
Dyfed Open Tech, County Education Office, Pibrwlywd, Carmarthen SA31 2NH. Tel: (0267) 235268 ext 4534/4512 or 24 hours: (0267) 235268. *EGS, DL.*
Pembrokeshire College of Further Education, Dew Street, Haverfordwest SA61 1TG. Tel: (0437) 5247.
St David's University College, University of Wales, Lampeter SA48 7ED. Tel: (0570) 422351. *HE, PTHE, MS, NOW, Occ.*
Trinity College, Carmarthen SA31 3EP. Tel: (0267) 237971. *HE.*
Welsh Agricultural College, Llanbadarn Fawr, Aberystwyth, Dyfed SY23 3AL. Tel: (0970) 4471.

Gwent

Adult education classes are run in 39 community centres, community colleges, adult education centres and leisure centres. Classes cost up to 50p per hour. There is no charge for basic education, or to people who are retired, unemployed, disabled or receiving social security benefits.

For further information contact: The Community Education and Leisure Section, Gwent County Council, Education Department, County Hall, Cwmbran, Gwent. Tel: (063 33) 67711 ext 411. (From 7 April 1987 County Hall's telephone number will be: (063 33) 838838.

Crosskeys College, Risca Road, Crosskeys, Gwent NP1 7EA. Tel: (0495) 270295. *DL.*
Ebbw Vale College of Further Education, College Road, Ebbw Vale, Gwent NP3 6LE. Tel: (0495) 302083. *DL.*
Gwent College of Higher Education, (Site of the Faculty of Management and Professional Studies, and the Faculty of Science and Technology), Allt-yr-yn Avenue, Newport, Gwent NPT 5XA. Tel: (0633) 51525. *HE,* (Site of The Faculty of Education and Combined Studies), Caerleon, Gwent NP6 1XJ. Tel: (0633) 421292, (Site of The Faculty of Art and Design), Clarence Place, Newport Gwent NP9 0UW. Tel: (0633) 59984.
Newport College of Further Education, Nash Road, Newport, Gwent NP6 2BR. Tel: (0633) 274861. *DL, MS.*
Pontypool College, Blaendare Road, Pontypool, Gwent NP4 5YE. Tel: (049 55) 55141. *DL.*
Usk College of Agriculture, Usk, Gwent NP5 1XJ. Tel: (02913) 2311. *DL, MS.*

Gwynedd

Adult education classes are run in community centres, secondary schools and one adult and community centre. Classes cost up to 95p per hour, the lower rate being 55p for vocational classes. There is a 50% reduction for the unemployed and free courses for pensioners in certain categories for vocational classes. Basic education is free.

For further information contact: Adult Education Office. Tel: (0286) 4121 ext 2177.

For adult basic education contact: Mr Robin Thomas on the above number.

Coleg Glynllifon, Clynnog Road, Caernarfon LL54 5DU. Tel: (0286) 830261 and 830733.
Coleg Harlech, Harlech, Gwynedd LL46 2PU. Tel: (0766) 780363. *ARC, HE Prep.*
Coleg Meirionnydd, Dolgellau, Gwynedd LL40 2SW. Tel: (0341) 422827.
Coleg Pencraig, Llangefri, Yns Mon, Gwynedd LL77 7HP. Tel: (0248) 722101.
Gwynedd Coleg Technoleg, Bangor LL57 2TP. Tel: (0248) 364186.
Normal College of Education, (Y Coleg Normal), Bangor LL57 2HQ. Tel: (0248) 352121. *HE.*
University College of North Wales, Bangor LL57 2DG. Tel: (0248) 351151. *HE, EM, MS.*

Mid-Glamorgan

Adult education classes are run in schools, community centres and colleges of further education. Classes cost 56p per hour. Basic education is free. Fee reductions or exemptions are offered to students who are retired, unemployed or disabled and in receipt of supplementary benefit.

For more information, including basic education, contact: Mr D Jones, County Further Education Officer, Education Department, County Hall, Cardiff. Tel: (0222) 820820 ext 3244.

Abercynon Adult Education Centre, The Old Secondary School, Ynysmeurig Road, Abercynon. Tel: (0443) 741332.
Aberdare College of Further Education, Aberdare CF44 8ST. Tel: (0685) 873405. *DL.*
Bridgend College of Technology, Cowbridge Road, Bridgend CF31 3DF. Tel: (0656) 55588. *DL.*
Merthyr Tydfil Technical College, Ynsfach, Merthyr Tydfil CF48 1AR. Tel: (0685) 3663, 4534 and 5399.
Mid-Glamorgan College of Agriculture and Horticulture, Pencoed, Near Bridgend CF35 5LG. Tel: (0656) 860202.
Polytechnic of Wales, Llantwit Road, Treforest, Pontypridd CF37 1DL. Tel: (0443) 405133. *PTHE, HE, Occ.*
Pontypridd Technical College, Ynys Terrace, Rhydyfelin, Pontypridd CF37 5RN. Tel: (0443) 3422. *NOW, MS, DL.*
Rhondda College of Further Education, Llwynypia, Rhondda CF40 2TQ. Tel: (0443) 432187.
Ystrad Mynach College of Further Education, Twyn Road, Ystrad Mynach, Hengoed CF8 7XR. Tel: (0443) 812929.

Powys
Adult education courses are run in colleges of further education, schools, community centres and village halls. Student fees are 32p per hour for vocational courses and 70p per hour for those considered non-vocational. Basic education courses costs 35p per hour. Reduced fees are charged to people who are retired, and those suffering hardship (such as unemployment) can request exemption.

For further information contact: Mr D W Hall, Area Education Office, 2nd Floor, Ladywell House, Park Street, Newtown, Powys SY16 1JB. Tel: (0686) 26521.

Coleg Howell Harris, Brecon College of Further Education, Penlan, Brecon, Powys LD3 9SR. Tel: (0874) 5252.
Montgomery College of Further Education, Llanidloes Road, Newton SY21. Tel: (0686) 27444. *MS, NOW, DL.*
Radnor College of Further Education, Llandrindod Wells LD1 5ES Tel: (0597) 2696. *DL, NOW.*

South Glamorgan
Adult education classes are run in 14 schools and community centres. O-level and A-level classes cost £23.50 for two hour classes per term year, or £35 for three hour classes, for over 18s; under 18s pay £5 for up to four courses. Non-vocational classes cost 76p per hour. Basic education costs £2 per class per term. Reduced fees are charged to people who are retired, unemployed, disabled or in receipt of supplementary benefit.

For more information contact: Education Department, Kingsway, Cardiff. Tel: (0222) 44291 ext 209.

For further information about basic education contact: Mrs Mair James, The Friary, Kingsway. Tel: (0222) 27472.

For further information about ESL contact: Mr R Mooneeram, 28 The Parade, Cardiff. Tel: (0222) 495578.

Adult Basic Education Centre, The Friary, Kingsway, Cardiff. Tel: (0222) 27472. *DL, MS.*
Barry College of Further Education, Colcot Road, Barry CF6 8JY. Tel: (0446) 733251.
Canton Adult Education Centre, 1st Floor, Severn Road School, Canton, Cardiff. Tel: (0222) 31652.
Combined Training Institute, University Hospital of Wales, Heath Park, Cardiff CF4 4XW. Tel: (0222) 755944.
The Community College, Old Hall, High Street, Cowbridge, South Glamorgan. Tel: (04463) 3831.
Penarth Adult Education Centre, St Cyres Comprehensive School, St Cyres Road, Penarth, South Glamorgan. Tel: (0222) 701569.
Rumney College of Technology, Trowbridge Road, Rumney, Cardiff CG3 8XZ. Tel: (0222) 794226. *DL, MS.*

South Glamorgan Institute of Higher Education, Cyncoed Road, Cyncoed, Cardiff CF2 6XD. Tel: (0222) 551111. *HE.*
South Glamorgan Women's Workshop, Edena House, East Canal Wharf, Cardiff. Tel: (0222) 493391. *Women's TW.*
University College Cardiff, University of Wales, PO Box 78, Cardiff CF1 1XL. Tel: (0222) 874000. *HE, EM.*
University of Wales College of Medicine, Heath Park, Cardiff CF4 4XN. Tel: (0222) 755944. *HE.*
University of Wales Institute of Science and Technology (UWIST), PO Box 68, Cardiff CF1 3XA. Tel: (0222) 372435. *HE.*
Welsh College of Music and Drama, Castle Grounds, Cathays Park, Cardiff CF2 3ER. Tel: (0222) 42854. *HE.*

West Glamorgan

Adult and community education classes are run in schools and community centres, in the four FE tertiary colleges and an adult education centre. Classes cost under 50p per hour for vocational classes and 53p per hour for non-vocational classes. Basic education is free. Reduced fees are charged for people who are retired, and classes are free for unemployed people and those in receipt of supplementary benefit.

For further information contact: Graham Smith, County Adviser, Community Adult Education, Bryn House, Walter Road, Swansea SA1 4PS. Tel: (0792) 470611.

Afan College, Margam, Port Talbot SA13 2AL. Tel: (0639) 882107. *DL.*
Bryn House Adult Education Centre, Walter Road, Uplands, Swansea SA1 4DS. Tel: (0792) 470171. *NOW.*
Gorseinon College, Belgrave Road, Gorseinon, Swansea SA4 2RF. Tel: (0792) 892037. *DL.*
Neath College, Dwryfelin Road, Neath SA10 7RF. Tel: (0639) 54271.
Swansea College (Tertiary), Tycoch, Swansea SA2 9EB. Tel: (0792) 206871.
Taibach Youth Centre, (Adult Prep Course), Margarn Road, Port Talbot SA13 2BM. Tel: (0639) 895672.
University College of Swansea, Singleton Park, Swansea SA2 8PP. Tel: (0792) 205678. *HE, EM.*

West Glamorgan Institute of Higher Education, Townshill Road, Swansea SA2 0UT. Tel: (0792) 203482. *HE.*
YMCA, Kingsway, Swansea SA1 5JQ. Tel: (0792) 55460.

Scotland

Education Guidance Service for Adults
NETWORK Scotland Ltd, 74 Victoria Crescent Road, Dowanhill, Glasgow G12 9JQ. Tel: (041) 357 1774.

Borders

The region's community education provision works in close conjunction with the Borders College of Further Education in the provision of adult education (vocational and non-vocational) courses. Certain informal classes take place in schools and village halls throughout the region. Fees are fixed at regional level for college-based courses and by individual centres for all others. Classes are not usually more than 50p an hour and there may be no charge in certain cases. Eligibility for fee reductions is decided at regional level for vocational courses but by individual centres for recreational courses. Unemployed people and under 18s will not usually pay full fees. Adult basic education is free and organised by the community education service.

For more information contact: The Education Department, Regional Headquarters, Newton St Boswells, Borders TD6 0SA.

For information about adult basic education contact: The Regional Organiser, Community Education Services, Thorniedem, Melrose Road, Galashiels.

Borders College of Further Education, Thorniedem, Melrose Road, Galashiels. Tel: (0896) 57755. *DL.*

Scottish College of Textiles, Netherdale, Galashiels, Selkirkshire TD1 3HF. Tel: (0896) 3351. *HE.*

Central

The adult education service organises classes mainly in school-based centres and the region's colleges at Alloa and Falkirk. Adult education is mostly free, although there may, in the case of some classes, be a nominal fee. Basic education is also free. There is an important community-based adult education programme working in six designated areas in Stirling, Alloa, Denny, Bonnybridge, Falkirk and Bo'ness. It is concerned with opening up provision and focussing on important issues.

For more information contact: Jeana Papamichael, Adult Education Co-ordinator, Hillpark Education Centre, Bannockburn, Stirling. Tel: (0786) 816205 ext 27.

Clackmannan College of Further Education, Branshill Road, Alloa, Clackmannanshire FK10 3BT. Tel: (0259) 215121. *DL, HE Prep, MS.*
Falkirk College of Technology, Grangemouth Road, Falkirk FK2 9AD. Tel: (0324) 24981. *DL, HE.*
University of Stirling, Stirling FK9 4LA. Tel: (0786) 73171. *HE, PTHE, EM, Occ.*

Dumfries and Galloway

Dumfries and Galloway College of Technology provides day and evening classes in vocational and non-vocational subjects. These are held mostly at the main Heathall centre but a few classes are offered elswhere in the area. There are plans for new developments at Stranraer and other regional centres. For more details contact the college principal. Non-vocational evening classes are organised by locally appointed management committees, which decide what to run and what fees to charge. Reduced fees are often available to retired or unemployed people.

For details of local organisers contact: the Principal Community Education Officer, 30 Edinburgh Road, Dumfries DG1 1JQ. Tel: (0387) 63822.

Barony Agricultural College, Parkgate, Dumfries DG1 3NE. Tel: (0387) 86251. *DL.*
Dumfries and Galloway College of Technology, Heathhall, Dumfries DG1 3QZ. Tel: (0387) 61261.

Fife

Informal further education is organised within the region's community education service. Courses are run in some 80 centres (mostly school-based) and further education colleges. Most centres have special facilities for disabled people. Fees work out at about 30p an hour for vocational courses and 50p an hour for non-vocational courses. Registered unemployed people and their dependants and the disabled pay no fees while retired people, single parents, under 18s and full-time students are entitled to a reduction in fees equating to 10p an hour fees. Basic education is free.

For more information contact: Mr D McNeill, Deputy Director of Education, Fife Regional Council Education Department, Regional Headquarters, Fife House, North Street, Glenrothes, Fife KY7 5LT. Tel: (0592) 754411.

Elmwood Agricultural and Technical College, Carslogie Road, Cupar, Fife KY15 4JB. Tel: (0334) 52781 ext 28. *NOW.*
Glenrothes and Buckhaven Technical College, Stenton Road, Glenrothes South KY6 2RA. Tel: (0592) 772233. *DL, EM.*
Kirkcaldy College of Technology, St Brycedale Avenue, Kirkcaldy KY1 1EX. Tel: (0592) 268591/7.
Lauder Technical College, Halbeath, Dunfermline, Fife KY11 5DY. Tel: (0383) 726201. *NOW, DL* (planned).
St Andrews University, College Gate, St Andrews, KY16 9AJ. Tel: (0334) 76161. *HE, EM, PTHE, Occ.*

Grampian

Classes for adults in the region are run by its five further education colleges and also in community centres and schools. Fees for vocational courses vary according to the level of the course but are between 42 and 70p an hour. Fees for non-vocational courses work out at £1.20 per hour. People receiving old age pensions are entitled to reduced fees for non-vocational courses while people under 18 and registered unemployed receiving benefit pay no fees if following a vocational course. The region's Adult Basic Education Unit organises basic education. No charge is made for individual tuition but £8.00 per year is charged for group tuition in refresher English and maths. An annual guide to evening classes is published in July.

For more information about adult classes, or about basic education contact: Mr Calderwood, Deputy Director of Education, Grampian Regional Council Department of Education, Woodhill House, Ashgrove Road West, Aberdeen AB9 2LU. Tel: (0224) 682222 ext 2549. *DL.*

Aberdeen College of Commerce, Holburn Street, Aberdeen AB9 2YT. Tel: (0224) 572811. *DL.*
Aberdeen College of Education, Hilton Place, Aberdeen AB9 1FA. Tel: (0224) 42341. *HE, DL.*
Aberdeen Technical College, Gallowgate, Aberdeen AB9 1DN. Tel: (0224) 640366. *DL.*
Aberdeen University, Regent Walk, Aberdeen AB9 1FX. Tel: (0224) 480241. *HE, EM, HE Prep, PTHE* (planned).
Banff and Buchan College of Further Education, Argyll Road, Fraserburgh, Aberdeenshire AB4 5RF. Tel: (0346) 25777. *DL* (planned).
Clinterty Agricultural College, Kinellar, Aberdeenshire AB5 0TN. Tel: (022479) 393.
Moray College of Further Education, Hay Street, Elgin, Morayshire IV30 2NN. Tel: (0343) 3425. *DL.*
Robert Gordon's Institute of Technology, Schoolhill, Aberdeen AB9 1FR. Tel: (0224) 633611. *PTHE, HE.*

Highland

Adult education in the Highlands is provided through the region's colleges, schools and community centres. In addition, distance learning is a significant form of provision. Fees for classes fall into the 30 to 50p an hour price range with reductions available to retired or unemployed people as well as those under 18. Basic education is provided free and is organised separately.

For more information contact: The Director of Education, Regional Buildings, Glenurquhart Road, Inverness IV1 5NX. Tel: (0463) 234121.

Duncraig Castle College, Plockton, Ross-shire IV52 8UA. Tel: (059 984) 229.
Inverness College of Further and Higher Education, 3 Longman Road, Inverness IV1 1SA. Tel: (0463) 236681. *HE, MS, NOW, PTHE, DL.*
Thurso Technical College, Thurso, Caithness KW14 7EE. Tel: (0847) 66161. *DL, NOW.*

Lothian

Community education courses in the region are held in a mixture of centres based in colleges, schools, community halls and arts centres as well as separate adult centres. Fees for vocational classes cost £25 per term year (including exam fees), whilst non-vocational fees are £14. Adult basic education is organised separately and provided free. Fee reductions are usually available to retired, unemployed or disabled people as well as those under 18. Lothian also runs a scheme for adults to study in some schools.

For more information contact: Community Education Section, Education Department, 40 Torphichen Street, Edinburgh EH3 8JJ. Tel: (031) 229 9166 ext 2124.

Dunfermline College of Physical Education, Cramond Road North, Edinburgh EH4 6JD. Tel: (031) 336 6001. *HE.*
Edinburgh College of Art, Lauriston Place, Edinburgh EH3 9DF. Tel: (031) 229 9311. *HE.*
Edinburgh University, Old College, South Bridge, Edinburgh EH8 9YL. Tel: (031) 667 1011. *HE, NOW, EM, MS, PTHE.*
Edinburgh Walk In Numeracy Centre, 67 Bread Stred, Edinburgh EH3 9AH. Tel: (031) 229 0382. *Drop-in Centre.*
Esk Valley College, Newbattle Road, Dalkeith, Mid Lothian EH22 3AE. Tel: (031) 663 1951/3. *DL.*
Heriot-Watt University, Edinburgh EH1 1HX. Tel: (031) 225 8432. *DL,MS, PTHE, HE.*
Kirk O'Field College Adult Learning Centre, Edinburgh University Settlement, 29 Guthrie Street, Edinburgh EH1 1JG. Tel: (031) 226 3801. *EGS, NOW.*
Leith Nautical College, 24 Milton Road East, Edinburgh EH15 2PP. Tel: (031) 669 8461. *DL.*
Moray House College of Education, Holyrood Road, Edinburgh EH8 8AQ. Tel: (031) 556 8455. *DL, PTHE, HE.*
Napier College, Colinton Road, Edinburgh EH10 5DT. Tel: (031) 447 7070. *HE, PTHE, DL.*

Newbattle Abbey College, Dalkeith, Mid Lothian. Tel: (031) 663 1921. *ARC.*
Oatridge Agricultural College, Ecclesmachan, Broxburn, West Lothian EH52 6NQ. Tel: (0506) 854387.
Queen Margaret College, 36 Clerwood Terrace, Edinburgh EH12 8TS. Tel: (031) 339 8111. *HE.*
Stevenson College of Further Education, Bankhead Avenue, Sighthill, Edinburgh EH11 4DE. Tel: (031) 443 7111. *TD Prep, DL.*
Telford College of Further Education, Crewe Toll, Edinburgh EH4 2NZ. Tel: (031) 332 2492 ext 244. *DL.*
West Lothian College of Further Education, Marjoribanks Street, Bathgate, West Lothian EH48 1QJ. Tel: (0506) 634300. *DL.*

Orkney Islands

Classes for adults are held in centres based on schools or community halls. Vocational classes cost 80p per hour and non-vocational classes £1 per hour. No fees are charged to the unemployed and pensioners; the disabled and under 18s pay half fees. Adults are welcome to join pupils for day classes, provided there is room in teaching groups. Adult basic education is free.

Kirkwall Further Education Centre, Grammar School, Kirkwall, Orkney KW15 1QN. Tel: (0856) 3535.
Orkney Education Department, Council Offices, Kirkwall, Orkney. Tel: (0856) 3535. *DL.*
Stromness Academy Further Education Centre, Stromness, Orkney KW16 3AW. Tel: (0856) 850259.

Shetland Islands

Community education on the islands is provided through 37 centres based in schools or community halls. Eight of these have special facilities for disabled people. The cost of courses works out at under 30p an hour with fee reductions available to retired people, those unemployed, and under 18s. Basic education is provided free of charge. Adults are welcome to join pupils for day classes.

Shetland College of Further Education, Gressy Loan, Lerwick, Shetland ZE1 0BB. Tel: (0595) 5514. *DL.*

Strathclyde

Community education and adult education in the region is administered through six divisional offices: Argyll and Bute, Ayr, Dunbarton, Glasgow Lanark and Renfrew. Each organises provision in a different way and fees vary. Some fees are set by the authority, but others are decided locally and have to be self-financing. In remote areas, minimum enrolment numbers may be lower than elsewhere. Basic education is provided free. Schemes are organised to allow adults to study in schools.

For information contact: Helen Munro, Adult Education Resource Unit, Adelphi Education Centre, 12 Commercial Road, Glasgow G5. Tel: (041) 429 8722.

Argyll Division, Assistant Principal Community Education Officer, Education Offices, 2 Tom-A-Mhoid Road, Dunoon PA23 7HN. Tel: (0369) 6918.
Ayr Division, David Rowan, Ayr Sub-regional Headquarters, Dumbarton. Tel: (0292) 266922.
Dumbarton Division, Aileen Finlay, Dumbarton Sub-Regional Headquarters, Dumbarton. Tel: (0389) 65151.
Glasgow Division, Glasgow Sub-regional Headquarters, 155 Bath Street, Glasgow G2 2SY. Tel: (041) 227 2680.
Lanark Division, Coral Devitt, Lanark Sub-regional Headquarters, Lanark. Tel: (0698) 454473.
Renfrew Division, Pat O'Neill, Renfrew Sub-regional Headquarters, Paisley, Renfrew. Tel: (041) 889 5454.

Anniesland College, Hatfield Drive, Glasgow G12 OYE. Tel: (041) 357 3969.
Ayr College, David Rowan, Ayr Sub-regional Headquarters, Ayr. Tel: (0292) 265184.
Barmulloch College of Further Education, Rye Road, Glasgow G21 3JY. Tel: (041) 558 9071.
Bell College of Technology, Almada Street, Hamilton, Lanarkshire ML3 0JB. Tel: (0698) 283100.
Cambuslang College, Janebank, Glasgow Road, Cambuslang, Lanarkshire G72 7BS. Tel: (041) 641 6197. *DL.*

Cardonald College, 690 Moss Park Drive, Glasgow G52 3AY. Tel: (041) 883 6151 or (041) 883 1119.

Central College of Commerce, 300 Cathedral Street, Glasgow G1 2TA. Tel: (041) 552 3941.

Clydebank College, Kilbowie Road, Clydebank, Dumbartonshire G81 2AA. Tel: (041) 952 7771. *DL, HE Prep.*

Coatbridge Technical College, Kildonan Street, Coatbridge, Lanarkshire ML5 3LS. Tel: (0236) 22316.

Craigie College of Education, Beechgrove, Ayr KA8 0SR. Tel: (0292) 260321. *HE.*

Cumbernauld College, Town Centre, Cumbernauld, Glasgow G67 1HU. Tel: (02367) 31811.

Glasgow College of Building and Printing, 60 North Hanover Street, Glasgow G1 2BP. Tel: (041) 332 9969. *HE.*

Glasgow College of Food Technology, 230 Cathedral Street, Glasgow G1 2TG. Tel: (041) 552 3751.

Glasgow College of Nautical Studies, 21 Thistle Street, Glasgow G5 9XB. Tel: (041) 429 3201.

Glasgow College of Technology, Cowcaddens Road, Glasgow G4 0BA. Tel: (041) 332 7090 ext 234. *HE, PTHE, MS.*

Glasgow School of Art, 167 Renfrew Street, Glasgow G3 6RQ. Tel: (041) 332 9797. *HE.*

Glasgow University, Glasgow G12 8QQ. Tel: (041) 339 8855. *HE, PTHE, EM, HE Prep, MS.*

Home Study Courses, Education Officer, 2 Tom-A-Mhoid Road, Dunoon, Argyll PA23 7HN. *DL.*

James Watt College, Finnart Street, Greenock, Renfrewshire PA16 8HF. Tel: (0475) 24433. *DL.*

Jordanhill College of Education, Southbrae Drive, Jordanhill, Glasgow G13 1PP. Tel: (041) 959 1232. *HE, DL, PTHE.*

Kilmarnock College, Holehouse Road, Kilmarnock, Ayrshire KA3 7AT. Tel: (0563) 23501.

Langside College, 50 Prospecthill Road, Glasgow G42 9LB. Tel: (041) 649 4991.

Motherwell College, Dalzell Drive, Motherwell ML1 2DD. Tel: (0698) 59641.

Paisley College of Technology, High Street, Paisley, Renfrewshire PA1 2BE. Tel: (041) 887 1241. *HE.*

Park Mains High School, Erskine, Strathclyde PA8 6EY. Tel: (041) 812 2801.

The Queen's College Glasgow, 1 Park Drive, Glasgow G3 6LP. Tel: (041) 334 8141. *HE, MS.*

Reid Kerr College, Renfrew Road, Paisley, Renfrewshire PA3 4DR. Tel: (041) 889 4225.

The Royal Scottish Academy of Music and Drama, St Georges Place, Glasgow G2 1BS. Tel: (041) 332 4101. *HE.*

St Andrews College of Education, Duntocher Road, Bearsden, Glasgow G61 4QA. Tel: (041) 943 1424. *HE.*

Springburn College, 110 Flemington Street, Glasgow G21 4EX. Tel: (041) 558 9001.

Strathclyde University, McCance Building, 16 Richmond Street, Glasgow G1 1XQ. Tel: (041) 552 4400. *HE, EM, DL, PTHE.*

Stow College, 43 Shamrock Street, Glasgow G4 9LD. Tel: (041) 332 1786. *PTHE.*

Tayside

The community education service in the region supports the provision of classes for adults through voluntary adult education associations. Fee levels for non-vocational courses vary between centres but all basic education is free. Many community centres also promote adult learning groups. The colleges of further education in Arbroath, Dundee and Perth also offer a wide programme of courses and classes.

Angus Technical College, Keptie Road, Arbroath, Angus DD11 3EA. Tel: (0241) 72056. *DL.*

Duncan of Jordanstone College of Art, Perth Road, Dundee DD1 4HT. Tel: (0382) 23261. *HE, DL.*

Dundee College of Education, Gardyne Road, Broughty Ferry, Dundee DD5 1NY. Tel: (0382) 453433. *HE, DL.*

Dundee College of Further Education, 30 Constitution Road, Dundee DD3 6TB. Tel: (0382) 29151. *DL.* Old Glamis Road, Dundee DD3 6LE.

Dundee College of Technology, Bell Street, Dundee DD1 1HG. Tel: (0382) 27225. *HE.*

Dundee University, Nethergate, Dundee DD1 4HN. Tel: (0382) 23181. *HE, EM, MS, PTHE.*

Dundee College of Further Education, Old Glamis Road, Dundee DD3 8LE. Tel: (0382) 819021. *HE, DL.*

Perth College of Further Education, Brahan Estate, Crieff Road, Perth PH1 2NX. Tel: (0738) 21171. *DL*.

Tayside Regional Council, Community Education Service, Tayside House, Dundee DD1 3RJ. Tel: (0382) 23281.

Western Isles

Classes for adults in the Western Isles are held in Lews Castle College. Fees cost around £1.20 an hour.

For more information contact: The Director of Education, Western Isles Islands Council, Council Offices, Stornoway, Isle of Lewis PA87 2BW. Tel: (0851) 3773.

Lews Castle College, Stornoway, Isle of Lewis PA86 0XR. Tel: (0851) 3311. *DL*

Northern Ireland

Education in Northern Ireland is administered by five appointed education and library boards. Adult education is provided by colleges, universities, the WEA and a number of voluntary organisations.

Education Guidance Services for Adults

Educational Guidance Service for Adults, Room 208, Bryson House, 28 Bedford Street, Belfast BT2 7FE. Tel: (0232) 244274.

Antrim

Antrim Technical College, Fountain Street, Antrim BT41 4AL. Tel: (084 94) 63916.

Greenmount Agricultural and Horticultural College, Antrim BT41 4PU. Tel: (084 94) 62114/5/6.

North Antrim College of Further Education, 2 Coleraine Road, Ballymoney, County Antrim BT53 6BP. Tel: (026 56) 62258/62339.

Armagh

Armagh College of Further Education, Lonsdale Street, Lisanally Lane, Armagh BT61 7HN. Tel: (0861) 522205.

Ballymena

Ballymena Technical College, Farm Lodge Avenue, Ballymena, County Antrim BT43 7DJ. Tel: (0266) 2871/5. *DL*.

Ballymoney

Ballynahinch

Ballynahinch Technical College, Church Road, Ballynahinch, County Down BT24 8LP. Tel: (023 856) 2369.

Banbridge

Banbridge College of Further Education, Castlewellan Road, Banbridge, County Down BT32 4AY. Tel: (082 06) 22289. *DL*.

Bangor

North Down College of Further Education, Castle Park Road, Bangor, County Down BT20 4TF. Tel: (0247) 962254/5. *DL*.

Belfast

Belfast College of Business Studies, Brunswick Street, Belfast BT2 7GX. Tel: (0232) 245891.

Belfast College of Technology, College Square East, Belfast BT1 6DJ. Tel: (0232) 227244. *DL, HE, PTHE*.

Queen's University of Belfast, University Road, Belfast BT7 1NN. Tel: (0232) 245133. *HE, PTHE, EM, Occ*.

Rupert Stanley College of Further Education, Tower Street, Belfast BT5 4FH. Tel: (0232) 52111. *HE Prep, NOW*.

St Mary's College of Education, 191 Falls Road, Belfast BT12 6FE. Tel: (0232) 227678. *HE*, or at Trench House, Belfast BT11 9GA.

Stranmillis College of Education, Stranmillis Road, Belfast BT9 5DY. Tel: (0232) 665271.*HE*.

University of Ulster, College of Art, York Street, Belfast BT15 1ED. Tel: (0232) 228515.
Univerty of Ulster, Belfast Campus, Magce Campus, Cromore Road, Belfast. *HE Prep.*

Castlereagh
Castlereagh College of Further Education, Montgomery Road, Belfast BT7 9JD. Tel: (0232) 797144.

Coleraine
Coleraine Technical College, Union Street, Coleraine, County Londonderry BT52 1QA. Tel: (0265) 54717/8.
The University of Ulster, Coleraine, County Londonderry BT52 1SA. Tel: (0265) 4141. *HE, HE Prep, PTHE, MS, Occ, EM, NOW.*

Cookstown
Cookstown Further Education College, Loy Street, Cookstown, County Tyrone BT80 8PE. Tel: (064 87) 62620.
Loughry College of Agriculture and Food Technology, Cookstown, County Tyrone BT80 9AA. Tel: (064 87) 62491.

Downpatrick
Down College of Further Education, Market Street, Downpatrick, County Down BT30 6ND. Tel: (0396) 5815.

Dungannon
Dungannon Further Education College, Circular Road, Dungannon, County Tyrone BT71 6BQ. Tel: (086 87) 22323. *DL.*

Enniskillen
Enniskillen Agricultural College, Enniskillen, Co Fermanagh. Tel: (0365) 23101.
Fermanagh College of Further Education, Enniskillen, County Fermanagh BT74 6AE. Tel: (0365) 22431. *DL.*

Kilkeel
Kilkeel Technical College, Greencastle Street, Kilkeel, Newry, County Down BT34 4BH. Tel: (069 37) 62582.

Larne
Larne College of Further Education, 32/34 Pound Street, Larne, County Antrim BT40 1SQ. Tel: (0574) 72268.

Limavady
Limavady Technical College, Main Street, Limavady, County Londonderry BT49 0EX. Tel: (050 472) 2334.

Lisburn
Lisburn College of Further Education, 39 Castle Street, Lisburn, County Antrim BT27 4SU. Tel: (084 62) 77225. *DL.*

Londonderry
Magee Campus, University of Ulster, Northland Road, Londonderry BT48 7JL. Tel: (0504) 65621. *EM, HE Prep.*
North West College of Technology, Strand Road, Londonderry BT48 7BY. Tel: (0504) 66711.

Lurgan
Lurgan College of Further Education, Kitchen Hill, Graigaron, County Armagh BT66 6AZ. Tel: (076 282) 6135.

Magherafelt
Magherafelt College of Further Education, 22 Moneymore Road, Magherafelt, County Londonderry BT45 6AE. Tel: (0648) 32462 and (039 67) 22451/23389.

Newcastle
Newcastle College of Further Education, Donard Street, Newcastle, County Down BT33 0AP. Tel: (03967) 22451 or (03967) 22451/23389. *MS.*

Newry

Newry Technical College, Patrick Street, Newry, Co Down BT35 8DN. Tel: (0693) 61071. *NOW*.

Newtownabbey

Jordanstown Campus, University of Ulster, Shore Road, Newtownabbey, County Antrim BT37 0QB. Tel: (0231) 365131. *HE, EGS, MS, PTHE, NOW, Occ, EM.*

Newtownabbey Technical College, Shore Road, Newtownabbey, County Antrim BT37 9RS. Tel: (0231) 64331. *MS.*

North Down College of Further Education, Victoria Avenue, Newtownabbey BT23 3EH. Tel: (0247) 812116 and 813742.

Omagh

Omagh Technical College, Mountjoy Road, Omagh, County Tyrone BT79 7AH. Tel: (0662) 45433 or (0662) 45433/45434.

Portadown

Portadown College of Further Education, 26–44 Lurgan Road, Portadown, Craigavon, County Armagh BT63 5BL. Tel: (0762) 337111.

Portrush

Northern Ireland Hotel and Catering College, Ballywillan Road, Portrush, County Antrim BT56 8JL. Tel: (026 582) 3768.

Strabane

Strabane Technical College, Derry Road, Strabane, Co Tyrone BT82 8DX Tel: (0504) 882317.

Channel Islands

Jersey

Adult education classes are run by the FE college and in one school-based centre. Classes cost up to 50p per hour, but special short courses can be a little more. Basic education is free. Reduced fees are charged to people who are retired or unemployed.

For information contact: The Education Department. Tel: (0534) 71065.

Highlands College, PO Box 142, St Saviour, Jersey. Tel: (0534) 71800. *DL.*

Guernsey

Adult education is provided by the adult education department of the College of Further Education and consists of a programme of about 180 classes (2500 enrolments). Classes are held in six Island secondary schools and provision, with the exception of a limited number of day classes, is evenings only. Fees are determined annually by the education council and there are reductions for the elderly, unemployed etc. Basic literacy and numeracy classes are free. All classes are advertised through a free prospectus with an Island wide distribution.

For further information contact: the Head of Department of Adult Education, College of Further Education, Route des Coutanchez, St Peter Port, Guernsey, Channel Islands. Tel: (0481) 27121.

Guernsey College of Further Education, Route des Coutanchez, St Peter Port, Guernsey. Tel: (0481) 27121.

Isle of Man

The Isle of Man College of Further Education offers a wide choice of vocational and non-vocational courses at centres based in Douglas, Peel, Castletown and Ramsey. Fees vary from £3 for one day Saturday classes, to £36 for a three term vocational course. Help with reading, writing, spelling and numeracy problems is available free.

For further information contact: The Principle, Isle of Man College of FE, Homefield Road, Douglas, Isle of Man. Tel: (0624) 23113.

Isle of Man College of Further Education, Homefield Road, Douglas, Isle of Man. Tel: (0624) 23113.

Booklist

Directory of further education
CRAC, Hobsons Limited, annual £39.95 (paperback).
Lists all FE and HE colleges, polytechnics and many specialist colleges (but not universities); with full course information.

The student book
Boehm, Wellings and Behr (eds), Macmillan, annual, 1987 edition £7.95.
Information on all places where you can study for a degree. Includes a description of each from a consumer's viewpoint.

Social services yearbook
Councils and Education Press, annual, 1986/7 edition £35.00.
Lists all social services departments, health authorities, citizens' advice bureaux, advisory services, councils for voluntary service etc.

The education yearbook
Councils and Education Press, annual, 1987 edition £35.00.
Names and titles of the main officials in each LEA.

The hospitals and health services yearbook
Institute of Health Services Management, 1986 edition £46.20.

Open tech directory
National Extensions College, £9.95.
Lists and describes all materials produced by Open Tech schemes.

British qualifications
Barbara Priestly (compiler), Kogan Page, annual, £18.00.
A comprehensive list of qualifications and awarding bodies.

Equal opportunities: a careers guide for women and men
Ruth Miller and Anna Alston, Penguin. Currently being updated. The next edition (available in September 1987) will be approximately £10.00.
Describes occupations with education and training requirements.

Careers encyclopaedia
Audrey Segal (ed), Cassell, 11th edition £19.95.

Occupations (replaces *Annual careers guide: opportunities in the professions, industry, commerce and the public service*)
COIC, annual, 1987 edition £15.00.

Index

Entries in *italics* are chapter titles.

Here's what you need to help you take what may be the first step towards another job!

Use them to cut out this page and order any of the products listed on pages 133 and 296

		Price	No. Reqd
WHAT ELSE series			
What can a teacher do except teach		1.95	
What else can a housewife do		1.95	
What can a nurse do		1.95	
What else can a secretary do		2.50	
What else can you do		2.50	
OCCUPATIONS '87		15.00	
JOB IDEAS		3.50	
WORKING IT OUT		1.00	
SPONSORSHIPS '87		1.25	
WORKING IN SERIES			
Accountancy	W163	99p	
Advertising	W145	99p	
Airports	W137	99p	
Animals	W184	1.95	
Arts (fine) and crafts	W162	99p	
Beauty and Health Care	W170	99p	
Books	W185	1.95	
Catering	W164	99p	
Children – work with	W151	99p	
Clothing/Fashion	W178	99p	
Community Care	W171	99p	
Computers	W182	1.95	
Construction – craft and manual jobs	W174	99p	
Construction – professions and technicians	W175	99p	
Dentistry	W190	1.95	
Design	W161	99p	
Electrical and Electronic Engineering	W149	99p	
Engineering Crafts	W160	99p	
Engineering Industry and its branches (Professional)	W143	99p	

		Price	No. Reqd
Engineering Industry – at work in the (Professional)	W144	99p	
Farms and Forests	W183	1.95	
Garages	W150	99p	
Gardening, Floristry and Horticulture	W180	1.95	
Hairdressing	W157	99p	
Home Economics	W188	1.95	
Hospitals	W167	99p	
Hotels	W165	99p	
Information Technology	W177	99p	
Insurance	W156	99p	
Journalism	W173	99p	
Laboratories	W139	99p	
Leisure	W176	99p	
Marketing	W147	99p	
The Media and Entertainment	W148	99p	
Money Business	W153	99p	
Nature Conservation	W186	1.95	
Nursing	W168	99p	
Offices	W166	99p	
Outdoor Jobs	W172	99p	
Performing Arts	W169	99p	
Photography	W140	99p	
Police	W159	99p	
Retail Management	W146	99p	
Science	W155	99p	
Self Employment	W197	1.95	
Servicing and Repair	W152	99p	
Shops	W158	99p	
Tourism	W189	1.95	
TV and Video	W179	1.95	

PLEASE USE BLOCK CAPITALS

NAME

FULL DELIVERY ADDRESS

POST CODE

TELEPHONE NUMBER PLUS EXTENSION

ORDER NUMBER/REFERENCE

SIGNATURE DATE

ORDERING GOODS – UNDER £15 IN VALUE

We are no longer able to invoice goods under £15 in value unless they attract VAT. If your order is less than £15 (excluding carriage) please send a cheque or postal order made payable to Manpower Services Commission to:

MANPOWER SERVICES COMMISSION
DEPT. CW, ISCO 5
THE PADDOCK, FRIZINGHALL
BRADFORD BD9 4HD

INVOICED ORDERS – GOODS OVER £15 IN VALUE

Please post to:

COIC, Room W1101
SALES DEPARTMENT
MOORFOOT, SHEFFIELD S1 4PQ.

Carriage will be charged at the appropriate rate.
VAT will be added.
If you live in a COIC bookshop area, send your order direct to the address on the reverse of this form.

CARRIAGE CHARGES

Please add the appropriate carriage charge. Goods up to the value of

£2 add 30p	£15 add £2
£4 add 50p	£30 add £3
£6 add £1	£100 add £4
£10 add £1.50	£100 and over £5

PRICES

The prices quoted in this list supersede all previous prices and offers. Charges for carriage may vary from time to time. Orders are accepted at the price ruling on the day of despatch.

DELIVERY

Allow at least 28 days for delivery.

CAREERS & OCCUPATIONAL INFORMATION CENTRE
Manpower Services Commission